Elizabeth Wormeley Latimer, A.C. McClur

Italy in the Nineteenth Century and the Making of Austria-Hungary and Germany

Elizabeth Wormeley Latimer, A.C. McClur
Italy in the Nineteenth Century and the Making of Austria-Hungary and Germany
ISBN/EAN: 9783743435490
Printed in Europe, USA, Canada, Australia, Japan
Cover: Foto ©ninafisch / pixelio.de

Manufactured and distributed by brebook publishing software (www.brebook.com)

Elizabeth Wormeley Latimer, A.C. McClur

Italy in the Nineteenth Century and the Making of Austria-Hungary and Germany

ITALY
IN
THE NINETEENTH CENTURY

AND THE MAKING OF

AUSTRIA-HUNGARY AND GERMANY

BY

ELIZABETH WORMELEY LATIMER

AUTHOR OF "FRANCE IN THE NINETEENTH CENTURY," "RUSSIA AND
TURKEY IN THE NINETEENTH CENTURY," "ENGLAND IN THE
NINETEENTH CENTURY," "EUROPE IN AFRICA IN
THE NINETEENTH CENTURY," ETC.

THIRD EDITION

CHICAGO
A. C. McCLURG AND COMPANY
1898

NOTE.

I HAVE stated, I think, several times in this book why the history of Italy is very hard to write. I need not repeat my reasons here.

It had been my intention to say to my large circle of readers (who seem almost my personal friends) that "Italy" would be the last volume in this Nineteenth Century series. Very probably it may be so. Yet, when I consider how picturesque a subject Spain would be, with its war of the Constitution; its Carlist struggles; the sad history of the Spanish marriages, and their consequences; King Amadeo; Alfonso XII. and his sweet wife, Mercedes; and the Regency of Queen Christina; also how acceptable some intelligible account might be of the connection of Spain with Cuban affairs (if such an account in the next twelve months should be procurable), I am tempted to undertake it.

It may seem to some that the chapters on Austria-Hungary and Germany have very slight connection with the story of Italy, yet I think it needs them. Without some brief account of contemporary events in those countries, my narrative would look to me like an unfinished seam left with a "ragged edge."

E. W. L.

BONNYWOOD, HOWARD CO., MD.,
    October, 1896.

CONTENTS.

CHAPTER		PAGE
I.	Italy early in the Nineteenth Century	9
II.	Pio Nono	40
III.	Southern Italy	59
IV.	Daniel Manin and his City	79
V.	Charles Albert and Northern Italy	92
VI.	Through Casa Guidi Windows	114
VII.	The Roman Republic	122
VIII.	Kossuth	150
IX.	Victor Emmanuel	173
X.	The Alliance with France	199
XI.	Garibaldi	221
XII.	Italy made — not completed	245
XIII.	Sadowa. Austria-Hungary	265
XIV.	Mentana	290
XV.	The Last Years of Victor Emmanuel's Reign	309
XVI.	The Papacy	327
XVII.	Brigandage and Secret Societies	349
XVIII.	King Humbert and his Reign	374
XIX.	The Italians in Abyssinia	395

LIST OF ILLUSTRATIONS.

QUEEN MARGHERITA	*Frontispiece*
EMPRESS MARIA LOUISA	*To face page* 28
POPE PIO NONO	40
KING FERDINAND II.	64
GENERAL PEPE	84
KING CHARLES ALBERT	100
FIELD MARSHAL RADETZKY	110
GIUSEPPE MAZZINI	126
LOUIS KOSSUTH	150
KING VICTOR EMMANUEL	173
COUNT CAVOUR	200
GIUSEPPE GARIBALDI	221
URBANO RATTAZZI	246
EMPEROR WILLIAM I.	266
PRINCE FREDERICK CHARLES	278
EMPEROR FRANCIS JOSEPH	284
PRINCESS MARGHERITA (afterwards Queen of Italy)	300
CARDINAL ANTONELLI	324
POPE LEO XIII.	338
KING HUMBERT	374
THE PRINCE OF NAPLES	392
FRANCESCO CRISPI	404
MARQUIS DI RUDINI	416
THE PRINCESS OF NAPLES	424

ITALY

IN THE NINETEENTH CENTURY,

TOGETHER WITH

THE MAKING OF AUSTRO-HUNGARY AND GERMANY.

CHAPTER I.

ITALY EARLY IN THE NINETEENTH CENTURY.

THERE is nothing more bewildering in the varied history of the nineteenth century than the story of Italy, and nothing at the same time more picturesque, soul-stirring and affecting. It is like a drama played on the world's stage, which we watch with breathless interest, following the moving story through many an act and scene.

Italy lost her ancient unity after the fall of the great Roman Empire. The peninsula became divided into sundry small states, each at enmity with its neighbors. Charlemagne and his successors, as Emperors of Germany and conquerors of the Lombards, claimed jurisdiction over Northern and Central Italy, its southern coasts were dotted by Greek colonies, each clustered round a city, governed by a nearly independent chief who owed nominal allegiance to the Emperor at Constantinople.

Early in the eleventh century some Norman knights on pilgrimage chanced to encounter a Greek exile from the town of Bari. Moved by his promises and by the story of his wrongs, they returned to Normandy and there collected a small force for the deliverance of Apulia from its oppressors. These Northmen did not come in their long ships, but crossed the Alps as pilgrims, and presented themselves in Apulia as knights, — horse-riding gentlemen. Their number was so small that they failed in their expedition against Bari and became a band of free lances wandering among the mountains and valleys of Southern Italy. Their discipline and prowess were speedily recognized and their assistance was sought in every domestic quarrel. They soon attracted to themselves other Norman adventurers, among whom were the sons of Tancred de Hauteville, — not the crusading hero of the "Gerusalemme Liberata," but a Norman gentleman, who had built himself a strong castle on the southern frontier of Normandy and called it Hauteville.

He had been twice married and was the father of eleven sons. His second wife had been a true mother to all these lads, and they were strongly attached to each other. As they grew to manhood it was agreed amongst them that two should remain at home to comfort and support their parents, and that the rest should go forth to seek adventures. They directed their steps to Southern Italy. Arrived there, they soon found themselves allied with certain Greeks in an attack upon the Saracens in Sicily. In this war William de Hauteville, the eldest son of Tancred, greatly distinguished himself.

Before long, troubles on the mainland recalled this William of the Iron Arm to Apulia. There Pope Leo IX., feeling his own territories in danger from such restless and ambitious neighbors, had invited an alliance with the German and Byzantine Emperors against them. A battle was fought at a place called Civitella, in which the Pope headed his own soldiers. Three thousand Normans routed a miscellaneous host, Count William and Count Humphrey, sons of Tancred, commanding their countrymen. The Pope fled, but was pursued and overtaken by the victorious Normans, who crowded round him, kissing his feet and imploring his benediction. Such conduct won at once the esteem and admiration of the pontiff, who gave up his alliance with the Emperors and conceived a warm friendship for the three elder sons of the house of Hauteville, William, Drogo, and Humphrey, who successively became the recognized heads of the confederacy of ten counts who had won cities for themselves in Southern Italy.

But the most brilliant of the family was Robert, known in history as Robert Guiscard. He was the eldest of the younger brothers, a born soldier and statesman, handsome, strong, valiant, and a devout churchman, — everything, in short, which made up the ideal of a perfect knight in that unpolished age. He had come into Italy with a small following, but his prowess and prestige soon became such that on the death of his brother Humphrey he was raised on a buckler by his countrymen and saluted chief of the Normans in Italy, and Count of Apulia.

Pope Leo IX. was dead, but his successor, Nicholas II., desirous to secure the friendship of this brave and brilliant Norman, " gave him the title of Duke, and the investiture of Apulia and Calabria, besides all the lands his sword might conquer, both in Italy and Sicily, from schismatic Greeks or unbelieving Saracens." Nor did his interest in Robert end here. He persuaded the other Normans in Italy to acquiesce in his new honors and accept his supremacy.

The Italian conquests of Robert accord with what was called subsequently the kingdom of Naples. The enterprising little republic of Amalfi, and Salerno, the chief seat of learning in Christendom at that time, acknowledged Norman Robert as their nominal protector, and he regarded them both with especial favor. He was at the height of his prosperity when Roger, his youngest brother, arrived from Normandy. He at once won the affection of his elder brother, who seems, however, to have been chary of pecuniary aid. Roger had set his heart on conquering Sicily from the Greeks and Saracens. He invaded it with only sixty followers, but his wife was with him. In after years he used to tell how they had had but one mantle, which they shared between them. Robert came over to help his brother as soon as he felt assured of his success. The Mahomedans in Sicily submitted to the conquerors, and the Pope put forth an extraordinary bull, not only investing Roger and his heirs with temporal sovereignty in Sicily, but making them in that island hereditary legates of the Holy See.

In 1081, ambition prompted Robert Guiscard to attempt the conquest of the Byzantine empire. His eldest son, Bohemond, best known to us as a crusader, commanded his naval forces, but the enterprise was not prosperous, and Robert made his way back to Italy. A second time he planned an invasion of the Greek empire, and fought the battle of Durazzo, when his men first encountered the Varangian guard, chiefly composed of Northmen in the service of the Emperor. Robert won the battle, but with considerable loss, and died not long after, when his subjects abandoned all idea of conquering Constantinople, and turned their energies soon after to the crusades and the crusaders.

Robert Guiscard was not succeeded by Bohemond, his elder son, whose mother he had divorced, but by a younger son, named Roger, on whose death Roger, the great Count of Sicily, became heir to his Italian dominions and took the title of "King of Apulia, Calabria and the Two Sicilies." He was the father of a long line of kings, and his successor, another Roger, who was only four years old when he came to the throne, further increased the renown of his family by successes against the Saracens on the coast of Africa. That model of all knighthood, Tancred the Crusader, was nephew of Robert Guiscard on the mother's side, and grandson of Tancred de Hauteville, the founder of his family.

The union of Naples and Sicily lasted many years, until German emperors interfered, claiming rights to the two kingdoms through an ancestress.

The Pope of that period, not liking the close proximity of a powerful Imperial house to his own Roman dominions, granted in 1254 the Two Sicilies to Charles of Anjou, brother of Saint Louis of France. The tyranny of the French led to the massacre of the Sicilian Vespers in 1282, when Spain, entering into the quarrel, conquered Sicily, separating it from Naples and uniting it to the kingdom of Aragon.

The Angevin kings held their often-disputed possession — the kingdom of Naples — with a firm hand until 1442. Then arose a fierce war between France and Spain for the possession of Naples, — a war which wrapped all Italy in a flame, and gave renown to the Spanish hero, Gonsalvo de Cordova.

The rule of the Angevin kings in Naples had not been entirely despotic; the old constitutions granted by the sons of Tancred to their subjects were held to be still in force, although the feudal system was established, but when, in 1505, the kingdom of the Two Sicilies became part of the Spanish monarchy, diets were no longer convened in Naples, the regal power increased, and with it the burdens of taxation. Things grew worse and worse under misgovernment for two centuries. At the Peace of Utrecht (1713) the Two Sicilies were again divided. Naples was given to Austria, Sicily to Savoy; but seven years later Austria acquired Sicily by exchanging for it the island of Sardinia.

Austria held her new possession only for a short time, Spain conquered the two kingdoms, which were then settled on the Infant Don Carlos, who, when he ascended the Spanish throne in 1759, conferred them on his third son, Ferdinand, then a babe, decreeing at the same time that they should never again be united to the Spanish crown.

King Ferdinand was King of the Two Sicilies (in possession or in exile) till 1825, which brings his fortunes and the fortunes of his kingdoms within the bounds of the history which this book is intended to cover.

The Popes, whatever might have been their political influence, were not temporal Italian princes till Pépin bestowed upon Pope Stephen II., about the year 755, the exarchate of Ravenna, which he had wrested from the Lombards; and in the twelfth century Matilda, a pious Countess of Tuscany, left her landed possessions — long called the Patrimonio di San Pietro — to the Pope, to be governed by him, not only as their spiritual head, but as their temporal ruler. But the Emperor of Germany, as the successor both of Charlemagne and the Cæsars, claimed temporal supremacy over any Italian dominions held by the Pope. This led to the celebrated disputes between Guelphs and Ghibellines. The Guelphs (as all readers of Italian history will do well to remember) were the party of the Pope; the Ghibellines were adherents of the German Emperor.

During the Middle Ages, Northern Italy was studded with free cities. The form of government called the Commune flourished in Italy. Each city governed itself and had a little tract of surrounding country over which it held sway.

Each city had its own army, its own alliances, its own laws, its own quarrels, its own exiles, and its own ambitions. Some cities were Guelph and some were Ghibelline. In the sixteenth century some were for France, and some for Spain. When I speak of Communism, I do not mean that in the Middle Ages the class that the French are pleased to call "the people" had any share in the Communal government of their native towns. The municipal government of these cities was in the hands of citizens, — the burghers of the city, — and sometimes one family made itself all-powerful, as the Medici in Florence, the Estes in Ferrara, or the Visconti in Milan. The most peaceful part of Italy was possibly Piedmont, together with its dependent duchy of Savoy; and yet it was the high road over which French armies were perpetually pouring south with designs on Milan and Naples. Venice and Genoa during those centuries were stable republics. Indeed, in the sixteenth century Venice had almost advanced herself to be what we should now denominate a "Great Power."

Those who have read Dante know something of the working of these aristocratic, or rather burghercratic communes. They know, too, how ardently Dante desired a United Italy, deprecating as he did the evils arising from the feuds of rival cities, — rivalries that are only beginning to die out in the present generation. Indeed, Mr. Senior, writing in 1851, records in his journal that an Italian gentleman had said to him that there could never be a United Italy, for that the

Pisans and the Genoese, the inhabitants of Lucca and Parma, the Romans and the Venetians, the Lombards and Sicilians, hated each other even more cordially than they hated the Austrians.

Any one who would like to get a good idea of life under the communal government of these free cities will find it in that most delightful of semi-historical novels Manzoni's " I promessi Sposi," or in Benvenuto Cellini's "Memoirs," or in George Eliot's " Romola." Or, for those who prefer pure history, Sismondi's " History of the Italian Republics " may be supplemented by Symonds's " Renaissance," which, however, deals principally with art and literature. I do not recommend Guicciardini's "History of Italy," remembering the old story that a cardinal, having betted with one of the Popes that no man living had ever been able to read Guicciardini's " History " all through, the Pope offered a criminal, condemned to death, a pardon if he would accomplish the feat. The man accepted the offer, but at the end of the second volume he returned the book, saying that on the whole he preferred to meet his doom.

By the middle of the seventeenth century, Austria had established her Ghibelline influence over the greater part of Northern Italy. She ruled Lombardy, and her influence was strong in Venetia, and the old free cities were hers. Tuscany was governed by an archduke of the imperial house; Parma, Modena, Placentia, Massa-Carrara, and all the rest of the little duchies (called at the present day collectively Emilia) had rulers devoted to the court and family at Vienna. But of all the ill-governed portions of Italy, the worst were the States of the Church in the centre of the peninsula, and tens of thousands of Italians lamented, with Dante of old, that the Pope's spiritual authority had been complicated by his being a petty temporal Italian ruler. Then came the French armies under Napoleon. They swept over Italy. The seeds of discontent sown by the oppression and misgovernment of Austro-Italian princes, began to sprout into a desire for the expulsion of foreigners, the establishment of constitutional government, and a United Italy.

"No country in Europe," says Mr. Probyn, "was more completely revolutionized by the wars and the policy of the first Napoleon than Italy. When at length he had become possessed of absolute power, all the old governments of the peninsula had been overthrown and were replaced by those of his own creation. The greater part of the kingdom of Piedmont and of the States of the Church, the republic of Genoa, and the duchies of Lucca, Parma, and Tuscany were incorporated into the French Empire. Eugène Beauharnais was made viceroy of a 'Kingdom of Italy,' composed of Lombardy, the republic of Venice, the duchy of Modena, the Pope's province of Romagna, and a portion of Piedmont. The kingdom of Naples received Joseph Buonaparte for its sovereign, and then Murat. These rulers were understood to act only as lieutenants of the French Emperor. Napoleon, in fact, governed the whole country from the Alps to the Straits of Messina."

French rule acted differently upon three classes of society in Italy. The peasants hated the conscription, and grudged the sacrifices they were compelled to make to support the imperial power of France, in which they had no national interest. Of the two they preferred the rule of the Austrians to that of the French. The Austrians were at least good Catholics. The Italian nobility, who from generation to generation had lived in apathy and idleness, suddenly found a stimulus in the many public offices to be filled by them under the administration of Napoleon; while professional men and the educated classes, not noble, rejoiced in the expulsion of the Austrians, in reforms in every department of the government, and in short in the new life of activity, prosperity, and hope that sent a thrill through the peninsula.

Not many Italians, however, voluntarily joined the armies of Napoleon; his promise at Milan that " he would make something of them, — that he would make them soldiers, and would lead them in six months as conquerors to the Tower of London," failed to waken their enthusiasm. Napoleon's aims were too evidently French; besides which Italians were not prompt to forget that when he had destroyed the old Republic of Venice in 1797 he had handed the city over, with insulting words to the detested Austrians.

Napoleon was crowned with the Iron Crown of Lombardy at Milan, and styled himself the King of Italy. The amiable and excellent Eugène de Beauharnais, was appointed his viceroy. For a time Eugène was popular, but his popularity did not survive the disasters of the campaign of Moscow, which fell heavily on the Italian contingent.

Lord Broughton (the John Cam Hobhouse who was the travelling companion of Lord Byron) says of Eugène :

"During the early part of his viceroyalty he had been much esteemed for a quality which is seldom found in men of high station and moderate capacity, — he listened to good advice, and was thus able to extricate himself from many difficulties. His conduct towards the Pope, for example, showed how capable he was of reconciling the interests of Napoleon with the temper of those whom he was called upon to control. He seems, however, to have been directed no longer by the same good sense or the same wise counsellors, when, during the retreat from Russia, he studiously neglected his Italian generals, and thereby forfeited the attachment of those on whom he was chiefly to depend in the coming struggle."

Much anti-French feeling was also excited in Lombardy by the activity of the Viceroy's ministers, Prina and Mejean, in raising the contingent of Italian troops for the campaign of 1813, and endeavoring, by all possible schemes of finance, to supply the French Emperor with money.

After the disasters of this campaign, Murat passed through Milan on his way to his kingdom of Naples. His money was exhausted, and he borrowed a thousand crowns from a Milanese merchant "to enable him," as he said, "to return to his capital with the equipment at least of a sovereign." In a moment of confidence he told this merchant that he had a scheme, now that the power of the Emperor was broken, of "collecting an army of eighty thousand men, marching northwards, raising the patriots in every province, and declaring the independence of Italy." The merchant was a Freemason, and communicated this secret to his lodge, whence it was at once made known to Prince Eugène, who was Grand Master of the Order in Lombardy. This caused bad feeling between Murat and Eugène, who had never been strongly attached to each other, and produced discord among their partisans, — an independent united Italy being the dream of almost all educated Italians. When Napoleon sent word to Milan that he released his subjects in Italy, and the Italians in his army from their oaths of allegiance, it seemed to many that the time was propitious for securing this boon. Eugène, on his part, meditated putting forth a declaration proclaiming the union of the States of Northern Italy, with himself as their constitutional king and France for their permanent ally.

But his scheme never reached a definite conclusion. Murat was marching northwards; leading patriots among the Lombards were already in communication with him; while the Austrians were advancing with promises to restore the ancient privileges of the Lombard kingdom, to be guaranteed solemnly by the word of the Emperor.

Affairs became more and more complicated in Northern Italy; some men were partisans of Eugène, some of Murat; while some believed the promises of Austria, and Murat had already become Austria's ally. England also sent a mixed force of English, Greeks, Calabrians, and Sicilians, under Lord William Bentinck to take a hand in the affairs of Northern Italy, — each party "assuming in turn the same generous character of liberators and friends; all professing themselves allies in the same pious enterprise, the emancipation of Italy from a foreign yoke."

Eugène at the head of sixty thousand men took up arms against these various "liberators"; but he was driven by the Austrians into Mantua, where, receiving news of the abdication of his stepfather at Fontainebleau, he proposed to Austria a suspension of hostilities. Milan was in a ferment. The Senate was in session. Some senators took the part of Eugène; some proposed a return to the rule of Austria; others proposed to accept an Austrian archduke, or any other prince except Eugène, as King of Northern Italy.

A most disgraceful riot took place in Milan on April 20, 1814. The mob surrounded the Senate-house, shouting, "The country and independence! Down with the French! Down with Eugène!"

The Senate in great alarm dispersed, a nobleman in the mob ran the ferule of his umbrella through a valuable picture of Napoleon in the Senate-house. The populace grew more and more excited. They rushed to the house of Eugène's finance minister, Prina, seized him, half stripped him and flung him from a window. Wounded and bruised, he contrived to escape into a friend's house, but the rioters surrounded it, and threatened to burn it down if he did not come out to them. He did so, exclaiming, "It matters little what you do to me. I am already a victim to your fury; but may my murder be your last."

These were, as it were, his dying words. The populace seized him, and beat him to death; though it has been supposed that he retained some life for about four hours, while they dragged his body through the streets by torch-light with savage execrations.

When news of the riot in Milan, and of this murder reached Eugène, he was utterly disheartened. A few members of the Senate who reassembled when the city became quiet, resolved to send a deputation to the Allied Sovereigns in Paris imploring them to select for them a sovereign "whose origin and qualities might make them forget the evils of their former governments." Eugène, meantime, ignorant of what had been resolved on in Milan, published a proclamation, declaring his readiness, if it were the will of the people, to take upon himself the cares of sovereignty. No notice was taken of this proclamation,— it died, as it were, still-born. It was never cancelled, contradicted, nor acted on in any way. Indeed, the ink with which it had been written was hardly dry before Eugène had signed with Field-Marshal Bellegarde, the Austrian Commander in Chief, on April 23, 1814, a convention by which he delivered up Mantua and his army to the Emperor of Austria. His soldiers were furious when they learned this, and proposed to arrest their late viceroy. But he had already secretly left Mantua, taking his treasure chest with him.

The Austrian general, when he took possession of his prize, appointed a regency, to last until informed of the intentions of the Allies. The people still entertained hopes that they might secure their independence, — that their deputies in Paris might be listened to. They trusted that English statesmen might move in their behalf, but Lord Castlereagh's only advice was that they should address themselves to their master, — the Emperor of Austria. The Emperor's answer was that he had conquered Lombardy and would issue his commands to her people from Milan. In vain, in their despair, such authorities as remained continued to petition for their country's political existence. Some counselled a wild scheme of insurrection, still hoping that the English, who were holding Genoa, would plead their cause. It was hoping against hope. On May 23, Marshal Bellegarde issued a proclamation announcing that Lombardy was taken possession of for the Emperor of Austria, and that he himself was appointed President of the Regency.

"When Lord Byron and myself," said Lord Broughton, "visited Milan two years after these events, the mistakes committed by the principal actors in them were acknowledged by all parties; but concerning the murder of Prina, and the riot or insurrection of the 20th of April, all were silent, because all were ashamed."

Venice and her dependencies on *terra firma*, otherwise called Venetia, had put herself under the victorious General Napoleon Bonaparte in 1797, by an act of abnegation on the part of the Great Council which seems almost incredible. She surrendered even before surrender was asked of her. Her patrician rulers became a provisional government, — a regency under the French Directory; her

Golden Book was burned, together with the ducal ensigns; and a fraternizing feast welcomed the French into the city. It was French for five months, and then Bonaparte, disregarding the rémonstrances of the French Directory, handed Venice and Venetia over to Austria by the Treaty of Campo Formio, October 18, 1797. Bonaparte's persistence in thus disposing of the ancient republic, which had maintained its position among nations for more than twelve hundred years, may have had some connection with the plan, at that moment ripening in his head, for the expedition to Egypt, and the establishment of himself on the throne of the Greek Emperors. Now that one hundred years have passed we may see reason to regret that he did not accomplish it. A French renegade Emperor in place of the Grand Turk might have relieved the nineteenth century from many of its difficulties.

Thus Venice was united to Lombardy. The rule of the Emperor of Austria, mild to his native Austrian subjects, was one of oppression and repression to all beyond the pale.

In 1820 and 1821 there were great stirrings of heart among educated men in Italy, who had almost all joined the secret society of the Carbonari. There were two branches of this society, one composed of Red Republicans, who approved assassination and fomented insurrectionary movements; the other, which called itself the Society for the Unity of Italy, had for its primary object the expulsion of the Austrians. To this society Lord Byron belonged, and almost all the men of letters in Italy. The Austrian police laid hands on as many of these gentlemen as possible in 1820 and 1821, — among them Silvio Pellico, author of the greatly admired tragedy of "Francesca da Rimini." He had committed no overt act of treason to the existing government, he was implicated in no conspiracy, but he was editor of a newspaper in Milan, the "Conciliatore," which aimed to keep alive the sparks of Italian patriotism. The association to which he belonged required no secret initiation. All the best patriots of Italy were involved in it, and their sole engagement was the formula taken on entering its ranks, "I swear to God, and on my honor, to exert myself to the utmost of my power, and even at the sacrifice of my life, to redeem Italy from foreign dominion."

Silvio Pellico, with other men of culture and refinement, was arrested in the autumn of 1820. For eighteen months they were kept in Italian prisons, perpetually undergoing interrogations, suffering inexpressibly from the fear that in the course of these examinations some chance word might be wrung out of them which would lead the authorities to suspect others. On February 22, 1822, he, with three others, was led forth to receive sentence of death on a scaffold in the Piazza of St. Mark in Venice; the sentence was then commuted to one of fifteen years' imprisonment in chains in the fortress of Spielberg, a convict prison on a mountain in Moravia.

There is no more touching piece of autobiography in any language than the "Le Mie Prigioni" of Silvio Pellico ("My Prisons"). It has been translated and re-translated into English and other languages. I read it with deep emotion when I was a school-girl. It stirred the very heart of Christendom.

"To Spielberg, that rock of sorrow," says the Countess Martinengo Cesaresco, "consecrated forever by the sufferings of some of the purest of men, Silvio Pellico, with Pietro Maroncelli, with nine or ten companions condemned at the same time, were the first to take the road. Here they remained for the eight years described by the author of 'Francesca da Rimini' in 'Le Mie Prigioni,' a book that served the Italian cause throughout the world. Even now, some Italians are indignant at the spirit of saintly resignation which breathes upon Silvio Pellico's pages, — at the veil which is drawn over many shocking features in the treatment of the prisoners. They do not know the tremendous force which such reticence gave his narrative. 'Le Mie Prigioni' has the reserve strength of a Greek tragedy."

Our countryman, Henry Tuckerman, says: —

"The political offenders in Lombardy in 1820 were subjected to the examination of commissioners notoriously venal and cruel. No opportunity was allowed them to prove their innocence; the slightest pretext sufficed to arouse suspicion, and, when this occurred, the arrest followed. Thenceforth the prisoner was allowed no intercourse with his family, his papers were seized, his associates were threatened, he was thrown into a slimy dungeon, or under burning leads; allowed only inadequate food, and when sleep, brought on by exhaustion consequent on these cruelties, came to his relief, he was suddenly roused at midnight, and urged, while in a state of half somnolency, to give up the name of a comrade, or to sign a paper which would prove his ruin. . . . The great idea derived from Silvio Pellico's memorial of his prisons, is that a man of rare endowments, of the deepest sensibility, and most pure aims, could be forcibly separated from the world of nature and humanity, — his sacred birthright, — invested with the livery of crime, denied communication with books, subjected to the greatest physical discipline, and moral isolation; — and although the author of this great wrong is scarcely alluded to, we revert to him for this very reason with the deeper indignation, and follow the pen of the generous martyr with the most profound sympathy. Wisdom could not have imagined, nor wit fashioned a work so well adapted to operate on public opinion, and yet so far from being the product of a vindictive mind. It is the simple overflowing of a frank and benign spirit, and by virtue of the very resignation, patience, love, and truth it breathes, it became a seal of condemnation to the Austrian government, and an appeal for the Liberals of Italy throughout the civilized world."

Maroncelli contracted a disease of the leg through the hardships he endured; amputation became necessary, but it could not be performed till permission was received from Vienna. After his release he went into exile in America, where he died, poor, blind, and with the loss of reason. Pellico, who died in 1854, devoted his latter years entirely to religion. Only men of iron fibre came out as they went in. The Spielberg prisoners always wore chains, and their food was so bad and scanty that they suffered from continual hunger, with its attendant diseases. Unlike the thieves and murderers confined in the same fortress, the State prisoners were given no news of their families. Such was Spielberg, — "a sepulchre without the peace of the dead."

Meantime, revolutions had taken place in Naples and in Piedmont. Of the former, as it belongs to the history of Southern Italy, I will tell in the next chapter; of Piedmont it may be proper to speak here.

The kings of Piedmont and Savoy, or (as they styled themselves after the year 1720) the kings of Sardinia, were descended from a knight of Northman descent, who came from Saxony. His name was Humbert (or Umberto) of the White Hands. Exiled from Court by reason of a quarrel with the Emperor, he built himself a castle among the hills of Savoy. When Conrad became Emperor of Germany, he gave this land in 1048 to Count Humbert. The Emperor Sigismund in 1417 made Savoy into a duchy. The Dukes of Savoy intermarried with royal families, and held a high place among the sovereign princes of Europe, less on account of their political importance than their personal character. One, Emmanuel Philibert, married a daughter of Francis I. of France, and his son, Charles Emmanuel, espoused a daughter of Philip II. of Spain; another, Victor Amadeus I., married a daughter of Henri IV. of France, while Victor Amadeus II., who in 1720 first assumed the title of King of Sardinia, married Anna Maria of Orleans, granddaughter of King Charles I. of England and Henrietta Maria.

Victor Amadeus, the second king of that name, but the third Victor Amadeus Duke of Savoy, ascended the throne in 1773 and had six sons. All grew to manhood, three were married, and succeeded each other on the Sardinian throne, but none had a male heir. Their names were Charles Emmanuel IV., who married Marie Adelaide Clotilde, sister of Louis XVI. and Madame Elisabeth; Victor Emmanuel I.; and Charles Felix. With Charles Felix the elder branch of the Savoy family died out in the male line. Charles Emmanuel abdicated in 1802 after some years of exile in Sardinia. Victor Emmanuel abdicated in 1821; Charles Felix succeeded him and died in 1830.

The next heir to the throne was young Charles Albert of Savoy-Carignan, a very distant cousin.

Savoy had been conquered by the French arms in 1792, and annexed to France as two departments; but by the treaties of 1814 it was given back to Piedmont by the allies; and to Piedmont was also annexed the former republic of Genoa, in spite of promises made to it by Lord William Bentinck, who held it for the English. Lord Castlereagh refused to ratify those promises and it was incorporated into a country for which it had for centuries entertained an especial aversion.

On January 11, 1821, a tumult took place at Novara, the work of some young students, who soon excited the populace. The rising was suppressed the next day by soldiers from Turin. But the revolutionary spirit was by no means subdued. A month later, at the dictate of Austria, several noblemen, leaders of the Liberal cause, were arrested in Piedmont, and thrown into prison. By March the revolutionary leaders proclaimed a Constitution, and unfurled the red, white, and green flag, the tricolor of United Italy. Turin then fell into the hands of the revolutionists. King Victor Emmanuel, who was absent from his capital, hastened back to it, determined at first to oppose the revolution; but finding that his army was of the same mind as those who were shouting for a Constitution, he decided to abdicate. The demand was universal for the Spanish Constitution. "Our hearts," said the insurgents, "are faithful to the king, but we must extricate him from his fatal counsellors; war with Austria, and the Constitution of Spain,— that is what the situation of the country and the people require." These, King Victor Emmanuel was unwilling to grant; he abdicated in favor of his only remaining brother, Charles Felix, who was then in Modena, and appointed his far-away cousin, Prince Charles Albert of Savoy-Carignan, who was next heir to the throne, Regent until Charles Felix could arrive. Then, with his family, he took the road to Nice, and Charles Albert, after some hesitation, proclaimed the desired Constitution.

The proclamation he issued said —

"In this most difficult moment it is not possible merely to consider what it is usually within the faculty of a regent to perform. Our respect and submission to his Majesty Charles Felix, upon whom the throne has devolved, would have counselled us to abstain from making any change in the fundamental laws of the kingdom, and would have led us to wait, so that we might know the intentions of the new king. But the imperious necessity of the circumstances being clearly manifest, and it especially behoving us to hand over to His Majesty his people in safety and happiness, . . . we have determined that the Constitution of Spain shall be promulgated."

The Regent then hastened to inform Charles Felix of what had been done, to which the King replied by protesting against any changes in the form of government introduced since his brother's abdication; he denounced the Constitution, and gave his subjects warning that his august allies would support him in his opposition to it. He appointed a new ministry, especially charged to punish all those who had striven to overthrow absolutism in Piedmont. He also summoned Charles Albert to repair at once to Novara and there make submission to him, together with his army.

Meantime, the Austrians, on the invitation of Charles Felix, marched into Piedmont; and Genoa, seeing resistance was hopeless, submitted. The King remained eight months in Modena before he visited his dominions, and Charles Albert, deeply in disgrace, was ordered to repair at once to Florence, and live there under the eye of his brother-in-law, Leopold of Tuscany, an Austrian archduke wholly out of sympathy with his revolutionary leanings. Nor was this enough. He was required to appease the allies, by serving in the French army which the Holy Alliance was about to despatch into Spain to put down Riego and the new Constitution.

The Congress of Verona took place in 1822. Strange to say, the inhabitants of that place made a great parade of their attachment to "their adored sovereign, the Emperor Francis of Austria," and welcomed their august visitors with enthusiasm. To be sure, there were four hundred police in the city to keep order, and ten thousand troops encamped around it. The sovereigns present were the Emperor Alexander, the Emperor Francis and his Empress, King Ferdinand of Naples, King Charles Felix of Sardinia, the Duchess of Lucca, the Archduke Ranieri, Viceroy of Lombardy, and the ex-Empress Maria Louisa. All sorts of fêtes and entertainments relieved their labors.

Lord Broughton says that, of all the sovereigns present, the Emperor Alexander took the most pains to ingratiate himself with the Veronese, by rambling about in pretended *incognito*, shaking hands with the ladies he happened to encounter in the streets, and giving sequins to the boys at play. He one day amused himself by carrying up coffee to his brother of Austria, and it was some time before Francis discovered that he was waited on by an emperor.

The Congress of Verona did not materially alter the political map of Europe as laid down by the Treaty of Paris signed May 30, 1814.

The arrangement of 1814 reinstated Pope Pius VII. in Rome, Victor Emmanuel I. in Sardinia, and Ferdinand III., Archduke of Austria, in Tuscany; while Parma and Piacenza were given to the Emperor's dethroned daughter, the ex-Empress Maria Louisa. Modena was restored to the Austrian Archduke Francis; Murat in 1814 had been allowed to return to Naples; but in 1822 the perjured Ferdinand was working his will both in Naples and Sicily, while Austria was supreme in Lombardy and Venetia. The independence of the tiny republics of San Marino and Monaco was graciously recognized, .while, at Verona, Genoa was confirmed to Sardinia, as was likewise that part of Savoy which in 1814 had been reserved to France.

Thus, all Italy, unless we except Piedmont, whose king was not absolutely deprived of all right to govern for himself, was Austrian, or governed by members of the imperial house of Austria, for even the Pope was held to be, in fact if not in theory, an Austrian vassal. There was thus, indeed, in one sense a united Italy, — an Italy united in misery, and, we may also add, in hatred to the rule of the Austrians. The seeds were being sown during this period which were to bear fruit in after years.

In 1831 there was an outbreak in Italy of revolutionary fervor. It was, in truth, for all Europe an important year. In it Charles Albert succeeded Charles Felix on the throne of Sardinia; Ferdinand II. (King Bomba) on the death of his father, Francis I., at the close of 1830 had become ruler of the Two Sicilies; Gregory XVI. became Pope. These were all personages who were to play important parts in Italy during the next twenty years. But even more important than the entrance on the scene of these potentates, was that of Giuseppe Mazzini.

He was born in Genoa on the day that the armies of Napoleon took possession of that city. His father was a physician. His mother was a woman whose life was devoted to companionship with her son. In 1831 he was but three-and-twenty, but he had already suffered seven months' imprisonment, in the fortress of Savona, for the suspicious tendencies of his political opinions. He was a Carbonaro, but was not in sympathy with the methods of the society; he abhorred its secrecies, its mysteries, and its ordeals of initiation. During his imprisonment at Savona he thought out a plan for a far simpler, and, as he hoped, a far more effective, organization, — that afterwards known as Young Italy. He had obtained his liberty before the death of Charles Felix, and was at Marseilles at the time of the accession of Charles Albert, to whom he addressed a letter, appealing to him to come forward and to put himself at the head of a national movement for the unity of Italy. Italian unity above and before all things was the object of Young Italy, — the form of government in a united Italy might afterwards settle itself. The oath taken by those who entered the society was, as we have seen, of the simplest kind. They were bound, by promise to God and by their honor, to do all in their power to promote the welfare and the unity of Italy, even should it be by the sacrifice of their lives.

Living at Marseilles, and there publishing a paper called

EMPRESS MARIA LOUISA.

"Young Italy," Mazzini made use of the facilities afforded him by the commercial relations of the place to aid his propaganda. One of his agents, serving on board an Italian merchantman, trading to Taganrog, on the sea of Azof, there met a young Italian whom he easily interested in the new society. It was Giuseppe Garibaldi. Cavour at the same date was in disgrace, having been removed from his work as an engineer officer in Genoa, on account of his political opinions.

Mazzini's personal convictions were in favor of a republican form of government. He believed that the will of the nation should rule, expressed through its elected delegates, — a noble thing not easily carried out when parties are governed by self-interest, and when disgust at the course of politicians puts the best men of the nation out of sympathy with affairs of state. The theory must be set to work before men can appreciate its difficulties.

Mazzini first became known to the public as the author of a letter addressed to Charles Albert imploring him to place himself at the head of the movement to bring about Italian unity. Mazzini was too good a patriot to insist on his own views. His wish was to see Italy united, free, and happy, whether under a constitutional monarch, or a republican form of government, though he believed always in his heart that the latter would be best.

Mazzini was a sincerely religious man. To him Catholicism was the national religion in a chrysalis state, and he could hardly be called a Catholic; but true religion, — faith in God and devotion to duty, because duty was obedience to God's will, — was the moving principle of his life in his early years. Carlyle, who, however he might worship deceased heroes, was seldom willing to admit into his Walhalla living men, said of Mazzini: —

"I have had the honor to know him for a series of years, and, whatever I may think of his practical insight and skill in worldly affairs, I can with great freedom testify that, if I have ever seen such, he is a man of genius and virtue, one of those rare men, numerable unfortunately as units in the world, who are worthy to be called martyr souls; who, in silence, piously in their daily life understand and practise what is meant by that."

And Mazzini, in a letter written about the same time, says of Carlyle :

"I have met upon my path — lonely enough, but I hope by choice — a Scotchman of mind and things, the first person here, up till now, with whom I sympathize and who sympathizes with me. We differ in nearly all our opinions, but his are so sincere and so disinterested that I respect them. He is good, good, good."

Mazzini's letter to Charles Albert, who did not wish to declare himself till wind and tide served, and who, indeed, under threat of an Austrian occupation of his kingdom, had just signed a document imposed on him by Prince Metternich, which bound him to make during his reign no radical or constitutional changes in the government of his kingdom, — this letter, written by an obscure exiled young student, did not move the King. He responded by an order for his arrest, should he again set foot in Piedmont.

Mazzini remained an exile in England, his "second country" he called it, and devoted himself to the good of the Italian working class immigrants in London.

He took a keen interest in the rescue and moral improvement of the children employed by organ-grinders. He opened a school for them in Hatton Garden,[1] which he mainly supported himself, in spite of his poverty, from 1841 to 1848.

In 1831 Italian hearts were stirred by the belief that the government of Louis Philippe had adopted what was called the principle of non-intervention. This meant not only that France would not take part in putting down any

[1] It was in 1846 that I was taken by Mr. and Mrs. George Putnam, in company with Margaret Fuller, then on her way to Italy, to a meeting held at this schoolhouse in Hatton Garden. Mazzini spoke, and we had an Italian improvisatore, and afterwards were taken into another room, where little Italian organ boys and white-mice boys, were swallowing yards upon yards of maccaroni. How little I realized the importance of the personages in whose company I found myself that evening! — though even then I was an enthusiast for Margaret Fuller's "Papers on Literature and Art."— E. W. L.

revolutionary rising in Italy, Spain, Germany, Poland, or elsewhere, but that she would prevent the interference of any other foreign government in any revolutionary movement. This was surely asking a great deal of France, which had her own affairs to settle, and a new dynasty to establish on her throne. Poland and Italy, Portugal, Spain, and Belgium, however, put their own interpretation on the policy of non-intervention, as enunciated by the first ministry of Louis Philippe; a portion of the Papal States broke at once into revolution; and, marvellous to say, the revolutionists looked to that unscrupulous intriguer and cruel despot, Francis of Modena, as the man to lead them, and in return he expected to be proclaimed King of Northern Italy.

Wise heads saw that the scheme was wholly impracticable, — not only impracticable, but subversive of better hopes; but patriotic enthusiasm is not to be checked by the cold considerations of wisdom. Count Joseph Orsi, in his interesting book of personal reminiscences, gives us an account of how Napoleon Louis and Louis Napoleon, sons of Louis Bonaparte and Queen Hortense, were carried away by the torrent, to the despair of their mother and father, who had been long separated, but were brought together at Florence by common concern for their two sons.

Napoleon Louis was remarkably handsome. Somewhat taller than a man of middle height, his figure and his gait were perfection.

"He had," says Orsi, "an expression of great intelligence and sweetness; and a keen look in his eyes, mingled with simplicity and kindliness, had made him the idol of society in Florence, and the dearly-loved son of his father, then living under the title of the Count de St. Leu. His education had been carefully attended to, and his stock of knowledge and his proficiency in foreign languages, and especially sciences, had brought the most eminent men in Florence to court his acquaintance and friendship. In horsemanship he was perfection."

Such is his portrait, painted by an admirer, early in the winter of 1831. He had recently married his cousin Charlotte, daughter of his uncle Joseph Bonaparte, and had every prospect of a happy life. But he and his brother, seized with the revolutionary enthusiasm prevalent in Italy, had taken the oaths as Carbonari, — not of that milder type that called itself Young Italy, or the Society of United Italy, but oaths of the advanced and secret kind of Carbonarism that resembles Nihilism, — that binds its members by strange oaths, demands secrecy and obedience, and holds killing to be no murder when inflicted on a recreant who has broken his vows.

The Prince, with all his attractive qualities, was wilful and determined, very hard to dissuade from any course on which he had decided. With the cause of regenerated Italy he was determined to stand or fall.

He declared to Orsi, whom he admitted into a sort of half-confidence, his full belief that the principle of non-intervention would be carried out by the new French government. It would check, he believed, the action of the Austrian government, and give free scope to the Italians to settle their own affairs. "One of the reigning princes of Italy," he said to Orsi, "whose name I am not at liberty to tell you, will shortly take the initiative in our affairs. We propose to form a Confederation of such States as will give in their adherence to our proposal, and it is expected that all will consent to form part of the project of establishing an independent state ruled by a constitution framed by and common to all. Should the scheme be successful, Rome will be the capital of the Italian Confederation, discharging its duties under the supreme presidence of the Pope."

The Prince believed in Louis Philippe's willingness to endanger his own crown to assist the cause of revolution in Italy. But Orsi, who had just returned from Paris, could not share these views. He was bidden, however, to a meeting to be held secretly in the house of Napoleon Louis, and was given leave to speak his mind to deputies who would come to Florence from other cities to be present.

The very day of the meeting it was rumored that the Austrians had taken the alarm, and were sending reinforcements to the fortress of Ferrara in Romagna, the Pope having given Austria the right to garrison it.

The brother of Ciro Menotti spoke first at the meeting, regretting the divergence in Liberal views, but believing that all patriots were in favor of insurrection at the proper time, — and that time had arrived, in his opinion.

Dictatorship, he said, was to be exercised by the Duke of Modena, until independence should be attained. The Duke's adviser and confidant was his own brother, Ciro Menotti. The Duke had for some time past been negotiating secretly with other Italian princes. On March 4 the insurrection was to break out in Modena, Parma, and Piacenza, which were to send volunteers to join the forces already manœuvring in Romagna. Austria would be shut up in her fortresses, forbidden by France to move.

"But," cried Count Orsi, "can you have placed your trust in the Duke of Modena? There is not a man or child, friend or foe — not a country, however far away from Italy, that has not heard of his standing as the most conspicuous champion of absolutism, cruelty, and lust for gold? His wealth is as great as his greediness for riches. His blind subserviency to the will of Austria and to the bigotry of Rome is notorious; and how your brother, Ciro Menotti, can have pinned his faith for the liberation of Italy to the Duke of Modena, and have made him our leader in the Italian movement, I am at a loss to understand. Tell him that the Duke is a master in treachery, — a man not to be relied on, that he would sacrifice his best friend to save his throne. Tell Ciro he is completely mistaken in his assumption that Austria will stand quietly a looker-on at what is taking place in Italy; and let him bear well in mind the responsibility and grief that will overwhelm his chivalrous nature at the sacrifice of so many lives, should the insurrection prove a failure."

Subsequently, on Count Orsi's remonstrating privately with the Prince, the latter pleaded his "engagements." "Engagements!" exclaimed Orsi, "and with whom?" "With the secret society of the Carbonari, of which both I and my brother are members."

That night poor Napoleon Louis and his brother, the

future Napoleon III., left Florence secretly, to join the insurgents who were in arms in Romagna.

Bologna had been surrendered to the patriots without resistance. The soldiers of the Pontifical army in garrison in the place even joined in effecting the change. The movement took possession without violence or bloodshed, of Romagna, Umbria, and the Marches. The citadel at Ancona surrendered at the first summons, its garrison disbanded, and the soldiers returned to their own homes. The Bishop of Rimini bore public testimony to the good order maintained in his revolted diocese.

But Austria soon put an end to all hopes founded on the possibility of her inaction. She sent troops at once into the revolted Papal States. Bologna and Ancona were at once reoccupied by Austrians, and the volunteer patriots soon learned that they were no match for disciplined soldiers of a regular army.

On hearing that the Austrians had entered Romagna, an evident proof that either Louis Philippe had given up the principle of non-intervention, or that the Austrian government had determined to march troops against the insurgents in spite of it, the Duke of Modena, perceiving the danger of his position, hastened to inform Menotti that, the intervention of the Austrians having altered the state of affairs, he declined to be implicated in the conspiracy. Ciro Menotti and his confederates, undaunted by the defection of the Duke, and acting on the assumption that they had to deal with a traitor, rose in arms against him, and took possession of several parts of his capital. The Duke brought his soldiers to put down the insurgents, who, being dislodged from the places that they occupied, took refuge in a house which they barricaded. The Duke ordered his artillery to storm the house, and to spare no one. The fight was long and bloody. The house, being built on pillars, became shaky. Some of the men in it jumped out of the windows, and were shot dead in the street. Ciro Menotti fell, dangerously wounded, and in that state was carried to the ducal palace; there he was secured in a carriage that was to take the Duke to Mantua that he might be under the protection of Austrian cannon and bayonets.

A few weeks after, when the insurrection had been completely quelled, the Duke brought Menotti back with him to Modena, and having caused a scaffold to be erected in front of Menotti's own house, had him executed upon it without trial.

The breaking up of the little army in Romagna had been promptly effected. The patriots were half armed, and had no experienced leader. Some escaped the fate of the less fortunate of their brothers in arms, who tried in vain to save their lives by taking to such small boats as they found upon the seashore. They were soon captured by Austrian cruisers, serving in the Adriatic, one of which was commanded by a naval officer named Bandiera.

The fate of those who were made prisoners is too dreadful to be dwelt upon. The Court of Rome vied with the Austrians for the privilege of torturing them, and executing them. Among the prisoners were many Roman subjects whom Austria refused to give up, asserting her right to them, having fought to save the Papal dominions from destruction. Between the two, the difference was rather in favor of Austria, as regarded the treatment to be expected by the unfortunate victims who were doomed to imprisonment. Those who were not shot at once underwent a sham trial, and were plunged, loaded with irons, into damp, dark prisons, — until a few saw light and liberty in the years 1847–48.

Both Napoleon Louis and Louis Napoleon had joined the insurgents. They fought bravely, and showed in several instances much military skill, but their presence was not acceptable to the leaders of the revolt, who still hoped for help and favor from Louis Philippe. Young Bonapartes in their ranks might tell against them. The Princes were required to repair to Forli, where they were kept in a species of captivity. There both became extremely ill. Their disorder was pronounced to be measles, a disease at that time prevalent in Northern Italy. But doubts have been thrown upon their case. They were Carbonari — they may have been considered recreant, or it may have been policy under the circumstances to get them out of the way. Napoleon the elder died. His brother, just risen from his sick bed, met their mother, Queen Hortense, a few miles out of Forli with the heartbreaking news. This effort and the emotion it occasioned were too much for him. He became desperately ill, and Queen Hortense was roused from her grief at the loss of one son by the necessity of doing all in a mother's power to save the life of the other.

She succeeded in getting him into Ancona, to a country house belonging to a member of the Bonaparte family. There she hid him and a friend of his, one of the proscribed, in a secret inner chamber, and nursed Louis through his illness, giving out, and even writing to his father (a precaution in case her letter should be opened), that she had got him off in safety to Corfu. She had provided herself with an English passport which carried them safely to Genoa, the proscribed friend and a faithful servant taking the part of the Englishwoman's two sons, while Louis, clad in livery, sat on the coach-box and directed the postilions.

Nearly one thousand persons in the little Duchy of Modena went into exile to escape the vengeance of the Duke, and more than five hundred were thrown into prison. The hanging of Menotti, with all its aggravations, united to other measures of the most cruel kind, made Francis of Modena so generally hated that he lived in constant fear and suspicion of those around him. Spies and informers flourished under him, the most innocent were not safe from denunciation. Even a man who had once saved the Duke's life, and was perfectly loyal to his person, was tried by court-martial and shot under a false accusation, — the Duke saying to his wife, the mother of eight children, while the ink was not dry with which he had signed the death-warrant, "I know the innocence of your husband, and even if he were guilty, I know well that gratitude would prevent my punishing him."

From 1831 to 1846, — that is, for fifteen years, — there was comparative tranquillity in the Italian peninsula, — the tranquillity that ensues when a victim stunned and bleeding lies helpless at the foot of his oppressor. Twice, however, during those fifteen years, Savoy was invaded by small bodies of exiled Italians, who thought to stir up revolutionary fervor, but these expeditions were mere raids, and in 1844 there was the brief sad episode of the rash attempt of the brothers Bandiera.

Restless and unhappy Italian exiles, who belonged to the order of Young Italy, planned hopeless revolutionary attempts. These did not succeed, nor was it likely that they should have been successful. "Devised by exiles at a distance from their country," says the Countess Cesaresco," "they lacked the first elements of success. The earliest of these attempts aimed at an invasion of Savoy; it was hoped that the Sardinian army and people would join the little band of exiles in a movement for the liberation of Lombardy."

The plans of the promoters of this ill-advised effort for Italian liberation were discovered before they were put in execution, and severe sentences of death and imprisonment were passed on those concerned in the conspiracy, even by Charles Albert, who felt himself obliged to secure the tranquillity of his kingdom by a certain submission to Austria, which had an army ready to occupy Piedmont if he gave her cause to do so. The brother of Ruffini (the author of "Doctor Antonio"), the bosom friend of Mazzini, committed suicide in prison, fearing he might inadvertently reveal in his examination the names of his associates.

Mazzini, who later deprecated rash attempts at insurrection, as leading only to the loss of precious lives that in due season might prove useful to their country, approved the plan of invading Savoy and Piedmont, and it was carried into effect in 1834. A Savoyard who had served in the Polish Revolution of 1831, Ramorino by name, had command of the expedition. He was accounted a good soldier, but was an inveterate gambler. He had crossed the frontier into Savoy with his handful of exiles, when he learned that a Polish reinforcement which he had expected to join him had been stopped on its way near the Lake of Geneva. He then considered the expedition hopeless, and effected his retreat, abandoning his followers, and advising their disbandment.

The expedition of the brothers Bandiera took place in the summer of 1844. It was disapproved and discouraged by Mazzini. Its object was to rouse Southern Italy.

The young men had been naval officers in the Austrian service, in which their father was an admiral. In 1831 he had arrested many of the Italian fugitives who in open boats were trying to escape to Corfu. The two young men had deserted their flag, but the Archduke Ranieri, then Viceroy of Lombardy and Venetia, made every attempt to win them back. Neither his promises of indulgence nor their mother's tears could move them. Their principal associates were Domenico Moro, who had been a comrade of theirs in a mixed force of Englishmen and Austrians in the Lebanon, after a massacre at Damascus, and the revolt of the Druses; Ricciotti, a young Roman of much promise; and Anacarsi Nardi, son of the chief minister of the Duke of Modena. The little band, which hoped to revolutionize the Italian Peninsula and drive the Austrians back over the Alps, amounted to twenty men. One of these twenty was, however, a traitor. They crossed the Adriatic from Corfu to Calabria, but the band of insurgents who they had been assured would meet them were nowhere to be found. Information had been furnished to the government of Naples by the traitor, a Corsican officer. They wandered for a few days in the mountains, then were surrounded and captured. Attilio and Emilio Bandiera were shot, together with Moro, Ricciotti, and Nardi. Their last words, heard above the rattle of the musketry, were *Evviva Italia!* They had been born on her soil, — and, rash as their enterprise had been, they died for her.

The traitor had a mock trial to save appearances, and was condemned to nominal imprisonment. "When he came out of prison he wrote to a Greek girl at Corfu, to whom he was engaged, to join him in Naples, that they might be married. The girl had been deeply in love with him, and had already given him part of her dowry, but she answered: 'A traitor cannot wed a Greek maiden. I bear with me the blessing of my parents; upon you rests the curse of God.'"

Of this ill-fated attempt of the brothers Bandiera Mr. Probyn says, in his "History of Italy":—

"Such was the spirit engendered by the wrongs of Italy. It was a spirit which led, indeed, to hopeless enterprises, and even to criminal acts, but it kept alive the national sentiment, it produced the great uprising of 1848, it survived the triumphs of the reactionary governments in 1849, it carried Italy through the conflicts, dangers, defeats, hopes, and successes, which, commencing with the Franco-Italian war of 1859, at length secured to Italy her unity and independence under the constitutional rule of the royal house of Savoy."

CHAPTER II.

PIO NONO.

ON the last day of May, 1846, Pope Gregory XVI. died. He had been a cruel temporal ruler, an indifferent Pope, and his enemies said that he was far from a good man. He was a very different Pope from the two who have succeeded him.

His death-bed was piteous. It is an old custom that when a Pope dies his apartments may be pillaged by his servants, who on this occasion were beforehand in their work, and the poor dying man was left utterly alone in his sick room, till a soldier on guard was persuaded to stay by him in his last moments, for charity's sake.

His death was welcomed by half the population of Rome, for the death of a Pope is generally succeeded by the release of political prisoners.

The prisons were crowded with men belonging to the best families in the Eternal City, and when it was reported that the Pope was very ill, mothers, wives, and sisters were hoping eagerly that he might not recover.

The death of Pope Gregory was officially announced by the usual ceremonies. The Cardinal Camerlengo, tapping the corpse three times upon the forehead with a golden hammer, asked His Holiness a question, and, receiving no answer, pronounced the Pontiff dead. Then the Pope's ring of the Fisherman was broken, and it only remained for the corpse to be embalmed, and lie in state.

The Conclave of Cardinals (the word *conclave* meaning literally under *lock and key*) were shut up in the Quirinal, each in his separate cell. They are always thus secluded

till the election of a new Pope has been made. Each day they take their places upon thrones in the Chapel, and after mass each cardinal gives in his scroll. In an inner fold he writes his own name, on the outer fold the name of the candidate he votes for. Two cardinals, appointed for the purpose, take the papers and read only the candidate's name. If no candidate has a two-thirds vote the scrolls are burnt up in a certain stove, and it is by smoke coming out of the chimney of that stove that Rome knows that a fresh vote has been taken, and that there is no election.

There were fifty-seven cardinals present in this Conclave; amongst them were Cardinal Mezzofanti, who knew fifty-six languages or dialects, and Cardinal Mai, whose fame for learning was world-wide, but in general the members of the Conclave (a few of whom, though Cardinals, were not in priests' orders) were indifferent men.

There was a by-law existing in 1846 that there could be only ten foreigners among the cardinals, — that out of the seventy, sixty must be Italians. At this time there were actually but five foreign cardinals, and none of these were present in the Conclave.

The two prominent parties were the party of Cardinal Lambruschini, who expected to receive the votes of the younger cardinals; while the older cardinals, who opposed Lambruschini, were under the leadership of Cardinal Fieschi; and a third party, attached to the Jesuits, was opposed to the election of any Pope who was a friar.

Austria and France had each its candidate. The Conclave was expected to be a very long one. To the astonishment of Rome and of the cardinals themselves, it ended in two days.

On the first ballot the cardinals forming the three different parties each voted for the candidate of their choice, and there was no election. The party of Cardinal Lambruschini was, however, the most powerful. Seeing this, his opponent, Cardinal Fieschi, became alarmed. Previous to the meeting of the Conclave he had directed his supporters, in such a case, to vote for some cardinal who had no prospect of being elected, in order to gain time. The leaders of the Jesuit party had done the same thing, and both parties, as they had had no opportunity of knowing the other's vote, fixed on the same man to serve their purpose.

The ballots were read. The Fieschi and the Jesuit cardinals united, outnumbered the cardinals who supported Lambruschini sufficiently to give a two-thirds vote to Cardinal Mastai-Ferretti, who no one had ever expected would be chosen. He was accordingly elected.

Shortly after, he was presented as the new Pope to the people, and selected as his title Pio Nono, or Pius IX.

Pio Nono's family had been always Liberals; a few generations back one of them had married a converted Jewess. The new Pope, Giovanni Maria Mastai, was the third son of his house. His elder brothers were in the Garda Nobile. He himself had been educated for a lawyer, but he did not "take to" learning, and, indeed, all his life was an indifferent Latin scholar. At Rome he fell in love with Clara Colonna, a very beautiful young lady, connected indirectly with the great Roman family of Colonna. She declined the addresses of Giovanni Mastai, though he was a handsome, elegant young man, and married a dragoon officer. The disappointment was severe. Mastai plunged for a time into dissipation, then renounced the study of the law, and his family got him an appointment in the Garda Nobile. But he was rejected as physically ineligible, because he had had epileptic fits.

This second disappointment was too much for him. He saw in it a sign from heaven, calling him to repentance. He changed his course of life, and resolved to enter the Church. His tastes were not for ecclesiastical learning, but for preaching the Gospel. He went out to Chili as a missionary. Afterwards, returning to Rome, he made the care of orphans his especial charge. He was made Bishop of Imola, and there was accused of betraying some of the unhappy patriots after one of their numerous and foolhardy abortive risings. He was certainly placed on a Commission to try them. He always said that he accepted the position with a view to their being treated with leniency. His enemies, however, accused him of "priestly treachery."

Among moderates he enjoyed the reputation of possessing liberal and moderate opinions, and a correct judgment, nor had he any toleration for the frightful temporal misgovernment of the Papal States, or the reactionary policy of Pope Gregory. He had read the books that were being passed from hand to hand among Italian Liberals, and his heart had been stirred by propositions for the federation of Italy under the headship of a Liberal Pope. When he went up to the Conclave he had carried with him some of the books containing patriotic, anti-Austrian, and Liberal opinions, intending to present them to whoever should be chosen Pope. A story is told that a white pigeon accompanied his carriage on his journey, and would not be driven away.

A month after his election the political amnesty appeared, and the political prisoners throughout the Roman States were released. The amnesty was hailed with rapture by the people. The Pope became their idol.

Here is part of a letter I received in those days from Mrs. Crawford, wife of the highly distinguished American sculptor, and mother of Marion Crawford, a novelist of whom America is justly proud.

My letter was dated at Frascati, July 26, 1846. After home news of herself and of her children, and telling me how she had left Rome for the summer season, she went on : —

"But indeed I must tell you how old Rome has waked up from a long, long sleep since the new Pope has come into power. The people have been in a state of excitement bordering on insanity, for about ten days since the Pope signed an edict by which fourteen thousand political prisoners in the Pontifical States were set at liberty."

Let me here interrupt Mrs. Crawford's letter to remark that fourteen thousand political prisoners in the Pontifical States represented one out of every twenty-six persons, including women and children. Mrs. Crawford continues : —

"There were only excepted priests, military men, or those who had been in the employ of the government, — all were freed at a moment's notice. When the edict was issued, late in the afternoon, a large number of people had assembled to witness a kind of ball-playing. The moment the young men heard of it they rushed from the place, formed themselves into a body, and marched directly to the Quirinal Palace, where they demanded of the Swiss Guard admittance to the presence of their Sovereign. This, of course, was refused. However, they insisted that the Swiss Guard should bear their message to the Pope, — that they had come to thank him for his generosity in liberating their countrymen. The Guard obeyed, and soon returned with orders to admit them into the inner courtyard, where, after a moment, the Pope appeared on a balcony. They all knelt while he blessed them, and then shouted their acclamations of joy.

"The same evening there was to be the canonization of a new Saint, attended with much beautiful music and imposing ceremonies, and most of the leading people of Rome were to be there to witness the ceremony. The new Saint's picture had been painted in brilliant colors, and hung over the door of the Church; the music and the services had begun, when the news of this glorious edict was whispered about among the people. The new Saint was forgotten, and with one rush they all — women and men alike — ran towards the Quirinal, seizing torches as they went, and their numbers continually increasing. At the Piazza Colonna they met with another immense body of people, who, actuated by a similar impulse, had also seized torches, and were on their way to the palace. They all reached the great square in front of the Quirinal about four o'clock at night. With one voice this sea of souls cried: *Fuori! Fuori! nostro Sovrano!* (Come forth! come forth! our Sovereign!) *Viva! Viva! Pio Nono.* There was a pause. Then they saw lights moving in the very extremity of the palace; they moved on from window to window, until they paused before that opening on to the great balcony looking over the Piazza. Then the blinds were thrown open, and between two lines of torches Pio Nono stepped forth, and the enthusiasm of the people knew no bounds. The Pope blessed them — a thing unheard of before at that hour of the night — and, after a few moments, he retired, waving his arms to the multitude till he was lost to view. My husband says it was one of the most beautiful and exciting sights he ever witnessed. It seemed to him almost a revolution. But the poor Saint awaiting canonization had to remain un-canonized all night. The following day the people in their enthusiasm detached the horses from the Pope's carriage, and drew it themselves along the Corso, ladies flinging handfuls of flowers upon him from the windows as he passed below. He was obliged to publish a paper requesting the populace, at the same time that he thanked them for their testimonials of esteem and affection, to moderate their transports somewhat. In Bologna they trampled under foot a portrait of Gregory XVI. at the same time that they are almost worshipping his successor, and I — yes, I! — have wept tears of joy for the thousands of happy hearts beating with new hope in consequence of the noble, generous conduct of this new Pope. Here he is surrounded with darkness, like a diamond glittering in some dim cave. He dares to be liberal-minded — to be generous — to attempt to shake off some of the dust of ages, to tear down the rank ivy which has overgrown and defaced the fairest portions of creation. Will not some unseen spirit bless the seed he scatters in the ground he ploughs?"

In Paris, little Parian busts of Pio Nono were sold everywhere, and it was my strong desire to possess one, greatly to the astonishment of my mother, who could not imagine what I wanted her to give me a Pope's bust for.

The amnesty was made much more liberal in consequence of the popular demonstrations of loyalty and gratitude. The populace had taken it for granted that it was general, in spite of the exceptions made in the proclamation, and the Pope did not resist their interpretation.

"Deep interest," writes a Roman who had a brother incarcerated at Rimini, "was felt in the liberated prisoners. When taken from their cells and brought into the light, among the huge crowd of their friends and relations they looked astonished and bewildered, as if suspecting that their triumph was but a dream. Many of them were entirely disabled and worn out by ill-treatment, and some were brought out blindfolded, upon chairs, because the light might have been too much for them. I saw, among those in Rome, a venerable old gentleman carried by four of his sons, all full-grown men, formerly his fellow-prisoners. A ray of joy illuminated his dying face, and his heart was overwhelmed with happiness at the imposing sight of the Roman people once more free, and evidently determined to maintain their freedom. I did not see my brother when he came out from prison, for he was in Rimini. My mother had been waiting there for the amnesty since she heard of the election of the Pope. 'They brought him to my arms,' she wrote to me, 'because he could not walk at all, or change his sitting position. The dampness of his dungeon had deprived him of the use of his limbs, and want of air and light made him look as pale as death. His sparkling black eyes were shut, because he could not bear the light. I need not say what I felt at this sight. But he was in excellent spirits, and bade me be of good cheer as he would recover in a few days. So thinks our excellent friend Doctor Michialis.'"

But though Pio Nono's popularity every day increased, he found himself beset by two opposing dangers. He was not a man of courage, not a man of political experience, and he had no adequate advisers. In Rome, surrounded by ecclesiastics, he stood almost alone.

The party of Young Italy, at the head of which was Mazzini, was resolved not to be satisfied with anything less than a republic in Rome, and a federation of Italian republics, with Rome for their City of Washington, to form a United Italy. To this, and to the expulsion of the Austrians, its members had pledged themselves by oath, and the reforms offered by the Pope by no means promoted their views.

On the other hand was the party of the Sanfedesti, — the Holy Faith party as it was called, — which opposed the reform of any abuses, however vile, as tending to encourage radicalism; and this party, never opposed by Austria, was sometimes strengthened by her active support. To Prince Metternich, the Austrian Prime Minister, a Liberal Pope seemed as abnormal as a United Italy. However, Pio Nono, while opposed by the Sanfedesti in Rome, and by the ruling powers in Vienna, had good friends in France and England. Lord Palmerston lent him all possible support, and enthusiasm in Paris went wild for him.

The Prime Minister of Louis Philippe in 1846 and 1847 was M. Guizot, and the French Ambassador at Rome was M. Guizot's son-in-law, Count Pellegrino Rossi.

It seems strange to find M. Rossi French Ambassador

at Rome, for he was an Italian who had been formerly a Professor at the University of Bologna. Pope Pius VII. exiled him in 1815 for his opinions, both political and religious, for he was (or became soon after) a Protestant. In Geneva he lived some years an exile, and there married one of M. Guizot's daughters. After 1830 he went to France, was naturalized as a Frenchman, and made Professor of Political Economy at the University of Paris. Louis Philippe subsequently made him a Peer of France.

In 1845 there was a general uprising in Europe against the Jesuits, — a persecution which in many instances was irreligious and unjust. However, exasperation against the Order rose in France to such a height that Louis Philippe determined to ask Pope Gregory to assist him in removing them from France, rather than that they should be expelled. For this purpose Count Rossi was sent as Minister Extraordinary to the Papal Court. The Pope was exceedingly angry that a rebellious subject of the Church, and an avowed Protestant, should have been sent to him on such an errand, and he refused at first to see him. Nevertheless, two months had not elapsed before Rossi had been presented to the Pope and had successfully accomplished his mission; and now, eighteen months later, he was in Rome strengthening the hands of a Liberal Pope, and preaching Liberal progress to the whole body of cardinals.

Meantime, Pio Nono, who was, as I have said, a man of little courage, and who, like most epileptics, had very little command over his nerves, was buffeted about by the strong contrary winds that blew around him. He would not give the Romans an Elective Assembly, but he nominated a sort of State Council of " good men and true," which met in August, 1847. It proved, however, a total failure; it was not empowered to legislate, and was incompetent to advise. The failure of this body to do anything to any purpose lost the Pope some of his popularity. His ministers, too, were repeatedly changed. From time immemorial all Cabinet Ministers in the States of the Church had been ecclesiastics. Count Rossi urged the Pope to choose some of his Cabinet from laymen. This was done; but events were now moving at railroad speed, and the truest friends of the Pope doubted his vigor.

In February, 1848, Louis Philippe had been driven from his throne, and with him fell his Prime Minister, M. Guizot, who became likewise an exile in England. Count Rossi upon this resigned his position as French Ambassador, and even as a Frenchman. He resolved to cast in his lot with his own countrymen. Revolution had broken out in Vienna. Prince Metternich had taken flight; the Italians in Lombardy and Venetia had rushed to arms. Charles Albert, King of Piedmont and Savoy, was preparing to join the Lombards and Venetians against their common enemy.

All this produced a ferment in Rome which terrified Pio Nono. He found that the concessions he had made were considered not half enough by his subjects, and he began to lament their ingratitude, and to bewail his disappointment.

Meantime, Rome and Young Italy throbbed with an enthusiastic wish to go to the assistance of their brethren fighting in Lombardy to drive away the Austrians. When the news of the outbreak in Vienna and the overthrow of Metternich reached Rome (March 21, 1848), a month after Louis Philippe had quitted France, a great tumult arose. Joy bells were rung; the Austrian flag was burned in public to the cry of *Evviva Italia!* Lawrence Oliphant, then scarcely more than a boy, has given us an amusing account of his participation in this work in his " Scenes in a Life of Adventure." He says: —

"Mutterings of the coming revolutionary storm had been heard all over Europe, and it was just bursting over Italy as we descended into that country at the close of 1847. On the day when I entered Rome for the first time, I passed cannon pointed down the streets, and found the whole town seething with revolution. I shall never forget joining a roaring mob one evening, bent I knew not upon what errand, and getting forced by the pressure of the crowd, and my own eagerness, into the front rank, just as we reached the Austrian Legation, and seeing the ladders passed to the front, and set against the wall, and the arms torn down: then I remember, rather from love of excitement than any strong political sympathy, taking hold, with hundreds of others, of the ropes which were attached to them, and dragging them in triumph to the Piazza del Popolo, where a certain Ciceruacchio, who was a great tribune of the people in those days, had a couple of carts laden with wood standing all ready; and I remember their contents being tumultuously upset and heaped into a pile, and the Austrian arms being dragged on the top of them, and a lady, — I think the Princess Pamphili Doria, — who was passing in a carriage at the time, being compelled to descend, and being handed a flaming torch, with which she was requested to light the bonfire, which blazed up amid the frantic demonstrations of delight of a yelling crowd, who formed round it a huge ring, joining hands, dancing and capering like demons; in all of which I took an active part, and going home utterly exhausted, with a feeling that somehow or other I had deserved well of my country. I remember, too, later, being roused from my sleep about one or two in the morning by the murmur of many voices, and looking out of my window and seeing a dense crowd moving beneath, and rushing into my clothes, and joining it, and being borne along I knew not whither, and finding myself at last one of a shrieking, howling mob at the doors of the Propaganda, against which heavy blows were being struck, directed by improvised batteringrams; and I remember the doors crashing in, and the mob crashing in after them, to find empty cells, and deserted corridors, for the monks had sought safety in flight. And I remember standing on the steps of St. Peter's when Pope Pio Nono gave his blessing to the volunteers that were leaving, as they hoped, for Lombardy to fight the Austrians, and seeing the tears roll down his cheeks."

Such reminiscences give us the seamy side of excited patriotism and the fervor of revolution.

The Pope's ministry had begun to enlist volunteers. To the usual banner of the Pontifical troops (a yellow flag embroidered with the Keys) they joined the tricolor of Italy — red, white and green. All Rome, intoxicated with joy, rang with the clash of arms. "The streets," says an Englishman who was present, "echoed to the music of warlike songs. The Pope and the religious orders presented large gifts in money to the cause of Italy. More than twelve thousand volunteers marched to the frontier to join the fray; among them were two of the Pope's nephews, and Pio Nono blessed them all as brave defenders of the Roman territory — and he blessed their cannon."

But then came the reaction. The young men of Rome had quitted Rome. Great pressure was brought to bear on Pio Nono. The Liberal Ministry insisted on a declaration of war against Austria, and that the Papal troops must cross the Po. Austrian influence at the Papal Court, and almost every cardinal, declared that the Pope must go back rather than go forward in his revolutionary career.

The history of what followed is not creditable to the courage or the statesmanship of Pio Nono. But indeed he dared not take a decided part either way. He put forth an allocution (as it was called) in such involved Latin that nobody could make out its real meaning. He fell into the strong hands of Cardinal Antonelli, who thenceforth governed him, and his career as a reforming Pope was over.

Still tossed about, however, by contrary advisers, Pio Nono placed Count Rossi, who was one of his new Council, at the head of a new Ministry, but this appointment was received with much disapproval from the priestly party, nor was it looked upon with favor by those patriots whose eyes were turning to Charles Albert as the possible saviour of his country. Rossi's reforms, too, attacked old-established rights and vested interests, and thereby raised against him a large crop of enemies in all ranks of the community; whilst the priestly party — the party of reaction — strove to inflame the populace against him by its cries: "What! Rossi, who is a Protestant! Rossi, a member of the infamous French Academy! Rossi, some of whose writings are in the Index Expurgatorius!" (the list of books prohibited in Rome).

On November 15, 1848, there was to be in Rome the solemn opening of the second session of the Deliberative Council.

"A little before one o'clock," says a Roman citizen, "I closed my office and went toward the building where the ceremony of the opening was to be performed. The huge square before it was covered with people. I saw a brilliant equipage crossing the square and entering the wide gates. It was the Prime Minister, Count Rossi. I was at the opposite end of the square, but, standing upon a piece of a broken column placed beside a gateway, I could see the wide entrance where the carriage stopped. Count Rossi got out of the carriage with two friends, and there were three servants in full-dress livery attending upon him. An unknown man among the crowd touched the left arm of Rossi, who turned his head with a quick movement; at this another tall fierce-looking man plunged a knife into his neck, and then calmly withdrew among the crowd that was pressing forward to see what had happened."

Who this man was, was not found out till six years after. Some said that the murderer was a brigand, hired by the Sanfedesti; others that Rossi had been condemned as a traitor by one of the secret societies. There seems to have been no just ground, even on the part of the most advanced Liberals, for personal hatred against Rossi, but his murder proved in the end to have been their doing.

The Countess Cesaresco, in her book on the " Liberation of Italy" says of this murder that it was " the most deeply to be regretted event in the course of the Italian revolution "; and adds : —

"As minister to the Pope, Count Rossi had made his influence immediately felt; measures were taken to restore order in the finances, discipline in the army, public security in the streets, and method and activity in the government offices. The tax on ecclesiastical property was enforced; fomenters of anarchy, even though they wore the garb of patriots, and perhaps honestly believed themselves to be such, were vigorously dealt with. If any one could have given to the temporal power a new lease of life it would have been a man so gifted and so devoted as Pellegrino Rossi, but the entire forces both of reaction and subversion were against him."

When news of the murder reached Pio Nono he shut himself up in the Quirinal, and gave orders to his Swiss Guard to admit no one to his presence but Cardinal Antonelli and the foreign ambassadors. Rossi's colleagues in the Ministry fled from Rome. There was neither a responsible Ministry nor any government in the city. The peace, however, was pretty well preserved during the night.

Next morning the Deliberative Council desired to send a deputation to the Pope. He refused to see them. They insisted, and a large crowd supported them. The crowd was fired on by the soldiery. It grew furious. A large body of the National Guard marched on the Palace, and pointed a cannon at the door of the Pope's private apartments. The Pope yielded. He received the deputation, appointed a new Ministry, and peace was restored. But Pio Nono prepared for flight.

Towards evening (November 25, 1848) he was visited by the Duc de Harcourt, the French ambassador, who had arranged the details of his escape with a beautiful Roman lady, Theresa Giraud, married to Count Spaur, the Bavarian ambassador, who was also in secret an agent of the government at Vienna. The plan of the Duc de Harcourt was to put the Pope on board a French steamer, then lying at Civita Vecchia, and to take him to France. The Austrian plan was, however, by no means that he should fall under the influence of revolutionary France, but rather that he should put himself under the protection of a power of extreme conservatism and far more in accordance with her policy.

The ambassador of France sought an audience with the Pope, while the doors of his private apartments were watched by sentinels of the Roman National Guard. The audience lasted several hours. On leaving, the Ambassador remarked, in the hearing of the sentinels, that His Holiness was very tired, and did not wish to be disturbed again that evening. The Duc de Harcourt during his audience had used every argument to persuade the Pope to adopt the plan arranged for him and to leave Rome.

Under his persuasions, Pio Nono went into his chamber, where his personal attendant Filippiani assisted him to exchange his white robes for the cassock of a mere priest. "He wept bitterly while doing so," says the writer from whom this account is taken. "The heart of the good shepherd bled for his ungrateful sheep, who had misunderstood his loving-kindness, and whom he was now abandoning to ravenous wolves."

This, however, was by no means the view of the situation taken by the Roman populace.

When dressed, the Pontiff flung himself upon his knees at the foot of his bed, and remained so long in prayer that his attendant was obliged to warn him that no more time could be spared. He rose at once, evidently strengthened and refreshed by those moments of devotion. On returning to the room where the Duc de Harcourt was still waiting, the latter, after a few words of encouragement, knelt and asked for the pontifical blessing. Then he hurried the departure of the Pope. Filippiani took a little bundle under his cloak containing a few private papers, the pontifical seals, his master's breviary, a few articles of clothing and a box containing some gold medals. They passed down a back staircase to a side door.

The Ambassador, meanwhile, remained alone listening anxiously to hear the wheels of the carriage which from an inner courtyard was to bear the Pope from the Quirinal. When, at last, he heard it drive off, he picked up some newspapers lying on a table, and from time to time read paragraphs aloud in as conversational a tone of voice as possible. By this means, and by the remark made in the hearing of the sentinels as he was going away, he secured some hours to the Holy Father during which his flight was unsuspected. By the time it was found out he was over the frontier.

Pio Nono, bearing in his bosom a golden ball which had once belonged to Pius VII. and which contained the wafers of the Eucharist, went, as I said, accompanied by Filippiani, along a secret passage to an old side door of the Quirinal which had been kept closed for many years. A faithful servant was upon the watch. At the proper signal he endeavored to open the door, but found he had not been provided with the right key. The Pope knelt down and prayed, while Filippiani went back to get the key changed.

At last the heavy wards turned back in the rusty lock, and

the fugitives passed out without having been discovered. They went through several dark passages, and at length reached a narrow staircase which led them into one of the interior courtyards of the Palace. There the carriage was waiting. "Good evening, comrades," said Filippiani to some National Guards who were posted there. "Good evening, Filippiani," they responded, without taking any notice of the priest who accompanied him.

As the Pope was getting into the carriage he came very near being betrayed by his footman, who, forgetting that his master must preserve a strict *incognito*, made a motion to kneel as the custom was at the papal Court. The Pope made him a quick sign, and happily the guards had not observed the blunder.

Over twenty of the Pope's servants had been in the secret, but not one betrayed him.

At last, by by-streets, the carriage reached a spot at which Count Spaur, the Bavarian ambassador, was waiting with another carriage. Here the Pope parted with Filippiani, and got into the carriage of Count Spaur. At the gate of the city they were asked to give their names. "The Bavarian Ambassador and Doctor Alertz, Professor of Theology," was the answer. "Where are you going?" "To Albano." "Pass," and the carriage was in a moment outside the city. The Pope, who sat silent, looked back and sighed deeply. Nor did he say another word during his journey.

At Albano, the Countess Theresa Spaur was awaiting their arrival. She had been there some hours with her son, a lad of fourteen and the Abbé Sebastian Liebl, a priest from Germany, who was her son's tutor. She had been growing very uneasy, till at last a message from her husband reached her, desiring her to change her route, and meet him at a little village called Arrica. She set out at once, and on reaching Arrica found five soldiers standing round her husband's carriage. The Pope had alighted and was leaning against a railing.

The Countess for a moment was overcome by fear. Then she summoned to her aid all her wits and all her courage.

She feigned to be exceedingly angry with her husband and the "Doctor," declaring it had been too bad of them to keep her waiting at Albano when they knew how she disliked to travel in the dark. Then she began talking to the soldiers, who were anxious to escort the Ambassador's carriage, saying that the road was not safe after nightfall. The party found it hard to decline their services. The Countess had not left her carriage, the Pope took his place beside her, her son and his tutor sat opposite to them, the Count and a footman mounted the box. Suddenly the Countess perceived with horror that the Pope had forgotten to change the white silk stockings that he wore, as Pontiff, for black ones. She also thought he would have done better to wear spectacles. However, no harm came of these blunders. The soldiers, satisfied with a donation, made their acknowledgments, by extreme politeness. They closed the carriage door; and, drawn by six good horses ridden by postilions, the travelling party galloped, — not toward Civita Vecchia, where the French steamer was waiting to receive them, — but across the frontier into the Kingdom of Naples.

The Pope sat on the back seat, with the Countess Spaur beside him. She was hardly able to restrain her tears. All the way as they went the Pope was praying, or reciting prayers from the Breviary with Father Liebl. As they crossed the frontier at Terracina, about eight o'clock in the morning, "he shed many tears, and thanked God for His protection," says Madame Spaur; "in the beautiful thanksgiving provided by the Church for deliverance from danger."

I have told at some length of the flight of the Pope because this account is from authentic sources.[1] It has been often falsely said that Pio Nono escaped disguised as a footman in livery.

In Rome other things at once commanded public interest and attention. Indeed, most people were glad of the Pope's escape, and quoted the proverb which says: If

[1] A paper by the Countess in the "Supplément Littéraire du Figaro."

your enemy wishes to flee from you, build him a bridge of gold.

Rome, deserted by its Pontiff, fell at once into the hands of the Republicans. A Constituent Assembly, that is, an Assembly called to make a Constitution, which was elected in defiance of the Pope's brief, assembled in February, 1849, — just one year after Louis Philippe's downfall, and two months after Louis Napoleon had been elected President of the French Republic.

This Assembly declared the temporal government of the Papacy to have fallen, in fact and in right, and established a Roman Republic.

But meantime terrible disasters to the Italian cause had been happening in both Northern and Southern Italy.

Austria had re-established her grip on Lombardy; King Ferdinand II. of Naples (whom history will always know as King Bomba) had resumed his brutal sway in Naples; the Roman volunteers who without orders had crossed the Po into Lombardy, had been crushed and cut to pieces; Piedmont had hard work to preserve her independence; Venice alone held out — as we shall see hereafter. All hopes of a United Italy were lost, whether as a Federation of Republics, or as a kingdom under one ruler.

The leading man in Rome among the populace, during the brief duration of the Roman Republic was named (or rather was popularly nicknamed) Ciceruacchio. He was a street orator, a sort of tribune of the people, a man of the old Roman stamp. He was a street truck-man by profession, and refused to leave his calling, or to be elected to any office, but whenever it was necessary to calm or to excite the mob he was on hand to do so. He had two sons, who assisted him. His subsequent fate, when the day of reckoning came, is a mystery. No one has ever known with certainty what became of him or of one of his sons.

Mazzini came to Rome as soon as the Constituent Assembly met, and was made one of a triumvirate to govern the Republic. But in the midst of Italian disaster, with Austria ready to march in upon her on one side, and a

Neapolitan army on the other, what could the poor little Roman Republic do? Her very existence — could she have continued to exist — would have compromised the prospect of a United Italy. To a United Italy Louis Napoleon was pledged. He therefore did not oppose a measure, passed through the French Assembly (which was largely Legitimist and Catholic), to send French troops to Rome, — ostensibly to keep the Austrians from getting possession of the States of the Church and taking cruel vengeance on the inhabitants, but really to sustain the Pope and throw a sop to Catholic Christendom.

On the morning of April 26, 1849, to the amazement of the Roman people, a French fleet anchored off Civita Vecchia. An officer came on shore, and begged permission of the Governor of the city to land a French army which was on board. "The French Republic," he said, "knows that you are threatened by an Austrian invasion, and has sent her soldiers to watch the progress of the Austrians in Italy, knowing that progress to be against the true interests of France."

The Commandant at Civita Vecchia openly expressed his suspicion that the object of the French was to restore the Pope and to destroy the Roman Republic. "That cannot be," replied the French officer; "the fifth article of the Constitution of the French Republic declares that she will never bear arms against the freedom of any people."

The French, therefore, were permitted to land at Civita Vecchia and at once proceeded to march upon Rome. The very flower of the Roman youth had, as I have said, been recently cut to pieces in battle with the Austrians beyond the Po; but the Garda Civile, the Roman National Guard, proceeded to make all possible resistance. They fought the French like lions, and at tremendous disadvantage. After two days of continuous fighting, General Oudinot and his French army were repulsed.

In those days our poor Margaret Fuller Ossoli was in Rome, and served with all other married Roman ladies in the hospitals. Ciceruacchio animated the populace. Barricades everywhere arose in the streets. Trees and gardens were destroyed, to give no cover to the invaders.

But victory over French Republicans availed Roman Republicans little. The French, unused to defeat, were furious. The French army was reinforced; the Austrians entered the Roman States on the north, the King of Naples on the southeast; even Spain sent her soldiers to aid the cause of the Pope, and on July 1, 1849, the City of Rome notified the French that it gave up resistance, though it would not capitulate. On July 3 the French took possession of the city, under protest from the Constituent Assembly, and the Pope was restored.

Louis Napoleon said afterwards that he had expected the Pope would have used his victory with mercy and moderation, but Pio Nono was now, — and forever after, — in spite of his kind heart and good intentions, the mere tool of Austria, doing whatever she might direct. Cardinal Antonelli governed. The Pope had been thoroughly frightened. He mistrusted himself and his people. Thenceforward he resigned himself to the position made for him, and, as a temporal ruler, did only what he was told.

During the first two years of the Pope's restoration there were two hundred and thirty people executed for their share in making Rome a republic for four months, besides all who died in the pestiferous air of the overcrowded prisons, where eight thousand were incarcerated. The number of the exiled was about twenty thousand, including those who fled for fear of being prosecuted.

There is no example in history of a more extensive vengeance taken by any civilized monarch restored to his throne. Besides these exiles, imprisonments, and executions, in the space of eight months six thousand youths of the best families in Rome had perished in battle. I say " of the best families in Rome," for all through the Italian struggle for independence the chief weight of effort, sacrifice, vengeance, disappointment, and despair fell on the cultivated class, not on the lower orders.

CHAPTER III.

SOUTHERN ITALY.

SICILY had derived a Constitution from Roger, son of her Norman conqueror. The Northmen lived in their own country under a rude constitutional government. Under all vicissitudes of fortune, thirty-four successive kings had respected it. It was reserved for King Ferdinand I., who ascended the throne in 1759, to destroy, in his hatred of all Liberalism, intensified by his horror of the French Revolution, this time-honored Constitution which the Sicilians held so dear.

It is no pleasure to Englishmen to recollect that this Ferdinand and his disreputable wife, Queen Caroline, were the royal pair protected by Lord Nelson, and bosom friends of Lady Hamilton, then wife of the British ambassador at Naples.

At eight years of age, in 1759, King Ferdinand received the throne of Naples from his father, Charles III. of Spain, and he grew up destitute of even the first rudiments of education, nor had he ever any knowledge of, or respect for, the commonest principles of government. He loved hunting, low company, and dissipation. He thought it good fun to sell fish in the markets of Naples disguised as a fisherman. He once opened a booth in his camp at Portici and sold wine and cakes to his soldiers, assisted by his queen and his courtiers. Writing his name bothered him so much that he had a stamp made to serve instead of his signature.

With this hatred for business, he was willing enough to turn over his power to his queen, daughter of Maria Theresa and sister of Marie Antoinette. Insatiable in ambition, courageous, energetic, dissolute, and vindictive, she was more like the Brunchildes and Frédégondes we read of in the annals of the Merovingians, than a woman of comparatively modern times. My father always called her "that vile woman," and he had known her when serving in the Mediterranean as an English naval officer.

It was in 1798 that the wrath of King Ferdinand was kindled against his Parliament in Sicily, and he resolved to put it down. It had refused to grant his demand for forty thousand dollars a month, *for so long as he might deem that sum necessary.* The Parliament objected, — not to giving the money asked, but to making the grant for an indefinite time.

The story of the kingdoms of Naples and Sicily is stirring, picturesque, and interesting during the first twenty years of the nineteenth century, but it cannot be told here. To Murat's reign, an Italian gentleman in 1850 told Mr. Senior, Naples owed all the progress it had made during the last three or four centuries. "He gave us," he said, "open legal procedure, the abolition of class privileges, the diminution of ecclesiastical property, and the few roads that we possess. Now all is going backward."

Ferdinand, when expelled from Naples by the French in 1806, took up his residence in Palermo. His administration in Sicily, which was absolutely despotic, provoked insurrection, and, without exactly abdicating, he was easily induced to rid himself of responsibility and annoyance by turning over the conduct of affairs in Sicily to his son Francis, the Prince of Syracuse.

Francis, under the advice, not to say the coercion, of his English protectors, granted Sicily a Constitution, and confirmed it by a solemn oath. This document is known in history as the Constitution of 1812. It was guaranteed to the Sicilians by the British Government, and during the two years that it was in force Francis was a popular king.

At the Congress of Vienna the Emperor Alexander had advocated the retention of Murat as King of Naples, saying that he "would not assist in restoring a butcher like Ferdinand to power." This broke the wicked old queen's heart; but the heart of her husband was set on regaining his two crowns, thereby deposing his son Francis, who had been acknowledged King of Sicily by the Sicilians. He succeeded in this, and abrogated the Sicilian Constitution,— Lord Castlereagh, who always espoused the cause of kings against their subjects, taking no steps to oppose him. Thenceforward, Ferdinand of Bourbon governed as he pleased, and Sicily became a hell upon earth for any man who desired progress or any kind of improvement, even of the most material description.

In 1820, a revolution in Spain forced another Spanish Bourbon, Ferdinand VII., to revive a Constitution framed by the Cortes during the brief reign of Joseph Bonaparte, and it became necessary for his kinsman, Ferdinand of Naples, as an Infant of Spain, to sign the document. Thus both the Spanish and the Neapolitan king became pledged to countenance constitutional government in Spain, and this excited the hopes of the Liberals in Naples.

I will give here the story of the uprising of 1820 in Naples, as it has been briefly told by John Webb Probyn, in his "History of Italy from 1813 to 1890."

"The desire for constitutional government spread rapidly through the Neapolitan kingdom. The army joined in the movement, and, under the leadership of General Pepe, united in a demand for a Constitution such as had been granted to Spain. The ministers urged King Ferdinand to yield. On July 6, 1820, he published an edict in which he declared that, the general wish of the nation having been made known to him in favor of a constitutional government, he, with the utmost willingness, gave his consent, and promised to publish the basis on which it should be founded within eight days.

"At the end of that time the Spanish Constitution was selected. General Pepe was placed in command of the army, and to him the King said: 'I would have granted a Constitution before if the utility of it, or the general desire for it, had been manifested. I thank God, who has permitted me in my old age to do a great good to my kingdom.'

"Some days after this, the King, having heard mass in the Royal Chapel, approached the altar, and in presence of the assembled ministers, courtiers, and others, took the oath to the Constitution. Then, fixing his eyes on the Cross, he added, of his own accord: ' Omnipotent God, who with infinite penetration lookest into the hearts of men and into the future, if I lie, or if one day I should be faithless to my oath, do Thou at this instant annihilate me.'

" His sons took the oath also, and they embraced one another with tears. What had taken place in the Royal Chapel was quickly known throughout Naples, and caused the utmost joy. On October 1 the Parliament was opened in person by the King, who was accompanied by the royal princes. The whole of Naples poured forth to greet them. The King's every look and gesture expressed his pleasure. Amidst a tumult of applause he ascended the throne, and with his hand outstretched on the Gospel, took once again the oath to the Constitution. . . . Festivities and fireworks expressed the general joy."

The Sicilian Constitution of 1812 was more liberal than the Spanish Constitution adopted in Naples, especially in matters relating to religion. The Sicilians wanted their own Constitution, not that which had been granted to Naples — and, indeed, aspired to a division of the two kingdoms. There was discontent and a rising in Sicily, and soon two events occurred which gave to the affairs of Italy a different turn.

The Allied Sovereigns, mindful of their engagement to crush all attempts to violate the provisions of the Congress of Vienna, and to put down, either by diplomacy or force, all efforts at revolution, appointed France to march an army in the name of the Holy Alliance into Spain, while Austria undertook to suppress constitutionalism in Italy. King Ferdinand received messages of decided disapproval from Vienna, and was summoned to a meeting with the Emperors of Austria and Russia at Laybach. He went accordingly, leaving behind him a special message to his Parliament, assuring them that, whatever might be the outcome of the conference at Laybach, he would "do all in his power in order that his people should remain in possession of a wise and free Constitution on the basis of a fundamental law that would secure personal liberty; no regard to be paid to privileges of birth in the matter of State rights; no taxes without the consent of the nation as legitimately represented; the power of the parliament to make all laws; the judges to be independent; the press virtually free; and ministers responsible. Furthermore," he continued, "I declare that I will never allow any of my subjects to be molested on account of any political matter that has happened." He further promised that he would, if necessary, return to Naples and defend it by force of arms.

On reaching Laybach he soon found that all that had passed during six or eight months in Naples was considered disorder and revolution, and if he could not bring back his subjects to rest content under a despotism, Austria, Russia, and Prussia were ready to march armies into the Two Sicilies as France was about to do into Spain.

The Austrians, indeed, by the will of the Allied Sovereigns had already quartered thirty-five thousand men in King Ferdinand's dominions, and they kept them there during the brief remainder of his reign and that of his son.

On March 15, 1822, King Ferdinand I. returned to his capital. "He re-established despotism, and condemned all who had taken part in the movement which had led to the establishment of a Constitution — that Constitution to which he himself had more than once solemnly sworn."

"During the years 1821 and 1822," says the historian Farini, "eight hundred citizens were for the cause of liberty condemned to death; more than double that number were sentenced to imprisonment, or to the galleys. Those driven into exile, or obliged to fly, were so numerous that it is impossible correctly to estimate their numbers; and nearly all bore their unmerited misfortunes with courage and fortitude."

King Ferdinand died in 1825; the reign of his son and successor, Francis I., lasted only five years. The former was the father of the Duchesse de Berri and of Queen Christina of Spain, neither of them being a lady *sans reproche*. During the brief reign of King Francis, his kingdoms may be said to have been held in possession by the

Austrians. He was succeeded by his son, Ferdinand II., commonly known to us as King Bomba, a name given him some years after his accession by the English "Punch," which conferred it on him when he showed no hesitation to bombard his own subjects in their own cities.

His first wife was the Princess Christina of Savoy, whom the Neapolitans adored as a good and gracious lady and almost a saint. She died early, however, after having given birth to a son, and her death was attributed to a brutal trick played on her a few weeks before her child's birth by her husband. His second wife was an Austrian princess. He was a tall, large-limbed man, of very commonplace intellect, and of the most determined despotic opinions.

In 1847, when Italy became excited by the astounding phenomenon of a Liberal pope, the Neapolitan subjects of King Ferdinand broke into insurrection at Reggio, protesting their loyalty to the King, but demanding a Constitution — the Constitution that had been granted to Sicily and then revoked thirty-five years before. Reggio stands on a headland near the Straits of Messina. A war steamer was sent to bombard the town, bombardment being King Ferdinand's favorite stroke of policy, and the insurrection was put down, its suppression being followed by horrible cruelties.

In a few months, however, when all Italy was in a blaze, King Ferdinand II. found himself obliged to grant his kingdom of Naples its desired Constitution, including a Liberal ministry and a National Guard. He also (possibly with a view of getting rid of fighting patriots) allowed an army of seventeen thousand volunteers to set forth to fight the Austrians in Northern Italy, under the command of General Pepe, who, however, received secret orders, after he had started, not to lead his troops across the Po.

"Unfortunately," says Lawrence Oliphant, "newspaper correspondence was then in its infancy, and posterity will have but a comparatively meagre record of the exciting scenes, and stirring events in these two great years (1848 and 1849) of Italian revolution. If it was distasteful to the Pope, as I, who saw the tears

KING FERDINAND II.

roll down his cheeks, deemed it was, to bless the volunteers with their banners and their cannon who were setting forth to fight the Austrians, it was still more hateful to the King of Naples to have to grant a Constitution to his subjects, and swear to keep it, upon crossed swords, which I saw him do with great solemnity in a church after a revolution which had lasted three days, and in which the troops refused to fire on the people. It was true he had no intention of keeping his oath, and broke it shortly afterwards, but the moment was none the less humiliating, and his face was an interesting study."

There is great difficulty in writing the history of Italy during the years 1848 and 1849, when the peninsula in every part was filled with revolutionary confusion. Each section, — and I think we may say there were eleven of them, — was making its own revolution at the same time; all picturesque, all filled with genuine patriotism and animated by enthusiasm, all hot-headed more or less, and all, alas! all ending in disaster.

In May, 1848, a quarrel among the deputies elected to the Parliament that was to meet in Naples excited the populace. Barricades were erected in the streets. Shots were fired. The guns of the forts bombarded Naples. The army was devoted to the King, who had been proud of his soldiers' military appearance, and the *lazzaroni* were on his side, stimulated by hopes of plunder.

The King and his party triumphed. The Chamber of Deputies was forbidden to meet, and constitutional government came to an end.

"On the evening of May 18, 1848," writes an eye-witness, "the most beautiful city of Italy presented a terrible spectacle. Palaces were burned and plundered; the streets were strewn with the dead and dying; the groans of the wounded were drowned by the obscene ribaldry of the soldiers and the populace; everywhere was squalid contention, in every family there was agitation, and in every breast was grief and dread. Liberty was extinguished. Reaction had begun."

The fighting of that day was but the beginning of many sorrows. Mr. Gladstone in the winter of 1850–51 made a journey to Naples, and stirred the heart of Christendom by letters, written to Lord Aberdeen in 1852, containing accounts of atrocities and prison cruelties that had come under his own observation in Naples and Sicily.

About the same time a book also was published which bore on the same subject, Ruffini's beautiful novel "Doctor Antonio." The Sicilians had been disappointed in their aspirations for autonomy. They were a restless and a reckless people. In the first seventeen years of King Ferdinand's reign, — from 1830 to 1848, — there were six risings in Sicily. One was in 1837, when, the cholera being in Naples, some quarantine regulations were put in force by the Sicilians. King Ferdinand, however, insisted that they could make no laws or regulations to prevent his doing what he liked in his dominions; and he sent a ship, loaded with the clothes and accoutrements of soldiers who had died of the cholera, to break the quarantine. The result was the introduction of the cholera into Sicily; thirty thousand people in Palermo alone are said to have died of it. The populace believed that their King had deliberately introduced the disease to decimate them, and to prevent insurrection. Absurd as this suspicion may have been, it roused all classes to fury and despair, and they broke into revolt immediately.

We may as well here tell the story of the insurrection of 1848 and 1849 in Sicily, returning to say a few words concerning events simultaneously taking place in King Ferdinand's Neapolitan dominions.

On January 9, 1848, when all Europe was ablaze for reform and freedom, the people of Palermo notified King Bomba that if, by January 12 (his birthday), he did not give them back their Constitution of 1812, they would break into insurrection.

The day opened with glorious sunshine. The forts and the shipping fired salutes in honor of the thirty-eighth birthday of their sovereign. But in a few hours the people of Palermo were as good as their word. They were fighting with the war-cry of "Long live the Constitution! Long live Pio Nono!"

The best men in Sicily headed the revolt, and for several days it went on. One success followed another. The Neapolitan troops, who garrisoned Palermo, very quietly submitted to be disarmed by the Sicilians.

While reading accounts of this insurrection in Sicily, I came upon a paper entitled "Cruelties in Sicilian Political Prisons." It described what the populace of Palermo discovered when they broke into the secret chambers connected with the offices of the police. The details (which I have since found elsewhere repeated) are too sickening to be recorded in this place, — too revolting to humanity.

About two weeks after the insurrection first broke out, the royal troops evacuated Palermo, the general in command setting free, before he left, all the brigands and other criminals confined in the prison. This, by a royal order, was always done on such occasions, and this time arms were distributed to the malefactors, that they might strike terror into the citizens. At first, however, this fiend-like policy failed to take effect. The miserable famine-stricken wretches, who crowded into Palermo in the gray dawn of a winter day, to the terror of the inhabitants, only asked for bread to appease their hunger, their jailers having left them on the verge of starvation, and the greater part of them asked permission to join the defenders of their country. This they were allowed to do, and for a while the solemn vows of subordination and honesty which accompanied their application were observed with singular fidelity. Many fought with great bravery, but when the first excitement passed away, most of them returned to their old habits, and, reinforced by other criminals and bandits, turned loose on Sicily from the prisons of Naples, became a frightful source of reproach and of disaster.

The King's army, when it evacuated Palermo, left desolation behind it as it marched along. Vineyards and gardens were destroyed, palaces and cabins were sacked and burned. Old men and the helpless were murdered, and their heads were carried on the march on soldiers' bayonets. But before long the Sicilians had their hour of revenge, and in their turn committed savage atrocities.

After a three days' march across the island the royal army embarked for Naples on the night of January 31, 1848, burning on the beach all the arms, clothing, and knapsacks that they could not carry with them, and killing many of their horses.

Unhappily the men of Palermo devoted the next month to rejoicings over their easy victory, instead of driving the King's forces from their great stronghold, the citadel of Messina. But they felt confident that England would interpose in their behalf, and would insist on the restoration of the Constitution which in 1812 she had guaranteed. Earl Minto, who was on a sort of travelling embassy at that time through the excited States of Italy, warmly sympathized with the Sicilian patriots, and went further in his promises of help than Lord Palmerston had authorized him to do. His negotiations between King Bomba and his revolted people utterly failed, and he took leave of the Sicilians, expressing his hope that "they would not suffer themselves to fall into the calamities of a republic."

On March 25, 1848, the Sicilian Parliament opened. It was no turbulent or extremely radical assembly. Archbishops, bishops, mitred abbots, noblemen whose ancestors seven centuries before had sat in the councils of the Norman Roger, composed its House of Peers. Its commons had been elected from the younger sons of the nobility, the general body of the clergy, professors from the universities, lawyers, and landowners. Men all over Europe believed that the knell of despotism was sounding in their ears. The Revolution of February in France, unexpected as it was even to its promoters, who sought only reform, had sent an electric thrill through Central Europe. Berlin and Vienna were in revolt; Italy had sprung into revolution like a giant refreshed from sleep; Milan and Venice had driven the Austrians from their walls; and Charles Albert was beginning his early victories. The Sicilian Parliament, having voted the deposition of King Ferdinand and the

Bourbons, decided to offer their crown to Ferdinand Albert Amadeus, Duke of Genoa, the second son of Charles Albert, stipulating, however, that he should take the name of Albert Amadeus, the very name of Ferdinand being hateful to them all. Louis Napoleon, not yet fully anticipating his higher destiny, had offered himself as a candidate, but no one gave him a vote.

A deputation was sent from Sicily before the final choosing of a king, to ascertain the feeling on the subject in the other Italian States. Everywhere the deputation met with cordial sympathy. Even Leopold of Tuscany promised to recognize the new kingdom. The Pope excused himself for not having been foremost in welcoming Sicilian independence, on the ground that he was a near neighbor to King Ferdinand, but promised to follow the lead of the other Italian States. He praised the humanity and generosity of the revolution, admitted its justice, and censured the conduct of King Ferdinand. "What better token do you desire than this?" he said, "I receive you — I embrace you, — I bless you, — and with you the whole of Italy!"

Meantime, a reaction had taken place in the affairs of Naples. King Ferdinand, urged by Austria, and supported by her armed force, had broken his oath to uphold the Constitution, had dismissed his Liberal ministers with insults and had recalled his troops from the Romagna, where they had been waiting impatiently for an order to cross the Po. Charles Albert had fought and lost the battle of Custozza; and had withdrawn his troops into his own dominions. Venice alone held out against the Austrians, and General Pepe,[1] with a small body of Neapolitan troops,

[1] In 1841 we were in Paris, and saw a good deal of General Pepe, then in exile. He was a tall, soldierly, gray-haired man, very intimate with our neighbors, Dr. and Mrs. Gilchrist, from Edinburgh. He spoke English fluently, but with an extraordinary accent, having engrafted a broad Scotch pronunciation on that of Italy. In 1841 I was wholly unacquainted with Italian politics, but the General interested my father very much. I was, however, struck by the complete misapprehension of the social workings of republican "liberty" in America, held by some of the exiles in Paris at that period, — men of intelligence of whom I saw a good deal. — E. W. L.

who refused obedience to the orders of their King, succeeded in reinforcing the garrison of that city.

The main body of King Ferdinand's troops returned to Naples, but were not suffered by an English fleet, then in Italian waters, to cross over into Sicily. The English squadron lay anchored off Naples to prevent any interference with the patriots of Sicily. The flag of the Sicilians was recognized, and in July, 1848, a French war steamer bore to Genoa the deputation that was to offer to King Charles Albert's second son the crown of Sicily. That young man was even more popular than his brother Victor Emmanuel. He was a brave soldier, a well-educated and accomplished gentleman, and he was in command of one division of the Piedmontese army. When the deputation, sent to offer him a crown, arrived in the Piedmontese camp, the Prince was not at headquarters. But the King, his father, promised that he should arrive the next day, and give the Sicilian deputation an official reception. Everything indicated to the embassy a happy conclusion of their errand, but the official reception on the morrow never took place. That night the Sardinians were surprised by the veteran Austrian general, Radetzky, and a series of rapid reverses forced Charles Albert to abandon Lombardy, and to retire into his own dominions. The Duke of Genoa was no longer an eligible candidate for the Sicilian throne.

The unexpected defeat of Charles Albert changed the policy of the English government. It was evident that Austria and despotism, and Austrian influence, were to triumph. England withdrew her protection from Sicily, and the army of King Ferdinand appeared before Messina.

For nearly eight months the guns of that citadel had been firing into the town. On Good Friday, 1849, when the inhabitants of Messina attempted to visit their churches, terrible havoc among them took place. After the Neapolitan fleet arrived, and combined with the citadel in bombarding the town, the inhabitants held out for five days. Then the troops of King Bomba forced their way into the ruined city. For three days, pillage, destruction, and all the other horrors of war went on. Then the commanders of the English and French fleets, who had been forced to look passively upon these things, joined on their own responsibility in a representation to the general in chief of the Neapolitan troops, imploring him to cease in the name of humanity.

Two miles of buildings had been burnt down, comprehending the most sumptuous palaces and churches. The fate of Messina sealed the fate of Sicily. Then came the news of Charles Albert's crushing defeat at Novara. Austria and her allies were triumphant over all the Italian peninsula, and the Sicilians had to await the dawn of a better day, — which came twelve years later, when Italy had learned many lessons which made her more fit to profit by reforms.

Had the revolutions of 1848 succeeded in Italy, there would have now been no United Italy, but a federation of petty states, kingdoms or republics, which, like the States of Italy in the Middle Ages, or the States of South America in our own day, would doubtless have exhausted their strength in quarrels with each other. During the long years of waiting for relief that followed 1849, the Italian people were educating for the change in store for them, and other nations were educating to rejoice when that change came to them.

When the general of King Bomba was about to destroy Palermo with his bombs as he had done Messina, the French Admiral interposed. By his mediation King Ferdinand was induced to promise the Sicilians a kind of Constitution, — one of his own sons as their Viceroy, a National Guard, and an amnesty, which should except only forty persons. The Sicilians submitted, — and not one of these promises was ever fulfilled.

Martial law was proclaimed the moment that the King resumed his power. Every man found with arms in his possession (even a fowling-piece) was at once shot. In a few days upwards of one thousand people were put to death for this offence alone. The prisons — the horrible prisons — were filled with political captives, and every ship that sailed from the Sicilian shores bore away fresh exiles. New taxes were imposed, and a fine of twenty millions of ducats laid on the Sicilian people, — "such being," said the ordinance, "the cost of insurrections."

Palermo was garrisoned by fourteen thousand troops to keep it quiet, and forty cannon in the citadel, always loaded, pointed down the streets. The power of the police was terrible; men were beaten to death on political suspicion. No modern inventions were permitted in Sicily. No railroads; no telegraph lines; no gas in the streets, though the inhabitants of the cities earnestly petitioned for it. No steamers were allowed to touch at the island unless they came from Naples. In order to keep the people in ignorance of political events, the mails and newspapers were often stopped altogether. The roads were purposely kept almost impassable. An officer of the royal army, having undertaken to repair a road, was reprimanded. The island seemed cut off from the rest of the world.

For seventeen years, in Paris, London, Genoa, Turin, Malta, and Nice lived the representative men of Sicily. Driven from home, from wealth and station, they bided their time, not altogether without hope, and in 1860 that time came.

As exiles they were at least happier than those who languished in the prisons.

To return for a moment to the year 1848 and the affairs of the kingdom of Naples. When, in February of that year, King Ferdinand took God Almighty to witness that he was sincere in his desire to govern as a constitutional king (having a few weeks before declared that he would rather put on the uniform of a Russian colonel than grant one inch to his subjects), he appointed a Liberal ministry, at the head of which was Carlo Poerio, one of a family of patriots. Carlo was born when his father was an exile after his share in the attempt to win a Constitution for his country in 1820.

"Poerio stands before the world as the typical victim of Neapolitan misgovernment," says the Countess Martinengo

Cesaresco, writing of Italian characters in those years of revolution : —

" The conspicuous position he so lately held as minister to the Crown, the large social circle by which he was known personally to be a man of high talent, and unblemished honor, not less than the extraordinary network of iniquity woven to obtain his conviction on a charge of high treason, contributed to give his case greater prominence than that of any other of the prisoners. It was known also of Carlo Poerio that his political views were strictly moderate, that reverence for law was at least as strong in him as love of liberty, and this was another reason why he attracted sympathy, especially in England, among those who most disliked revolutionary methods."

When King Ferdinand resumed despotic sway in Naples, being secure of the assistance and sympathy of the Austrians, now victorious in Lombardy, and in their struggle in Hungary, he summarily dissolved the Parliament, which had sat six weeks.

" He resumed his absolutest sway, rejoiced at the overthrow of that Italian liberty which he had promised to aid ' by all his forces by sea and land,' and became one of the firmest supporters of Austrian influence and despotism."

Farini, the most trusted Italian historian of the period, writes : —

" Naples became the prey of his furious rage ; whoever was known for his love of Italy, and fidelity to the Constitution, was either obliged to find refuge on board foreign ships from the snares of police agents, and so seek safety in exile, or, afflicted with every kind of moral and physical evil, was thrown into prison with criminals. . . . There was no guarantee for civil rights, no legal check, no shame in the government — nothing but insolent tyranny."

This might seem exaggeration were it not fully corroborated by impartial witnesses. Here is the state of affairs in Naples at the close of 1850, as given to Mr. Nassau Senior by an Italian resident in Naples : —

"No one in any class of society is safe. A mere denunciation to the police may occasion his arrest, and when once imprisoned he may be forgotten."

No sooner did Ferdinand find it would be safe to throw himself into the protecting arms of Austria, than, as I have said before, he summarily dismissed his Liberal Ministry, and set up a reactionary one. A little later, when he felt himself still more secure, every one of his late Liberal ministers was put under arrest, two only excepted, Troja and Manna, who, having some personal influence with members of the new Cabinet, were only placed under strict police surveillance, and thus, at the close of 1850, Mr. Senior and his friends, Mr. Gladstone and De Tocqueville, found them.

Speaking of Scialoja, a distinguished Roman scholar, who was then in close confinement in the dungeons of St. Elmo, Troja said to Mr. Senior : —

"They are afraid of his eloquence if he remains in the country, and of his pen if he quits it: so they keep him, and may keep him forever, in prison, visible only at intervals to his own relations, — and you are not to suppose that a Neapolitan prison resembles a prison in any other part of the civilized world, except, perhaps, Rome. Even before trial, the prisoners are chained together, two and two, in irons never taken off for any purpose whatever, and weighing between thirty and forty pounds. The cells at the Vicaria, holding three persons each, are about eight feet square, receiving light and air from a hole in the top, far below the level of the ground, reeking with damp, and swarming with vermin. In Nisida there are rooms not twenty feet square in which seventeen or eighteen persons have been confined for months, fed only on the blackest bread, and soup of which you could not bear the smell. And these are untried persons — persons whom the laws of every other country treat as innocent, and detain only to insure their safe custody. In Procida, in Ischia, and in the other islands which fringe the coast, the prisons and the treatment in them are worse even than in Naples."

On December 20, 1850, Mr. Senior was taken to the tribunals where forty-two political prisoners were being tried, the principal of whom was Carlo Poerio, whom eighteen months before the King had seemingly trusted as a friend. The trial took place in the old part of Naples in an enormous palace built by the Angevin kings.

Next day an Italian friend, himself compromised, brought Mr. Senior the act of accusation against the forty-two prisoners whose trial he had seen going on the day before. Many of them were accused of crimes with which the others were not charged, — some, for instance, of having in their possession forbidden books, others tricolor scarfs, others forbidden weapons. But all were charged with being members of the Society of United Italy, having for its object the subversion of all existing sovereignties in the peninsula and the conversion of Italy into one federal Republic.

"The two important prisoners," said the Italian gentleman, "to punish whom the trial is got up, are Poerio and a man of letters named Settembrini. The judges by whom they are tried have been carefully selected, they have also received some broad hints as to their personal responsibility in the matter of conviction. . . . Of four judges who voted for the acquittal of some political prisoners at Reggio, — persons against whom there was absolutely no evidence, — two were immediately dismissed without pensions, and the other two were removed to an inferior court in the most savage part of the Abruzzi. Neapolitan judges cannot be expected to resist such a pressure as this."

Poerio had been warned in July, 1849, but, doubtful whether it was a warning from a friend or a trap laid by the police, he took no notice of it. The next day he was placed under arrest, and eighteen months after, sentence was passed upon him of twenty-four years in chains, and a fine of six hundred ducats. It was thus that Mr. Gladstone saw him on the island of Nisida, in 1851, when he wrote his celebrated letters on this subject to Lord Aberdeen. These letters in the end produced their effect. In 1859, after nine years of imprisonment, Poerio was suddenly released. King Ferdinand had grown weary of being bothered about him. He returned to the world broken in health, and with a permanent wound in the leg where his irons had eaten into the flesh. After his release he was never heard to utter a bitter word against the King, or any of his other persecutors. He was, though associated with criminals, at least spared the most intolerable of the miseries that fell on some of his fellow-sufferers. He was allowed to choose a prisoner with whom he was to be chained, and he chose a friend, — a physician.

The prison of Settembrini was on the rocky island of San Stefano, opposite to Gaeta, about thirty miles distant from the shore. The only building on the island was the prison, in which, when Settembrini reached it, there were seven hundred and fifty-eight men confined, including twenty-eight political prisoners. These were lodged in ninety-nine cells, of which the largest measured about sixteen spans. The political prisoners were not placed by themselves, but scattered through the building, among the worst class of thieves and murderers.

"Into this dwelling, — into this society," says the Countess Cesaresco, " entered Settembrini, a man full of gentle refinement, of home affections, and of elegant tastes, in the early morning of a chilly 6th of February, 1851. Here, by the royal clemency he was to abide *for life*."

Three years later, on the anniversary of that day, Settembrini wrote in his journal : —

" My body and my clothes are soiled ; it is of no use to try and keep them clean ; the smoke and dirt make me sickening to myself. My spirit is tainted. From association with those around me I feel all the hideousness, the horror, the terror of crime ; had I remorse I should come to believe that I too was a criminal. My spirit is being defiled. It seems to me as if my hands were also foul with blood and theft. I forget virtue and beauty.

"Oh my God ! Father of the unfortunate, Consoler of those who suffer, oh ! save my soul from this filth, and if Thou hast written that I must here end my sorrowful life, oh ! let that end come soon . . . I fear to become vile ; I fear my soul growing perverted. How can I come before Thee thus ? . . . The world knows not, nor can it conceive — few are those who know and feel — that the first of all possible and imaginable griefs is to watch the ruin of one's own soul!"

Settembrini was never allowed to leave his crowded dungeon.

"I cannot see the sea or the earth," he says, "I see only the little space of sky above the prison, and yet, by the milder air, and by the wonderful purity of the heavens, I feel and remember the return of the fourth spring that finds me here."

There seems to have been no restriction on his use of pen and paper, or, the jailers, having no direct orders from the government, may themselves have inclined to mercy. He procured a copy of the works of Lucian, and the translation of that book, together with an introductory life of the author, occupied him during the last five years he passed in prison. His work was published in 1861, when it was considered the best rendering ever made of a prose classic into Italian. "A translation," he said himself, "should be a work of art;" and such he had endeavored to make his Lucian.

When nearly ten years had passed, the King, moved by the same impulse that had induced him to release Poerio, that is, becoming weary of the remonstrances and expostulations that had never ceased to worry and annoy him since the publication of Mr. Gladstone's letters, set free, unexpectedly — and as if by a caprice — sixty-six of his five hundred political prisoners. Settembrini was one of these. They were embarked on board a Neapolitan war vessel, which, off Gibraltar, was to transfer them to an American ship bound to New York. But a son of Settembrini, a young officer in the Sardinian royal navy, disguised as a cook's mate, and passing for a Spaniard, obtained a berth on board of her. As soon as the Sicilian war vessel was out of sight he stepped on the quarter-deck in the full Sardinian naval uniform, and insisted that the vessel should be delivered over to him.

"The audacious scheme was crowned with complete success, and amid the hurrahs of the crew, and the wild antics of the negro cook, who had lost his assistant, the ship's head was turned in the direction of Queenstown."

Settembrini stayed in London, giving lessons in Italian for a year. Then he joined his beloved family in Florence, till, in the fulness of time, Naples claimed admittance into the Italian fold. He was then charged by the Neapolitans with the mission of offering their crown to Victor Emmanuel, of whom in later days he used to say: —

"Without a king who loyally guided the patriotic movement, Italian unity would never have been accomplished. It was useless to speak of federation. Unity alone could have given us liberty and independence, because in unity alone a nation has consciousness of its strength."

Settembrini retired into private life after the unity of Italy was accomplished, accepting, however, the post of Professor of Italian Literature in the University of Naples. His views on public matters were rather conservative than radical, and he was opposed to an extension of the suffrage among the ignorant. When old and broken in health he was appointed a Senator, and he made a last effort as a matter of duty to go to Rome, "to speak on what he considered the most vital question affecting New Italy, — that of the excessive and crushing taxation. He saw how dangerous was the inclined plane on which Italy had stepped, how misleading the theory that, because she was now a great nation, she must spend in proportion with her greatness and not with her means."

Full of plans for his lectures, serene and gay to the last, he died quietly in his chair on November 3, 1877.

CHAPTER IV.

DANIEL MANIN AND HIS CITY.

VENICE had been a Republic since the latter part of the fifth century, and a proud, aggressive oligarchy for five hundred years, when Napoleon put an end to its republican existence in 1797. It had shone gloriously as a star among the nations, but by the time it met its fate it had deserved its downfall.

> Mourn not for Venice — though her fall
> Be awful, as if Ocean's wave
> Swept o'er her. She deserves it all,
> And Justice triumphs o'er her grave.
> Thus perish every king and state
> That runs the guilty race she ran,
> Strong but in fear, and only great
> In outrage against God and man.

Napoleon gave Venice to the Austrians by the Treaty of Campo Formio, but during his subsequent wars he recovered it, and annexed it to Lombardy as part of his kingdom of Italy. While his power lasted, Venice was not badly governed. It is true that she did not relish incorporation with Lombardy, and that her people felt the oppression of taxation and conscription under the French system.

By the Congress of Vienna, Venice was once more handed over, together with Lombardy, to Austria. The especial value of Venice to that country was its situation at the head of the Adriatic Sea. Venice and Trieste were Austria's sole outlets to the ocean. Venice became her great naval station. The arsenal, so vividly described by Dante, was invaluable to her navy, and of all her possessions the one she was most disposed to hold with a firm grasp was

St. Mark's city. Between Lombardy and Venetian territory she had erected, or rather strengthened, four immense fortresses, which, in the eyes of military men, made her hold on Lombardy and Venetia almost secure. These fortresses — Mantua, Verona, Peschiera, and Legnago — formed what was called the Quadrilateral, and play no inconsiderable part in the history of Italy from 1848 to 1867.

In no part of Italy, not even in Milan itself, was the rule of the Austrians more detested than in Venice. Not even, in after years, could the rule of the gallant and gentle Archduke Maximilian reconcile Venetians to the loss of what they called their independence, though there had been little individual liberty under the rule of the Council of Ten.

After the Treaty of Vienna had settled the boundaries of the states of Europe, Venice, held down firmly by an immense Austrian garrison, was very quiet for a good many years, but in 1844 the rash invasion of Calabria by the brothers Bandiera, who were of Venetian birth and of an old patrician family, moved the hearts of their countrymen to profoundest sympathy.

The last of the Doges was named Manin. In 1797, when Venice was handed over for a brief season to the Austrian Emperor, before Napoleon became King of Italy, he dropped fainting from emotion while attempting to pronounce the oath of allegiance to the house of Hapsburg, and in a few hours he died. During his dogeship a leading Jew in Venice had been converted to Christianity, and according to custom, had, on being baptized, taken the surname of his sponsor. The son of this Jew was christened Daniele, and he went by the surname of Manin. He had very delicate health, and was fair, with light hair and blue eyes. He was a lawyer by profession, and an exceedingly fine speaker. From his babyhood he had been brought up to hate the rule of Austria. In 1830 he drew up a paper exhorting the Venetians to join the revolt that was then preparing in Modena and Romagna. But this revolt suddenly failed, and Manin's authorship of the dangerous document was not discovered.

He then devoted himself to social and commercial reforms. A railroad was projected between Venice and Milan. The Viceroy of Lombardy wanted it to take a route that would be of advantage to the Austrian military position in the Quadrilateral; the Italian bankers, who were to advance the funds, wanted it to take another line. Manin was appointed their advocate to oppose the Austrian governor. The affair ended in the company being dissolved, and the railroad was not made for many years.

In 1846, Mr. Cobden, the English apostle of free trade, visited Italy, and the great men who were afterwards leading Italian statesmen took his cause up warmly, — in Genoa, D'Azeglio; in Bologna, Minghetti; in Turin, Cavour; and in Venice, Manin and his friend Tommaseo.

In January, 1848, a month before the overthrow of Louis Philippe, both Manin and Tommaseo, who had pleaded for reforms, were arrested for high treason. This led to Venetian demonstrations of hatred against Austria. Two months later, the French revolution having been accomplished, half Europe being agitated by political excitement, and Vienna itself in revolt against its Emperor, the Venetian populace assembled under the windows of Count Palffy, the Austrian governor, and demanded the release of Tommaseo and Manin. The governor, after some resistance, yielded, saying at the same time: "I do what I ought not to do." The people, in a tumultuous crowd, rushed over the Bridge of Sighs; they burst open the door of Manin's prison, but he refused to come out till he had seen the warrant for his release. This was produced, and then, in his prison garments, borne on the shoulders of the crowd, he was carried to the glorious Piazza of St. Mark, where — no one ever knew by whom — the red, white, and green colors of Italy had been hoisted on those historic pillars, where for long years the yellow and black colors of Austria had waved.

"I know not yet," said Manin, addressing the crowd around him, "to what events I owe my liberation, but I can see that love of country and national spirit have made great strides since I went into prison. But forget not," he added, "that there is no true or lasting freedom without order; and of order you must make yourselves the jealous guardians. Yet there are times pointed out by the finger of Providence when insurrection is not only a right but a duty."

In three or four days news came that all Lombardy was in a blaze. About three thousand Venetians assembled armed. "Let every one who will not implicitly obey me, depart," said Manin. The Austrian governor, Count Palffy, who was not personally unpopular, endeavored to appease the multitude by telling them that a Constitution was to be granted to Venice, and that nothing would please him better than to be their first constitutional governor. But the people had gone beyond a desire for reforms; they demanded the expulsion of their foreign masters. Count Zichy, the Austrian general, had to withdraw his troops, and Count Palffy was constrained to deliver up his powers into the people's hands. These officers were both loyal gentlemen, but they were Hungarians by birth, and doubtless felt more sympathy with the revolted Venetians than would have been the case had they been of Austrian blood.

How Manin seized the celebrated Arsenal by surprise, how he drew to light the grand old banner of St. Mark, and, marching with it in triumph to the great Square, proclaimed the Republic of Venice, I have not space to tell, though it is a picturesque and stirring story, — with a tender sadness in it too, when we read of Emilia, Manin's little girl, looking with tears in her eyes at her father in his triumph, because her heart prophesied that his ruin would soon come.

Bit by bit the Austrian authority was yielded to the new Dictator. The Austrian garrison was sent away from Venice, bound not to serve again during the war, but when all this was accomplished Manin's strength failed. For five days he had suffered physical torture, and when his followers would have again carried him in triumph, he exclaimed in his anguish, "Leave me at least this night to rest, or I shall die."

Meantime, the great Austrian general, Radetzky, an old

man and a consummate soldier, had been forced (March, 1848), after five days of tumult, to withdraw his garrison of fifteen thousand men from Milan, the capital of Lombardy. Pio Nono was still believed to be a patriot. Roman troops, bearing the tricolor flag of Italy, had publicly received his blessing, and were marching on the Po. The Duke of Modena and the Duchess of Parma had fled into Austrian territory, and even Ferdinand of Naples found himself forced to allow his army, under General Pepe, reinforced by patriotic volunteers, to approach the seat of war.

There were three parties among the Italian patriots. One believed that Italian independence could not be achieved without the help of some powerful foreign ally, — probably France, on whom the hopes of Italy were set until French troops landed to support the Pope at Civita Vecchia. Another, with Charles Albert, King of Sardinia, at its head, took for its motto, *Italia farà da se*, — that is, Italy will manage for herself. The third was the republican party, of which Mazzini was the chief, which wished a confederation of Italian republics. To this party seems to have belonged Manin. Nevertheless he, in the end, accepted the proposal to unite Venice to the dominions of Charles Albert, saying that the first thing to be considered was the expulsion of the Austrians; and that forms of government could be considered when Austria's power in Italy was destroyed. Accordingly, in June, 1848, it was resolved by an assembly, elected by universal suffrage, and convened by Manin in Venice (the *terra firma* Venetia was in the hands of the Austrians), that the newly-formed Republic should acknowledge Charles Albert as its leader, and constitutional King. But in a few weeks the tide of war had turned, and Charles Albert had been forced to sign an armistice, one of the stipulations in which was the renunciation of Venice.

"When this news reached the city," says the Countess Cesaresco, "Venice was plunged in a ferment of sinister agitation. Excited crowds rushed about the city clamoring for Manin, and crying 'Down with the royal government!' They threatened Charles Albert's commissioners with violence, and it was only when Manin declared that he would stake his life upon their honesty and patriotism, that the crowds became more calm, and acceded to his request to wait patiently while he held a consultation as to what was to be done. . . . The consultation over, Manin went out to the people, and told them how things stood. 'The day after to-morrow,' he said, 'The assembly of the city and province of Venice will meet to appoint a new government. For these forty-eight hours I govern!' His hearers were electrified with joy."

When the Assembly met, its wish, together with that of the populace, was to make Manin Dictator. He objected that he had no military training or experience. A triumvirate was therefore formed, of which he was the head.

Now Venice had to prepare for a siege. A small part of the Neapolitan troops under General Pepe, had, as has been said, refused to obey the orders of King Ferdinand to return home and assist in putting down the rebellion in Sicily. They threw themselves into Venice, and strengthened its garrison. The Roman volunteers, under their leader, General Durando, had crossed the Po in spite of orders, and soon after had been cut to pieces by the Austrians.

The details of the siege of Venice, which lasted from August, 1848, to August, 1849, need not here be told; the particulars of military operations are rarely interesting to the general reader, who looks only to their results. But I think I may add a very touching episode of the war in those days.

My sister, living in Venice, sent me the documents concerning it some years ago, saying that she thought I might make some literary use of them; but having afterwards mentioned the story to Mr. Browning, he seemed to her so desirous to make a poem on the subject himself, that she wrote to me to return the papers for his use, which, of course, I did, being unwilling that the unfortunate hero should lose the immortality which a poem by Mr. Browning would have conferred on him. I copied the documents, however, before parting with them, and, as Mr. Browning never accomplished his wish of writing a poem on the subject, I here add a translation of the papers.

GENERAL PEPE.

"The holy reverence in my heart," says the Venetian narrator, "concerning the glory and honor of my country, impels me to recount a most unhappy episode in its history. It is a story that might well move every heart, — even the least emotional, — to pity. It happened in Venice, May 30, 1849, toward the close of the celebrated siege.

"The heroic enterprise of the principal actor in the story, which might well serve to illustrate one of the grandest pages in the annals of a generous people, was marred not only by cruel Fate, but by men still living, who have paid their debt of gratitude to the hero's memory by forgetting him and his exploit altogether. This oblivion has gone so far that he almost rests under a false, dishonorable suspicion, — a stain which history should make speed to wipe away. Let us, therefore, with the pride of true Italians, rehabilitate our hero's memory.

"After the heroic defence of the fort of Malghera, the government of the Republic, convinced that outside resistance would be useless, decreed that the position should be abandoned, ordered the withdrawal of the troops, and continued the defence of Venice on the second line.

"The piazzale in the middle of the great bridge over the lagoon had been the central point of our fortifications, and, with the little islands to its right and left, formed the front of our line of defence facing the enemy, while at San Giuliano and at Malghera after its evacuation, and all along the shores of the lagoon on *terra firma*, the enemy continued to construct new batteries to bear upon our second line of defence, and on the city.

"During the terrible siege and bombardment of Malghera, the officer in command of our troops conceived the idea of destroying that part of the bridge that was contiguous to one of the islands, considering it perilous to our defences. But Venetian officers at that period were not unanimous, and the opinion of Colonel Milani, of the engineers, which was unfavorable to the proposed destruction of the bridge, or rather of its fortification, prevailed.

"However, as soon as Malghera was evacuated, the destruction of that part of the bridge became an absolute necessity. A corps of sappers and miners were at once ordered to set to work to blow it up by means of mines already prepared.

"On the morning of May 22 the mines were sprung, but the explosion did not produce the effect anticipated. General Girolamo Ulloa therefore set to work to consider the best mode of repairing the mines, so as to succeed in destroying several arches which had only been partially shattered by the explosion. Before anything could be done, it was desirable to ascertain the precise condition of the mines that had not exploded, and the amount of ruin effected on the arches, also what quantity of material it would be necessary to transport, and that promptly.

"The immense peril of accomplishing this investigation under the hot fire of the Austrian cannon and musketry, the former of which might at any moment send the bridge and those examining it into the air, daunted even the boldest and most noble-hearted among the defenders of Venice. It was, however, essential that a man brave and intelligent should undertake the enterprise.

"When the general in command had decided on the necessity of a forlorn hope, a young patriot at once volunteered. He was a mason, Agostino Stefani, from Budoia, near Sacile, and was accepted with high praise by General Girolamo Ulloa, after he had explained to that general the heroic project he had conceived.

"In company with another volunteer, Stefani went forth on his hazardous undertaking. Having received their instructions, they embarked on a small boat, and rowed toward the shattered arches. They had taken every precaution to escape the Austrians' vigilance, and they safely reached their destination. There they set to work carefully to observe everything. But in their enthusiasm having leaped upon the *débris* of the shattered bridge, they were observed, and drew upon themselves the fire of the enemy, who, anxious to hinder their work, did their best to kill them.

"With great regret they were forced to abandon their task, and under a terrible fire they rowed back to the shore.

"But Agostino Stefani, regardless of peril to himself, and full of warm affection for his country, conceived the idea of alone attempting the enterprise which the enemies of Italy had forced him to abandon.

"With this generous purpose he set to work to obtain from the authorities a fresh permission. It was granted to him this time, by Colonel Enrico Cosenz, subsequently a general, but then the officer in charge of the second line of the Venetian defences.[1] He believed that the heroic self-devotion of this brave man, who risked his life for the salvation of his beloved

---

[1] He was a Sicilian by birth, and subsequently a distinguished officer among the Red Shirts, with whom Garibaldi invaded the Two Sicilies.

country, could not remain without results, and he authorized him to make the attempt over again.

"Agostino, therefore, stepped into his boat and rowed out very slowly. Bold, calm, and undaunted, he reached the ruined arches of the bridge. With one bound he was up on the structure the arches of which had been imperfectly destroyed, and although he was again perceived by the Austrians, who directed against him a more furious fire than before, he did not desist, but imperturbably fulfilled the duty for which he had volunteered, — happy and proud that he could risk his life in aid of his country and his besieged fellow-citizens.

"But a great and unexpected misfortune awaited him. He had accomplished his heroic mission, and, returning joyfully to his boat, which so far had escaped injury from the fire of the Austrians, he began to row towards Venice.

"Suddenly a shot shivered one of the planks of his boat, and it sank under him. He fell into the water, but his courage did not desert him, and he endeavored to swim toward Venice, whence he had come.

"Unhappily the set of the current was against him; and the long distance exhausted his strength so much that he gave signs of perishing. . . .

"Meantime, a small reconnoitring party of Venetians, who were patrolling the banks of the lagoon, had been aware for some time that a man was at work alone by himself upon the bridge and its ruined arches. With prompt suspicion they imagined him to be an enemy, and continued carefully to observe his actions. They now waited for him to come ashore at a point not far from the outposts of the Austrians.

"Seeing him, however, about to sink, they went out to him in their boat, and took him out of the water. They marched him to the Battery Pio Nino, where at that moment General Girolamo Ulloa chanced to be. There they informed this officer that, having seen this man making his way toward the Austrian outposts, they had pursued him, picked him up, and arrested him.

"It was only proper to inquire into these circumstances, great caution at such times being necessary. The general, therefore, ordered that Stefani should be sent forthwith to the vigilance committee, guarded by a sufficient escort, on the boat of two brothers who were scouts, named Zanini.

"As the boat put off from the Battery Pio Nono, a rumor most unhappily got about that the prisoner was a traitor and a spy. A party of roughs gathered on the bank, beside themselves with cruel thoughts of vengeance, and began at once to stone the unfortunate Agostino.

"The Zanini and the escort seeing their own danger, and fearing that the vengeance of the mob might fall upon themselves, flung their prisoner overboard.

"In vain Agostino tried several times to get back into the boat; he was every time beaten off with oars, besides being struck down with stones hurled against him by a furious crowd on the bank of the lagoon. Thus assailed, the unhappy man sank dead under his sufferings, and life was hardly extinct when Colonel Enrico Cosenz, commander of the inner line of defence, arrived in haste. He had given the permit to Agostino, and had been watching his movements on the bridge. Perceiving that something had gone wrong, he hurried to the place where the tragedy had been enacted, and learned with horror the barbarous fate that had befallen his young hero."

The fortress of Malghera had held out during twenty-three days of incessant bombardment, Haynau and his army of twenty-five thousand men having concentrated their attack on this position. One-fifth of the garrison of the fort had been killed or disabled. When the place was no longer tenable it was so quietly evacuated during the night of May 29, that the Austrians knew nothing of the retreat of the garrison till the morning. It was deep sorrow to the remainder of these gallant men to leave the place they had defended. The gunners with tears kissed their guns before they spiked them. Happily Haynau was not there to take possession of the ruined fortress. He had been ordered to Hungary, where he put the last touches to his reputation for brutality. The ruins of Malghera fell into the hands of Count Thurn, an Austrian general who could appreciate the bravery of its defence, and made no secret of his profound admiration of the way in which it had been conducted.

As the siege of Venice went on, money was needed, and all kinds of sacrifices were made by the inhabitants. Ladies brought their jewels to the treasury, gondoliers' wives their silver hairpins. Twelve thousand soldiers were clothed by private subscription, two citizens giving one hundred thousand lire ($20,000) apiece. One young marquis presented his palazzo. General Pepe gave his dearest possession — a picture by Leonardo da Vinci. Manin sent in all his silver, two dishes, two coffee-pots, and a dozen forks and spoons. Little children came with their toys, or went dinnerless that they might bring their mite. The very convicts made up a purse for their country. But it was all in vain.

Manin was the idol of the people, and was called by them the Star of Italy. Once when they thought he was being ill-treated by other members of the government, a roaring mob surrounded the assembly, and threatened to burst in the doors. Manin, sword in hand, with his son Giorgio at his side, stood in the doorway, and told the rioters that if they intended to disgrace their Venice thus, they must pass over his and his son's dead bodies.

Early in March, 1849, when things had grown very desperate, Manin was made Dictator. Cholera and hunger were in the city, — the Austrian host without. On accepting the position — refused by all others — Manin told his countrymen that if the civic guard had no longer confidence in his loyalty he should lay the burthen down: "I ask frankly, has the civic guard faith in me?" he cried. The whole Piazza resounded with a thundering "*Si!*" "Then," continued Manin, "come what may, say of me 'This man was misled,' but never, 'This man misled others.' I have deceived no man. I have never spread illusions which were not mine own. I never said I hoped when I had no hope."

After Manin was made Dictator the war-cloud seemed to lighten for a moment. Charles Albert again took the field — and then he was defeated at the battle of Novara!

In July, 1849, the Austrians, who had hitherto bombarded only forts, began to throw bombs into the city, the cholera increased, and hunger, after twelve long months of siege, quenched the courage of the Venetians. Resistance became hopeless. A capitulation was signed, August 24, 1849. "A more honorable capitulation," wrote General Pepe, "could not have been obtained if Venice had had remaining in her gunpowder and provisions for a whole year, instead of only for one day."

Forty leading citizens, together with all officers who had served in the Austrian army, were required to leave the city. Manin, of course, was one of the forty exiles. At midnight, he, his wife, son, and little Emilia went on board the French steamer "Pluton," which carried them away, all but one, into lifelong exile. Manin was penniless. Some friends had pressed on him a little money, but he shared it with exiles still poorer than himself. His wife died of cholera on board the "Pluton," and with his two motherless children, one of them very ill, he made his way to Paris. There, great man as he had been, he had to support himself by giving Italian lessons, while day by day his Emilia faded before his eyes. But it was not till 1854 that she died. Her last words were: "My darling Venice! I shall never see you again."

Her father survived her three years. In those later years he became more and more convinced that the best government for a United Italy would be a popular king. It rejoiced his heart to see the Italian colors blended with the French and English flags in all demonstrations of rejoicing over the success of the Crimean War.

He died in 1857, at the age of fifty-three. Had he lived nine years longer he would have witnessed the independence of a United Italy.

Two days after Manin quitted Venice, Marshal Radetzky, the commander-in-chief of the Austrian forces in Italy, entered the city, amid "the silence of a bewildered population," says an Austrian eye-witness; and for seventeen years the same silence and bewilderment continued.

On Thursday, July 5, 1866, the Austrian colors were hauled down from their great flagstaffs before the Palace of Saint Mark, and on October 18 the colors of the kingdom of Italy were hoisted in their stead.

Manin, his wife, and child had been buried in Ary Scheffer's tomb at Montmartre, but after the liberation of

Venice their remains were carried back to their dear native city, and rest together in an elaborate sarcophagus. A statue was erected to Manin opposite his former house in Venice. He is represented in the act of addressing his fellow-citizens, and the Lion of Saint Mark is nestling at his feet.[1]

[1] This chapter of my history was written some years ago, probably before the Countess Evelyn Martinengo Cesaresco wrote her interesting and pathetic book, " Italian Characters,"— certainly before its publication. But on reading and consulting that book recently, I found, to my surprise, that what its author had written of Manin and what I had written were almost identical. In recopying my narrative I have left it as I had written it, adding only a few passages, that I have marked as quotations from the book of the Countess. I can only account for this similarity between my chapter and a book I had never seen, by supposing that the Countess and I worked from the same material. Such a coincidence is not foreign to my experience, having occurred once before in my literary life. In 1882 I published anonymously a No Name novel,—a story called " My Wife and my Wife's Sister." It turned on the history of an adventurer and criminal, Pierre Coignard, who was tried and convicted of crime and fraud in Paris in 1818. His story made much noise at the time, and, in describing the scenes at his trial, I worked as closely as possible to contemporary and official reports. Shortly after the book was published, a distinguished literary man pointed out to Messrs. Roberts that at least twenty pages of the book were a bold plagiarism from a story, " Dans la Peau d'un Autre," by Gaboriau. I had never heard of " La Peau d'un Autre." I had read only one short story by Gaboriau. We had worked from the same material, making the trial of Pierre Coignard adhere as nearly to the truth as possible. My only regret was that my saintly heroine Angélique should have figured as a tigerish adulteress in Gaboriau's story.

CHAPTER V.

CHARLES ALBERT AND NORTHERN ITALY.

CHARLES ALBERT, Prince of Savoy-Carignan, who, as we have seen, represented the House of Savoy in the male line on the death of his remote cousin, King Charles Felix of Sardinia, was the son of Charles Emmanuel, Prince of Savoy-Carignan and of a lady described variously in genealogical tables as a princess of Courland, or as a princess of Saxony. She was indeed Christina, daughter of Charles, Prince of Courland, and Countess Françoise Krazinska, a lady of good family in Poland. Very lately a charming little book, the "Journal" of this lady has been published in this country. Prince Charles of Courland was at the time of his secret marriage to Françoise Krazinska, heir *expectant* of the Polish throne. He did not obtain it, however, but with his wife — his marriage was then acknowledged — went into exile in Saxony, where Charles Emmanuel courted their daughter and married her. Charles Emmanuel was the only Prince of the house of Savoy who made any concessions to the French when they took possession of Savoy. In return they gave him a pension, and he lived for a few years near Paris; he then died, leaving his only son, Charles Albert, to the care of a wilful mother, who had adopted revolutionary ideas of liberty and equality. She is said at one time to have appeared in the streets of Turin dressed in the extreme of revolutionary fashion, with her young son in her arms. After Charles Emmanuel's death she married a French husband, M. de Montléart, and it is said that both she and this gentleman showed little interest in the training of the child. His education was for the most part very irregular, though occasionally his mother tried on him experiments adopted from the educational theories of Rousseau. Unhappy, neglected, and estranged from the mother whom he could not love, the boy grew up sad and silent, an object of dislike and distrust to at least one of his royal cousins, Charles Felix. He had been instructed to call these distant kinsmen "uncles," but Charles Felix never spoke of him but as "that little vagabond."

Miss Godkin, in her "Life of Victor Emmanuel," says, however: —

"Charles Albert spent some time at a military school in Paris, and at the age of sixteen was made by Napoleon a lieutenant of dragoons. His education was completed at Geneva, under the direction of a very able Protestant divine. For all his liberal education, Charles Albert was as devout a Catholic as any of his predecessors. His nature was profoundly religious, and his faith was firmly, indissolubly fixed in the Catholic Church. His political principles were liberal, just, generous, his love of his country sincere. The conflicting elements of love of country and love of the Church warring in his soul, made him melancholy, reserved, incomprehensible, incomplete."

Strange to say, the only person who seemed to bestow much thought or consideration on the presumptive heir of Piedmont was Prince Metternich. He concocted a scheme by which the eldest of King Victor Emmanuel's four daughters should marry her uncle, Francis of Modena, who, having been deprived of his intended bride, Maria Louisa, by her marriage with Napoleon, had remained a bachelor. The Salic law in Piedmont, when the time came, was to be set aside in favor of this lady and her husband, and thus Austrian influence over all Northern Italy would be complete. The Duke of Modena imprudently let out the secret of this scheme at the Congress of Vienna, when Prince Talleyrand, alarmed at the preponderance it would give to Austria in Italy, and looking upon Piedmont and Savoy as buffer States between France and Austrian Italy, opposed the scheme, and the rights of Charles Albert were formally recognized.

The young Prince was invited to visit the camp of the allies, an invitation that his kinsman, Charles Felix, although he detested and mistrusted the lad, characterized as a scheme designed to get the only male heir in any branch of the house of Savoy either debauched or killed. The young Prince was therefore called to the Court of Victor Emmanuel I., and definitely acknowledged as his uncle's heir. In due time he was married to the Archduchess Maria Theresa of Tuscany, at Florence, who, on March 14, 1820, gave birth to a son, Victor Emmanuel, the future King of Italy.

To learn what the condition of Italy was about this period, we might refer to the letters of Prince Metternich himself, a statesman of great general information and sagacity, but we may better quote, perhaps, M. de Chateaubriand, as an unprejudiced authority.

"It is not," he says, "some poor devils of Carbonari, excited by the actions of the police, and hung without mercy, who will revolutionize the country. The most false reports of the true state of things reach the ears of the governments. They are prevented from doing what they ought to do for their own safety by being led to believe that all discontent arises from the conspiracies of a handful of Jacobins, whereas it is the effect of a permanent and general cause. Such is the real position of Italy. Every one of the states, over and above the general dissatisfaction which fills all minds, has some cause of discontent peculiarly its own. Piedmont is delivered up to a fanatical faction, the Jesuits; the Milanese territory is devoured by the Austrians; the dominions of the Pope are ruined by bad administration; at Naples the weakness of the government is only saved by the cowardice of the people. The antipathies created by territorial divisions add further to the difficulties of an internal movement. But if some impulse came from without, or if some Prince on the Italian side of the Alps gave a Constitution to his subjects, a revolution would take place, for everything is ripe for revolution."

Victor Emmanuel I., King of Sardinia and Piedmont, and Duke of Savoy, found himself in 1814 in possession of all the former dominions of his family, together with the important city of Genoa and its dependencies, which, much against the will of its inhabitants, had been also given him.

On March 10, 1821, eight years before Chateaubriand wrote the passage I have quoted, a revolutionary rising took place in Alessandria, a strongly fortified position on the frontier of Piedmont adjoining Austrian Lombardy. The cry was raised of "King and Constitution," coupled with "Down with the Austrians!" At once the spark kindled a flame in Turin and Genoa. The King came in haste to his capital, bringing with him Prince Charles Albert. Arrived at Turin, he assembled a council. A soothing proclamation was issued, which, however, had no effect. The revolutionists still demanded a Constitution. At that very moment came news from the congress of the emperors at Laybach, that the Holy Alliance would not suffer any fresh "liberty" in Spain or Italy, and that if any people succeeded in extorting a Constitution from its sovereign, its country would be invaded by the Powers, who had guaranteed that there should be no change in the condition of things established by the Congress of Vienna.

This put an end to the Constitution sworn to by King Ferdinand of Naples, and appalled Victor Emmanuel, King of Piedmont and Savoy.

Meantime, the flag of Italy had been hoisted on the citadel of Turin, and had been hailed with enthusiasm by the inhabitants. Charles Albert, whose associations had been with young men accounted Liberals, with whose aspirations he was believed to sympathize, was sent, in the King's name, to demand the surrender of the fortress. He received in reply: "Our hearts are faithful to the King, but we wish to deliver him from perfidious counsels. War with Austria, a Constitution like that just granted in Spain, are the wishes of his people."

Perhaps had the Revolutionists known more about the Constitution "just granted in Spain," they would not have found its adaptation to Piedmont so satisfactory. It set aside the Salic law, and would have made the Duchess of Modena and her detested husband heirs of the reigning king, to the exclusion of his brother, Charles Felix, and Charles Albert, the young Prince of Savoy-Carignan.

In his perplexity, King Victor Emmanuel called together his military chiefs, and asked them to tell him the state of feeling in the army. All answered for the fidelity of their soldiers to the person of the King, but they declined to answer for them further.

After three days of vacillation, the kindly old King abdicated. He had refused to let such troops as were faithful to him fire on his subjects. He took leave of his people, appointing Charles Albert regent until the arrival of Charles Felix, the new sovereign. The Queen had desired to be regent, and was greatly disappointed. At the Congress of Vienna, Victor Emmanuel had pledged himself to the Allied Powers never to grant a Constitution to his people, and seeing that they would not be satisfied without one, he thus endeavored to escape responsibility.

He retired to Nice after his abdication, and Charles Albert was left for a few days to hold the reins of government. Those few days, however, sufficed to give the Piedmontese their earnestly desired Constitution.

The ministry of the late king counselled the regent to proclaim at once the Spanish Constitution. He hesitated, — but he did so. His proclamation ran thus : —

"In this most difficult moment it is not possible merely to consider what it is usually within the province of a regent to perform. Our respect and submission to His Majesty Charles Felix, upon whom the throne has devolved, would have counselled us to abstain from making any change in the fundamental laws of the kingdom, and would have led us to wait, so that we might know the intentions of the new King. But the imperious necessity of the circumstances being clearly manifest, and it being equally behoving on us to hand over to His Majesty his people in safety and happiness, and not torn in pieces by factions and civil war, we have determined, having well considered all the circumstances, acting in harmony with our council, and hoping that the King, moved by the same considerations, will invest this our decision with his sovereign approval, that the Constitution of Spain be promulgated, and observed as the law of the State, with such modifications as shall, by the National Representation, in concert with His Majesty the King, be determined on."

His Majesty the King, who was then staying with his kinsfolk in Modena, was furious at this action of the Regent, — a young man whom he hated, distrusted, and despised. He repudiated at once all idea of granting a Constitution to his kingdom, and ordered Charles Albert to repair to Novara, bringing with him all the troops he could collect. "I shall see," he said, "by the promptitude of your obedience, whether you are still a prince of the house of Savoy, or whether you have ceased to be one of them."

Charles Albert obeyed the King, and, with a few troops in his train, went submissively to Novara, that spot on which in his despair and anguish he did his best to court a soldier's death in after years. For five months, Charles Felix would not enter his capital. By the time he did so, constitutionalism had been put down, and Austrian troops had been summoned to support his authority.

When Charles Albert presented himself to his kinsman at Modena, Charles Felix refused to see him, but ordered him at once into exile at Florence, where ruled the brother of his wife, the Grand Duke Leopold of Tuscany. He also favored a scheme for setting aside the claims of Charles Albert to the succession. But this was opposed by Louis XVIII., who held his crown by right of legitimacy, and by the Emperor of Russia. Finally in 1825 the matter was settled, when Charles Albert signed a paper pledging himself to make no alterations in the government of his kingdom, when he should receive it, at the death of the reigning king.

In the late "International Review," appeared in 1880 a paper signed Luigi Monti, giving so graphic an account of the arrival of Charles Albert at Florence in disgrace and exile, that I cannot do better than insert it here.

"On a cold, dreary morning in the winter of 1822, several travelling carriages, escorted by dragoons, entered the city of Florence, and, through the Boboli gardens, came to the private entrance to the Pitti Palace. From the first one there alighted a tall, thin, stiff young man of military air, and of distinguished appearance, but with a sad, severe, thoughtful countenance. He helped from the carriage a handsome blonde lady, who, though speaking with the purest Tuscan accent, yet revealed by her complexion and features her Teutonic descent. On the landing at the top of the short stairway, stood the Grand Duke of Tuscany, with his family and household, to receive the new-comers. But before the lady would ascend the few steps, she waited for the next carriage to draw up; then taking from the arms of a nurse a child not quite two years old, she walked hastily up the steps, and with deep emotion rushed into the outstretched arms of the Grand Duke, who embraced her tenderly.

"The aristocratic, sober man was Charles Albert, Prince of Carignano, the lady was his wife, Maria Teresa of Austria, daughter of the Grand Duke; the child was Victor Emmanuel of Savoy, the future King of Italy. But why were they thus escorted by dragoons, who seemed to prevent intercourse with the people, while serving as a guard of honor? Why were they so privately received? Why did the Grand Duke, who greeted the Princess so warmly, scarcely notice the Prince, her husband, who followed her into the apartments, like an attendant, and then left her, bowing with glacial politeness, as if he were a family culprit? Why, after a few weeks of almost secluded residence, and the birth of another child, did he leave his family in Florence, and go to Spain, there to serve in the army of the Spanish king against the Constitutionalists?

"Prince Charles Albert of Carignano, of the younger branch of the house of Savoy, was the presumptive heir to the kingdom of Sardinia by the failure of male heirs in the elder branch, — a most extraordinary case, and almost a providential one. His training had been wholly military and religious. On the failure of all hopes of heirs in the elder branch in 1815, at the age of seventeen he had been married to Maria Teresa of Austria, daughter of the Grand Duke of Tuscany. Neglected at Court, he had sought solace in books of history and chivalry, and in the society of men of liberal ideas. His youthful fancy led to visions of Italian independence. He joined that division of the Carbonari whose aim was a federation of Italian States with constitutional governments, and he looked forward to the day when he could openly work for the cause of Italy. He took for his motto, — though in secret, — *J'attends mon astre.* Unhappy man! The star flashed several times on the horizon of his career, but it was destined never to rise and shine forth, except over the head of the child whom we have just seen held in his mother's arms on the palace stairs."

Charles Albert had continued, even after his marriage, to be a continual object of anxiety to Prince Metternich, who kept close watch upon him. He had never taken oaths to the Carbonari, as Louis Napoleon and his brother had done, but his intimates were not only men who held the opinions adopted by that order, but members of the order itself; and when Austria in 1822 and 1823 entered on a persecution of all the men of learning, influence, and especial probity, who were, or were suspected of being, Carbonari, Prince Metternich was extremely anxious to fasten the accusation of belonging to that society on the young Prince of Carignano. To this end, when Count Confalonieri, head of the society, had been sentenced to death, and had his sentence commuted to imprisonment for life at Spielberg, he was amazed, on reaching Vienna, on his way to that fortress, to find himself conducted to a luxurious apartment, where every comfort was provided for him, marred only by his chains. There Prince Metternich in person visited him, and, by every promise, cajolery, and threat that he could think of, endeavored to extort some of the secrets that concerned the Carbonari,—above all, Was the Prince of Carignano in any way associated with that order?

Needless to say, Prince Metternich extracted nothing, and Confalonieri went on his way to the same captivity as Silvio Pellico.

"Charles Albert, though a prince of the blood, was made to atone for his defection from Court absolutism by serving against the Constitutionalists in Spain, thus discrediting himself forever, it was hoped, with Italians of liberal opinions. He fought bravely, for he came of a martial race, and when the spirit of battle was upon him, he distinguished himself by his bravery at the taking of the Trocadero. But when he returned from Spain, despair seemed to have settled on his sad, severe countenance, which seldom changed, or smiled. He was a sad, silent man, suspected by the Liberals, who accused him of deserting their cause, suspected by the Austrians, and by the other princes of Italy, for his liberal opinions."

Charles Felix reigned till 1830. In his youth he had earnestly desired to be a monk, but things had been ordered otherwise. During his reign Piedmont may be said to have been ruled by the Austrians and the Jesuits. The cry that a few years later arose against the latter throughout Europe, was loud and fierce in Piedmont, and often probably unjust in lands where their political influence was bitterly resented.

Charles Albert, who came to the throne on his kinsman's death, was a mystery to all men. He gave no cause of complaint to the Austrians, he imprisoned followers of Mazzini, he caused the self-exile of young Cavour. Silent and impassive, nothing seemed to interest him but the discipline of his army, the care of his finances, and the education of his sons. "Traitor" and "double traitor" he was called. No man knew what to make of him.

The truth appears to be that Charles Albert, in very difficult circumstances, kept his own counsel, but his views were probably these: he did *not* want a federation of Italian republics with a Liberal Pope at its head, but he *did* want Austria to be driven out of Italy, and a United Italy (Northern Italy at least) made into a kingdom, with himself as its constitutional king. For these things he bided his time, and opposed those patriots who dreamed of republics, or made untimely attempts at revolution.

There were three very great men in his little kingdom, though two of them were not known beyond it up to the year 1848, — Count Camillo Cavour, General La Marmora, and the Marquis Massimo d'Azeglio. The latter was the author of a well known Italian romance called "Ettore Fieramosco."

These men were all true patriots, but wise and statesmanlike, opposed to rash enterprises, and to premature republicanism. Their motto was: "Let us first make Italians, and then make Italy." To this end they were all working to carry out material improvements, the construction of railroads, the regulation of commerce, the promotion of education, and so on.

KING CHARLES ALBERT.

Count Camillo Cavour was the third son of a noble Piedmontese father. When hardly out of college he was suspected of political leanings that were too patriotic, and for ten years his family were glad to have him live out of Italy, principally in France and England, studying their systems, particularly agriculture, to which he devoted himself on his return home. In this his history is like that of his great rival, Prince Bismarck, and he was like him, too, in this, that at one period of his life he was very "wild."

About 1846 he devoted himself to journalism in Turin, and thenceforth came forward as a politician. In 1834, when in disgrace at Court, he wrote to a friend that he hoped nevertheless some day to gratify all his ambitions, for in his dreams he saw himself Minister of Italy. Charles Albert seems to have had his eyes upon him, for, on some one asking him, "Why is not Cavour in the Cabinet?" he answered, "The time is not yet come for Cavour."

D'Azeglio was a Constitutionalist, opposed to the wilder projects of Mazzini. His family was illustrious, and Charles Albert had been on terms of affectionate intimacy with them.

In 1845 a change came over Italy. The enterprise of the brothers Bandiera, foolish and wasteful of life as it was, had stirred men's hearts. D'Azeglio, after a tour of inspection in the Papal States and central Italy, in which he had held intercourse with all the chief Liberals and perceived a sure prospect of a general rising against Austria, came to Turin, and had several private interviews with Charles Albert. The austere King listened to all the faithful patriot confided to him without replying, till at the last moment D'Azeglio, as he was leaving him, said: "Sire, I am going back to central Italy, — what reply shall I there make to my friends?" The sad face of the King suddenly brightened, his eyes flashed, and, seizing D'Azeglio's hand, he whispered in a low tone, as if afraid he might be overheard, "Marquis, tell your friends that, when the hour comes, I will stake my crown, my life, and the lives of my sons for Italian independence!" Then, as if terrified at having said so much, he hastily withdrew.

In 1846, as we have seen, the hopes of Italy revived after the election of Pio Nono. February, 1848, was a month of great events throughout all Europe. On February 8, two weeks before the French Revolution overthrew Louis Philippe, Charles Albert of his own motion offered his subjects a Constitution, or, as it was called a *Statuto Fondamentale*, and changed the national colors from those of the house of Savoy to red, white, and green, the tricolor of Italy. In the same month Leopold of Tuscany gave his subjects a Constitution.

Charles Albert, by first hoisting the Italian colors, placed himself at the head of the popular movement in Italy. He had fifty thousand trained soldiers in his army, and there were nearly one hundred thousand well-disciplined Italian soldiers in the ranks of the Austrians in Lombardy, all ready to desert at the first trumpet call.

Charles Albert was brave, patriotic, and thoroughly in earnest. His frame was hardy, his habits abstemious, and his recreations were active and manly. He had seen war, but not in the way it would be supposed an Italian patriot would have done, for he had drawn his sword in Spain in favor of despotism. He was a splendid soldier, but no general; nor had he genius. He was hampered by the poverty of his people, — though he had carefully hoarded their finances, — by the strong clerical party which disapproved his patriotism, and by the distrust of the advanced Republicans, who, although they assisted him as soldiers, set themselves against him personally in every way. Besides this, we must remember that before Italy could win her independence she had, besides the Austrians, who were enemies enough, five native princes to conciliate or overcome, — Ferdinand of Naples, Pio Nono of Rome, Leopold of Tuscany, Francis of Modena, and the Duke of Parma.

Charles Albert was, in 1848, fifty years old. His wife was a pious, gentle lady, sister of the Duke of Tuscany, kinswoman consequently of the Emperor of Austria. They had two sons, Victor Emmanuel, and Ferdinand Albert Amadeus, Duke of Genoa. These young men had had for their military preceptor Alfonso de La Marmora, who was subsequently the commander of the Sardinian army in the Crimean War. In one respect La Marmora was not a favorite with Charles Albert, being aggressively anti-clerical, whereas the King was, from his early training and family sympathies, greatly under the influence of the Jesuits, and the strongly clerical party. Though politically he went against them, he deeply suffered from it in his own mind.

It was early in 1847 that Milan, the capital of Lombardy, began to make such patriotic demonstrations of hatred to the Austrians as were possible without incurring the interference of the police. Milan society was gay and brilliant at that time, but if any Austrian officer or official was admitted to a ball at the house of a Milanese nobleman, his host knew well that he would have to retire to his country seat, as none of his friends in Milan would continue to visit him.

There was an obsolete by-law in Milan that smoking was not allowed in the streets. Every patriot gave up smoking (and a terrible sacrifice it must have been to him) because a large part of the Austrian revenue was derived from a monopoly in tobacco, and if an Austrian officer were seen smoking on the street, he was subjected to all manner of persecutions.

The whole peninsula, all through 1847, was in a state of unrest and of expectancy, and when, in February, 1848, Charles Albert granted Sardinia a Constitution, and the French Revolution overthrew *bourgeois* ascendency in France and its citizen king, Venice revolted from its Austrian rulers, and all Italy burst into a blaze. Those were the days when Mrs. Browning watched the progress of events in Tuscany through Casa Guidi windows.

The Austrian general in Lombardy was Radetzky, a man past eighty, who had served under the Russian general, Suwarrow, against armies of the French Republic in Italy fifty years before, and had fought Napoleon in all his wars. The youngest officer on his staff could hardly keep up with the old Marshal in his rides. Though his hair was snow-white, his eyes had not lost their fire, nor his mind its quick decision. He was the idol of his Austrian soldiers. Never depressed by defeat, never elated by victory; clement to the vanquished, and, though a leader in civil strife, one who never stained his hands in the blood of the defenceless or unresisting. He knew, when the insurrection burst out in Lombardy, that he must depend upon himself, — his Emperor had enough to do with troubles in Hungary and insurrection in Vienna.

The revolution in Milan broke out on the 18th of March, 1848, and for five days there was the most desperate street fighting ever known.

"In all quarters of the city," says the Countess Cesaresco, whose husband in those days marched to Milan at the head of a band of rustic followers, "barricades sprang up like mushrooms. Everything was freely given for their construction, the benches from the Opera House La Scala, the beds of the seminarists, the court carriages found hidden in a disused church, building materials of a half-finished palace, grand pianofortes, valuable furniture, and the old kitchen tables of the artisan. . . . In the first straits for want of arms, the museums of two ancient families were emptied by permission of their owners; the crowd brandished priceless old swords and specimens of early firearms. More serviceable weapons were obtained by degrees from the Austrian killed and wounded, and from the public offices which fell into their hands."

"The very foundations of the city were torn up," wrote Field Marshal Radetzky, in his official report, "not hundreds, but thousands of barricades crossed the streets. Such circumspection and audacity were displayed that it was evident military leaders were at the head of the people. The character of the Milanese had become quite changed. Fanaticism had seized every rank and age in both sexes."

And yet, with all the excitement in those five days of fighting, the Milanese population showed wonderful forbearance.

Radetzky ordered the evacuation of the town at last, and marched his thirteen thousand soldiers out of it in the night of Wednesday, March 22. His garrison had consisted of eighteen thousand men, but five thousand of these, being

Italians, had deserted and joined the Milanese, while volunteers from all the neighboring towns marched in to strengthen the patriot party.

Wild was the enthusiasm of the Milanese at their success. They established a Provisional Government, and Charles Albert, declaring war against Austria, marched his Sardinian army to their aid.

Charles Albert had no personal reason to complain of Austria, but he was animated by the general Italian feeling against Italy's foreign masters, and, like others, saw the finger of God in the events that were taking place. Besides, he could not but be sensible that, if Italy became a united kingdom, he was the chief who would be placed at its head.

Charles Albert's army was in many respects well equipped and very efficient. His light infantry was among the best in the world. His want was the lack of generals of experience, for in those days La Marmora and Dabormida had not come to the fore.

The Austrians retreated from one strong position to another, till they made their final stand on the line of the river Mincio, defended by the fortresses known as the Quadrilateral, — Mantua, Peschiera, Legnago, and Verona. The Tyrolese remained enthusiastically faithful to their Austrian rulers, and were of great assistance to the Austrian commander.

I must leave others to tell the details of the campaign of 1848 in Lombardy, — how the tug of war swayed sometimes in favor of Radetzky, sometimes in favor of Charles Albert. The latter got his army within the celebrated Quadrilateral, took Peschiera, one of its great fortresses, and shut up the Austrians in Mantua and Verona.

By the middle of the summer of 1848 the advantage was with Charles Albert. He had been offered the crown of Northern Italy, but had refused it, deeming the offer premature. Venice had put herself under his authority, and for a brief space was governed by his commissioners.

But he sorely needed reinforcements, and they were hard to obtain. There had been, as we have already seen, a strong body of Neapolitans under General Pepe despatched ostensibly to his assistance; but secret orders had forbidden their general to lead them across the Po. When orders, in the spring of 1848, were received by the Neapolitan troops to return home, the larger part obeyed. When the Pope, on April 29, declared that he would not make war on Austria, the Roman patriots under General Durando crossed the frontier. They were met by the Austrians not far from Bologna. Being without military experience, they were cut to pieces. Among them were three thousand of the Pope's Swiss Guard, who fought brilliantly, losing two hundred out of every thousand men.

Radetzky had about forty-four thousand men besides his sick and his soldiers in garrison. The Piedmontese army numbered about the same, but many were undisciplined volunteers, who could be little counted on in actual warfare. Charles Albert had, however, the advantage of being in a country that was friendly to him. On July 24 and 25, 1848, took place the battle of Custozza, and Charles Albert lost it. It was fought in a heavy rain, and the Sardinian army was weakened by having too long a line to defend. The next day, however, Charles Albert so manœuvred as to snatch from the Austrians all the fruit of their victory. But after that the situation changed. The King was unable to provision his army, and when his soldiers had suffered from hunger for three days, he was compelled to retire, and to surrender the great fortress of Peschiera, which it had cost him so much to gain.

He continued his retreat to Milan,—a retreat which greatly discouraged his army; and the republicans and foreign volunteers began to cry "Treason!"

Radetzky closely followed the retreating army. "But," says Alison, "the troops of Charles Albert, though finally worsted, exhibited the courage in disaster which is the most honorable attribute of soldiers. All, however, was unavailing." The decree of Providence had been pronounced, and Italy was again for seventeen long years to pass under the Austrian dominion.

Charles Albert, finding it would be impossible to save Milan, made his preparations. A capitulation was proposed and discussed, on the 5th of August, but no sooner did the Milanese find out what was at hand, than they assembled tumultuously before the King's quarters, shouting: "Death to the Piedmontese! War to the death with Austria! A war of the barricades!"

Shots were fired in at the King's windows, and the Piedmontese soldiers were so exasperated at the conduct of the Milanese, that it required all the efforts of their officers to restrain them from charging the crowd, and avenging the insults heaped on their sovereign.

And yet one can hardly blame the unhappy Milanese, who were to be delivered in a few hours into the hands of their enemies.

The King was rescued from the fury of this exasperated mob by the gallantry of La Marmora, who, seeing the danger increasing every moment, rushed out into the street, and, by sheer intrepidity, forced his way through the mob, collected a body of soldiers, returned with them to the King's quarters, and carried him off in safety. When they returned to Turin, the Queen asked to see Colonel La Marmora.

"M. le Chevalier, you saved the King's life! I shall preserve the recollection always in my memory," she exclaimed, with trembling lips, as La Marmora kissed her hand, with the deep respectful sympathy which with him seldom found its way into words.

"It was not only the King I wished to save," he said afterwards to a friend, "but the population of Milan from a horrible crime, the consequences of which would have been fatal to Italy."

The authorities of Milan, dreading indiscriminate plunder, or rash and useless resistance to the inevitable, on the departure of the Piedmontese army, requested that, before it left, the soldiers would remove the barricades.

The Piedmontese army on August 6 quitted Milan before daybreak, and the Austrians entered it in triumph by ten o'clock the same day.

"They swept by in superb order, in their white uniforms, to the triumphant strains of military music," says Alison, "and amidst the deathlike silence of all who witnessed their entry. The dreams of the enthusiasts had passed away, — the vision of Italian independence had melted into air, — the iron had entered the very souls of the Milanese."

Ten years more of suffering, and Milan was free; seven years later and all Lombardy, Venetia, Tuscany, and the group of little duchies sometimes called Emilia, were under the rule of Charles Albert's son; a little longer and the dream of a United Italy was accomplished. One thinks of the old Hebrew verse, as it stands in Cranmer's version of the Psalms, in the Book of Common Prayer: "O! tarry thou the Lord's leisure; be strong, and He shall comfort thine heart, and put thou thy trust in the Lord!"

Shortly after this, an armistice for a year was concluded at Salasco, in which Charles Albert renounced any jurisdiction over Venetia, and the little republic was left unassisted to fight out her own quarrel.

Eighteen hundred and forty-eight was a sorrowful year for the King. The clerical party urged on him that all his misfortunes were in punishment for his opposition to the clergy. His mother and his wife supported this opinion, and left him no peace "for the good of his soul."

One of his ministers died, and no priest in Turin would give him the last sacraments; while all over Italy rose the cry: "We have put our trust in princes, and in vain; — the war of the people is about to commence!"

The revolutionary fires burnt higher than ever. It was in 1848 that Rossi was stabbed, and that the Pope crossed his frontier, self-exiled into the kingdom of Ferdinand of Naples. Then the Roman Republic was proclaimed.

The two leading republicans in Italy were Mazzini and Garibaldi. Mazzini was made the leading triumvir in the Roman Republic; Garibaldi had been engaged in forming a volunteer corps at Genoa, the headquarters of republicanism in Italy, the city least loyal to Charles Albert in his dominions. He did not foresee the future. He did not foresee his friendship for the son of Charles Albert, but stigmatized that monarch and his Piedmontese at this period, as " moderate traitors."

At the opening of the spring of 1849, in spite of the remonstrances of the French and English ministers at Turin, Charles Albert resumed preparations for war. " I must declare war," he said, " or abdicate and see a republic established but to fall."

On March 12 the armistice terminated. Charles Albert's army, notwithstanding his utmost exertions, was not efficiently equipped, and largely consisted of new levies. It had one hundred and thirty-five thousand men, *on paper*, but he could bring only eighty-three thousand fighting men into the field. The noisiest patriots clamored for a foreign general, complaining of former leaders as aristocratic do-nothings; and a Polish refugee with a name that he never made sufficiently illustrious to tempt the world to pronounce, was set over the Piedmontese army. The theatre of war was to be that great and fertile plain of Lombardy watered by the river Po, — one of the garden spots of the whole earth.

On March 18, Radetzky, after cautioning the inhabitants of Milan to give no cause of offence to the Austrian government during his absence, as he would soon come back in triumph and take account of how they had behaved, marched out of Milan in all his glory, and took the road that would lead him into the dominions of the Sardinian king. Germans, Austrians, Bohemians, Tyrolese, Italians, Magyars, Poles, and Croats were in his army, and when the signal to march was given, " the bands," says a spectator, " struck up enlivening airs, and all, in the finest order and the highest spirits, moved with a proud step, confident of victory."

They crossed the river Ticino, and were on Piedmontese soil. " The fate of Italy seemed sealed," says Alison, " for sixty battalions of infantry, forty squadrons of cavalry, and one hundred and eighty-six cannon, — in all fifty-five thousand well-appointed combatants, — had entered, unopposed, Charles Albert's territory."

The fatal difference between the Italian and the Austrian armies was, that the one had a general on whom it could thoroughly depend, while the other, — the Italian army, — had next to no leader at all. The general who should have opposed the Austrians was Ramorino, the same who in 1834 had made an abortive attempt to invade Savoy at the head of a small body of Poles and Mazzinists. He was said to be the illegitimate son of the great Marshal Lannes. With the foolish idea of copying a celebrated military movement of his father's, he crossed the Po in defiance of his instructions, and left the road to Turin open to the enemy. The Austrians came on, gaining small advantages at every step, which disheartened the young Italian troops, till both armies met near the city of Novara.

Charles Albert drew up his army with as much skill and in as advantageous a position as circumstances would allow. Fortune wavered from side to side for some hours. The sons of Charles Albert distinguished themselves by their bravery — so did the Austrian Archdukes in the other army, who were serving under Radetzky. But in the end the day was won by the Austrians. The reserve of the Piedmontese army, under the Duke of Genoa (Prince Ferdinando Alberto Amadeo), performed prodigies of valor, and did all that men could do to arrest the disorder and cover the retreat of the defeated army. But Radetzky had been reinforced, and his numbers, as well as his discipline, were against the Italians.

" The day was lost, and a general retreat became unavoidable. Twelve guns were taken by the Austrians in their pursuit, but very few prisoners. The old soldiers of Piedmont retired, firing at intervals, and in admirable order, the Genoese and Lombard new recruits fled in utter confusion, and for the most part, disbanded, and were never heard of more. In the town of Novara, into which the defeated army poured during the night, the most dreadful confusion prevailed. Plunder immediately began. The cavalry charged the fugitive crowds through the streets, and they were soon streaming in wild confusion over the roads to the mountain towns of Duomo, Ossola and Arona, the only refuge left open to them."

FIELD MARSHAL RADETZKY.

All retreat to Turin was cut off. They had nowhere to retire to but the inhospitable barrier of the Alps, where little food was to be had, and where the defiles would have soon made the roads impassable for a retreating army. Only an immediate armistice could save them.

All through the day Charles Albert had borne himself like a gallant soldier. About seven in the evening, when the battle was evidently irretrievably lost, he permitted General Durando to lead him away. But even then he lingered under the walls of Novara, where bullets were falling fast, hoping that one would strike him, saying, "General, this is my last day; — let me die!"

About nine o'clock, when prevailed upon to withdraw into the town, he assembled such of his principal officers and counsellors as he could collect together, and declared to them that he was unalterably resolved to abdicate in favor of his son Victor Emmanuel, the Duke of Savoy. "I have sacrificed myself," he said, "for the Italian cause. For it I have exposed my life, that of my children, and my throne. I have failed. I am aware that I am the sole obstacle to a peace that has now become necessary for our State. I could not bring myself to sign it. Since in vain I have sought death, I give myself up, a last sacrifice to my country. I lay down the crown, and abdicate in favor of my son."

After this, he dismissed his attendants, sat down and wrote a farewell letter to his wife, and at one in the morning presented himself at the Austrian outposts, where he narrowly escaped being fired on with grape shot. He gave his name as a Piedmontese gentleman, bearer of despatches to Count Thurn. When he reached that general and made known his name and rank, great was the astonishment of the Austrians. He was allowed at once to pass the Austrian lines. He passed one night in a convent on the mountains, spending his time in prayer. Then he made his way to Nice, and thence to Oporto, where he died of a broken heart a few months after. The last words spoken by him on Italian soil were: "In whatever time, in whatever place, a regular government raises the flag of war with Austria, the Austrians will find me among their enemies as a simple soldier."

At the opening of the campaign, at the close of a long conversation *tête-à-tête* with the Marquis Pallavicini, one of the amnestied Spielberg prisoners, Charles Albert had said, as he embraced the ex-prisoner at parting, "You and I had always the same thought. The independence of Italy was the first dream of my youth. It is my dream still. It will be till I die."

General Pepe, writing only a year later, for Italians disappointed, humiliated, and inclined to cry "Treachery!" emphatically expresses over and over again his high confidence in the honest purposes and patriotism of Charles Albert.

"It is my firm conviction," he says, "that there was no treachery in him whatever, and that all Italy should be grateful to the Piedmontese army, and still more to Charles Albert and his two sons, who, without hesitation, exposed their lives and fortunes for the Italian cause, without being discouraged by the misfortunes of the first campaign. Italians! there is no citizen who more than myself has had occasion to show how much more he is devoted to his country than to kings. From kings I desire nothing; nor could I, without being wanting to myself, accept any personal favors from them. Nevertheless, I repeat that we should all remember Charles Albert with gratitude, as well as his sons, who valiantly followed him to the field of battle, and who cannot now ever deviate from the line of policy embraced by their father, without exposing themselves to dishonor and the loss of their throne."

And it is thus that poetry has spoken of Charles Albert, who, having sought death in vain, laid down on the last battle-field his sword and crown: —

> "He stripped away
> Th' ancestral ermine ere the smoke was cleared,
> And, naked to the soul, — that none might say
> His kingship covered what was base, and bleared
> With treason, — he went out an exile; — yea,
> An exiled patriot. Let him be revered. . . .

> For he was shriven, I think, in cannon smoke;
> And, taking off his crown, made visible
> A hero's forehead. Shaking Austria's yoke,
> He shattered his own hand and heart."[1]

Almost the first words the new King, Victor Emmanuel, uttered as a sovereign were worthy of the son of his father, — worthy of himself. Pointing his sword toward the Austrian camp, he exclaimed, "*Per Dio! L'Italia sarà!*" "In the name of God, Italy shall yet be!"

[1] Mrs. Browning.

CHAPTER VI.

THROUGH CASA GUIDI WINDOWS.

VICTOR EMMANUEL had sworn that Italy should *be!* — though all things round him as he took that oath seemed adverse to his hopes. The year 1849 was a sorrowful one for Italy, even as 1871 was for France.

In the summer of 1849, Rome was besieged, and the little republic crushed, by Frenchmen acting in the name of another republic. After seventeen months' absence at Gaeta, Pio Nono, under the protection of the French, returned to the Quirinal, and resumed his temporal sovereignty; Ferdinand of Naples also went back to his capital to wreak vengeance on his revolted subjects; Bologna in the Papal States, and Brescia in Lombardy were occupied by the Austrians, Marshal Haynau commanding in the assault on the latter city. His name alone would suffice to tell what woes fell on its inhabitants. Venice had better treatment. She held out until the close of August, 1849, and was then suffered to make an honorable capitulation. At the close of May, 1849, the Grand Duke Leopold returned to Tuscany, escorted by the Austrians, and with them made a triumphal entry into Florence, at the head of the troops who had fought at Novara, each man wearing a sprig of green from that sad field, as he strode on through the streets of Florence. Garibaldi was a fugitive and his "Thousand" were disbanded; Francis of Modena, Charles of Parma, and Charles Louis, Duke of Lucca, were safely back in their own dominions. Of these things a brief account must be given in this chapter, — a chapter, it may be, of shreds and patches, — while the next will be devoted to the troubles of the same year in the Austrian dominions, best told in a brief biography of Kossuth. We may then return to Victor Emmanuel, and pursue his career up to 1866, the date of the battle of Sadowa. The writer of Italian history, as well as the Italian patriot, has cause to sigh for a United Italy.

After the surrender of Charles Albert, the Austrians turned their attention to the punishment of Brescia, a city of Lombardy, and therefore in revolt against its Austrian Emperor. Other cities in Lombardy, seeing resistance hopeless, had made terms with the Austrians, but the fire of patriotism burned strongly in Brescia. "She had," says the Countess Martinengo Cesaresco, whose husband was a Brescian, whose ancestor, indeed, commanded in that city while it still held out — "a love of liberty which was an hereditary instinct from her long connection with free Venice, where hatred of the foreigner, planted by the ruthless soldiery of Gaston de Foix, had gone on maturing for three centuries. In Brescia, with a single mind, the inhabitants resolved upon as desperate a resistance as was ever offered by one little town to a great army."

The Austrian troops were commanded by a skilful general of Irish descent, named Nugent. He died in the midst of the bombardment, but, struck with admiration for the forty thousand inhabitants of the little city which defied a victorious army eighty thousand strong, he left, on his deathbed, by his will, all his fortune to the city he was endeavoring to conquer. Field-Marshal Haynau succeeded him. Haynau was already known in Brescia, where he had been appointed military governor after Austria had resumed her authority a year before.

He reported to his government the attack he made upon the city after its bombardment, and the narrative may be best told in his own words.

"It was," he wrote, "a most murderous fight, a fight prolonged by the insurgents from barricade to barricade, from house to house, with extraordinary obstinacy. I could never have believed that so bad a cause could have been sustained with so much perseverance. In spite of this desperate defence, and although the assault could only be effected in part, and with the help of cannon of heavy calibre, our brave troops, with heroic courage, but at the cost of many lives, occupied a first line of houses. But as all my columns could not penetrate into the town at the same time, I ordered the suspension of the attack at nightfall, limiting myself to holding my ground. In spite of that, the combat continued late into the night. On April 1, in the earliest morning light, the tocsin was heard ringing with more fury than ever, and the insurgents opened fire with an entirely new desperation. Considering the gravity of our losses, as well as the obstinacy and fury of the enemy, it was necessary to adopt a most rigorous measure. I ordered that no prisoners should be taken, but that every person seized with arms in his hands should be immediately put to death, and that the houses from which shots came should be burnt. It is thus that conflagrations, partly caused by our troops, partly by the bombardment, broke out in several parts of the city."

The Countess Martinengo Cesaresco, who has almost the authority of an eye-witness, speaks thus: —

"From the nobles to the poorest, all did their duty. The horrors of the repression make one think of Khartoum. Not even in Hungary, where Haynau went to continue his 'system,' did he so blacken his own and his country's name as here. In a boy's school, kept by a certain Guidi, the master's wife, his mother, and ten of his pupils were slaughtered. A little hunchback tailor was carried to the barracks to be slowly burned alive. But stray details do not give the faintest idea of the whole."

Count Martinengo, after the Austrians were in possession, escaped from the city by the assistance of a band of young butchers who organized his flight. It took him ten days to reach safety, and he had many hairbreadth escapes on his perilous way. A prize of 3,000 florins was set upon his head.

Among all the States of Italy, after the territories of that fair land had been portioned out by the Congress of Vienna, Tuscany was the most tranquil, the most prosperous, the best governed. There political fugitives from other States sometimes found refuge. Its Grand Duke was unlike other

Bourbons; he was far from being unpopular with his subjects, and many Italians thought that, in the event of securing Italian unity or a northern and central Italian kingdom, it might be well to place him on the Italian throne.

In 1847, when Pio Nono was granting reforms in his dominions, the Grand Duke, almost unsolicited, granted his subjects greater freedom of the press, and an improved civil code. An assembly of wise men, — men of character and authority, — was summoned to take into consideration further reforms, and the organization of a Garda Civile, or National Guard. On September 5, 1847, a procession of twenty thousand Florentines marched to the Pitti Palace to express enthusiastic gratitude to their Duke. But Prince Metternich lost no time in reprimanding the Grand Duke, and disapproving of his new policy.

The revolution went on, Rome to all appearance, leading the way. In February, 1848, when Europe was ablaze, Duke Leopold promised a Constitution, and appeared among his people in the uniform of a colonel of the Civic Guard. On March 13, 1848, a revolution in Vienna drove Prince Metternich into exile. Then came the murder of Count Rossi, the flight of the Pope, and disasters to the army of Charles Albert in Lombardy. It seemed probable that Austria would regain her ascendency in Italy. Leopold had already authorized the calling into existence of an Italian Constituent Assembly, which should offer plans for the federation of the various Italian States, and on January 10, 1849, he opened a Tuscan Parliament as a preliminary measure. Then he grew frightened, and, pleading impaired health, removed with his family from Florence to Siena. Thence, under pretence of taking a drive, he set off for a seaport on the Mediterranean, whence, a month later, he repaired to Gaeta, where the Pope and Ferdinand of Naples were awaiting the turn of events which would restore them to their capitals.

After the battle of Novara, the Austrians, heartened by their successes in Northern Italy, marched into Tuscany, and restored Leopold II. to his archducal throne.

Mrs. Browning saw all these events from Casa Guidi windows, and there is no account of what passed during those days in Florence so vivid as hers. From those windows she gazed down upon the crowds that greeted the Grand Duke's reforms in September, 1847, — accepting them as the first-fruits of his new Liberalism.

The exultant Florentines passed the house in orderly procession, banners waved, music played, and thousands of voices joined in patriotic songs. The magistrates passed by, the insignia of their office glittering in the sun; the great crowd shouted frantically at the sight, while from the windows all along the route hung blue and green and scarlet draperies, and ladies flung down flowers, wreaths, and bay leaves on the heads of those they recognized, as the procession passed their houses. Especially were the lawyers greeted in this way.

Then followed deputations from every local division of the archduchy, each with its banner, on which was emblazoned the emblem of its city, — the she-wolf of Siena, the hare of Pisa, the golden lion of Massa, the silver one of Pienza, the war-horse of Arezzo, and so on.

It took three hours for the procession to pass Casa Guidi, while the crowd that looked on, filled with patriotic emotion and enthusiasm, laughed, shouted, wept, and fraternized with one another. And Mrs. Browning cried : —

> "Oh! heaven, I think that day had noble use
> Among God's days! . . ."

When the procession had reached the Pitti Palace, Duke Leopold came forth upon the balcony to receive their greetings. He had his little children by his side, and said something of his hope that they would some day govern Tuscany in accordance with the good-will of the people, making Florence prosperous and happy. There were tears in his eyes and on his cheeks, "good, warm, human tears," said Mrs. Browning.

> "I like his face. The forehead's build
> Has no capacious genius, — yet, perhaps,
> Sufficient comprehension ; — mild and sad,
> And care-full nobly. Not with care that wraps

Self-loving hearts, to stifle and make mad,
 But care-full with the care that shuns each lapse
Of faith and duty. . . . So, God save the Duke!
 I say with those who that day shouted it."

Alas! a few weeks passed and the scene changed. Margaret Fuller, then in Italy, wrote thus of the disappointment of the Florentines when they found that the concessions of the Grand Duke did not come up to their expectations : —

"The first announcement of the regulation for the Tuscan Civic Guard terribly disappointed the people. They felt that the Grand Duke, after suffering them to demonstrate such trust and joy on the feast of September 5, did not really trust on his side, — that he meant to limit all he could. They felt baffled, cheated. Hence, young men in anger tore down at once the symbols of satisfaction and respect, but the leading men went among the people, exhorting them to wait till a deputation had seen the Grand Duke. The people listened at once to the men who, they were sure, had their best good at heart, — and waited. The Grand Duke became convinced, and it all ended without bloodshed. If the people continue to act so, their hopes cannot be baffled."

So wrote an American lady, full of faith, hope, charity, and enthusiasm. She did not yet know her Italy as Mrs. Browning knew it, who, gazing from Casa Guidi windows, viewed with different sensations the outburst of civic rapture when the Duke, lately the popular idol, fled to Gaeta.

"From Casa Guidi windows I looked out —
Again looked, and beheld a different sight . . .
 Long live the people! How they lived and boiled
And bubbled in the caldron of the street!
 How the young blustered, nor the old recoiled.
And what a thunderous stir of tongues and feet
 Trod flat the palpitating bells, and foiled
The joy guns of their echo; . . .
 How down they pulled the Duke's arms everywhere;
How up they set the café signs to show
 Where patriots might sip ices in pure air, —
(The fresh paint smelling somewhat!). To and fro
 How marched the Civic Guard, and stopped to stare
When boys broke windows in a civic glow.
 How rebel songs were sung to loyal tunes,
And bishops cursed in ecclesiastic metres. . . .

How of Guerazzi men cried: 'There's a man!
The father of the land, — who truly great
   Takes off that national disgrace and ban,
The farthing tax upon our Florence Gate,
   And saves Italia as he only can!'
How all the nobles fled, and would not wait
   Because they were most noble; — which, being so,
The Liberals vowed to burn their palaces,
   Because free Tuscans were not free to go.
How grown men raged at Austria's wickedness,
   And smoked, while fifty striplings in a row
Marched straight to Piedmont for the wrong's redress.
   Who says we failed in duty, — we who wore
Black velvet like Italian democrats,
   Who slashed our sleeves like patriots; nor forswore
The true Republic in the form of hats?
   We chased the Archbishop from the Duomo door;
We chalked the walls with bloody caveats
   Against all tyrants. If we did not fight,
At least we fired muskets in the air
   To show that victory was ours of right.
We met, — had free discussion everywhere
   (Except, perhaps, in the Chambers) day and night.
We proved the poor should be employed, — 't was fair, —
   And yet the rich not worked for; everywhere
Pay certified, — yet payers abrogated; —
   Full work secured, yet liabilities
To over-work excluded; — not one bated
   Of all our holidays, that still at twice
Or thrice a week are moderately rated.
   We proved that Austria was dislodged, or would
Or should be; and that Tuscany in arms
   Should, would, dislodge her; ending our old feud.
And yet to leave our piazzas, shops, and farms,
   For the simple sake of fighting, was not good.
We proved that also. 'Did we carry charms
   Against being killed ourselves, that we should rush
On killing others? What! desert herewith
   Our wives and mothers?— was that duty? Tush!'
At which we shook the sword within the sheath
   Like heroes, — only louder."

Well might Charles Albert, who had known popularity and popular contumely, say that one was as little to be regarded as the other. Our Shakespeare knew the class that Italians call *il popolo*, the French *le peuple*, and whom he calls " mechanicals."

The battle of Novara had been fought.

> "From Casa Guidi windows, gazing then
> I saw, and witness how the Duke came back, —
> The regular tramp of horse and tread of men
> Did smite the silence, like an anvil black
> And sparkless. With her wide eyes at full strain
> Our Tuscan nurse exclaimed: 'Alack! Alack!
> Signora, these shall be the Austrians!' 'Nay,
> Be still,' I answered, 'do not wake the child.'
> For so my two-months baby sleeping lay
> In milky dreams upon the bed, and smiled. . . .
> Then, gazing, I beheld the long-drawn street
> Alive from end to end, full in the sun
> With Austria's thousands, sword and bayonet,
> Horse, foot, artillery; cannon rolling on
> Like blind, slow storm-clouds, gestant with the heat
> Of undeveloped lightnings. Each bestrode
> By a single man, dust-white from head to heel,
> Indifferent as the dreadful thing he rode. . . .
> So swept, in mute significance of storm,
> The marshalled thousands; not an eye deflect
> To left or right, to catch a novel form
> Of Florence city, adorned by architect
> Or carver; or of beauties, live and warm,
> Scared at the casements; — all, straight forward eyes
> And faces, held as steadfast as their swords . . .
> While every soldier in his cap displayed
> A leaf of olive. Dusty, bitter thing! —
> Was such plucked at Novara, as 't is said?"

Thus Leopold, Archduke of Austria, Grand Duke of Tuscany, came back to Florence. He was restored by Austria as a despotic sovereign. Ten years later, when war was about to break out with Austria he refused a proffered alliance with France and Piedmont, though the leading statesmen in Florence, men who to a certain extent enjoyed his confidence, Ricasoli and Capponi, did their best to persuade him to unite with his people in favor of the national cause. But he again preferred exile and the protection of Austria. He left Florence and took refuge in the Austrian camp. A provisional government was formed which placed the Tuscan forces at the disposal of Victor Emmanuel, and shortly after the Tuscans by a *plébiscite* acknowledged him their king.

CHAPTER VII.

THE ROMAN REPUBLIC.

THE course of history may in most cases be compared to the course of a river, sometimes rapid, sometimes sluggish, but in almost all cases it has a main stream, flowing steadily on its way from source to mouth. Such is not the case with the history of Italy. For more than ten centuries its main stream had divided and subdivided into numerous branches, and any writer who may set himself to tell its story must frequently go back to the point from which he last started if he would produce an intelligible and interesting narrative of any of its principal events.

Thus, though I have already said a few words concerning the Roman Republic, much remains to be told, especially as the history of its brief existence brings a new character upon the scene, — Garibaldi, who was Italy's most popular hero for almost thirty years.

Patriot as he was, Garibaldi's lack of statesmanship, and superabundance of unenlightened sympathy and enthusiasm, would assuredly have made shipwreck of the cause of United Italy had there not been wiser men to say him nay. Happily, being susceptible to personal influences in an extraordinary degree, his enthusiasm was in a manner regulated by steadier minds. Thus, by turns, Mazzini, Pio Nono, Charles Albert, and for a time again Mazzini, were the objects of his trust and admiration. To them succeeded Cavour and Victor Emmanuel (though personal liking he never gave Cavour). These held him in leash for some years, after which he professed himself a friend and follower of Victor Hugo, Rochefort, and French Red Republicans. But he always declared himself to be the Rè Galantuomo's affectionate and personal friend. The form of government in which he seems most steadily to have believed, was a Republic, with himself as its dictator. Constitutionalism he neither accepted nor understood.

He displayed the same unenlightened enthusiasm in his religion. While he early threw off his allegiance to the church of his fathers, he yet wrote and spoke, while under the influence of his noble friend, the patriotic Barnabite monk, Ugo Bassi, like a truly religious man. Later, he attacked in ferocious language, not only the Roman hierarchy but all those who looked on priests as their spiritual fathers. In his earlier campaigns he would suffer his followers to commit no pillage of churches, no desecration of sacred things, while during his French campaign in 1871, the sacrileges they committed caused the peasantry of the Vosges to consider them bandits rather than allies.

However, to go back to Rome, as it was on the morning of November 24, 1848, when its inhabitants awoke to learn that the Holy Father had abandoned the Quirinal and had crossed the Neapolitan frontier.

We cannot but sympathize with the self-exiled Pio Nono; we sympathize with his deserted and bewildered subjects. But the first thing the Roman people thought to do was to make a joyful demonstration. In the course of it they collected the wooden confessionals from the churches, with the intention of burning them on the Piazza del Popolo. Ciceruacchio, however, mounted the pile, and, addressing the crowd, said : " I formerly thought it would be a good thing to burn these monuments of corruption to our wives and daughters, but our leading men fear that the smoke of their burning may hurt the eyes of European diplomatists and dispose them against us. They understand the matter better than we do; therefore let us obey them."

When Ciceruacchio spoke he was invariably obeyed. But the crowd was not to be balked of its bonfire, so it turned its vengeance against the guillotine.

Pio Nono's first act on reaching Gaeta was to excommunicate those he held to be his enemies, — his late ministers and others, more especially all who might take part in any clamor for universal suffrage.

This brief was forwarded to all bishops in the Papal States, but few of them seemed inclined to publish it. The insurgents, however, secured a copy, and gave it the widest circulation.

As usual, the Roman people made a demonstration, first, however, electing by universal suffrage a Roman Constituent Assembly. Then they amused themselves by performing a funeral ceremony over the Pope's brief of excommunication, after they had burnt it publicly. They then proceeded to excommunicate the Pope himself, and to cut him off from all Christian sympathy and communion.

The flight of the Pope and the resignation of his ministers left Rome for a time without any kind of legal government and with a prospect of anarchy. The Assembly did not meet till February 5, 1849. Meantime, it was largely owing to the influence of Ciceruacchio that order was preserved in the city. The Pope had, indeed, left behind him a letter exhorting the people to preserve order in the absence of any lawful authority, and very remarkably that order was maintained.

"Of great help in quieting the people's passions," says the Countess Cesaresco, "was Ciceruacchio. He never put on black cloth clothes, or asked to be admitted into the Ministry, according to the usual wont of successful tribunes. He had the sense of humor of the genuine Roman *popolano*, and it never came into his head to make himself ridiculous. His influence had been first acquired by works of charity in the Tiber floods. Being a strong swimmer, he ventured where no one else would go, and had saved many lives. At first a wine-carrier, he made money by letting out conveyances and dealing in forage, but he gave away most of what he made. He opposed the whole force of his popularity to a war of classes. *Viva chi c'ia, e chi non c'ia quattrini!*" (Long live who has money and who has none!) was his favorite cry. Once when a young poet read him a sonnet in his honor, he stopped him at the line 'Thou art greater than all patricians,' saying that he would not have that published: 'I respect the nobility and never dream of being higher than they. I am a poor man of the people, and such I will always remain!"

Two hundred representatives made up the Assembly. Of these a large number were lawyers, some were rich landowners, two were Jews, two were priests, and one was a monsignor. They at once confirmed the deposition of the Pope as their temporal ruler, and then came the question of a new form of government. The majority were in favor of a Roman Republic; a few were for delaying action, as they hoped Charles Albert, who had retired into Piedmont after the armistice that followed the battle of Custozza, would again take the field against the Austrians in the spring. These, however, were overruled. More radical views prevailed. The populace was delighted to make the occasion an excuse for a Roman holiday. They illuminated their city, they gave vent to transports of joy.

The decree of deposition ran thus : —

"I. The Papacy has fallen in fact and in right from the temporal government of the Roman States.

"II. The Roman Pontiff shall have all necessary guarantees for the independent exercise of his spiritual power.

"III. The form of government in the Roman States shall be a pure democracy, and shall take the glorious name of the Roman Republic.

"IV. The Roman Republic shall have such relations with the rest of Italy as the common nationality demands."

This decree was published February 9, 1849, and the colors of Italy superseded the banner of the Papacy, with its crossed keys. It was not until March that Mazzini arrived in Rome. He entered the Eternal City (where he had never been before) as a Roman citizen, having been made such by an especial decree. Garibaldi, too, had been summoned, and reached Rome about the same time with his somewhat disorderly legion, which had been recruited to strengthen Charles Albert in his war with the Austrians.

Mazzini, and two others, Armellini and Saffi, men whose names never became world-famous, were elected triumvirs. The good order they maintained in Rome was as creditable as it was surprising. "That at such a time," wrote Mr. Henry Lushington, "not one lawless or evil deed was done would have been rather a miracle than a merit, but on much concurrent testimony it is clear that the efforts of the government to preserve order were incessant, and to a remarkable degree successful." He adds that the streets were far safer for ordinary passengers under the triumvirs than under the Papacy.

The little Roman Republic had expected to wage war with Austria, Spain, and Naples. It never occurred to her people that their dangerous enemy was France. However, on November 28, 1848, when news of the Pope's flight reached Paris, Cavaignac, who had been dictator of the French Republic since the riots in June of the same year, suggested to the French Chamber of Deputies to send troops to Civita Vecchia for the protection of the Pope from all or any of his enemies, whether Austrians or Red Republicans. The Republican ministry deprecated such intervention. The Pope and his friends were negotiating for the formation of a league for his support between Austria, Spain, and Naples. Doubtful of the precise intentions of the French Republic, Pio Nono refused to take any part in the scheme of the French Assembly. "If you say openly that you are going to give me back my temporal power, well and good. If not, I prefer the aid of Austria," was his reply to overtures made him on the part of the French government.

Mazzini, who for some time past had been fomenting a republican spirit in Rome, had come from Paris, fresh from the excitement of a French Revolution. He believed in assurances he had received from that advanced Republican, Ledru-Rollin, a member of the provisional government, who alternately opposed Lamartine and allied himself with him. Ledru-Rollin felt enthusiastic sympathy for all "Red Republicans," and he assured Mazzini that the French,

GIUSEPPE MAZZINI

faithful to that clause in their new Constitution which bound France never to bear arms against the freedom of any people, would give Roman Republicans their fullest sympathy and support. Louis Napoleon Bonaparte was elected President of the French Republic, December 10, 1848, and Mazzini and his party argued that since he had fought and suffered for Italian liberty in 1831, and had been bound by the most solemn oaths to do all in his power to help Italy to deliver herself from the yoke of the foreigner, he would not neglect this opportunity of championing the Italian cause.

Mazzini at once, therefore, despatched a mission to the Northern Powers and to England and France. He felt confident of securing from the two last, if not active help, at least neutrality. But this mission gave the Romans little ground for hope. A naval expedition was being already fitted out at Toulon for Italian waters; on April 26, 1849, it appeared off Civita Vecchia. An officer came on shore and begged permission of the commander of the city peaceably to land some troops that his vessels had on board. These troops, he said, had been sent by the French government to assist Rome and the late Papal States to defend themselves against the Austrians, the progress of that power being a menace against France.

The commander at Civita Vecchia had less faith in French Republicans than Mazzini had; he openly expressed distrust of their intentions, but at last, by promises and arguments, the French troops obtained permission to land, and almost immediately took their way to Rome.

General Oudinot was their commander. He was son of that Marshal, — the Duc de Reggio, — who had served in all Napoleon's campaigns, and who had died about eighteen months before.

Rome had never stood a siege since the days of the Duke of Bourbon and Benvenuto Cellini, — in other words, thirty-seven years before the birth of William Shakespeare. Its defences were very poor. Garibaldi and his men were recalled with all speed from the Neapolitan frontier. But had it not been for Mazzini's confidence in French Republicans, more time might have been allowed him as General in Chief to make ready to receive the invaders. The Roman Constituent Assembly passed a unanimous decree to "repel force by force." This decree was announced to the assembled Roman people by the whole body, standing together in an open square, and Mazzini added that all Europe was now against them, but that it was for Romans to oppose a desperate resistance to a despotic league.

Barricades were thrown up in the streets, and the approach of the French was waited for with great determination; but the Romans were very insufficiently armed,—many had only pikes, or ancient arquebuses.

On April 31, at nine in the morning, the advanced guard of the French was seen approaching. It had been Oudinot's plan to reach the gates at an early hour, to take possession of the city before midday, hear high mass at St. Peter's, and banquet in the Vatican.

The Romans expected the attack on the side of the Hill Janiculum, that having been considered the key to the defence since the days of Lars Porsena. The gate on that side is the gate of San Pancrazio, where Garibaldi was stationed, awaiting attack, but the French general, learning that the Vatican gardens were defended only by National Guards, made his first assault in that direction. His forces were twice repulsed,—both parties after the first attack having received reinforcements.

As the French retreated, Garibaldi and his legion rushed out of the San Pancrazio gate and fell upon them. The struggle was terrible. The Romans fought, knowing that they were holding out against hope, that victory itself would make their ruin more sure. But this time also they conquered. The French troops, veterans from Africa, turned their backs and fled. The Romans took five hundred prisoners; the French a single man, Ugo Bassi, the monk, who, kneeling by the side of a sorely wounded comrade, would not abandon him. The French had come on unprovided with surgeons, ambulances, or medicines. General Oudinot demanded an armistice, and begged for medical assistance. Both were accorded him, and the Romans sent him back all his unwounded prisoners, receiving in return their own Ugo Bassi.

Hospital service was well organized in Rome, under the superintendence of a lady very prominent in those revolutionary days, the Princess Belgiojoso. The sick were attended by Roman married ladies. One hospital was put under the care of our own countrywoman, Margaret Fuller, then in Rome, awaiting the turn of political events for a propitious moment in which to announce to her family and friends her marriage to the young Marquis Ossoli.

"Night and day," says Mrs. William Story, "Margaret was occupied, and, with the Princess, so ordered and disposed the hospitals that the organization was truly admirable. All the work was skillfully divided, so that there was no confusion or hurry, and, from the chaotic condition in which these places had been left by those who had previously had charge of them, they brought them to a state of perfect regularity and discipline. Of money they had very little, and were obliged to give time and thought in its place. From the Americans in Rome they raised a subscription for the wounded of either party, but besides this they had scarcely any means to use. I have walked through the wards with Margaret, and seen how comforting was her presence to the poor suffering men. 'How long will the Signora stay?' 'When will the Signora come again?' For each one's peculiar tastes she had a care; to one she carried books; to another she told the news of the day; and listened to another's oft-repeated tale of wrongs, as the best sympathy she could give. There were some of the sturdy fellows of Garibaldi's legion there, and to them she listened as they spoke with delight of their chief, of his courage and skill, for he seemed to have won the hearts of his men in a remarkable manner."

Margaret herself says, in a letter to Ralph Waldo Emerson : —

"It was a terrible battle — that of April 30 — fought here from dawn till the last light of day. I could see all its progress from my balcony. The Italians fought like lions. It is a truly heroic spirit that animates them. . . . Many, especially among the Lombards, are the flower of the Italian youth. . . . The Palace of the Pope on the Quirinal is now used for convalescents, — some are French, some German, and many Poles.

Indeed, I am afraid it is too true that there were comparatively few Romans among them."

Notwithstanding the hostile conduct of the French, Mazzini still had faith in both the influence and sympathy of Ledru-Rollin. Garibaldi would gladly have received permission to consummate his work. "I said I would drive these French troops from the walls of Rome," he cried, "and now I would promise that not one of them should reach their vessels."

Garibaldi, in March, 1849, had been on his way with about thirteen hundred Red Shirts to join Charles Albert in Lombardy. When near Ravenna he received news of the battle of Novara, and the evacuation of Milan. He paused, therefore, taking a position at Rieti, whence the Republican authorities in Rome sent for him and his legionaries. He had entered Rome during the month of April, and his arrival there is thus described by Gibson, the English sculptor: —

"Those who witnessed the entrance of Garibaldi's legion, saw one of the strangest scenes ever beheld in the Eternal City. The men wore pointed hats with black waving plumes; thin and gaunt, with their faces dark as copper, with naked legs, long beards, and dark hair hanging down their backs, they looked like a company of Salvator Rosa's brigands. Beautiful as a statue amidst his extraordinary host rode the chief, mounted on a white horse, which he sat like a centaur. He was quite a show, every one stopping to look at him."

"Probably," writes another Englishman, "a human face so like a lion, and still retaining the humanity nearest the image of its Maker, was never seen. Garibaldi wore the historic red shirt, and a small cap ornamented with gold. The origin of the red shirt was given a few years since in the reminiscences of an English naval officer. The men employed in the great slaughtering and salting establishments in the Argentine provinces wore scarlet woollen shirts. Owing to the blockade of Buenos Ayres, a merchant in Monte Video had a quantity of these red shirts on hand, and, as economy was a great object, the lot was bought up cheap for the Italian legion, with little prevision that their wearers would make the *camicia rossa* immortal in song and history."

During the armistice between Oudinot and the Roman government the Austrians, advancing from Ferrara and

Modena, had taken Bologna and Ancona. Spain had landed troops in Naples, to keep the subjects of King Bomba quiet, while he himself, with an army of ten thousand men, advanced towards Rome. The Neapolitans had reached Albano when Garibaldi, with four thousand light horse, rode secretly from Rome to meet him and surprise him. The legionaries rode on South American saddles; the back of each could unroll, and form a small tent, which at night was sufficient for its owner's protection.

On May 8, the four thousand encountered Ferdinand's ten thousand troops. The rout of the Neapolitans was complete. "Not a Neapolitan soldier," wrote Daverio, chief of Garibaldi's staff, "is to be found on the soil of the Roman Republic, and the King has gone back to Gaeta, to pour his sorrows into the heart of the Pope." This success, however, nearly cost Italy dear, for Garibaldi was wounded in the hand and the foot.

The chief of the staff was mistaken on one point. Ferdinand had not gone further than Velletri, where he claimed that the battle of Palestrina was his victory, not his defeat, and ordered a *Te Deum* to be sung in Naples.

Garibaldi returned to Rome after this battle, fearing a surprise on the part of the French. It has never been explained why the Roman Republic chose this moment to displace its victorious general, and to give the chief command of its forces to an obscure soldier, General Roselli. Perhaps the extreme party in Rome were growing jealous of Garibaldi's influence and popularity. Perhaps his known opposition to Mazzini on the subject of the dependence to be placed upon French faith, was the cause of it. At any rate he accepted his new position without remonstrance, saying, "Whoever gives me a chance of fighting, if only as a common soldier against the enemies of my country, him will I thank." But the remembrance of this slight rankled in his breast to the day of his death, — though, as he was consulted by Roselli on important occasions, he remained virtually, though not in rank, commander in chief.

On May 16 Garibaldi marched with ten thousand men

against the Neapolitans at Velletri. This time their defeat was so decisive that even King Bomba could advance no claim to victory. He only took credit to himself for unexampled rapidity in his retreat.

Garibaldi was about to pursue his success and march on Naples, when he was hurriedly summoned back to Rome.

When the news of Oudinot's repulse before the walls of Rome reached Paris, intense was the indignation and excitement of the French. Bitter disputes arose in the Chamber as to the wisdom of the expedition, but there was but one feeling among Frenchmen, viz., that they would not quietly accept defeat. Defeat marred the prestige of the new President and his party; the triumph of a republic under the rule of Mazzini would strengthen the Red Republican party in France. M. de Lesseps (son of a gentleman who had been French Consul-General in Egypt in the days of Mehemet Ali) was sent at once to Rome as Envoy Extraordinary, not to the triumvirs, but to the Roman Republic. His instructions were vague; they amounted to a direction to do the best he could. The real object of his mission has always been supposed to have been to gain time for reinforcements to reach General Oudinot. Mazzini, however, who believed himself well informed as to the secret politics of the French Republicans, daily expected some new revolution, or *émeute*, in Paris which might overthrow Louis Napoleon, and place Ledru-Rollin in the Presidential chair. His first interview with de Lesseps was somewhat undiplomatic, but dramatic and singular.

Mazzini was lodged in the Palace of the Consulta, to which de Lesseps repaired secretly at dead of night.

" The doors of the Palace seem to have been left open. There were guards, but they were all asleep. The French diplomatist traversed the long suite of splendid apartments opening into each other without corridors until he reached the simply furnished room where, on an iron bedstead, Mazzini slept. De Lesseps watched him sleeping, fascinated by the beauty of his head as it lay in repose. He still looked very young, though there was hardly a State in Europe where he was

not proscribed. When de Lesseps had gazed his fill, he called
'Mazzini! Mazzini!' The triumvir awoke, sat up, and asked
if he had come to assassinate him! De Lesseps told him his
name, and a long conversation followed. One thing, at least,
that de Lesseps said in this interview was strictly true, namely,
that Mazzini must not count on French republican soldiers
objecting to fire on republicans. 'The French soldier would
burn down the cottage of his mother if ordered to do so.' The
discipline of a great army is proof against politics."

De Lesseps believed his steps to be dogged by a French
ex-convict, probably with a view to his assassination. He
complained of this to Mazzini, who said he could do nothing. Then de Lesseps had recourse to Ciceruacchio, who
guaranteed his safety.

This interview between Mazzini and the future engineer
of the Suez Canal took place in one of the first nights of
the month of June. Very soon after, de Lesseps made an
agreement with the Roman government, the text of which
was as follows : —

"I. The help of France is guaranteed to the populations of
the Roman States. They consider the French army a friendly
army which comes to aid in the defence of their country.

"II. In accord with the Roman government, and without
mixing itself up in any way with the government of the country,
the French army will take such exterior quarters as may be
convenient, as well for the defence of the country as for the
health of the troops. Communications shall be free.

"III. The French government guarantees against all foreign
invasion the territories occupied by its troops.

"IV. It is agreed that the present compromise must be submitted to the ratification of the French Republic.

"V. In no case can the effects of the present agreement
cease until fifteen days after the communication of the non-arrival of the ratification."

As, by article IV., it was agreed that the present compromise should be subject to the ratification of the French
Republic, de Lesseps sent it off at once to Paris, and submitted it in the meantime to the approval of General
Oudinot.

The general absolutely refused to agree to, or to be bound by, these conditions. To attack and take Rome was for him a point of honor. Besides, he had received secret instructions from Louis Napoleon, who had written: "Our soldiers have been received as enemies. Our military honor is at stake; I shall not suffer it to be assailed. Reinforcements shall not be wanting to you."

M. de Lesseps, who had been much pleased with himself for the success of his diplomacy, hastened to Paris in great excitement, assuring Mazzini that all could be arranged, — he had not a doubt of the acceptance of his terms of pacification. The answer came, however, in the person of M. de Courcelles, who was sent by the French government to disavow the proceedings of M. de Lesseps, "who had exceeded his instructions."

Then General Oudinot gave notice of the cessation of the armistice, and that he would again attack the city. "Only," he added, "with a view of giving our fellow-countrymen who are desirous of quitting Rome, the means of doing so with ease, I shall, at the request of the French embassy, postpone my attack on the Piazza till Monday morning."

But very early Sunday, when the soldiers and citizens of Rome were asleep, the French, stealing gently up to the Roman outposts, suddenly surrounded two of them and took the men, stationed by Garibaldi to defend them, prisoners. The Romans retook these outposts, which commanded the gate of San Pancrazio, but they were soon after lost again. The besiegers had now thirty-five thousand men; the Romans nineteen thousand.

General Oudinot drew his troops closer and closer round the doomed city. He bombarded it day and night. One night one hundred and fifty bombs fell within the walls. Many noble buildings were shattered, many works of art destroyed. Shells fell even into the hospitals, where French and Roman soldiers alike were cared for.

The feast on St. Peter's day was celebrated according to custom by the illumination of his Cathedral, the flag of

Italy flying from the summit, in the midst of a tremendous thunderstorm, and still the fighting, bombarding, and destruction went fiercely on. All knew that it was no use. Much of the noblest blood of Young Italy had been spent in that week's fighting, but still Mazzini urged his Romans to fight on. His zeal had become fanaticism.

"I feel profoundly for Mazzini," wrote Margaret Fuller; "he has become the inspiring soul of his people. He saw Rome, to which all his hopes through life tended, for the first time as a Roman citizen — and was to become in a few days its ruler. He has animated her, he sustains her to a glorious effort, which, if it fails this time, will not in the end. His country will be free. Yet to me it would be so dreadful to cause all this bloodshed, to dig the graves of these martyrs! Then Rome is being destroyed; her glorious oaks, her villas, haunts of sacred beauty that seemed the possession of the world forever, — the villa of Raphael, the villa of Albani, home of Winckelmann and the best expression of the ideal of modern Rome, and so many other sanctuaries of beauty, — all must perish lest a foe should level his musket from their shelter. *I* could not — *could not!* . . . Oh! Rome, my country! — could I imagine that what I held dear was to heap such desolation on thy head! . . . I did not see Mazzini during the last two weeks of the republic. When the French entered, he walked about the streets to see how the people bore themselves, and then went to the house of a friend. In the upper chamber of a poor house I found him. He had borne a fearful responsibility; he had let his dearest friends perish. In two short months he had grown old: all the vital juices seemed exhausted; his eyes were all bloodshot, his skin orange; flesh he had none; his hair was mixed with white; his hand was painful to the touch; yet he had never flinched, never quailed, but protested in the last hour against surrender. Sweet and calm, but full of a more fiery purpose than ever; in him I revered the hero, and owned myself not of that mould."

On the morning of June 30, when the bombardment had lasted a week, Garibaldi was sent for by the Assembly. He was called from the midst of a *mêlée* where he had been dealing blows right and left as if possessed by some supernatural power. Those around him said it was impossible he could much longer have escaped death had it not been for the message from the Assembly.

"When he appeared at the door of the Chamber the deputies rose and burst into wild applause. He seemed puzzled, but looking down upon himself he saw the explanation. He was covered with blood, his clothes were honeycombed by balls and bayonet thrusts. His sabre was so bent with striking that it would not go more than half way into its sheath. What the Assembly wanted to know was whether the defence could be prolonged. Garibaldi had only to say that it could not. They voted, therefore, the following decree: — 'In the name of God and of the People, the Roman Constituent Assembly discontinues a defence that has become impossible, and remains at its post.' At its post it remained till the French soldiers entered the Capitol where it sat, when, yielding to brute force, the deputies dispersed. Mazzini, who would have resisted still, when all resistance was impossible, wandered openly about the city as in a dream. After a week his friends induced him to leave Rome with an English passport."

Oudinot did little in the way of vengeance. That was reserved for the Papal authorities when, some months later, they returned to Rome. In 1851 a Conservative newspaper in Florence published the statistics of the victims. Two hundred and thirty people were executed during the first two years after the Pope's return. It is said that he laid each death-warrant at the foot of a cross, and, if nothing happened to indicate the clemency of the Almighty, it was signed. Many more died in the crowded prisons, where eight thousand prisoners were huddled together. The number of exiles was over twenty thousand, including most of the leaders and others who fled through fear of being prosecuted.

Margaret Fuller wrote: —

"I cannot tell you what I endured in leaving Rome; abandoning the wounded soldiers; knowing that there is no provision made for them when they rise from the beds upon which they have been thrown by a noble courage, and where they have suffered with a noble patience. Some of the poorer men, who are bereft even of the right arm — one having lost both the right arm and the right leg — I could have provided for with a small sum. Could I have sold my hair, or blood from my arm I would have done it. Had any of the rich Americans remained in Rome they would have given it to me; they helped nobly at first in the service of the hospitals when there was far less need, but they had all gone. What would I have given that I could have spoken to one of the Lawrences or the Phillipses; they could and would have saved the misery. These poor men are left helpless in the power of a mean and vindictive foe."

Rome had fallen; Charles Albert had fallen; Italy had fallen, — all Italy save Venice; and she fell a few weeks later. Austrian despotism ruled Italy from the Alps to the extremity of the peninsula. The independence of Italy seemed a lost cause. Prayers, sacrifices, and blood had apparently failed to save her. All things had turned out as those who prayed and suffered hoped they would not do. Short-sighted are we mortals, who "see not the bright light that is behind the clouds" — who do not realize that all these prayers and sufferings help on the desired end.

Pride in their own brave struggle raised Italians in their own eyes, and drew to them the sympathy of other nations. The taunt *Les Italiens ne se battent pas* was disproved. By the woes and disappointments of 1848 and 1849, Italians were ripening for the coming deliverance. As Mr. Probyn says: —

"So fell Rome; her soldiers fighting to the last extremity; her people vying with each other in maintaining the glorious but unequal struggle; her rulers firmly rejecting every dishonorable compromise or proposal; and, as firmly, declaring that Italians, and Italians only, had a right to decide what should or should not be the government under which they would live. Assuredly such men are rightly held to have deserved well of their country."

I have sometimes thought that I could understand Garibaldi, from having known and loved and honored a man of his own stamp, — a man with the heart of a little child, a man whose judgment followed the lead of his quick sympathies, a man of eagerness, vehemence, and energy, who could accomplish *anything*, provided a calmer mind gave his energy direction, or, rather, turned to use whatever it effected. Like Garibaldi, he was a man of the sea; a man who had "seen cities and men"; a man of varied information, acquired by himself; who, while overflowing with the milk of lovingkindness, both for man and beast, was nevertheless the "good hater" whom Dr. Johnson loved. But all his hatreds were impersonal. Brought into contact with any man's good qualities, he at once loved him; but tyranny, meanness, cruelty, and oppression were abhorrent to his very soul. Like Garibaldi, no thought of himself seemed to have any influence on his plans or his decisions. He was lavish of money when he had it, but spent it all on others. He was a man whom those who loved him most and knew him best, always held to be unfitted for any position which involved complicated responsibility. He was beloved by all who knew him; but those who served under him adored him most. He was influenced by every man who made an appeal to his noble impulses. Of "sober judgment" he had none.

Giuseppe (or Joseph) Garibaldi was born in Nice in the year 1807. He was the son of a small trader who owned a coasting vessel. His ancestors had been seafaring men from generation to generation. The name of Garibaldi was inscribed on the Golden Book of the Old Republic of Genoa, but it was also borne by humble fishermen.

The father and mother of the future hero and patriot were pious, industrious, but unthrifty, people; who brought up a large family in a small way. Their son in after years held them to have been "priest-ridden." They had intended to devote him to the service of the Church, thinking him too frail for active occupation, but all his bent was for the sea. He had one teacher, a priest, whom he did not like, — and another, a civilian, who gave him a taste for study. He loved books, was a good classical scholar, and in after years acquired the various European languages, learning them by use and by experience, rather than with dictionaries and grammars. He was a splendid swimmer, and on more than one occasion, while still a lad, distinguished himself by saving men from drowning.

At the age of twenty-one he found himself mate on board

a brig bound for the Black Sea. He had adventures enough upon this voyage to supply materials for the most sensational of dime novels, but what most concerns us is that a member of the new order of "Young Italy," lately founded by Mazzini, took him in hand at Taganrog, on the Sea of Azof, and filled his heart with that enthusiasm for Italian independence which was the aim and glory of his life in days of suffering and days of honor.

On his return to Italy he made the acquaintance of Mazzini, who extended over him that charm of personal influence which he seems to have done over all who approached him. The result was that Garibaldi took part in the ill-advised invasion of Piedmont from Switzerland, and also in a conspiracy which was to effect a revolutionary rising in Genoa. Both failed. Garibaldi earned sentence of death from the Piedmontese government, and quitted Italy in 1836 for South America.

At Rio Janeiro, by the help of friends, he fitted out a small trading vessel, but his temperament was not suited to commerce, and he never prospered as a trader. It suited him better to enter the service of Don Gonsales, President of the Republic of Rio Grande, a province on the left bank of the La Plata which had broken off from the empire of Brazil.

For ten years he fought by land and by sea among these obscure, turbulent, semi-civilized republics, where he had every opportunity to learn leadership in guerilla warfare, where he daily ran startling risks, and distinguished himself by deeds of daring.

No good end seems ever to have been the aim of all this warfare ; men fought apparently because they wished to kill each other, and Garibaldi made himself a dreaded name as the foe of the Brazilians. He had collected a small band of Italian exiles, who made him their commander. He had also his love-affairs, and married Anita, whose name is associated with his in all dangers and sufferings, but who survived only for a few weeks the siege of Rome.

Anita bore him four children during their life together on

the shores of the La Plata. Menotti, his eldest boy, was named after the victim of Francis of Modena; then there was Ricciotti, called after a young man shot with the brothers Bandiera; and there were two daughters, one of whom, with her nurse, was burned to death when a baby. This loss to the day of his death Garibaldi never ceased to lament. The other daughter was Theresita.

At last he quitted Rio Grande, and went to Monte Video, the capital of another republic on the La Plata, sometimes called Uruguay, sometimes the Banda Oriental. So long as the provinces on the shores of the La Plata were Spanish dependencies, Buenos Ayres exercised a sort of supremacy over the others. When they achieved their independence, Buenos Ayres desired to convert them into a confederacy, and to be its head. This federation was bitterly opposed by Uruguay with its capital Monte Video, which was also the commercial rival of the city of Buenos Ayres. A desultory war had been carried on between Uruguay (or the Banda Oriental) and Buenos Ayres for several years before Garibaldi arrived in South America; at that time General Rosas was dictator in Buenos Ayres.

This is not the place to enter into any account of Rosas, or the complicated wars he waged with neighboring republics. In 1845 I made my *coup d'essai* in magazine writing by an account in an English review of Rosas, Buenos Ayres, and Monte Video. I had a large quantity of excellent material given me by English naval officers fresh from service on the La Plata, and they also directed my attention to other documents, which I saw in the British Museum. The stories told of the cruelty, brutality, and arrogance of Rosas seem so incredible, that of late years they are supposed to be exaggerations. I can only say I found them corroborated by reliable men, Englishmen and Frenchmen, officers and residents. I will offer one extract by way of specimen from a pamphlet by a French officer.

"Heads of respectable citizens of Buenos Ayres have been rolled about in carts, or displayed on butchers' stalls; nay, more, there was an official dispute with a French admiral, invested with high diplomatic authority, to decide whether one of these heads thus cut off was a French head or a Spanish one. That of Zelarayan, brought from the southern frontier, was exposed in Rosas' drawing-room; and Lucian Manella, his brother-in-law and a general, dared to insult Mr. Mandeville, the English Minister by showing him the *salted ears* of Colonel Bórda, sent from Tucuman by D. Manuel Oribe."

This Oribe had been at one time President of Monte Video. General Riviera was his rival. On Riviera's obtaining the Presidential office, Oribe went over to Rosas, and joined him in invading Uruguay. The savagery of this war was horrible. Garibaldi, with his Italian legion and his friend Azani, joined the forces of President Riviera, though I do not remember to have seen his name in any of the documents that I consulted.

England and France were appealed to by Riviera, and joined to put a stop to so horrible a war. Rosas was driven into exile, Uruguay became an independent State, and Buenos Ayres was left to become the chief city and province of the Argentine Republic. I am unable to say how many revolutions it has undergone since that day, together with wars, triumphs, and reverses, — financial and otherwise.

Every mail had brought to Monte Video news of stirring events in Italy. Garibaldi, like all others, hailed with delight the liberal views attributed to Pio Nono, and, together with his friend Azani, he addressed to him a letter in which they offered him their own services, and those of their Italian legion.

"If, then," the letter ran, "to-day our arms, which are not strangers to fighting, are acceptable to your Holiness, we need not say how willingly we shall offer them in the service of one who has done so much for our country and our church. We shall count ourselves happy if we can but come to aid Pio Nono in his work of redemption, we and our companions, for whose concurrence we give our word, and we shall consider ourselves privileged if we are allowed to show our devotedness by shedding our blood. . . . There remains for us but to beg your illustrious and venerable Highness to forgive us for thus troubling

you, and to accept the expression of the deep esteem and unbounded respect with which we subscribe ourselves your devoted servants, "G. GARIBALDI.
"F. AZANI."

The Pope returned no answer, and the aspiring patriots were deeply disappointed. They, however, proceeded to organize an expedition to assist the cause of Italy. The Italian legion would not as a body volunteer. The leaders secured only eighty-five men, and of these, twenty-nine deserted.

Garibaldi, with Anita and their children, accompanied by Azani, who was slowly dying of consumption, embarked on Garibaldi's little ship, the "Esperanza," for the Mediterranean. On touching at Alicante, great news met them. They heard that Charles Albert had granted a Constitution to Piedmont, and was in arms against Austria; that Turin was wild with joy; that the cry of *Evviva la casa di Savoja!* was ringing through Northern Italy. There was news, too, of the Revolution in France; of the flight of Metternich from Vienna; of revolt in Hungary; of insurrection in Berlin. Even Ferdinand of Naples had been forced to give his people a Constitution.

Garibaldi hoisted the Italian flag upon his little schooner. Anita made it out of half a counterpane, a red shirt, and a bit of old green uniform, and the "Esperanza" sailed gaily into Nice. There Garibaldi's old mother, though she welcomed her son, was by no means pleased with her new daughter-in-law. The so-called marriage of Garibaldi and Anita had been very irregular. The old lady insisted on a proper marriage ceremony; but she never became reconciled to the younger woman.

Azani died soon after they landed. His death was a great sorrow to Garibaldi. But in May all the glorious news that they had heard at Alicante seemed clouded with disaster. Pio Nono had blighted the hopes of his enthusiastic friends. The King of Naples had forsworn himself, and ordered his troops to return home. Charles Albert had been left alone to fight the Austrians, and Mazzini was using his utmost efforts to create new difficulties for him by spreading disaffection in Piedmont, decrying constitutional government, and advocating republicanism.

It was at this time that Garibaldi, though still under sentence of death, requested an interview with the King of Piedmont. Charles Albert received him cordially, but replied, in answer to his offers of service, that he must consult his ministers. Garibaldi's former association with Mazzini probably made the King distrustful.

Considering Charles Albert's answer a repulse, Garibaldi went into Tuscany, and there began to organize an independent corps. Radetzky, subsequently speaking to a Piedmontese about the war, said frankly: "The man of all others who could have served your cause the best you refused to recognize." And what was worse, the seeming slight threw Garibaldi back into the ranks of the radically revolutionary party.

Garibaldi raised a large body of volunteers in Tuscany. They were no sooner collected than he received a summons from the Milanese to help them to defend their city, Charles Albert's army having been forced to retreat into Piedmont after the lost battle of Custozza.

Mazzini, as we have seen from his conduct when a Roman triumvir, did not adopt the principle of *reculer pour mieux sauter*. He and his followers shouted loudly *Traitor!* against the King. D'Azeglio said of this crisis: " Since Lombardy and Venice would not unite, I told the King that his duty, the good of Italy, the welfare of the cause, required that he should retreat to Piedmont and defend it."

"But," says Mr. Bent, "Charles Albert, like Garibaldi, first went to the defence of Milan, and the Milanese, urged on by the disaffected party within their walls, received him with stones and curses. From the agents of Mazzini, the King, who had been fighting for the cause of Italy, fled for his very life."

Before Garibaldi could reach Milan, news came to him of the conclusion of an armistice between the King of

Piedmont and the Austrians, and, deeply indignant, he turned aside into the mountains, hoping to carry on a guerilla warfare against the foreigners and to be ready for the next emergency.

His band of volunteers dwindled to two hundred and fifty, with whom, rejecting an offer from Charles Albert of a high post in the Sardinian army, which was being reorganized, he started for Venice, to assist Manin. At Ravenna, however, news reached him which turned his steps towards Rome. How he arrived there, and what he did there, has been told already. A few words must be said of what befell him and the volunteers, now amounting to three thousand, with whom, on July 2, 1849, he quitted the defeated and despairing city.

The capitulation had been signed, and next day the French were to make their entry. Then Garibaldi, having assembled all troops and volunteers in Rome in the great square before St. Peter's, thus addressed them: "Soldiers! that which I have to offer you is this: hunger, thirst, cold, and heat; no pay, no barracks, no rations, but frequent alarms, forced marches, charges at the point of the bayonet. Whoever loves our country and glory may follow me!"

His design was to make his way into Tuscany, where he hoped to rouse the slumbering spirit of the people. Anita, though she was near her confinement, and little in a state to travel, insisted on sharing danger at his side. Ciceruacchio and his two sons joined him, almost all the officers of his legion, and Ugo Bassi, the monk, his chaplain and fast friend. Garibaldi took a small sum from the Treasury to support his troops till they should be out of the Roman States, but to supply his own wants and those of Anita, he sold his watch. His faithful negro servant, who had followed him from Monte Video, had been shot through the brain not many days before.

Tuscany proved unwilling to welcome them, though for the moment she was a republic, but an Austrian army was on the frontier ready to march into the duchy on any pretext or provocation. Then Garibaldi hoped he might reach

Venice, but he was hotly pursued by the Austrians over the Apennines, and at last decided to take refuge in the little mountain republic of San Marino and there disband his men. San Marino is not far distant from Rimini, and not many leagues from the Adriatic Sea. It has only seven thousand inhabitants, and, of course, would have been unable to resist Austrian invasion. The authorities sent food to Garibaldi's men, and offered to receive them if they would disarm, and enter their republic not as soldiers but as refugees. This offer was accepted, and in the end each man was furnished with a passport, and a small sum of money to pay his way to his home. The passports, however, did not always meet with respect.

Garibaldi addressed his men for the last time, and then posted on the church door a proclamation.

"Soldiers! We have arrived in a land of refuge; we must maintain an irreproachable conduct towards our generous hosts, since it will gain for us the respect due to our misfortunes. From the present moment I release all my companions in arms from every engagement, leaving them free to re-enter private life. But, I would remind you, it is better to die than to live as slaves to a foreigner. "GARIBALDI."

The next night, Garibaldi, finding that his presence made it probable that less favorable terms of capitulation would be granted by the Austrians to his followers, left San Marino secretly by night, and made his way to a little port on the shore of the Adriatic. He hoped to reach Venice by boat. He was accompanied by Anita, Bassi, Ciceruacchio and his younger son (the other had been killed a few days previously), and a party of officers.

They procured thirteen fishing boats, and started for Venice. But a storm arose. Some of the boats were captured by Austrian cruisers, and four were forced back to land. The party, on landing, separated, for the Austrians were in close pursuit. The remainder of the story shall be related as Mr. Theodore Bent has told it in his "Life of Garibaldi" : —

"The shore where the four boats put in was swarming with Austrian scouts, sent to trace the fugitives. Anita was lying a little way off the shore, concealed in a corn-field, her head resting on her husband's knee. Leggiero, an old comrade of Garibaldi's in South America, was their only companion. He kept guard over them, so as to give notice if he saw any white-coated Austrians lurking near. Garibaldi, stricken with grief, watched the gradual ebbing away of that life whose every hope and joy had been so closely bound up with his own. . . . Later in the day, when the Austrians had disappeared, some peasants, struck by the piteous sight of the husband bearing his sick wife in his arms, yielded to his entreaties to fetch medical aid, brought a cart on which the dying woman was placed, and, carried over rocks and by-paths (for the Austrians were upon the roads), they reached at last the estate of the Marquis Guiccioli. Garibaldi then carried Anita to a peasant's cottage, where a bed was hastily prepared, and no sooner was Anita placed thereon, than she expired, leaning on Garibaldi's arm. Stricken by so great a bereavement, Garibaldi, caring not what his own fate might be, could scarcely be roused to understand that the Austrians were close upon him. With a supreme effort he tore himself from the remains of her who had loved him but too faithfully, and with weary step and aching heart pursued his flight. The peasant fulfilled a promise Garibaldi exacted from him of burying Anita under the shade of the pine groves, but unfortunately her little dog discovered the remains of his mistress, scarcely cold, under the newly turned sod, and revealed the place to the Austrians. The peasant was arrested for having harbored rebels."

Finally Garibaldi and his friend Leggiero, by mountain passes and through many dangers, reached Ravenna; thence, finding there was no chance of reaching Venice, and no hope of a rising in Tuscany, they contrived to reach Spezia, and on September 6, after two months of wandering, Garibaldi and his companions arrived in the kingdom of Charles Albert and presented themselves at Genoa to General La Marmora, who received them kindly, though he lodged them in prison. They were held to be dangerous guests in the present position of Piedmont, and after a short time, during which Garibaldi paid by permission a visit to his aged mother and three children at Nice, he was set at liberty, but courteously requested to leave Italy. He passed over to Sardinia, where he wandered in the mountains, and was hidden for a while on the rocky island of Caprera, his future home. Eventually he sailed for New York from Liverpool. In New York he obtained employment from a tallow-chandler, and occupied himself for eighteen months in making candles, without, however, he tells us, making much proficiency in the business.

In 1852, New York was a haven of refuge for revolutionists whose hopes had set in dark clouds of disappointment. Ledru-Rollin came, and Louis Blanc, and many others, Frenchmen and Italians, who thought it no shame to engage in any employments that would relieve them from the necessity of receiving charity.

At the end of eighteen months of New York life, Garibaldi went to Peru, and commanded trading vessels both on the Pacific and Atlantic oceans. At last, when the Piedmontese government became more settled, and the flag of Italy took part with the flags of France and England in the Crimean war, Garibaldi came back to his own land. With such money as he had made in his trading expeditions, he made a home for himself among the rocks of Caprera.

His extreme republicanism had been modified by his experiences, and his advice to his followers and fellow-patriots was now: "Look to Piedmont as the hope and example of Italy."

A few words must be said of the monk Ugo Bassi — of whom some one has remarked that he seemed to be compounded of St. Francis of Assisi and Savonarola. In his early career he had been a hero in Sicily, risking his life freely among those stricken by the cholera, and preaching sermons which stirred the very hearts of his hearers. An enthusiast for Italian independence, a believer in Pio Nono, who had declared him to be a man after his own heart, his hopes sank after the Pope's flight to Gaeta, and he joined Garibaldi's legion at Rieti, before it marched to Rome. In every encounter he rode foremost, often on a fiery horse, in uniform, but with the cross of his order suspended from his neck, and with no weapon but his crucifix. His mission was to animate his men, to shrive the dying, or bear wounded men (whom he often carried upon his horse) out of reach of the enemy. When his beloved leader quitted San Marino he was in the boat with him and Anita, but he quitted them when the party, rescued from the tempest, scattered on reaching shore. Ciceruacchio and his remaining son went into the great pine woods round Ravenna. The fate that befell them was long a mystery. Soldiers in the Crimean war had a report that Ciceruacchio had been seen dealing out wine to the Sardinian soldiers. But subsequently — long after — it came to be believed that Ciceruacchio and his boy, together with seven other fugitives, one of whom was a priest from Genoa, had been captured and summarily shot, by an Austrian lieutenant in command of a scouting party of Croats. The story ran that the lad stirred after he was thought dead, and another bullet was sent through his body.

Bassi and a wounded officer, Livraghi, had almost reached safety, when, utterly exhausted, they paused for a little rest. They were captured, and handed over to the Croats, who carried them to Bologna, Bassi's native place, heavily chained. On the wall of his prison at Commachio, Bassi drew a picture of Christ upon the cross, writing beneath it: —

"Ugo Bassi here suffered somewhat, glad in spirit through the knowledge that he had committed no crime. Livraghi, a captain of Garibaldi, was here too, and shared in everything."

Livraghi was a Lombard, and had served in the Austrian army, but there was no case against Bassi; not even arms were found on him, only his crucifix, his breviary, and a leather case containing the last cantos of a poem he was writing, "La Croce Vincitrice." But many Italian priests had joined the revolutionists, and it was determined to make him an example. It is said that Pope Pius, who had loved him, was much affected by his death.

Twelve priests had been called to sign his death-warrant, as his execution seemed to be an affair of the Church.

They were all Austrian military chaplains, but three of them, Hungarians, refused to sign.

On August 9, the execution took place, but it is said that Bedini, the papal legate at Bologna, gave orders that first Bassi, having been a priest, should be "desecrated," by his head, that had been tonsured, being flayed, and also the hand which had held the consecrated wafer. This is not in all accounts of Bassi's death. Let us hope it may not be true.

The officer told off to give the word of command to the firing party could not utter it. Another officer took his place, but Bassi, raising his eyes to Heaven, said calmly: "I am ready," and in a moment he fell dead.

Ten years later, Garibaldi, when Central Italy was a free kingdom, visited Bassi's grave in the great pine woods of Ravenna, immortalized by their connection with Dante and Lord Byron; there, too, was the grave of Anita. Her body had been removed to a little chapel in the neighborhood of the hut where she died.

The bones of Ciceruacchio (Angelo Brunetti by name) and those of his son, or what are supposed to have been theirs, were removed to Rome, with every mark of honor and affection. They now rest on the Janiculum, with the Eternal City lying at its feet, and all around a glorious view of the Campagna.

CHAPTER VIII.

KOSSUTH.

THE struggle for independence in Hungary, which went on in the years 1848 and 1849, simultaneously with the effort made in Lombardy and Venetia to throw off the Austrian yoke, may not, *a priori*, seem to belong to the history of Italy, and yet it is so closely connected with it that I feel myself excused for interrupting the main narrative by interpolating it here.

The story of the emancipation of Italy from Austria would be unintelligible without an account of the battle of Sadowa, and the causes that led to it in 1866; and to understand Sadowa, we need to know what events distracted the Austrian Emperor's dominions eighteen years before, when the Emperor Nicholas sent armies to his assistance in Hungary, and offered to dispatch other troops into Lombardy to overwhelm Charles Albert. This offer, however, was declined. Old Marshal Radetzky considered himself quite equal to the task, and, as we have seen, he successfully accomplished it.

A brief biography of Louis Kossuth, probably the brightest comet of our nineteenth century, will afford us, I think, the best means of learning all we may here need to know of the abortive attempt at a Hungarian revolution.

The life of Kossuth was almost coeval with that of the nineteenth century. He was born in 1802. The years in which his name became a household word throughout Europe and America were in the middle of the century, and his death took place almost at its close. His father was a Magyar nobleman of small estate, and he was a Protes-

LOUIS KOSSUTH.

tant. Young Louis graduated at a Calvinist college when he was seventeen, and at once commenced the study of law.

He was twenty-nine when the cholera, which spread over Christendom in 1831, broke out in Hungary, and, as usual, the peasantry attributed the pestilence to the Jews and to the nobles. It was then that Kossuth came forward into public sight. Up to that time he had chiefly distinguished himself in field sports. But such sports make the nobleman and the peasant personally acquainted. Kossuth knew the class he had to deal with, — the people whose hearts he was to touch by burning and persuasive words. Wherever the cholera raged in its worst form, he appeared to calm the fears and combat the delusions of the stricken people.

A year later he was sent to the Hungarian Diet by some princess as her proxy, having liberty to vote, but not to address the assembly. There, as he sat silent, listening to the debates, there came to him the idea of reporting them. It was against law and custom to print such reports, but Kossuth wrote them out with his own hand, and, after the manner of the ancient news-letters in England, they were read aloud in clubs and public places throughout the towns and villages of Hungary. When the labor of writing from sixty to eighty such letters a week became too great, Kossuth set up a lithographic press. This was promptly suppressed by the government. He continued his paper, therefore, in manuscript, and, as the use of the post-office was denied him, its circulation was intrusted to colporteurs. The paper soon became of great national importance, rousing political discussion and forming public sentiment, especially on the question of the abolition of serfdom. It created a national public opinion where, up to that time, public opinion had been timid and local.

The Austrian government, becoming alarmed at this spread of national feeling in Hungary, suppressed the paper, and ordered the arrest of Kossuth, although, being a Hungarian nobleman, he could not be legally imprisoned until he had been convicted of crime. In spite of this, he was incarcerated without trial, and when, in 1839, he was at last tried, he was condemned to a further period of imprisonment.

Having thus brought the biography of Kossuth to the time when he became dimly visible to the public eye, I will offer some account of Hungary, that ancient Dacia whence came the bravest gladiators of imperial Rome. Long before Rome became imperial, however, barbaric tribes had penetrated into the dense forests of this region, and, under the name of Gauls, swept down on Greece, pillaged its Temple of Delphos, and, afterwards invading Italy, outraged the Conscript Fathers in Rome.

About the time of the Christian era, Pannonia was added to the Roman Empire, and Dacia about a century later. As soon as Rome had possession of these provinces civilization set in. Magnificent roads and aqueducts were constructed, the forests were cut down, agriculture was introduced, and Roman military colonies were planted in suitable places. There is still standing part of a magnificent bridge built by Trajan over the Danube.

When the Roman Empire fell, and the Roman legions were withdrawn from the remote provinces, all kinds of races poured into Dacia, among them Goths and Visigoths. These were converted to Christianity not many years after their settlement in their new quarters, and after Christianity came medieval civilization, which, however, was very far behind that which had prevailed in Dacia during the palmy days of its occupation by the Romans.

Next came the Huns, from the borders of far-off China, under their great king, Attila, with his Mongolian features. He threatened Constantinople, and he sacked Rome. He was called The Scourge of God. After thoroughly humbling the Romans, he required them to send ambassadors to him at his residence in a forest on the frontier of Poland. These ambassadors kept a minute journal of all they saw during their journey, and at the intrenched camp where Attila held court, surrounded by his Huns.

The descendants of the Roman military colonists called

themselves Roumans. The Huns, although they gave their name to Hungary, soon sank into an inferior race. Nevertheless, a second detachment of them, known in history as Avars, spread terror at one time all over Germany, and even threatened Belgium. These Avars were a handsome people of light complexion, bearing little personal resemblance to the Huns. They dressed like that race, however, except that they tied their long hair with colored ribbons.

The Magyars followed the Avars from the plains of Asia about the time of Alfred the Great. At first Europeans believed them to be the Gog and Magog of prophecy. They were of the same blood as the Finns, and a branch of their race had settled in Scandinavia.

The Finns make hardy sailors, and, although they have shown no literary development since their settlement in Europe, they brought with them one of the world's early epics, the " Kalewala," written in a metre, of late years imitated by Longfellow in " Hiawatha."

The Magyars were likewise cousins to the Turks. A cousinly friendship between Turks and Magyars exists even to the present day, and adds to the puzzles and difficulties of modern diplomacy in the settlement of the Eastern question.

In the early part of the tenth century, the Magyars were nearly as formidable to the broken empire of Charlemagne as the Huns under Attila had been to the remnants of the mighty empire of Rome. Otho the Great, however, defeated them, bearing in his hand the sword of Constantine, and spreading the banner of Saint Maurice, besides having with him a spear-head, made of four nails of the true Cross, for which the Duke of Burgundy had given a province of his duchy. The Magyars were driven back into Hungary, where they soon began to form a settled government under dukes of their own. The chief point in their Constitution, if we may so call their unwritten law, was that all Magyars governed, and that all men of other races (and there were eight or more different races in Hungary) were of no political importance. All great questions were decided by an assembly of Magyars on horseback in the plains near the river Theiss, and all Magyars were eligible to take part in these deliberations.

The first great Magyar chief was Arpad. His grandson was a Christian, and made great efforts to convert his heathen subjects, but this work was not accomplished in his reign; it was, however, in that of his son, St. Stephen, who was named Stephen because the first martyr, in a vision, before his birth, desired he should bear that name, and predicted that he should be numbered among the saints of God.

The Pope, towards the close of St. Stephen's reign, sent him a crown, — since known as the crown of St. Stephen, — the most precious possession of the Hungarians to this day.

All political power, as I have said, was in the hands of the Magyars. Their King was elected, and no Magyar was bound to obey the sovereign till he had been crowned with St. Stephen's crown and had taken an oath to maintain all the Magyar's liberties and privileges.

Besides the King, there was always a sort of sub-king, called a Palatine, elected for life. There was a Diet with two Chambers, in which only Magyars sat, and the Diet, — not the King, — had the privilege of making war or peace. There were also county assemblies, which taught men self-government; and thus Hungary and England were the only really constitutional monarchies in Europe during the Middle Ages.

The history of Hungary and of its early kings is interesting and picturesque, but there is no space to tell it here. There was a continual struggle going on between the kings and magnates, for the latter would never suffer any infringement of their privileges, while, of course, the kings were always endeavoring to get a little more power.

At one time, not long after Dante's death, early in the fourteenth century, Charles of Anjou was King of Hungary, and his connection with Naples involved Hungary in the affairs of that unquiet kingdom. When the Ottoman Turks came into Europe, the Magyars alternately fraternized with them and opposed them.

From the beginning of their history as a European people the Magyars have had a deep and abiding hatred of all Slavonians. The Slavs are of the same race as the Russians. They surround Hungary, inhabiting Servia, Croatia, Dalmatia and Bosnia, while they form part of the lower class in Roumania and Hungary.

The Slavs are commonly of the Greek Church, the Magyars were Roman Catholics, though, when Protestantism began to spread, many of them sided with the Reformation.

The Magyars, being a race of warriors, strongly objected to having a female sovereign, but Louis the Great, who had been King of both Hungary and Poland, left, in 1389, his Polish crown to his daughter Mary, and the Magyars chose her for their *King*, insisting, however, that she should sign herself Maria Rex, and not Maria Regina. She married Sigismund, King of Bohemia, who afterwards became Emperor of Germany (the Super-Grammaticam of Mr. Carlyle). Their only child, Elizabeth, married Albert, Archduke of Austria, and by this marriage Austria fast acquired an interest in the affairs of Hungary. Albert succeeded Sigismund about the year 1438 as Emperor of Germany, King of Hungary, and King of Bohemia. But Albert's reign was short. He left a young wife and infant son. It was then that his widow Elizabeth, dreading a forced marriage that would impair the rights of her little boy, carried him off, and the crown of St. Stephen with him. The faithful lady who had charge of both left a record of the perils of the journey. The narrative is here of the nature of an episode, but as it has really some bearing on the history of Kossuth and the Hungarian Revolution, and as it is extremely interesting and curious, I take leave to relate it here.[1]

"Seventy-six years after the presentation by the Pope of a crown to St. Stephen another crown was given to the King of Hungary by one of the Greek emperors. It was combined with the more precious crown, whose arches were sur-

---

[1] I have not been able to consult the original narrative, and am therefore largely indebted to Miss Yonge's "Book of Golden Deeds" for an account of the crown, and its adventures.

rounded by this golden circlet. The crown was so precious on account of the privileges it conferred that it was kept in the vaults of a certain strong castle on the Danube, about twelve miles from the cities of Buda and Pesth. It was laid in a case placed in a chest with many seals, and a seneschal had his bed in a chamber where was the door leading to the vault.

"Now, Elizabeth, Queen of Hungary, was at the time of her husband's death expecting a new babe, who, she hoped, would prove a little king. She was therefore most anxious to avoid marrying a certain King of Poland, proposed to her by the magnates, and was resolved to take all means in her power to prevent his being crowned King of Hungary.

"She took Helen de Kottenner, one of her ladies, into her confidence, proposing to her, while the seneschal was sick, to steal the crown. 'The Queen's command,' says Helen, 'sorely troubled me, for it was a dangerous venture for me and my little children, and I turned it over in my mind what I should do, for I had to take counsel but of God alone, and I thought if I did it not, and if evil arose therefrom, I should be guilty before God and the world. So I consented to risk my life in this difficult undertaking, but desired to have some one to help me.'

"That 'some one' was hard to find, but at last a Magyar gentleman, brave and devoted as herself, was found to aid her. The Queen went with all her ladies to the strong Castle of Komorn, and when there she sent back Helen and the faithful gentleman to the castle where the crown was kept, under pretence of packing up some of her things.

"At midnight, every one being asleep, Helen admitted her confederate to the room which led to the vaults, which, although now appropriated to the seneschal, had been beforetime a lady's chamber. He brought with him a faithful servant, 'bound to him,' Helen says, 'by the strong tie of the same Christian name.' He had also files in his shoes, and plenty of wax candles. The men went into the vault, breaking and filing chains and locks as they went on, for there were many doors to pass, and Helen staid on the watch, her heart beating at every sound, and vowing a pilgrimage to the Virgin if their enterprise escaped discovery. At last the men reappeared with the crown. Day was beginning to break. It was almost time for their journey to begin. They had replaced the broken chains and padlocks with others they had brought with them, and the Queen had given them the royal signet and her keys.

"They took the crown into the chapel, where they found a big velvet cushion. They took out half the stuffing and put in the crown. When this was done, the gentleman bade his servant take the cushion and put it into the Lady de Kottenner's carriage. Then they started on their journey back to Komorn, with much luggage, and several of the Queen's ladies, who were not in the secret, in company. Crossing the Danube on the ice, they broke through, and the crown and Helen came very near being lost together, after all.

"They reached Komorn just as a son was born to the Queen. There were great rejoicings, and the babe was named Ladislas, after an early King of Hungary, who for his goodness and piety had been canonized. The Magyars were not satisfied, however. They did not wish for an infant king and a regency. The King of Poland claimed to have been elected King of Hungary, and at the head of his troops was drawing near to claim the widowed Elizabeth as his bride.

"No one had discovered the abstraction of the crown, and Elizabeth's plan was to take her babe to Alba Regale, the Royal City, and there have him crowned. She sent to Buda for cloth of gold to make him a splendid coronation robe, but as it did not arrive in time, Helen, sitting in the chapel with bolted doors at night, made him a splendid garment out of a vestment once worn by his grandfather Sigismund. It was red and gold, with silver spots, and she made everything he needed, even to the little shoes.

"By this time, however, the Queen had heard that she would probably be intercepted by the Polish party on her way to Alba Regale, and was terribly afraid they might discover the crown. But Helen, saying that the King was even more important than the crown, proposed that the two should travel together. She wrapped the crown in a cloth, and hid it under the mattress of the King's cradle, with a long spoon for mixing his pap upon its top.

"It was the week before Whitsuntide, 1440, when the Royal party set out on their journey, escorted by some magnates opposed to the Polish marriage. They crossed the Danube in a large boat. Then the Queen and her little girl were placed in a carriage. The ladies, including Helen, rode; while the baby in his cradle was carried by four men. But poor little Lasla, as Helen calls him, screamed so loud that she was forced to dismount and carry him through a deep swamp in her arms.

"The danger of attack was so great that when, in the next stage of their journey, the baby King was put into his mother's carriage, 'we all,' says Helen, 'formed a guard around it, that if any one should shoot we might receive the shot.' The little

King proved a troublesome traveller, and either Helen or his nurse had to carry him on foot nearly all the next day through dust and wind and a pelting storm.

"After five days' journey they reached Alba Regale, or Pressburg, five hundred gentlemen coming out to meet them, and Helen, carrying her little King, who was twelve weeks old, surrounded by these magnates, holding naked swords, rode into the town.

"They passed into the church through the choir door, which was then closed, according to Hungarian custom, until another king should arrive to be crowned. The Queen swore to the Constitution, in the name of her son. Then he was confirmed; then he was knighted, held in Helen's arms, and the old Hungarian nobleman who dubbed him knight, struck with such force that the blow falling on Helen's arm severely hurt her. Next the Archbishop anointed the baby King. Next they dressed him in his red and gold coronation robe, and put on his head the holy crown, 'and the people admired to see how he held up his head under it,' said Helen. But the poor little man could have had small pleasure in his coronation, for Helen tells us that 'the noble King all through it wept aloud.' Helen held him on her lap while the crown was held upon his head; then he was seated on a throne, after which, at last, he was carried from the church in his cradle, the crown and other regalia being borne before him."

The crown of St. Stephen had many other adventures, though after this it was kept in an apartment of its own, protected by two guardians, though it was locked into an iron chest, and the door of the apartment was of iron.

The greatest Hungarian of the fifteenth century was John Hunniades. He was a natural son of the Emperor Sigismund, and bore for his arms a crow carrying a ring in its mouth, in allusion to a ring given his peasant mother by her royal lover, and said to have been carried off by a crow. He also took the surname of Corvinus. All his life he fought the Turks, guarding the frontier of his country.

Ladislas, the King crowned in his babyhood, showed great ingratitude for the services of Hunniades, putting to death his two eldest sons. This bitterly incensed the Hungarian people, who, when Ladislas died, chose Matthias

Corvinus, son of Hunniades, as their king. He is known in history as Matthias the Just, and is celebrated for his superb palace and library. He, however, was a bitter persecutor of the Hussites, and undertook a crusade against them. He was the idol of his people, spoke five languages fluently, and set up the first printing press in Hungary. He left no children, and the King of Poland was next called by the Magyars to their vacant throne. The king who succeeded him was the King of Bohemia, and an Archduke of Austria. He perished while escaping from a lost battle with the Turks; and Hungary lay at their mercy. Then the Magyars offered to purchase the assistance of the Emperor Charles V. by giving their crown to his brother Ferdinand.

From that moment, for three hundred years, the history of Hungary in its connection with the house of Hapsburg was one of incessant disputes, the Austrian rulers striving to do away with Hungarian privileges, in order to make Austria and Hungary one nation, — the Hungarians protesting that they were a separate people, with rights and privileges and a Constitution of their own. Each king swore to protect these rights when he was crowned with the crown of St. Stephen, and no king was legally their sovereign till he had been so crowned.

The Austrian policy was to excite race jealousies, to stir up the Slav races that surrounded Hungary to make war on her or to rebel against her, and so far as possible to Germanize the Hungarians, discouraging every indication of nationality in customs, dress, and language.

Protestantism flourished at this period in Hungary, but even Catholic priests and Catholic nobles desired toleration, while the Hapsburgs never ceased their efforts to stamp out the reformed religion.

The most successful effort made to denationalize the Magyar nobles was unconsciously the work of Maria Theresa. We all know the story of her appeal to the Hungarian Diet, and of their response, "Let us die for our king, Maria Theresa!" After this, she greatly loved her Hungarian subjects, and a number of the Magyar nobles gathered round her in Vienna, where they learned to consider that their national dress and speech were barbarous. Napoleon, in his wars with Austria, in vain endeavored to detach the kingdom of Hungary from its allegiance to Maria Theresa's successors; and, when the Napoleonic wars were over, the fidelity of the Magyars was rewarded by a total rejection of the Hungarian claims to their ancient liberties and privileges. These were considered dangerous to the tranquillity of the rest of the Austrian dominions.

But the more the Emperor of Austria endeavored to denationalize his Hungarians, the more closely they adhered to their ancient ways. In particular they were outraged because the Magyar language had given place, by imperial decree, to Latin in all public documents and political debates.

In 1830 the Hungarians were greatly excited, first in the spring by the opening of steam navigation on the Danube, secondly in July by the revolution in France. Again they made demands for the restoration of ancient privileges, and for the use of the Hungarian language in public documents and law courts, but again they were refused.

There was one privilege, dear to Magyars, that the modern reform school of Hungarian nobles was anxious to efface. No Magyar could be taxed. All taxes were paid by their inferiors. Now Buda and Pesth, as we all know, form practically one city, but the Danube runs between them. There was no bridge over the Danube at this point, and the chief reformer, — whose name, Szechenyi, it is unhappily hard to pronounce, — took the matter in hand, built the bridge, and charged a toll of a few cents to be paid by every one who passed over it, noble and peasant alike. Great was the opposition, great the indignation of the nobles, — but the toll on that bridge was the entering wedge of reform. One old magnate wept bitterly, and said that he would never cross the bridge, for in its erection he foresaw the downfall of the Hungarian nobility.

At last, in 1844, after a fierce struggle between the Magyars and the Croatians in behalf of their respective tongues, Magyar was declared to be the national and official language.

It was at this time that Louis Kossuth's connection with politics began. It was principally for disseminating the views of a noble who advocated better treatment for the peasantry, and for complaining that the government would not allow landowners to ameliorate the condition of their serfs by means of legislation, that Kossuth found himself in prison.

The Austrian Empire was composed of more nations distinct from each other in language than any other, except Turkey. In 1848 it contained about eight millions of Germans, nearly eighteen millions of Slavs, five and a half millions of Magyars, and about as many Italians. The policy of the Austrian Cabinet was to govern by dividing, — to set race against race, and creed against creed.

After 1830, Hungary had seemed to awaken like a giant refreshed, — railroads and steamers were introduced, the nobles (after the victory of the toll-gate had been carried) consented to pay taxes. Banks were opened, the theatres were filled, and books were published. As I have said, Kossuth started journalism and reporting. His paper, though carefully moderate, kindled a flame that was to burn fiercely and steadily.

In 1847, the Emperor of Austria, as King of Hungary, opened the Diet, all the imperial family being present, and he answered the loyal addresses in Magyar, to the great delight of the Hungarians. The Archduke Stephen was chosen Palatine, that office being vacant. But still the Diet insisted on presenting a petition to the Emperor for the redress of grievances. Kossuth, who had signally failed as a public speaker a few years before, now began to display that eloquence in which he has been unrivalled by any man in modern times. If he was unequalled even when he spoke in English, what must have been that eloquence when he spoke in his native tongue! French, German, and Italian he spoke as well as he did English. A writer on Hungary once said : —

"As he surpassed all others in information, research, and knowledge of his country, besides familiarity with the statistics, historical lore, policy, government, and institutions of foreign countries, — particularly England and America, — so also he surpassed all men in command of language. There was no chord in the national heart which he did not touch with a master hand. He never pointed out an end without pointing out the means as well. He never unveiled a defect without holding up the remedy."

There were three parties in Hungary when the revolution of 1848 broke out : — the Austrian party ; the Moderates, who only wanted to secure the old constitutional privileges of Hungary ; and the Radicals. To the constitutional party Kossuth belonged, though he was in advance of some of its members, — Francis Deàk, for example, to whom the cause that Kossuth lost has been indebted for its resurrection and victory.

When news came from Paris of the fall of Louis Philippe, Kossuth urged upon the Diet that the right moment had come to put pressure on the Emperor and to insist on Hungarian reforms.

Meantime, revolution had broken out in Vienna, Metternich had fled away to England, and the Emperor was disposed to do anything to pacify his people. He promised his Austrians trial by jury, freedom of the press, publicity of proceedings in the law courts, and parliamentary representation.

On this, the Hungarian Diet resolved to send a deputation to Vienna, with Kossuth at the head of it. The Palatine the Archduke Stephen, an excellent man, and a true friend to Hungary, formed a ministry which included Kossuth, Deàk, Count Batthyani, Prince Paul Esterhazy, and others.

The Emperor, after a little hesitation, confirmed the appointment of this ministry, and the work of reform went on.

"By unanimous votes in both houses, taxation was equally distributed, and perfect toleration in religion was secured. The nobles gave up all right to exact feudal labor from the peasantry, and, in fact, made the peasants a free gift of half the cultivated land in the kingdom, so that each peasant family owned from thirty to forty acres. Every man who owned $150 worth of property had a right to an electoral vote. The Diet also introduced other reforms."

But alas! — there was war on the southern and western boundaries of Hungary. The Slav provinces, Croatia and Transylvania, wanted to be separate nationalities; Croatia, now that changes were to be made, had no wish to remain part of Hungary. Austria encouraged these views, that she might weaken Hungary, whom she distrusted and feared. The Croats rose under Joseph Jellachich, recently created Ban of Croatia, — that is, Viceroy, — and he sent word to the Archduchess Sophia, the Emperor's sister-in-law, whose influence was all-powerful in the Palace, that he was marching to the assistance of the Emperor.

The Hungarians felt themselves deeply outraged by the ingratitude and defection of the Croats, and prepared to resist their invasion. A levy of two hundred thousand men, and a grant of twelve million florins for war purposes were voted by the Diet, and wild was the enthusiasm when Kossuth exclaimed fervently: "If your energy equals your patriotism, I will make bold to say that hell itself cannot prevail against Hungary!"

Alas!—there was energy enough, and patriotism, but there were divisions among them. The patriotism of the country was divided. Hungary claimed Croatia, which disputed her claim; Transylvania looked for freedom under its own princes; and certain other provinces rose also in revolt, so that Hungary had not only to make head against the Austrians for the recognition of her own constitutional rights, but had to fight what she considered insurgent provinces.

Then Hungary had no leader, soldier and statesman, as Italy had in Charles Albert, then fighting the Austrians.

Kossuth was at that time unknown to Europe, and his name carried with it no weight beyond the Hungarian border.

Again, it was not clear to Europe what Hungary was fighting for. Was it for its ancient Constitution, and the privileges of the old Magyars, which had been set aside by the nineteenth century aspirations of the peasantry? Half the Hungarian leaders favored a republic, and half were for the old constitutional monarchy. Again, every other government in Europe, except Russia, had its hands full of its own troubles in 1849. Italy, as we have seen, was in a blaze of war, bitterness, and revolution; Spain was in vain looking for a ruler; France was still tempest-tossed; Germany was beset with revolutions and revolutionists, with no Prince Bismarck in that day at her head. Russia alone had attention to bestow on the affairs of Hungary, and it was her assistance that Austria invoked.

Panslavism was growing strong in Russia at that period, and the idea of a Panslavonic empire had its promoters and agents even in the United States. The peoples opposed to it were the Magyars and Roumanians, who both hated the Slavs, and at any time preferred Turkey to Russia. The Slav peoples whom Russia desired to assimilate were Poles, Croatians, Transylvanians, Servians, Bosnians, Herzegovinians, and the semi-Slav Bulgarians. In Hungary, Wallachia, and Moldavia, there was likewise a considerable population of Slavs, who, if encouraged and assisted, might get the upper hand of the dominant Magyars. So the Emperor of Russia was well pleased to march his armies through Moldavia, and extinguish an independent spirit in the kingdom of Hungary.

The populace of Vienna, led by young students from the universities, had been ready enough to make a revolution, but it lacked the purpose, steadiness, and union that would have carried it on. Dissensions allowed time to Prince Windischgrätz to organize the Emperor's army and to recover Vienna. Then the Emperor, who had declared Jellachich and his Croatians rebels against his Hungarian kingdom, welcomed them to Austria as his allies. The Hungarian army, which had hesitated to march over the frontier into Austria, did so at last. It was ill disciplined, and, in spite of its frantic valor, was defeated. Then the Emperor proceeded to take vengeance both on Vienna and Hungary. He was a weak man, but a conscientious one. When it was urged upon him that Hungary must be reduced to the rank of an Austrian province, he declared that he could not break the oath he had taken when St. Stephen's crown was placed upon his head. He therefore abdicated, and left the task of annihilating the kingdom of Hungary to Francis Joseph, his successor. This young man had been popular with the Hungarians. He spoke Magyar well, having had a Hungarian tutor. He refused to be crowned King of Hungary, or to take any oath to support its Constitution, and very soon the Diet passed a Declaration of Independence, and set up a Committee of Defence *pro tem.*, its Provisional Chief Executive being Kossuth. The Catholic clergy joined the patriotic movement.

The five principal generals in Hungary were Bem and Klapka, — who had come forward to defend Vienna, — Görgey, Guyon, and Dembinski. Of the five, two were Poles. Görgey of these generals was by far the greatest. He was one of those leaders who possess magnetic influence over their soldiers, and his tactics in war were as brilliant as those of Napoleon, but he was hampered by civilians in the Committee of Defence, and grew restive and irritable. Besides this, he was jealous of the other generals, and perpetually quarrelled with those either under or above him. Kossuth endeavored " to make things work," as we say in colloquial language, but his task was herculean.

The brilliant generalship of Görgey defeated the Austrians. Jellachich retired to Croatia with his followers. Meantime, Lombardy and Venetia were in revolt, and all the strength of Austria was needed in Italy.

The Hungarians had almost believed their independence won, when Francis Joseph called to his aid the Emperor of Russia, and a Russian force of two hundred thousand men, marching through Moldavia, entered the eastern provinces of Hungary.

Then nothing could exceed the miseries of the Hungarians. The Servian and Hungarian peasants, without leaders, engaged in a guerilla warfare all along the border line. The combatants were as savage as Red Indians, and far less disciplined. Every man fought for his own hand.

Meantime, Marshal Haynau was recalled from Italy, where he had perpetrated all kinds of cruelty at Brescia. Flogging women in public was one of the atrocities that drew on him the disgust of all the world.

I think it probable that the only names connected with the revolution in Hungary well known to the general public are those of Haynau the Austrian, and Kossuth. Haynau may thank the workmen at Barclay and Perkins's brewery in London for his unenviable notoriety.

Hungarian ladies (like other ladies when they believe their sons and husbands to be fighting in a patriotic war) were enthusiasts in the cause whose justice they maintained. When, after a while, Hungary lay prostrate at the feet of the Austrians, vengeance began, — and the ladies of Hungary were not spared in the day of retribution.

The chief military punishment in Austria is for the offending soldier to "run the gauntlet," or rather not to *run*, for he is forced to walk, stripped to the waist, at the pace of a military march, down two lines of soldiers armed with rods, who strike him as he passes. This punishment was inflicted by Haynau's orders on high-born Magyar ladies and on nuns. They were stripped like soldiers to the waist, but were sometimes allowed a light shawl to cover their shoulders. Thus they passed down the rank, stepping firmly, generally without word or groan. Sometimes a soldier would refuse to strike, and was punished on the spot for contumacy.

There were many such atrocities committed, but not by the Russians, or under any Austrian general except Haynau. "Punch," then in his young days, took up the subject, and the heart of all England was stirred against Haynau by several of his pictures.

A year or two afterwards, Marshal Haynau met with retribution. He visited London, but was refused admission to the clubs and had to content himself with sight-seeing. At Barclay and Perkins's brewing establishment he was vigorously assaulted by their burly workmen, and, although their treatment of him was brutal in the extreme, every man and woman in England in their hearts applauded them.

After the Russian army invaded Hungary, Görgey despaired. With divided counsels, divided ends, and dissensions among their generals, with Serb and Croat populations against the Magyars, and revolt in the frontier provinces, Görgey thought that Hungary could not hope to succeed, and that it would be a crime to prolong the struggle.

For many years in all Hungarian books Görgey was called a traitor for his conduct. He was said to have thrown up the cause out of spite to other leaders. When the cause of Hungary grew desperate, he had been called upon, in August, 1849, to assume the post of Military Dictator, and the Committee of Defence resigned, refusing to participate in any steps looking to submission.

Görgey surrendered his Hungarian army, August 13, 1849, at Villagos to the Russians, — his officers breaking their swords, and his troopers shooting their horses, after hugging and kissing them. Kossuth and the other leaders passed over the frontier into Turkey.

"Those among us," said an English paper in 1885, "who remember the particulars of the Hungarian War of Independence, will recall that the Hungarian commander in chief, Arthur Görgey, was the scapegoat sent out into the wilderness with all the sins and sorrows of that unsuccessful struggle upon his head. It was not enough that two of the most formidable military powers of Europe had joined their forces to crush the Hungarians; they were betrayed, — so the world was assured, — by the foremost soldier in their ranks, the general to whom Kossuth, in a moment of misplaced confidence, had intrusted the future of his country. No one who is unfamiliar with the excitable and emotional races of Southern Europe would appreciate the readiness with which the words "betrayed" and "traitor" spring to the lips of all men on experiencing a reverse. *Why* Görgey should have turned traitor, his accusers never knew; but it was taken for granted that the motive for his surrender was unworthy."

The capitulation at Villagos, where twenty-four thousand men, with one hundred and forty cannon, laid down their arms before the Russian commander (who had an enormously superior force), was for the Hungarian nation what the humiliations of Metz, Sedan, and Paris were to the French people. By it two delusions, dear to the Hungarian heart, seemed in danger of being blown aside. First, that Hungary alone in arms might defy all her enemies; secondly, if she could not, that the free peoples of the West would interfere to save her. The theory of Görgey's treason came opportunely to save the *amour-propre* of the nation.

Probably at that time Hungary never could have succeeded in establishing her independence. She has it now, though it was not secured under conditions that satisfied her great patriot, Kossuth. Her chief difficulty in 1849 lay in her divided counsels. From the first, Kossuth and Görgey had differed as to the proper aim and scope of her aspirations. When, after the Russians entered Hungary, military disasters began, Kossuth abdicated and left the country, but his rival remained and capitulated.

From 1849 to 1867, when a reconciliation took place between Hungary and its King, the Emperor of Austria, Görgey was kept under Austrian *surveillance*, and was never allowed to revisit his home. About Christmas, 1884, some old Hungarian officers sat discussing the surrender of Villagos, and, finding that they all agreed in exonerating Görgey, they determined to collect the opinions of their surviving comrades. The result was that on Christmas Day they presented a paper to General Görgey, signed by nearly all the officers then living of his army, declaring that in capitulating at Villagos he had altogether acted as became a soldier and a patriot.

What consolation this must have been to the heart of the old soldier who had lived thirty-five years under the weight of unmerited opprobrium!

After Görgey surrendered to the Russians, the great fortress of Komorn, in a bend of the Danube, held out under General Klapka against the Austrians. When informed of the surrender of Görgey, he asked for the cessation of hostilities for a month to send out and receive information. That information convinced him that he could do nothing but surrender. He did so, making excellent terms for his garrison, — which the Austrians violated in every respect.

When the Russians, shortly afterwards, retired, Austrian vengeance began. Count Louis Batthyani, one of the leading men of Hungary, whose course had been always as conservative as it was possible for that of a Hungarian patriot to be, perished on the scaffold. Out of thirty-four Hungarian generals, twelve were shot or hanged; three were imprisoned for life, and the rest became exiles. Scaffolds were erected in all the cities, and the executioners, in green uniforms, were kept frightfully busy. These executions, which might more properly be called judicial massacres, went on for some months.

I have heard from those who have visited Hungary that the people, their country homes, and way of life, strongly resemble those of Old Virginia.

Kossuth, with five thousand men, among whom were Generals Guyon, Bem, and Dembinski, escaped over the frontier into Turkey. Russia and Austria demanded the fugitives. Sultan Abdul Medjid consulted France and England. He was counselled to do his best to protect the refugees, but if Austria invaded Turkish territory, England and France would not promise to help him. Under these circumstances, the Sultan proposed to the Hungarians to declare themselves Mahomedans, when, of course, he could not deliver them up to the infidels. To become a renegade and to enter the Turkish service had been no unusual thing among Hungarians. The great general, Omar Pasha, was one of them. How many of the five thousand men who accompanied Kossuth accepted the Sultan's proposal I do not know. Generals Bem and Dembinski did; Kossuth, a Protestant, refused peremptorily;

Guyon was made Pasha of Damascus. Both he and Bem died in the Turkish service. A price was set, not only on Kossuth's head, but on the heads of his wife and his three little children. His wife, however, after many perils and adventures, joined him in Turkey, and was sent with him to Asia Minor. The little boys were seized and imprisoned at Pressburg, where their treatment was so severe that Haynau himself interfered on their behalf, and they were sent to their father.

A few months later, Senator Foote offered a resolution in the United States Senate that our country should intervene on behalf of Kossuth and his companions. Both England and America offered to send a war vessel for their use, but Kossuth chose that of America, the Mississippi, on board of which, with his wife, children, and a party of his friends, he embarked for America. On leaving Turkey, Suleiman Bey, who had been appointed to watch over them, said: "You are free. You will find friends everywhere. Do not forget those who were your friends when you had no other."

Kossuth and his party did not, however, reach America on the Mississippi. The weather was stormy, and Madame Kossuth suffered so terribly from sea-sickness that the ship put into Marseilles for her relief. Kossuth hoped to cross France by land on his way to England. But during his residence in Turkey he had shown signs of affiliation with Mazzini, and the French Republic, already embarrassed by that leader of revolutionary ideas declined to give him passage. Kossuth was exceedingly hurt by this refusal. The people of Marseilles in boats crowded round the Mississippi, offering him wreaths of laurel. He addressed them from the poop in a French speech, but his address contained some impolitic and uncourteous allusions to the man whom he called Monsieur Louis Napoleon Bonaparte. Kossuth little foresaw that in ten years he would fall for a while under the charm of Monsieur Louis Napoleon Bonaparte, advanced to the dignity of Emperor of the French.

The Mississippi landed her passengers, by their wish, at Gibraltar, whence they went in an English steamer to England. In England Kossuth remained from October 26 to the middle of November 1851, receiving addresses, silken banners, and public dinners. He was not in good health, having broken down before the fall of Hungary, and was glad, while in England, to seek medical aid. He became the idol of all classes in England, his marvellous fluency of speech greatly contributing to this result. He lauded the Queen and the Constitution of England, while at the same time he expressed the hope that Hungary would one day be a Republic. At Liverpool he was requested to give his opinion of Socialism. "I can," he said, "understand Communism, but not Socialism. I have read many books on the subject, but never could make out what they really mean. The only sense that I can see in Socialism is inconsistent with social order and the security of property. . . . I am firmly resolved to use all the influence that Providence may place in my hands in the next great struggle, in such a manner that no doctrines shall rule the destinies of nations which are subversive of social order."

To America Kossuth had been invited as the guest of the nation. He reached the harbor of New York, December 5, 1851, — three days after the *coup d'État* in Paris made the will of Louis Napoleon supreme over the French people. Madame Kossuth, Monsieur and Madame Pulsky, and several Hungarian gentlemen came with him.

In Washington he was received with honors such as had been offered to no man save Lafayette. He made addresses and received public dinners in all the large cities of the Union. Nothing could exceed the enthusiastic admiration of his hearers; but he failed wholly in the object of his mission. Neither the government nor individual citizens could be prevailed on to give him material aid to raise another revolution in Hungary. Everywhere he went he spoke of the dangerous and growing power of Russia, and professed himself a republican. He also paid tributes of personal gratitude to the Sultan of Turkey, and to the English people; the English government had refused to recognize him as a public character.

At Cleveland he spoke of the resources of Hungary. "She has," he said, "no public debt, a population of fifteen millions, a territory of more than one hundred thousand square miles, abounding in the greatest variety of Nature's gifts, if only the doom of oppression were taken from her. She has rich mines of gold, silver, copper, quicksilver, antimony, iron, salt, sulphur, nickel, and opal. She has the richest salt mines in the world, where it costs but twenty-five cents to extract one hundredweight of the purest rock salt, which is sold by the government for from two to more than three dollars. The government? No! — there is no government in Hungary! It is usurpation, now sucking out the life-blood of the people, crushing the spirit of freedom by soldiers, hangmen, and policemen, — and harassing the people in its domestic life and the sanctuary of family life, with oppression worse than any American can conceive."

It was thus in 1852. In this year, 1896, the Hungarians are celebrating their millennial jubilee with overflowing hearts of thankfulness and wild enthusiasm. But it is only indirectly to Kossuth that this end is due.

After his return from America he retired to Turin; and we shall again meet with him in Italian history.

KING VICTOR EMMANUEL.

CHAPTER IX.

VICTOR EMMANUEL.

AT the close of the year 1849 there seemed a pause in the history of Italian affairs. It was like the celebrated official announcement: "Order reigns in Warsaw," when that city lay bound and bleeding, life and spirit crushed out of her, at the feet of her oppressor. Rome had fallen before the army of the French, and the Pope was preparing to return from Gaeta, where he had been holding Court with King Bomba, turned out of Naples, and the Archduke Leopold, self-exiled from Tuscany. Bomba went back to his dominions to practise untold cruelties upon his subjects for another ten years; Leopold, more mild, went back to Tuscany and governed thenceforth like a well-behaved Archduke, virtually a vassal of Austria. Venice and Lombardy had been given back to the hated "stranger."

The government of Austria had always been milder than that of the large majority of Italian princes, so long as her subjects submitted to her rule; but towards men of liberal opinions her course was horribly severe. King Charles Albert had been totally defeated by Radetzky, at Novara; he had abdicated that same evening, when he rode off into the Austrian camp to surrender himself, and then proceeded to Oporto, to the dominions of his son-in-law, the King of Portugal, where he lived in strict privacy, and died of a broken heart a few months after. His remains now rest in Piedmont, in the mausoleum of the princes of the house of Savoy.

His son and successor, Vittorio Emmanuele (Victor Emmanuel), was proclaimed King almost upon the battlefield.

Shaking his sword towards Austria, he swore that Italy should yet be a nation, — "*Per Dio! Italia sarà!*" — It seemed a vain boast at the moment. Sardinia was utterly defeated, Italy utterly prostrate, — and yet the gallant King at the bottom of the box of ills saw hope.[1]

The line of the Dukes of Savoy, — subsequently Kings of Piedmont and Sardinia, — had sprung from a Norseman, Humbert (Umberto) of the White Hands. They were all brave, hardy, and domestic. All bore traces of their Northman origin, and Victor Emmanuel was a true son of his race. His mother was a princess of Tuscany, sister of Leopold the Grand Duke; his boyhood had been spent in a villa near Florence, while his father was constrained to expiate his liberalism by serving against the Constitutionalists in Spain. In that villa was born his dear brother Ferdinand Albert Amadeus, the Duke of Genoa.

The two boys were very strictly educated according to the old rules of the house of Savoy. Their chief preceptors were Monsignor Charvaz, afterwards Bishop of Genoa, and Dabormida, then a Piedmontese officer, afterwards a general and minister of State. Another officer, La Marmora, also assisted in their education. They were both boys of strong affections and remarkable intelligence, but Ferdinand was more studious than his brother. Victor never took kindly to book-learning. They had the highest love and veneration for their noble ancestry, — a feeling that they must never fall short of what should be expected from a son of the house of Savoy. Theirs was that grand feeling of *Noblesse oblige*, than which there is no higher worldly motive.

Victor Emmanuel, when he grew up, was of middle stature, broad-shouldered and powerful, with a dark skin, brown hair, a snub nose, and heavy under-jaw, — not handsome, — as a Savoyard peasant woman told him once, exclaiming when he informed her that he was the King:

---

[1] If any of my readers wish to know the history of Victor Emmanuel, *Il Rè Galantuomo*, more minutely than I can tell it here, I recommend them to read it in the "Life of Victor Emmanuel," by G. S. Godkin, a small volume published by Macmillan and Co.

"You need not try to deceive me with such talk; I will never believe that our dear, sweet, pretty queen, would have married so ugly a man!" He wore a full brown beard and an immense moustache. Kindliness and good feeling beamed from his brown eyes. He had married his cousin Maria Adelaide, daughter of the Austrian Archduke Ranieri, Viceroy of Lombardy. Her mother was his aunt, Charles Albert's sister. The Princess Adelaide was very pious, and suffered much from the Church's hostility to her husband and his opposition to the temporal claims of the clergy in his kingdom. The war between her husband and her family nearly broke her heart, but she never set herself openly in opposition to her husband, or to those Italian interests that he had in charge. She was beautifully charitable, and a devoted wife. Her husband was deeply attached to her, though history cannot but record that his morals were loose with respect to women, and his infidelities must have cost her many a heart-pang. In that, as in other things, he was very like Henri Quatre, — the *Vert Galant*. The pair had five children who survived their infancy. Humbert (Umberto) now King of Italy; Amadeus, who became King of Spain when Leopold of Hohenzollern refused the crown, and abdicated when convinced that only a native prince would satisfy the Spaniards; Maria Pia, who married the young King of Portugal; the Princess Clotilde who sacrificed herself in marriage to Prince Napoleon Bonaparte, for the good of her country; and a lame boy, Odone.

Victor Emmanuel's feelings, when he found himself King of Piedmont and Sardinia, must have been bitter in the extreme. A more miserable inheritance could hardly have been transmitted from father to son. "I did not desire to be King," he said, a few days after, to the English ambassador; "I have no taste for the profession. It seems to me a miserable one, and at the present day very difficult."

The first thing to be done was to arrange an armistice with Austria, for Piedmont could fight no longer. Marshal Radetzky made Victor Emmanuel all kinds of tempting offers if he would give in his adherence to the Austrian policy in Italy, and abrogate his father's gift of a Constitution to his subjects. "Marshal!" the young King answered vehemently, "I would sooner lose a hundred crowns than break my word to my people. What my father has sworn to I will maintain. If you wish a war to the death — be it so! I will call my nation to arms once more, and you will see what Piedmont is capable of in a general rising. If I must fall it shall be without shame. My house knows the road to exile, but not that to dishonor!"

The old Austrian marshal, to the day of his death, always spoke of Victor Emmanuel as "that noble fellow."

The terms exacted by the Austrians for a cessation of hostilities were considered hard; very like those which the Prussians exacted afterwards when the French armies had been disheartened and defeated in the Franco-Prussian war, — an indemnity of eighty thousand francs, and possession of certain frontier fortresses till the money should be paid.

The people of Piedmont and Savoy were so bitterly disappointed by defeat, so overwhelmed by these hard conditions, that not a cheer greeted the new King on his entrance into his capital. Thus ran his proclamation : —

"Citizens!— Untoward events, and the will of my most venerated father, have called me, long before my time, to the throne of my ancestors. The circumstances under which I hold the reins of government are such that nothing but the most perfect concord amongst us all will enable me (and then only with difficulty) to fulfil my only desire, the salvation of our common country. The destinies of nations are matured in the designs of Providence, but man owes to his country all the service he is capable of; and in this debt we have not failed. *Now* all our efforts must be to maintain our honor untarnished, to heal the wounds of our country, to consolidate her constitutional institutions. To this undertaking I conjure all my people; to it I will pledge myself by a solemn oath, and I await from the nation the exchange of help, affection, and confidence.
"VICTOR EMMANUEL."

With the greatest difficulty the Chamber of Deputies was brought to consent to the conditions of the armistice, even when the old Chamber had been dissolved, and a new one, chosen fresh from the people, had taken its place.

All over Italy the extreme party, — the party of Mazzini, — raised the cry of "Traitor!" against Charles Albert and Victor Emmanuel. "I am ashamed of myself now," wrote one in after years, on remembering that he had once written, in relation to Victor Emmanuel, that " it might be wise to *use*, but not to *trust* the King."

If it was hard to get a Piedmontese parliament to consent to the terms of the armistice, it was harder still to induce it to ratify the terms of the treaty of peace. In vain Austria modified somewhat the conditions of indemnity and cession of territory, which bore with crushing force on Piedmont, in hopes that the little nation would consult its own interests by surrendering in return a stipulation it was desirous to make, *i. e.*, that the hundred thousand Italians from Lombardy and Venetia who had come over into Piedmont to fight under her sovereign should be amnestied by the Austrian government. After five months the dispute resulted in a compromise. A few leading men were exempted from the amnesty, the rest were suffered to return home.

But Austria was not disposed to treat her unloving subjects with mildness. The very day after the promulgation of the amnesty a street riot took place in Milan, on the occasion of the Emperor's birthday, and the Countess Cesaresco gives us a list of seventeen persons, — all of them of what we should call the respectable classes, — who were publicly beaten with rods, and for these rods the Milanese municipality had to pay thirty-nine florins. Among the persons so beaten were two young women, opera-singers, one aged eighteen, the other twenty. Among the men were barristers, artists and students, a watchmaker, a lithographer, a bookseller, and a domestic servant. Sixty strokes of the Austrian stick were generally enough to prove fatal. Many of these persons were condemned to receive fifty.

But, though the peace had been signed by the King, the Parliament still held out, and Victor Emmanuel and his ministers dissolved the Chamber.

The King made a stirring appeal to his people, which, Cavour said, saved the country. "The country was roused to a sense of duty and citizenship," says Miss Godkin, "and sent up moderate and sensible men who had the true interests of their country at heart."

At this time, too, Victor Emmanuel was saddened and embarrassed by a new difficulty. Genoa took the opportunity of revolting from Piedmont. The garrison was driven out of the city, and for a few days Genoa was in the hands of the extreme republicans, when La Marmora was sent to put the revolt down.

Victor Emmanuel's first ministry had comprised Gioberti, the priest whose eloquent pamphlet on the abuses of government in the Papal States had first roused liberal feelings in the breast of Pio Nono, while he was yet the Cardinal Mastai-Ferretti. A somewhat more conservative ministry succeeded. At the head of it was the statesman, artist and novelist, the Marquis d'Azeglio, though he was still unable to stand, being disabled by a wound received while fighting the Austrians at Vicenza. It is said that some one having suggested Camillo Cavour as a man who might be called upon to form a ministry, the King replied, "The time for Cavour is not yet."

Victor Emmanuel, unlike Louis Napoleon, had always superior men around him, — men to aid, but not to rule him, for, as M. Thiers said of him, when he came to know him, " C'est bien le souverain le plus fin que j'ai connu en Europe." D'Azeglio, Cavour, La Marmora, Balbo, Dabormida, and others of the same stamp, were the men who enjoyed his confidence.

One day, d'Azeglio, talking alone with him, said that there had been few honest kings in the world. "You mean by that," said Victor Emmanuel, "that I am to begin the series?" "Your Majesty has sworn to the Constitution, ·· and you thought of all Italy, not Piedmont only. Let us continue in that path, and hold that a king must keep his word." "Well, in that case," said Victor Emmanuel, "the profession seems an easy one to me."

A few days after this the census-taker in Turin called on the King with his paper. Under the heading of "Profession," Victor Emmanuel wrote "Rè Galantuomo." It is the name he has been known by ever since, — The honest King! And *galantuomo* means even more than honest; it means valiant for the truth.

As long as Pio Nono continued at Gaeta, Victor Emmanuel endeavored to call him back, by letters and ambassadors, to his old path of patriotic reform. But the ambassadors were rarely admitted to an audience, and the letters were answered with stinging rebukes. The Pope was committed in all things temporal to the influence and policy of the Austrians. The priest was stronger in him than the patriot. Before Victor Emmanuel had been long upon the throne he had a desperate illness, and this, although it gave hope to Mazzini's party of extreme republicans, drew back to him in some measure the affection of his people. The peace with Austria that had been signed and ratified was, as the King said of it, "hard, but not ruinous." Balbo called it an armistice which would hardly last ten years. It remained to consolidate the constitutional institutions of the country, and, in the sailors' phrase, to "stand by" for the next duty which might be indicated by events.

One of the first things needed to make the Constitution work, was to treat all men as equal under the law. To effect this, some priestly privileges had to be abolished. Piedmont, indeed, retained more of such privileges than any other European State, even in Italy. The priests claimed the medieval right of affording sanctuary, and no priest could be tried in any case, civil or criminal, except in a court, called Foro Ecclesiastico, where bishops only sat as judges.

Sicardi, the Minister of Grace and Justice, who was to propose and carry through these laws, which bore his name, was sent to Gaeta to confer with the Pope concerning them. The Pope and his advisers affected afterwards to believe that he had never said a word concerning the concordat during his embassy, meaning, it is to be supposed, that the matters on which he had been sent to treat lay outside the concordat, — *i. e.*, the agreement between the Church and the government of Piedmont concerning the limits of temporal and spiritual power. The negotiation, at any rate, between the courts of Turin and Gaeta came to nothing, and the ministry at whose head was d'Azeglio, and among whose members was Santa Rosa, a statesman of sincere piety and a pure life, passed the Sicardi laws. Their objects were to make priests amenable to the law of the land, except in what referred to their spiritual functions; to limit the wealth amassed by convents and religious corporations; to check the multiplication of convents, and to diminish the number of feast days; to deliver education from the sole control of the clergy; and, lastly, to permit civil marriages, all those not performed by the parish priest having been previously illegal, and the children born of such unions illegitimate.

Undoubtedly such changes were distasteful to the whole body of the clergy, and to many sincerely religious persons, especially women. Reading Lord Broughton's letters, or Mr. Nassau Senior's journals from Italy, about this period, we see how society in Piedmont was stirred to its depths by the prospect of what to many seemed sacrilege and robbery. Great excitement resulted from the death at this time of Santa Rosa, who, though a sincerely religious man and a good Catholic, was denied the last sacraments by his parish priest, under direction from his bishop, unless he would repent of having favored laws so obnoxious to the Holy Father and the clergy. Santa Rosa would not recant, and died without absolution. It was deemed expedient to make examples. The convent of the order to which the priest belonged who refused him the last sacraments was suppressed, and the Bishop of Turin and two others, who persisted in opposing the execution of the Sicardi laws, were sent into exile. Wealth taken from the convents was devoted to educational and charitable purposes, but this kind of spoliation rarely advances the cause of religion. It stirs up strife and worldliness in both parties. But Piedmont was almost at the end of her resources, and men, as well as nations, do sometimes what it were best that they should not do, under the pressure of want of funds.

The passage of the Sicardi laws cost much anguish of heart to Victor Emmanuel. Many of those who surrounded him thought he was sacrificing his faith as a Christian by endeavoring to meddle with the privileges of the Church. He suffered terribly, five years after his accession, when, in 1854, both his mother and his wife were dying. He was passing from one sick bed to the other, and both women, especially his mother, were urging him, for his soul's sake, not to set himself in opposition to the Holy See. But Victor Emmanuel stood firm. The Queen Dowager and Queen Consort died within a week of each other, and two weeks later died the Duke of Genoa, Victor Emmanuel's beloved brother Ferdinand. To support the King under these sorrows, the good Archbishop of Genoa, Victor Emmanuel's old tutor, Monsignor Charvaz, hastened to him, for to feel himself cut off from the Church at such a moment was agony to Victor Emmanuel. "They tell me," said he to the Archbishop, in a voice broken by sobs, "that God has stricken me with a judgment, and has taken from me my mother, my wife, and my brother, because I consented to these Sicardi laws, and they threaten me with greater punishments. But do they not know that a sovereign who wishes to secure his own happiness in the other world ought to labor for the happiness of his people on earth?"

D'Azeglio, speaking of him at this time, says:

"I found him thinner by half than he had been. His waistcoat, which used to be tight, I could put my hand into, and still it hung about him. But with the exception of a couple of days he attended to business, and signed documents, saying to me: 'I am King; it is my duty.' Certainly, he appears fifteen years older. However, the stuff, physical and moral, is strong, and I have no fears."

Both the mother of the King and his wife were admirable women. Though the latter was the daughter of an Archduke of Austria, she had at heart the interests of Italy, and had never attempted to influence her husband in opposition to them, except in this matter of the Sicardi laws. She had borne her husband five children, was devoted to his interests, and, in the end, was popular with his subjects. He was, as has been said, truly attached to her, though, unhappily, his wayward fancy caused him to desert her often for other women. Some little excuse may be found for him in the life that he had been compelled to lead at his father's Court during the early days of his marriage.

A story which made much noise in Turin during Charles Albert's lifetime, is thus told by the Countess Cesaresco. She relates the anecdote when speaking of the little sympathy or enthusiasm felt for Victor Emmanuel in Piedmont, on his accession.

"Victor Emmanuel was not popular. The indifference to danger which he had shown so conspicuously during the war would have awakened enthusiasm in most countries, but in Piedmont it was so thoroughly taken for granted that the princes of the house of Savoy did not know fear, that it was looked upon as an ordinary fact. The Austrian origin of the Princess, his wife, formed a peg on which to hang unfriendly theories. It is impossible not to compassionate the poor young wife, who suddenly found herself queen of a people who hated her race, after having lived since her marriage the most dreary of lives, in the dismallest court in Europe. At first, as a bride, she seemed to have a desire to break through the frozen etiquette which surrounded her; it is told how she once begged and prayed her husband to take her for a walk under the Porticos of Turin, which she had looked at only from the outside. The young couple enjoyed their airing, but when it reached Charles Albert's ears, he ordered his son to be immediately placed under military arrest. The chilling formalism which invaded even the private life of these royal personages, shutting the door to 'good comradeship,' even between husband and wife, may have had much to do with driving Victor Emmanuel from the side of the Princess, whom, nevertheless, he loved and venerated."

Possibly Charles Albert but too well remembered the scandal caused by his "emancipated" mother when she walked the streets of Turin in revolutionary costume, with her infant in her arms.

The Marquis Massimo d'Azeglio quitted his post of Premier in 1852, worn out by physical suffering and the mental anxieties of his high position. When he made the announcement of his resignation to the King, he recommended that Cavour, who was then in the Cabinet as Minister of Agriculture, should take his place. Victor Emmanuel remarked that though he had no objection to Count Camillo Cavour, his other ministers had better take care, for he was the man who would turn them all out before long.

Camillo Cavour, whose biography is the history of Italy from henceforth to the day of his death in 1861, was the younger son of a noble Savoyard house, descended, like the kings, from Norman ancestry. He got into trouble while serving as a military engineer in Genoa in his early youth, and in 1835 was sent by his family away from Italy for several years. A curious paper was found in the police archives at Milan, speaking of him when he was about to return home as a young man of great ardor and talent, but of very dangerous political opinions, and recommending that he should if possible not be permitted to re-enter any part of Austrian Italy, or, if his passports were all in order, that his luggage, clothes, and person should be carefully searched, as he was more than likely to be the bearer of revolutionary communications.

About the same time Cavour wrote to a friend who had written to him to express her sympathy : " But I can assure you that, notwithstanding this, I shall make my way. I own I am ambitious, and when I am Minister I hope to justify my ambition. In my dreams I see myself already Prime Minister of Italy."

During his absence from his own country he lived principally in England, a country for which he felt and expressed such high esteem that in after years his enemies called him Lord Camillo. He wrote a book on Ireland, and devoted himself to the study of agriculture, into which, — although he called agriculture the refuge of all defeated parties," — he threw himself " with as near an approach to enthusiasm as his uneffusive temperament allowed." He earnestly deprecated the absenteeism of landed proprietors, and considered wiser and more liberal cultivation of the land the best barrier against discontent and revolution.

No less was he interested in commerce. Mr. Cobden on his visit to Italy in 1846, to advocate free trade, found in him an earnest disciple, and when made Minister of Commerce in the early days of Victor Emmanuel, he carried those convictions into effect. He was earnest in opening railroads through Piedmont. He projected the Mont Cénis tunnel, which was popularly considered a wholly impracticable project. But his King presided at the inauguration of the work in 1857.

"We must submit, wait, and prepare" was the saying of another great Italian after Novara, and this saying might have been called Cavour's watchword.

Cavour was never a popular man, but, after his elevation to the premiership, it soon came to be understood that he had arranged affairs in such a way that only himself could manage them, and that necessarily, therefore, they must be left in his hands.

He made an alliance with Marquis Rattazzi, leader of the Left, though he was himself a Constitutionalist and a Conservative, and he encouraged Rattazzi to push the principle of the Sicardi laws somewhat further than had been intended at the time of their first conception. By degrees he arrived at such political importance that he and Victor Emmanuel, between them, seemed to hold not only the affairs of little Piedmont, but of all Italy in their hands.

In 1855, while Victor Emmanuel was overwhelmed with sorrow for the bereavements that had taken place in his own family, the treaty was signed which elevated Sardinia almost to the rank of a Great Power, and was in its results the making of Italy, — I mean the treaty of alliance between England, France, and Sardinia, by which the latter bound herself to help the two other allied powers in the

Crimean War. Things were not going on prosperously for the Allies in the Crimea, and they were glad to accept help. Sardinia had her own causes of enmity against Russia. The Emperor Nicholas had treated her young sovereign with contempt. He it was who had taken upon himself to stamp out the revolt against Austria in Hungary. He had offered to do the same in Italy, but his proposal was declined.

It was the terrible winter of 1855; the English and French armies were lying round Sebastopol. It had been proposed at first to place the small Sardinian army, fifteen thousand men, under the King's brother Ferdinand, the Duke of Genoa, but on his death the command was given to General La Marmora, although he wholly disapproved of the expedition. It needed the eye of a statesman to pierce the future and approve the plan. La Marmora's disapproval, indeed, appeared justified when, almost as soon as his soldiers landed, cholera broke out amongst them, and Alessandro La Marmora, his own elder brother, dearly beloved, died of it almost immediately.

The Sardinian troops did good service in the Crimean War; their discipline and soldierly qualities extorted great praise from their allies, and General La Marmora became a hero. They were not at the Alma, Balaclava, or Inkerman, but their behavior at the battle of Tchernaya wiped off forever the reproach that had been bandied about in Europe: *Les Italiens ne se battent pas.*

In November, 1855, Victor Emmanuel, accompanied by Cavour, and by d'Azeglio, set out on a visit to Paris and to England. He had been very ill, having persisted in swimming his horse across a river, when heated with hunting, rather than wait for a boat. It was thought, as we sometimes say in homely phrase, " that he might be better for a change."

The Emperor and Empress of the French were most cordial to him on his arrival in Paris, showing him all kinds of delicate attentions, — for instance, everything provided for his own use bore the arms of the house of Savoy.

D'Azeglio in his apartment found four of his own paintings, — d'Azeglio had been an artist when in early life he was an exile. But the most important thing in the visit was the Emperor's question: What can be done for Italy? — a question he and Cavour were to settle between them two years later, in their celebrated secret interview at Plombières.

Then, too, it was that Manin's heart rejoiced, as he saw the tricolor of Italy white, green, and red, blended everywhere with the tricolor of France and the ancient flag of England. Victor Emmanuel had steadily refused to yield to the persuasions of Austria that he should give up this national flag, which symbolized his hopes of a United Italy, and return to the plain blue banner of Piedmont. In Paris, too, Cavour had several interviews with Manin, then sinking into his grave from disease, poverty, and sorrow. Manin fully agreed with Cavour's views and with his policy, declaring that the first thing to be aimed at was the deliverance of Italy from the foreigner, and he assured Cavour that if the house of Savoy would be true to Italian liberty he would, though a Republican, willingly give his allegiance to a king of that house, if Italy wished to place herself under his constitutional rule. He deprecated the plottings of Mazzini, and wrote three admirable letters to him, disapproving the use of such methods as the Carbonari, the Internationals, the Nihilists, and the Anarchists have been known to adopt and sanction, dwelling especially on the folly and wickedness of political assassinations.

When Victor Emmanuel and his ministers visited England, the Queen and Prince Albert were warm in their welcome. When the Queen bestowed upon her guest the order of the Garter, the beautiful Duchess of Sutherland said that, of all the Knights of St. George that she had ever seen, he was the only one who would have had the best of it in a fight with the Dragon.

Victor Emmanuel seems to have had at this time some idea of taking a second wife, could he have obtained the hand of Princess Mary of Cambridge, but she preferred to marry the Prince of Teck and to take up her residence in England.

The King and his suite were enchanted with everything in England except the climate. The mountaineer of Savoy did not mind it, but d'Azeglio says: "I suffered the agonies of the *inferno* with neuralgia." The Lord Mayor gave the Sardinian King a banquet in the City, when Victor Emmanuel replied to his welcome in French, for he was not an English scholar.

In December, Turin welcomed her King back again; appreciating him all the more because it found how much he was appreciated in other lands.

Sebastopol had fallen on September 8, 1855, though it was nearly a year before the war was fully ended. Then a European Congress was assembled in Paris to settle the affairs of Europe. Nothing was done about Italy, but Cavour was encouraged by the English and French plenipotentiaries to present a picture of the wrongs of the peoples of that land, their condition, and the cruelties practised in Naples, Sicily, and the Roman States. Then came the return of the Sardinian soldiers from the Crimea. Three thousand had died of cholera or in the field. It must have been hard for them to understand how, on the shores of Southern Russia, they were fighting for the independence of Italy, but they did their duty faithfully and bravely, and by their help Sardinia had made for herself two good friends, having given her assistance to France and England in the hour of their necessity. All Italy was full of admiration and congratulation for the gallant little army which had so well maintained the national honor, and, in spite of the jealous watchfulness of their governments, Lombards, Venetians, Tuscans, Romans, and Neapolitans raised a subscription to give Victor Emmanuel one hundred cannon for his fortress of Alessandria, close on the frontier of Piedmont and Lombardy.

Victor Emmanuel and Cavour had two sets of enemies; the Austrians, supported by the reactionary party; and the Republicans, or followers of Mazzini. It was not long after the Crimean War that England, — Italy's best hope, — deserted her in a measure, by making a treaty of alliance with Austria, and so blighting, apparently, men's hopes of a United Italy.

In 1858 occurred Orsini's Carbonari attempt against the life of Napoleon III., and republican attempts on Victor Emmanuel's life were talked of, though he had never been a Carbonaro. Constancy, wisdom, and patience had still to be the motto of Cavour and of his master; perhaps we may express their policy in the words of their own proverb, *Chi va piano va sano, chi va sano va lontano;* or in words of wisdom addressed by a long-suffering uncle to Orsini himself: "Felice, remain quiet. Love your country, but love her to do her good, and not to cause her sorrow;" and again, "Undertake nothing without seeing your way clear to success. When you do not, it is a crime to attempt any revolt or rising." But these views were not held even in Piedmont by Italian exiles from other States. Men bred in secret societies had no patience, and were all the time endeavoring to precipitate events which they could see approaching. There was very little statesmanship among the Reds of Italy, — or, indeed, among the Reds of other lands, so far as I have studied them or known them.

Felice Orsini may be considered a typical rash, restless revolutionist. All his life he never kept himself out of hot water, not even long enough to court his wife, or pass his honeymoon. Conspiracy was his element, his business in life, his joy and his diversion.

Orsini was born in the Roman States in 1819. His father had served under Napoleon and made the campaign of Moscow. He had a severe fall on his head when two years old, was unconscious for forty-eight hours, and this may have had something to do with unbalancing his mind. He was christened Theobaldo, but was always called Felice. When twelve years old, living with his uncle at Imola, he joined in the morning with schoolboy zeal and pride in revolutionary demonstrations in the streets, and in the afternoon was enthusiastic in his admiration of the Austrian soldiers who marched into the town to put down the revolutionists. It was the year 1831, and, as we have seen already, all Central Italy was making attempts to effect political change. Felice's next escapade was running away to join the French who were occupying Ancona, in the hope that he might be accepted as a drummer-boy. He was brought home, however, and had his ears boxed, an indignity which his spirit of independence bitterly resented. In short, a more troublesome young lad probably never existed. When about fifteen he professed himself a "Liberal," in a great measure probably out of opposition to his uncle, who was a personal friend of the Bishop of Imola, Cardinal Mastai-Ferretti, — the future Pio Nono.

Of himself he says grandiloquently: "I learnt in Roman history the greatness and valor of my country in ancient times, and I imbibed the principles of the old republican valor; the ancient Roman heroism woke an echo in my heart." No doubt these ideas falling into a hotbed of self-will, vanity, recklessness, and a boy's eagerness for notoriety, and love of risk, made him the man who passed his life from prison to conspiracy during the next twenty-four years. He possessed himself of a pair of pistols, he associated with Liberals, he talked aloud as he heard them talk in secret, he openly despised priests, and filled his uncle with terror, for it was a time when spies flourished in Romagna, a "time of accusation, arbitrary trials, and universal terror."

One of the pistols that Felice treasured unknown to his uncle, went off accidentally one day and killed the family cook, who entered the room as he was hurriedly loading it. This caused great grief and consternation. The police hurried into the house, the accident was suspected to have had some connection with politics, and the lad was arrested. It might have gone very hard with him had it not been for the interposition of the Bishop, toward whom, however, he showed little gratitude in after years.

He was sent out of the Papal States for six months, and then the affair blew over, but strong influence was brought to bear on him to induce him to enter a religious order, the Jesuits apparently, the clergy thinking that they might make something of him, could he be tamed by their discipline, and inspired with religious enthusiasm.

He next became a student at Bologna, where he wasted his time, and studied little, except fencing and gymnastics. When he was about nineteen, he read Thiers's "Histoire de la Révolution Française," which filled his whole soul with enthusiasm for the principles of '89, and for the heroes and the literature of the same period. He saw in every youth who pleased him one ready to become a hero, — but who, to develop into a hero, must begin as a conspirator. His first chance to strike a blow against tyrants occurred, he thought, in 1843. He heard of an intended revolt in Barcelona, and endeavored to get there and take part in it, but by his uncle's vigilance his plan was frustrated. Shortly after, there was plenty to be done near home; activity increased among the Liberals; the severity of the papal government knew no bounds. Orsini joined a secret society, and drew up plans for revolutionary projects; one of these plans fell into the hands of the authorities, and in May, 1844, he was arrested, chained, tried, and sent to the galleys for life, but subsequently, on the election of Pio Nono, he received pardon through the amnesty.

On Orsini's release, as Liberalism under the first months of Pio Nono's reign seemed to be taking care of itself in Rome, he turned his attention to Tuscany, joined a revolutionary committee, and worked to stimulate risings and so provoke reforms. When Florence grew too hot for him, he went back to Imola. Up to that time, he says, he had had no personal connection with Mazzini.

Before long he was in Rome, and was enrolled among the volunteers who, with the papal troops, marched to assist Charles Albert in his war with the Austrians. Next came the Pope's flight and the establishment of the Triumvirate to govern the Roman Republic. Rome itself was kept in good order by Ciceruacchio during its republican days, but anarchy and disorder in the provinces were terrible. Orsini was recommended to Mazzini, — who ruled over his two co-triumvirs as Napoleon did over his colleagues when First Consul, — as a man of great zeal and energy, and he was sent to Ancona to put down political assassinations and other enormities, with a high hand. Orsini's mode of government, especially his arbitrary imprisonments, drew on him the fury of the citizens and of many of the inhabitants of the surrounding country. A sort of civil war broke out in Ancona, but Orsini seems to have fulfilled his mission, and boasted when he prepared to leave Ancona that he had succeeded in restoring order, which, in that province, had before wholly disappeared.

Orsini was next sent to Ascoli, where brigands were causing much disturbance, crossing the frontier back and forth from Naples. They threatened the town with sack and murder if they should be denied provisions and ammunition.

But meantime the French were besieging Rome, and the Austrians were advancing to supersede the Roman republican government in Ancona, to which end they allied themselves with the brigands. Orsini, at last, finding that he could not hope to reach Rome with his soldiers, left his officers to effect a capitulation with the Austrians, and escaped in disguise to Genoa.

He continued to work actively as an agent of the revolutionary party. He wandered on revolutionary missions, and in various disguises, into many parts of Central and Northern Italy. He had a share in the rising at Genoa which gave so much trouble to Victor Emmanuel, also in that miserable rising in Milan, which brought Austrian rods down on the backs of many persons, guilty or innocent, who took, — or seemed to take, — part in it. Frequently he was threatened by those whom he had treated with scant consideration at Ancona, and was pronounced no Liberal.

In 1850, Orsini was with Mazzini in Nice, where preparations were being made for an important rising against the government of Louis Napoleon, and arrangements for a revolutionary loan were in progress. This movement was directed from London. Its plans looked well enough on paper, but failed wholly in execution. An Italian and a French column were to be assisted by many exiled Germans and Poles.

The scheme having failed, Orsini, for about the first and only time in his life, had an interval of quiet, though he wrote to Mazzini begging to be employed in any desperate service. He spent his time at Nice, chiefly in the society of English families, and perfected himself in the English tongue. He also saw much of the wife of a German poet, Madame Emma Herwegh, to whom he subsequently owed his life.

"But conspiracy," he says, "took me before long from my friends and my studies." Mazzini wrote: "I keep my word, and intrust to you a most dangerous undertaking." This was to effect a rising throughout Northern Italy, but the whole thing was badly planned. The refugees in Genoa, on whom the execution of the scheme mainly depended, were distrustful and half-hearted. They did not confide in the practical good sense of Mazzini. They believed him to be a man of theories and not of action. The attempt was made by a few individuals only; some were punished; the whole affair failed, although Orsini still continued to act as "walking delegate" in the cause of conspiracy and revolution. The government of Piedmont finally arrested him at Nice, and then decided to banish him. He went to London, and there took rank as a leading Italian patriot, and was one of those exiled revolutionists assembled at the celebrated dinner given to Kossuth by Mr. Saunders, the American consul. Garibaldi, Ledru-Rollin, Mazzini, and Pulsky were among the other guests on the occasion.

After a brief stay in England, Orsini was off again on another mission. This was to land a cargo of arms at Massa. The arms were indeed landed, but orders had gone wrong. The two hundred young men who obtained them (with very little ammunition) were not disposed to obey Orsini, when he cried "Follow me! and we will attack the first band of carbineers we meet." They answered this foolhardy proposition by the cry, "No! By Heaven, we will not die the death of the brothers Bandiera!" So the affair was over, — happily this time without useless shedding of blood. Even Orsini learned something by experience, and ceased to approve Mazzini's methods, saying: "What can an expedition of thirty, forty, or a hundred exiles do?"

Nevertheless, Mazzini having proposed to him "to take part in a brilliant affair in the Valtellina," he announced himself ready, and prepared for an expedition into Southern Switzerland and Northern Lombardy. His associates were an Italian and a Hungarian. Mazzini was to be director in chief of the expedition. Orsini and his colleagues were to take charge of its military affairs. But the Valtellina proved to have no thought of rising. Everything went wrong. The Swiss police captured Orsini, but, by help of a Swiss servant girl and a Russian lady, he contrived to escape. He wandered about Switzerland for some time, contriving to avoid recapture, while others were arrested.

Next, in September, 1854, Mazzini put forth a new plan — I need not give its details, though the plan lies before me, but its object was to organize a band of death, — "eighty young men, robust and decided," armed with daggers, who should, in parties of three, go into Austrian camps, associate with the officers and soldiers, create no suspicions, and wait quietly till, on a day and hour agreed upon, each should thrust his dagger into the heart of an Austrian officer. "For," says Mazzini, "when the Austrian army has lost its officers, it is lost."

Orsini was ready, though with some misgivings, observing that "against the Austrian oppressor who does not scruple to violate every oath and every law of justice, Italians are justified in using every means in their power to put the oppressor down."

The eighty young men, however, were not to be found. Orsini next set out for Transylvania and the Danubian provinces, where regiments, composed of Lombards in the

Austrian service, might be found. His mission was to stir up mutiny in these regiments, and induce the soldiers to kill their officers, — a task analogous to that undertaken three years later in India, for which those engaged in corrupting Sepoy troops were blown from guns.

However, Orsini did not carry out his mission. He was recognized by a Jew, arrested soon after he reached Hungary, and sent in chains to Vienna. Thence he was consigned to the strong fortress of Mantua, and placed in one of the condemned cells, though before trial.

Here he contrived to find means to correspond with his friend, Madame Herwegh, and to procure from her money, opium, and saws. He seems to have been treated with considerable indulgence, both by his jailers and the authorities, — he says, " because they found that I was not a man who tried to parry, but was a known and approved enemy. I speak frankly. I know my fate, and I am prepared. I have declared that I love my country — that I will compromise no one."

He sawed the bars of his cell, and on the night of March 26 he prepared to escape. But when he gazed down the immense height that he would have to descend into the ditch, and reflected that he would then have to mount the counterscarp, his heart failed him. He had previously tried to stupefy both jailers and sentinels by opium, but his plan had failed.

Two days later, however, he made the descent.

Here is his own account, published afterwards in an English paper : —

" In twenty-four days I had cut away seven of the inside bars, and one of the outside ones, and had extracted from the wall eight bricks, which I hid in the straw of my mattress. As for the cord, I had thought of that before. On February 1, I had kept back without my jailers' knowledge the sheets I ought to have sent to the wash, and on the 1st of March I kept back the towels, which were as wide as the sheets and a little longer. By cutting these in strips I made my cord. . . . On the night of March 30 I lay still on my bed till after the last visit of my jailers, at half-past one. Then I let myself down by the cord.

When about six yards from the ground I felt I could no longer sustain myself. I looked at the depth below me, and let myself drop. A sort of swoon came over me. . . . I had injured one foot and was lame, but I dragged myself round and round the castle in the ditch, hoping to escape into the lake, but it was barred by a grating."

Then he endeavored to climb the side of the ditch, which was eighteen feet high, but he fell back exhausted. He lay in the ditch till dawn, when some peasants passed, to whom he called, saying he had been drunk overnight and had fallen over the embankment. They helped him out, and he lay all day concealed in some long reeds. He had, apparently, confederates in the city who provided him with food, a razor, and some brandy, and at nine o'clock in the evening he was dragged (for he could not walk) to a yard where he was covered with straw. There he remained eight days while pursuit was hot, but at last he got away to Genoa, and thence back to England. Here he was made a kind of hero. He published a book on "Austrian Prisons"; he gave lectures all over the country. He was handsome, — the *beau idéal* of a conspirator, with flashing eyes, and long black hair. Many people invited him to their houses and were kind to him, among them a Mr. Thomas Alsop. Walter Savage Landor also received him as a guest at his house in Bath.

I have told the story of Orsini at some length, — a length disproportioned, it may seem, to its importance, — because it shows so clearly what Victor Emmanuel and Cavour had to contend with from the hot-headed republicans who accepted the lead of Mazzini. From the hour of Victor Emmanuel's accession to 1859 there was a perpetual eruption of conspiracy going on in all parts of Italy, under the active superintendence of Mazzini, who, however, strange to say, never seems to have adventured himself personally in these revolutionary risings. Cavour and Victor Emmanuel found it harder to deal with these hot-headed revolutionary compatriots than even with the Austrians. They crossed the well-laid plans of statesmanship in every direction. While the rulers of Piedmont were strengthening their bonds of alliance with the Emperor Napoleon, and believed that the foreign aid they deemed essential, if Italy would cope with Austria, would come by way of France and its Carbonaro Emperor, " that sovereign was regarded by no inconsiderable number of Italians as the greatest, if not the sole, obstacle to their liberation," and with many the idea arose that the greatest service that could be rendered to their country would be the removal of this sovereign from the political scene. Then would a French Republic be established after the pattern of that of 1792, — and would carry propaganda throughout Europe, sweeping away tyrannies, and establishing republics everywhere.

Mazzini offered Orsini further employment in Italy, but Orsini answered, somewhat coldly, that when he again ventured his life in the republican cause he should prefer to act by himself.

He, however, wrote to Cavour, asking for a passport to return to Italy, offering to place himself at the service of the Sardinian government, provided it would leave off wavering and show its unmistakable purpose of achieving the independence of Italy.

Cavour was not going to have his hand forced by a restless and irresponsible individual. He returned no answer, though he said later that the letter was a noble one.

Then Orsini determined to act for himself. He procured the assistance of two men, one a Dr. Simon Barnard, who made explosive bombs for him in Birmingham; the other an Italian named Pieri, who was to assist him in flinging the bombs.

Having taken out a passport in London in the name of Thomas Alsop, he proceeded early in January, 1858, to Paris, and on the 14th of January, just as the carriage containing the Emperor and Empress was drawing up to the opera-house, he flung his missiles. No less than one hundred and fifty-six persons were wounded; ten were killed, and five hundred and sixteen wounds were inflicted by the explosion; but the Emperor and Empress were hardly harmed. Prince Ernest of Saxe-Coburg was awaiting the arrival of the imperial party at the opera-house, and has given in his memoirs a very graphic description of the scene.

Orsini, when asked, on his trial, what he had expected would happen had he succeeded in killing the Emperor, answered: "We were convinced that the surest way of making a revolution in Italy was to make a revolution in France, and that the surest way of making a revolution in France was to kill the Emperor."

From the very first days of his reign, Napoleon III. had been perplexed by his relations to Italy. He and his brother had taken the oaths of Carbonari, they had even fought for Italy in 1831. It has never been certain that Napoleon Louis did not die by a Carbonaro's knife, instead of by the measles; and it is probable that the Emperor knew that if he failed to do anything to promote the cause of independence in Italy assassination surely awaited him.

Besides this, his sympathies were sincerely enlisted in the Italian cause. The affair at Rome had been a great disappointment to him. When the Romans defeated a French army it would have been as much as his throne was worth to refrain from obtaining a victory over them. He said repeatedly that he had never expected the Pope on his return would take cruel vengeance on his revolted subjects. He endeavored to press on him reforms, and clemency; and he was never easy under the position in which events at Rome had placed him. It should never be forgotten, even in judging Louis Napoleon's policy, that he was a kindhearted man.

"Everything," says the Countess Cesaresco, "was done to make Orsini a hero in the eyes of the French public. Jules Favre defended him, pleading, not for the life, but for the honor of his client. Orsini's own letter to the Emperor from his prison, produced a powerful impression, not only on him to whom it was addressed, but on the public; there was a dramatic interest created in the man who, disdaining to crave clemency for himself, tried a last supreme effort in appealing for the country he had loved so well. 'Deliver my fatherland,' was the conclusion of the letter, ' and the blessings of twenty-five million citizens will be with you.' "

The Emperor made every effort to save Orsini, but his ministers and the Chambers insisted on his execution ; doubtless Orsini himself may have approved it. There is no question that he had much communication with the Emperor through Pietri, the chief of police, who was an Italian, and it is said that the Emperor visited him at Mazas before his execution.

Thus the fears, the sympathies, the policy of Napoleon III., all prompted him to make speedy alliance with Victor Emmanuel on behalf of the independence of Italy, and he sent Orsini's letter to Cavour.

On the scaffold, Orsini was upborne by the strongest hope that the fulfilment of his life's wish, the independence of his country, would not be postponed long. It is said he had received a solemn promise to that effect from the Emperor Napoleon.

CHAPTER X.

THE ALLIANCE WITH FRANCE.

IT was in July, 1858, five months after the execution of Orsini, that Cavour received an invitation from the Emperor Napoleon to meet him secretly at the little summer resort of Plombières, situated in the Vosges, and not far from the old conventual settlement for royal and distinguished ladies at Remiremont.

Some sharp words had passed between Count Walewski and Cavour on the subject of the overflow of restless, scheming Italian exiles into Piedmont; and while Cavour maintained the dignity and independence of Piedmont in his correspondence on this subject with other diplomatists, he introduced a bill into the Piedmontese Parliament to punish conspirators who laid plots in that country against the life of any sovereign.

This harboring of exiles gave great offence to Austria, and relations between Piedmont and herself became so dangerously strained, that England and Russia proposed a European congress to preserve peace. There were fierce disputes concerning the composition of this congress, Austria at first insisting that Piedmont should take no part in it; then that she could only appear in it as a *secondary Power*, while, meantime, both Piedmont and Austria armed for war, and their troops stood facing each other on the Lombard frontier. No congress, however, took place.

The Emperor and Cavour, at their meeting in July, came to an understanding, but the Emperor stipulated for profound secrecy, and also that Austria must be the aggressor in the coming war.

On New Year's Day, 1859, words spoken by the Emperor to the Austrian ambassador at his reception gave indication of what might be at hand in the coming year; while Cavour labored to keep his own outspoken sovereign from raising premature hopes in Italy on New Year's Day, when he, too, received diplomatists and deputations. There was no Austrian ambassador at Turin at that time; diplomatic relations with Vienna had been for some months broken off. While the King received the ambassadors and senators, he kept closely to the instructions of Cavour, but when it came to the turn of the city magistrates, out of the fulness of his heart his mouth spake, in spite of prudence. "Forgive me," he said afterwards to Cavour, "I followed your advice as long as possible, but I really could not keep in any longer. The magistrates alluded to the important events of last year, — I told them that I looked for more important events in the year to come." Cavour, who had a strong sense of humor, laughed loud and long.

The Piedmontese Parliament was to assemble ten days later. The King was to open it with a speech from the throne. Cavour insisted that he must not say anything that might give the alarm to Austria, or sound like a declaration of war. "Then, if I cannot speak clearly, I had better say nothing," said the straightforward sovereign, but the more diplomatic Cavour succeeded at last in convincing him that *something* must be said, and they spent the ten days composing together a speech "that should unite brevity and clearness, prudence and boldness, frankness and reticence." A draft of the composition was forwarded to the French Emperor for his approval, and he added the few memorable words at the close. "We are not insensible to the cry of anguish that comes to us from other parts of Italy." When Victor Emmanuel uttered these words, with flashing eyes and startling emphasis, the Chamber and the spectators went wild with enthusiasm. This is what has been said of the scene by one who witnessed it.

"At every pause the speech was interrupted by clamorous approbation, and cries of *Viva il Rè!* But when he came to

COUNT CAVOUR.

the words 'a cry of anguish,' — *un grido di dolore*, — there was confusion indescribable. Senators, deputies, spectators, all sprang to their feet with a bound, and broke into passionate exclamations. The ministers of France, Russia, Prussia, and England were utterly astonished, and carried away by the marvellous spectacle. The Neapolitan ambassador turned pale. We poor exiles did not even attempt to wipe the tears that flowed copiously from our eyes, as we frantically clapped our hands in applause of that King who had remembered our griefs, and had promised us a country. . . . He reigned in our hearts, and was already our King!"

From all parts of Italy came young volunteers of all classes to join the army that was to resist the troops of hated Austria. Garibaldi had been already summoned from Caprera, and was charged to raise a corps called Hunters of the Alps. The only Italians who did not rejoice were those who formed what was called the Clerical Party, and Mazzini and his immediate followers. They saw in the movement nothing but dynastic ambition on the part of Victor Emmanuel, and prophesied, — too truly, — the loss of Savoy and Nice to Piedmont.

For, in truth, the help of France, which was essential to resuscitate Italy, had to be paid for. The Emperor's Italian projects, though dear to himself, were not popular in France, and something had to be done to propitiate the French people. It was one of the cherished projects of Napoleon III. to make the eastern frontier of France what it had been under his uncle; and he demanded of Victor Emmanuel the cession of Nice and Savoy to France, in return for his assistance in humbling the power of Austria in Italy. He also is thought to have had projects of making a descendant of Murat king of the Two Sicilies, and his cousin, Prince Jerome Napoleon, ruler of Tuscany. He demanded the hand of the Princess Clotilde, Victor Emmanuel's eldest daughter, for this cousin, a man more than twice her age, of disorderly life, rough manners, and fantastic opinions.

Both these conditions were terribly distasteful to Victor Emmanuel. Savoy was the cradle of his race; his motherless daughter was very dear to him. It is true that there was to be a *plébiscite* in Savoy and Nice to see if the people would willingly belong to France or not, and the free consent of Princess Clotilde was to be a condition of the marriage.

The poor young girl could not but feel repugnance to her fate, but she was a true daughter of Italy, and when Cavour set before her how the assistance of the French Emperor in the cause of Italy depended upon her, — the Iphigenia of modern history, — she consented. When Cavour related what had passed between them to a friend, he spoke of the courage and self-devotion of the young girl with tears in his eyes. The marriage took place January 29, 1859, — there could not have been much time for bridal preparations, — and the married pair set off at once for Genoa, on their way to France.

Princess Clotilde found a warm friend in the Empress Eugénie, and a coarse, hard man in her husband. One sees a little glimpse of their married life in an anecdote that is told of them at the deathbed of the old king, Jerome Bonaparte. He was dying without religious consolations, and, in the absence of his son, Prince Jerome Napoleon, a priest was brought in, who prayed and administered to him the last sacraments. Prince Napoleon came in just as this was over. "Do not be angry with Clotilde," said the Empress, "I sent for the *curé*." The Prince glared angrily at the women, and left the room, banging the door behind him.

Poor Princess Clotilde had two boys and a daughter. Her eldest son, Prince Victor Napoleon, is the cousin to whom the Prince Imperial left any rights he might have to the French throne. Princess Lætitia has rather scandalized Protestantism by marrying (under a dispensation) her uncle, the widowed Duke of Aosta. The Princess Clotilde escaped from Paris on the same night as the Empress Eugénie, in September, 1870, but she refused to use any subterfuges, saying: "A daughter of Savoy can know no fear." After that she lived in Italy. Every year her husband and herself met for a few weeks at some watering-place, that they might together take counsel as to the welfare of their sons.

However, to return to the war. The treaty with France having been signed shortly after the marriage, and war preparations being well advanced, it became a great object with Cavour and his King that Austria should take the first step toward a declaration of hostilities, since French assistance was only to be sent to Piedmont in case she was attacked by her powerful enemy.

There were many diplomatic negotiations to prevent the war, England being very much averse to any further disturbance of the treaties of Vienna, which gave Austria, directly or by influence, control over Italy. Cavour made a journey to Paris to see the Emperor, and to Berlin to visit the King of Prussia. On his return to Turin the people received him with an ovation. Next morning he was beginning to tell the King all about his popular triumph after nightfall, when Victor Emmanuel interrupted him. "I know all about it, my dear Count," he said. "I was in the crowd, unrecognized in the darkness, shouting till I was hoarse, *Viva Cavour!*"

On April 23, 1859, Austria cut negotiations short by sending her ultimatum to Sardinia. The little kingdom was summoned to disarm in three days, otherwise her powerful neighbor would declare war.

The King made his will, appointed his cousin Eugenio, Prince of Carignano, to be regent, told his people that Napoleon III. was his ally, and ended his proclamation with the words: "We confide in God and in our honesty of purpose. We confide in the valor of Italian soldiers, and in the alliance of the noble French nation. We confide in the justice of public opinion. I have no other ambition than to be the first soldier of Italian independence. *Viva l'Italia!*"

Before leaving Turin, the King called to him Count Nigra, and confided to him his children. "Here is my testament," he said. "If I should be killed, open it, and see that my will is executed. I will try to bar the road to Turin, but if I should not succeed, and the enemy advances, remove my family to a place of safety, and scrupulously follow my instructions. In the Gallery of Arms you will find four Austrian banners taken by our soldiers in the war of 1848, and placed there by my father. . . . If need be, abandon everything else, — valuables, jewels, archives, collections, — but save the banners. So that they and my children are safe, the rest does not matter."

Next morning a solemn service was held early in the Cathedral, the King kneeling at the altar, asking Heaven's blessing on his enterprise; then, accompanied all along his road by the cheers and acclamations of his people, he passed on to the frontier fortress of Alessandria, defended by its hundred cannon that Italian patriots had given him by subscription.

"It was fine," wrote an eye-witness, "to see him ride up the ranks of his soldiers, or in the midst of his people, as he acknowledged with dignity their enthusiastic *evvivas*, — but, finest of all, when, in the heat of battle, he flung himself with impetuous valor on the enemy."

And a French officer describes him thus, as he entered Alessandria: —

"A great noise was heard; we distinguished the tramp of horses, and cries of enthusiasm. A minute after, I saw King Victor Emmanuel. I recognized his countenance by its rugged features, such as one might see by many a humble fireside. There was that eye, ardent, yet soft, which darted a straight, bold glance over a provokingly aggressive pair of moustachios. . . . From this day forth I shall think a king on horseback in a moment of danger is a sight to make the heart beat. Lamartine once said, 'Horses are the pedestals of princes.' I shall never forget Victor Emmanuel as I first saw him on horseback, with his sabre by his side, breathing freely and joyously the warrior air of Alessandria, as an atmosphere suited to his lungs. Other memories, as well as mine, will preserve this image."

La Marmora remonstrated with the King about rushing into danger. Victor Emmanuel, in a moment of irritation, answered him rudely. But La Marmora, undeterred, got a friend who was a civilian to speak on the same subject. "Say to the gentleman in whose name you have addressed me," said the King, "that in a few days I must send to death who knows how many thousand men. I have not the courage to send *them* to meet death, if I do not act so as to let them see that the cause is such as deserves we should all meet it if need be, and that I myself am ready to do so." These words produced a most inspiriting effect upon the soldiers.

The first action of the war was very near being disastrous to the Sardinian army, and led to a fierce altercation between La Marmora and his sovereign. La Marmora's advice prevailed, however; a panic impending among the troops was stayed, and next day Victor Emmanuel wrote La Marmora an affectionate apology. Had Napoleon III. had such men about him, history might have been very different.

On the 30th of April, 1859, French troops began to arrive at Turin, and on May 13 the Emperor himself, with his Imperial Guard and the remainder of his army, landed at Genoa. The Italians warmly welcomed the French troops, and the two sovereigns conceived a sincere friendship for each other.

The plains that lay between the frontier and Turin were soon flooded, the farmers assisting the soldiers to destroy their own property with enthusiasm. But letters written from the Austrian camp assert that the Piedmontese peasantry, oppressed by the weight of taxes, showed themselves very willing to welcome the Austrian troops, provided they paid for what they took from them. No money, however, seems to have been able to procure for the Austrian commander, General Gyulai, any information. His army, on its entrance into Piedmont, was sadly in need of spies.

The inundation of the fields, assisted by rainy weather, greatly impeded the Austrian advance, and gave time for the concentration of the French troops with the Sardinians.

Volunteers from all parts of Italy, — nobles, peasants, students and professional men, flocked to the standard of the Italian king, and these were mainly put under the command of Garibaldi, who, from this time forward was truly and personally attached to the Rè Galantuomo.

His corps carried on a guerilla warfare in Northern Lombardy, in the neighborhood of the Lakes of Como and Maggiore, while a division of the French army under Prince Napoleon had been landed at Leghorn, to operate in the duchies of Parma, Modena, and Tuscany.

The first battle of the campaign was fought May 20, at Montebello between the Austrians and the Sardinians. The second took place May 31, at Palestro, and was very stoutly contested. The valor of the French Zouaves, and the daring of Victor Emmanuel, however, decided the fortunes of the day. In the thick of the fight, when victory was doubtful, Victor Emmanuel was seen galloping to the front, sword in hand, waving on French and Italians to defend an important bridge. The sight of their King inspired the Piedmontese with fresh ardor and the Zouaves, with a cry of *Vive l'Empereur!* threw themselves precipitately along with their allies upon the enemy.

" The Zouaves were lost in admiration of Victor Emmanuel's gallantry. He was the first of Zouaves, they said, for he would listen to no reason. The French standard-bearer fell at his feet struck by two balls, but he rushed on into the midst of the fire, regardless of the remonstrances of the Zouaves. It was imprudent and rash, for too much depended on his life to give him any right to risk it inconsiderately. At one moment he was in the greatest peril; from thousands of breasts rose a cry of terror; the Zouaves, the staff-officers, the Bersaglieri, all, with horror in their faces, threw themselves upon the enemy."

The day was won, and the king was safe. That night the Zouaves elected King Victor Emmanuel a corporal in their third regiment, and sent to his headquarters the cannon they had taken from the enemy. These he forwarded to the Emperor, and sent heartfelt thanks to his new comrades. Next day Napoleon said to him: " Now that you belong to my army, I have a right to reprove your imprudence. If you act again as you did yesterday I shall put you under arrest."

As Victor Emmanuel the next day walked over the battlefield, saddened by the terrible sights he saw there, he came to where a young Roman lay dying. At sight of the King his eyes brightened. "Raise my head," he said. "Let me look at him again — my hero! — my King!" Then, as the King bent over him, he whispered: "God bless you, Savior of Italy! By this blood, by the glory of your throne, by the memory of your martyred father, I conjure you to make our whole country free!" The King, with tears, renewed his vow, holding the dying soldier's hand, as he bent over him.

About four days later, on the 4th of June, was fought the battle of Magenta. The troops engaged in it were chiefly French and Austrians. It was not a brilliant victory; both armies fought well, but there were faults of generalship on both sides. The battle was fought upon the soil of Lombardy, the allied forces having crossed the boundary line, the river Ticino.

"It was in the little village of Magenta that the fight raged the hottest. There, in the narrow streets, in the gardens and inclosures, among the whitewashed, red-roofed houses, under the loopholed walls of the cemetery, Austrian and Frenchman, Jäger and Zouave, fought bayonet to bayonet, while from roofs and windows a sharp fire poured down upon the combatants below. A volume might be written on the storming of Magenta, so many were the tales told at the time of the desperate courage displayed on either side. . . . Slowly the daylight deepened into twilight, for a terrible storm had raged during the day, and a red sunset was now glowing in the west. As night fell, the Austrians drew off from the battlefield, but it was late before the last shot was fired and silence fell.

"Along the fields blazed the watch-fires of the Austrian bivouacs. Those of the French illumined with their flickering light the ground they had won. A crescent moon looked down from a clear sky. Here and there along the field flashed the lanterns of the fatigue-parties who were already collecting the wounded, — for, heaped in the villages and scattered over the fields, ten thousand Austrians and Frenchmen lay wounded, dying, or dead." [1]

The day after the battle of Magenta, the French and Sardinian troops, with their respective sovereigns, entered Milan, the capital of Lombardy. Lombardy, with an outburst of enthusiasm, implored Victor Emmanuel at once to declare himself its king.

Victor Emmanuel unfortunately had, as we have seen, an inconvenient habit of saying too much. In the proclamation in which he accepted the crown of Lombardy, he said: "The Emperor of the French, our generous ally, worthy of the name and genius of Napoleon, wishes to liberate Italy from the Alps to the Adriatic." This sentence, which was received with enthusiasm, led a few weeks later to bitter disappointment.

The Emperor Napoleon had been greatly moved by the paroxysm of enthusiasm with which he and the King of Piedmont had been received as saviors in Milan, and is said to have exclaimed: "How this people must have suffered!" He, too, took the occasion to put forth a proclamation to "the Italian people," saying: —

"Your enemies, who are also mine, have endeavored to diminish the universal sympathy felt in Europe for your cause, by causing it to be believed that I am making war for personal ambition, or to increase French territory. If there are men who fail to comprehend their epoch, I am not one of them. . . . True greatness lies in the moral influence which we exercise, not in sterile conquests. . . ." And the proclamation ended with the words: "Tomorrow you will be the citizens of a great country."

In Milan, Victor Emmanuel and Garibaldi met for the first time.

"Hitherto," says Miss Godkin, in her "Life of Victor Emmanuel," which I have freely quoted, "Garibaldi had earned a rep-

---

[1] "The Making of Italy," by the O'Clery. The author served subsequently among the Pontifical Zouaves. His book is inimical to Victor Emmanuel, and written from the point of view of the Holy See.

utation somewhat like that of the Irishman who, on landing in America, cried out: 'Is there any government in this country? — because if there is, I'm agin it!' But thenceforward, with a few intervals of distrust and disappointment, he yielded to the love and admiration he felt for Victor Emmanuel. To a king like Victor the voluntary homage of this wild republican was very pleasing, and Garibaldi was not insensible to the tone of brotherly equality with which he was met by *il Rè Galantuomo.* The king put the gold medal for military valor on the breast of the brave general, who was proud to receive it from his hands, not because he was a king, but because he was a hero and a patriot."

On June 24 took place the last battle of the war, the fight at Solferino. The Italians call it the battle of San Martino, for their part of the action was carried on, on a hill of that name. General Gyulai had been displaced, and the young Emperor Francis Joseph commanded in person, but the Austrians fought apparently without any fixed plan, and the different divisions seem to have had little idea of what was being done by the others. The most bloody part of the work was at San Martino, where the Sardinians were confronted by the division commanded by the best of the Austrian commanders, General Benedek. Piqued by a piece of impertinence on the part of Baraguay d'Hilliers, the French marshal, who was commanding at Solferino, Victor Emmanuel made incredible exertions to secure possession of the San Martino hill. "Children!" he said to his soldiers, "we *must* take San Martino, — or it will be San Martino with us!" — thus alluding to a custom which made St. Martin's day, like the 1st of May in New York, a day of general moving.

The battle ended in a frightful storm, preceded by a moving wall of yellow mist, not uncommon in that country, which the French took for the advance on their flank of a large column of Austrians. They were thrown into great confusion, and a panic began, especially among the baggage train, but the Austrians were already crossing the Mincio into Venetia, and a few more days were to end the war.

Among the Austrian dead was a lad whose musket had

never been loaded. He died whispering to the man who killed him that he was a Venetian who had been forced to serve the Austrians, but would never fire on his countrymen, and preferred to be killed by them. He died clasping the Bersagliere's hand. After the fight was over, his countrymen stripped off his white Austrian uniform, and buried him reverently with their own dead. Mrs. Browning wrote a poem on this incident, called "The forced Recruit."

It has been always believed that the frightful scenes witnessed by Louis Napoleon on this battlefield, where twenty-five thousand men were killed or wounded, largely influenced him to bring the war to a close. He was naturally tender-hearted, and all accounts describe the scene of carnage on which the sun rose the next day as most horrible.

"And," says Countess Cesaresco, "even a field of battle with its unburied dead speaks only of a small part of the miseries of a great war. Those who were at that time at Brescia, to which town the greater portion of the French wounded, and all the worst cases were brought, still shudder as they recall the dreadful human suffering which no skill or devotion could do more than a very little to assuage. The Brescian ladies turned with one accord into sisters of charity. Every house, every church, became a hospital; everything that gratitude or pity could do, was done. But many were to leave their bones in Italy, and how many more to go home maimed for life, or bearing with them the seeds of death!"

Louis Napoleon's policy was full of surprises, but no surprise was ever so great, so sudden, so unprovided against, as that which startled Europe like a thunder-clap three days later.

The Emperor had sent his confidential friend and aide-de-camp, General Fleury, to the Emperor Francis Joseph, who was then at Verona, asking for a cessation of hostilities!

It is now nearly forty years since that cry of "Hold!— Enough!" fell on the ears of the allied armies and the Austrian forces, each of which fancied itself still certain of victory. We know more now than astute diplomatists did then, and can better appreciate the Emperor's motives.

First, then, he found the war more and more unpopular in France; even victory had failed to excite any great show of enthusiasm. French tax-payers, and the fathers and mothers of peasant families, asked what was France to gain for all this expenditure of money and blood? Secondly, the next step in advance would place the French army within the Quadrilateral. The Austrians had fought splendidly during the last month; what might they not effect when assisted by stone walls? and a repulse upon such ground might bring disaster irretrievable. Thirdly, the Emperor had realized that inadequacy and incapacity reigned in every one of his departments for military supply. The deficiencies which became patent to all Europe twelve years after were becoming apparent in this earlier campaign. But his strongest motive for making an immediate peace, and not completing the fulfilment of the promise Victor Emmanuel had made in his name, — that Italy should "be free from the Alps to the Adriatic," — was at the time a diplomatic secret. It is now matter of history that Germany, always watching her opportunity to make the Rhine her boundary, had massed troops on her western frontier, and was about to attack France, in the absence of her Emperor, as the natural ally of Austria.

On the evening of the 6th of July, only seven weeks and six days after Napoleon had landed with the flower of his forces at Genoa, a rumor spread that Fleury had been sent with a message to the Emperor Francis Joseph at Verona. Victor Emmanuel knew nothing of it, nor had Louis Napoleon confided in his generals. The next day General Fleury came back with news that the Emperor of Austria accepted the armistice. He, too, had his reasons for bringing the war quickly to a close, even at the cost of Lombardy. " Further secrecy was impossible, and like lightning the news flashed through the world."

Apparently without consulting Victor Emmanuel, the two emperors met at Villafranca, and arranged the terms of the armistice. It was not a treaty, — the treaty was signed some months later, when Louis Napoleon could feel more sure of his plans.

The news of the armistice struck Cavour like a thunderbolt. He was in Turin at the time, but he hurried with all speed to headquarters, hearing on every side as he travelled alone and *incognito*, in hired vehicles, curses both loud and deep on the Emperor who had so unexpectedly deceived them, nor was Victor Emmanuel himself spared.

In 1848 Lombardy had refused to accept freedom on condition that she should give up Venetia, which, for the sake of its maritime advantages, was of great value to Austria; and now was she, in her hour of hope and triumph, to accept as a boon from the French Emperor the same terms?

In Venice itself the news was received with indignation and despair. The very morning that the armistice was signed at Villafranca, her citizens, standing upon her Campanile and on their highest towers and roofs, had watched for the coming of the French fleet which was that very day to bring them reinforcements, and to fulfil, as they believed, the promises held out to them. They saw the French ships in the offing, steaming and sailing towards them. Hope was high, when all at once there came a change of course. The ships headed suddenly on an opposite tack, and sailed or steamed away. Their commander had received counter orders. Venice and Venetia were left to fight the whole power of Austria alone.

Cavour had been wholly unprepared for the cessation of the war. For the first and only time he lost his self-command. When he reached the presence of his King, he raged and stormed with fury, declared that his sovereign ought to refuse Lombardy, and when he found that his arguments, his reproaches, and his grief availed nothing, he left the King's presence, having given in his resignation. In three days he had grown older by many years.

But the King did not despair as Cavour did. He looked forward to the future, and events justified his faith. He had done all in his power, when he heard of the terms of the armistice, to persuade his ally to carry on the war, but the Emperor was immovable. He said, indeed, in private, that "from the Alps to the Adriatic" was only to be postponed, and he made his promise good seven years after, but the disappointment in 1859 was so great that Italians have never forgiven him, and have been, I think, ungenerously and ungraciously ungrateful to his memory.

"*Povera Italia!*" exclaimed the King, when his remonstrances proved of no use; and then he added: "Whatever may be your Majesty's decision, I shall always feel grateful for what you have done for Italian independence, and you may count on me as your friend."

But Cavour, though no longer in office, could not restrain his feelings. "Your Emperor has dishonored me," he said, in Kossuth's presence, to M. Pietri, Napoleon's Chief of Police. "Yes sir, he has dishonored me!" And after painting the situation with all the irony and scorn of which he was master, he added: "If need be I will become a conspirator, a revolutionist; but the treaty proposed by your master, the creation of an Italian Confederation, shall never be executed, — a thousand times No — never!"

The preliminaries of the treaty of peace between Austria and France, had opened with the words, "The Emperor of Austria and the Emperor of the French will favor the creation of an Italian Confederation under the honorary presidency of the Holy Father." Further, it was provided that the rulers of Tuscany, Parma, and Modena should return to their duchies. It was stipulated that they were not to punish their subjects, and the Pope was to be persuaded to make some reforms as a temporal ruler.

But, although the treaty of Villafranca was to restore the Grand Duke Leopold to Tuscany, the Romagna to the Pope, and the Dukes of Parma and Modena to their dominions, it made no provision for putting them back in spite of their subjects' will, and their people utterly refused to receive them. As Prince Albert wrote: "What statesman could adopt measures to force Austrian rule again upon delighted free Italy?"

The inhabitants of these States of Central Italy had already elected Victor Emmanuel as their King, and had prayed him to accept them as his subjects. This, for diplomatic reasons, he had considered premature, but he sent them each a "Commissioner," and favored their forming provisional governments, which kept good order, — though they protested against the disposition made of them by diplomacy. During the interregnum, the only violence that occurred to mar the behavior of the people was the murder at Modena of a particularly obnoxious minister of the departed Duke.

Victor Emmanuel, though he did not accept the proffered crowns, sent a general and certain high officers to the provinces; and permitted Garibaldi to take his volunteers into Tuscany. That general by no means agreed with La Marmora and Fanti, generals bred in schools of discipline and regular warfare. He wanted to invade the States of the Church, and it seemed impossible to restrain him. But Cavour had by this time returned to his old post; he had been recalled by the King quite unexpectedly. Their bitter quarrel had never been healed; they had never met since that stormy interview in which words had been spoken hard to forget, even between equals. But Cavour knew himself to be essential to the cause of Italy. He did not suffer wounded pride to stand in the way when he might do her service. He obeyed the summons. Both King and minister acknowledged the intemperance of their speech in the late quarrel, and regretted their estrangement. At once Cavour found himself restored frankly to the old confidential footing with his sovereign. He advised the King to send for Garibaldi to Turin; where by his personal influence he might induce the fiery leader to forget the affronts offered him by other generals, and to refrain from his design of invading the Papal States, by pointing out to him why any invasion of the Pope's frontier would complicate Italian affairs, in the eyes of Europe, and render Italian independence more difficult to attain. Garibaldi gave up his scheme, but resigned the command of his volunteers, and retired for a time to his island of Caprera. Before quitting the shores of the Adriatic he made a pious pilgrimage to the chapel in the pine forest near Rimini, to which the remains of his wife Anita had been removed. He had taken another wife a few months before, during his campaign with his Alpine hunters. A young woman, daughter of the Marquis Raymondi, in a man's dress, brought him important information, and insisted on being rewarded by his hand in marriage. In vain Garibaldi protested that he wished for no wife, that his heart was with the dead mother of his children; the woman carried her point. At the very door of the church, after the ceremony, Garibaldi discovered that he had been entrapped, that she and her friends had trusted to his kind-heartedness to conceal the consequences of a shameful intrigue carried on with her by one of his officers. Garibaldi quitted her at once, and was subsequently divorced from her. He was, however, with difficulty dissuaded from adopting her child.

In August, 1859, Victor Emmanuel went privately into Lombardy. The Treaty of Peace being not yet signed at Zurich he could not enter it as its sovereign. While in Milan he wished to visit the good and great Manzoni, author of that most beautiful of Christian and historical novels, "I Promessi Sposi" ("The Betrothed"). Here is what Manzoni said of their interview: —

"I see in the King's character the hand of Providence. He is exactly the sovereign needed to accomplish the resurrection of Italy. He has rectitude, courage, incorruptible honesty, and disinterestedness. He seeks not glory or fortune for himself, but for his country. He is so simple, — never caring to appear great, — that he does not meet the admiration of those who seek to find in princes theatrical actions and grandiloquent words. He is natural because he is true; and this makes his enemies say he is wanting in royal majesty. To found Italian unity he has risked his throne and his life."

But Victor Emmanuel's troubles were far from being over. There remained the affairs of Central Italy to be settled, involving the keen displeasure of the Pope.

For some years there had been a great and happy change in some of the governments of Italy. Leopold of Tuscany had been a mild ruler; the Duchess of Parma, who governed as regent for her son, had been considerate of the welfare of her subjects; while in Lombardy and Venetia, on the retirement of Marshal Radetzky, in 1857, in his ninety-third year, the Archduke Maximilian had been appointed viceroy. I have told the unhappy story of this prince elsewhere.[1] Countess Cesaresco says of him:—

"A more naturally amiable and cultivated prince never had the evil fate forced upon him of attempting impossible tasks. Just married to the lovely Princess Charlotte of Belgium, he came to Italy radiant with happiness, and wishing to make every one as happy as he was himself. Not even the chilling welcome which he received damped his enthusiasm, for he thought the aversion of the population depended on undoubted wrongs, which it was his full intention to redress. He was to learn two things:— firstly, that the day for reconciliation was past,— there were too many ghosts between the Lombards and Venetians, and the house of Hapsburg; secondly, that an unseen hand beyond the Brenner would diligently thwart each one of his benevolent designs. The system was, and was to remain, unchanged. It was not carried out quite as it was in the first years after 1849. The exiles were allowed to return, and the sequestrations were revoked. It should be said, because it shows the one white spot in Austrian despotism,— its civic administration,— that on resuming their rights of ownership the proprietors found that their estates had not been badly managed. But the depressing and deadening influence of an anti-national rule, continued unabated. Lombardy and Venetia were governed, not from Milan, but from Vienna. Very small were the crumbs which the Viceroy obtained when he went on a journey to Austria, expressly to plead for concessions. It is sad to think what an enlightened heir to the great Austrian Empire was lost when Napoleon III. and his own family sent Maximilian of Hapsburg to his death at Queretaro."

But while ameliorations were taking place in the administration of Lombardy, Tuscany, and Parma, the rule of the Duke of Modena had been as bad as ever. So was the

---

[1] *France in the Nineteenth Century.*

Pope's temporal government in Romagna; and, as to Naples, all Europe was ringing with the words of Mr. Gladstone to Lord Aberdeen.

It is difficult to follow the geography of the States of the Church, called, after their annexation to Piedmont, together with the smaller duchies, Emilia. Romagna was the most northerly, with its five cities, Ravenna, Forli, Imola, Faenza, and Rimini. Then there were the Marches, of which the chief towns were Ancona and Perugia; and south of the Marches lay what was called the Patrimony of St. Peter.

The temporal power of the popes had been of gradual growth, having no connection with their spiritual power, whether we consider them as bishops of Rome, or heads of the Roman branch of the Catholic and Apostolic Church.

The city of Rome, until the middle of the fourteenth century, belonged to the Empire, and was only the residence of the popes. The first actual territorial possession of the pontiffs was the exarchate of Ravenna, presented to Pope Stephen III. by King Pépin, who had won it from the Lombards. The gift was confirmed by Charlemagne, who added to it two provinces, Perugia and Spoleto. The popes, having thus become temporal Italian princes, were desirous of increasing their dominions. Henry III. of Germany added another duchy to their provinces, and, A. D. 1115, Matilda, Countess of Tuscany, made them that gift since called St. Peter's Patrimony, so lamented by Dante. Still, Rome was theirs only by sufferance; their episcopal residence not their rightful possession till the middle of the fourteenth century, when it changed masters, being torn from the Emperor by a revolution. In 1532, Clement VII. gained the Marches of Ancona, and in 1626 the duchy of Urbino, which had belonged to the family of Pope Julius II., was annexed to the Holy See. The last additions to the Papal States were made about 1680. Pope Paul III. had owned two provinces, which he gave to the Duke of Parma; but one of the Duke's descendants pawned them, and, being unable to redeem his pledge, Pope Innocent XI. took possession of them in the name of the Holy See. It will thus be seen that the temporal power of the Church had no spiritual origin. At first its possessions were divided into thirteen provinces, and subsequently into what were called thirteen delegations.

The Treaty of Villafranca, which confirmed the armistice of the 8th of July, was to be submitted to a conference at Zurich. The Villafranca treaty was between the French Emperor and his ally, and Austria; no mention had been made in it of the cession of Savoy and Nice to France, — indeed, Nice had not been named between Cavour and the Emperor at Plombières. The first mention of it had been made in the last words spoken by Napoleon to Victor Emmanuel before he left Turin. "We shall think no more of Savoy *and Nice.*" His promise had been only half kept. He could not demand full payment for work left undone. But. Louis Napoleon had at heart the formation of an Austro-Italian Confederation, of which the Pope should be the honorary temporal head, while he, whose soldiers alone maintained the Pope's authority in Rome as an Italian prince, would naturally exercise a predominating influence in the Confederacy.

A congress was projected to settle the affairs of Central Italy, but it met with powerful objections from three quarters, — first, from all the people of these states, who with one voice had elected as their king Victor Emmanuel; secondly, from the Pope, who refused to give up any portion of the papal territory, and declined to have anything to do with the congress; and, thirdly, from England, Lord John Russell, then Minister for Foreign Affairs, saying: "We are asked to propose a plan for parcelling out the peoples of Italy, as if we had any right to dispose of them;" while, fourthly, Victor Emmanuel wrote to the Emperor a powerful protest against the congress, saying: "I am bound on my side by honor in the face of Europe, by right and duty, by the interests of my house, of my people, and of Italy. My fate is joined to that of the Italian people. We may succumb, but we will never betray. . . . The apostasies of princes are always irreparable. I am moved to the bottom of my soul by the faith and love which this noble and unfortunate people has reposed in me, and rather than be unworthy of it I will break my sword, and, like my august father, throw my crown away. Personal interest does not guide me in defending the annexations. The sword and the progress of events have borne my house from the summit of the Alps to the banks of the Mincio, and those two guardian angels of the Savoy race will bear it further still, — if it please God."

Alas! the price exacted for the realization of these hopes, was the renunciation of the cradle of his race, and of Nice, which, as some one has said of it, "lets France within Italy's front door."

The Pope, who, as G. S. Godkin says, "refuted — if ever monarch did — Macaulay's saying that 'no one can be a good man, and a bad king,'" held long correspondence with Victor Emmanuel on the subject of what adherents to the Pope's claim to temporal power called his " robberies " in the legations. He ended by excommunicating the King, his officers, and any of his subjects who had concurred in the scheme of annexing to Piedmont any portion of the Papal States.

In this there is no question that Pio Nono was acting according to his conscience, and his language was dignified and temperate. All his letters, even after his bull of excommunication, ended with promises to pray for his erring son, which, no doubt, he faithfully did. But his consecration oath bound him, as he believed, to transmit intact the Papal States to his successor.

Nothing, however, could repress the course of events, and Victor Emmanuel became King of Northern Italy, including Piedmont, Tuscany, the duchies, and the legations, — Naples remaining under its new sovereign, Francis II., son of the lately deceased King Bomba, while the Pope, under the protection of the French, retained Rome, and a small portion of his territory.

Then came the bitter moment for Victor Emmanuel when he had to give up Savoy and Nice to France. Savoy was French in language, and had always looked to Paris rather than Turin as its metropolitan city, but Nice was Italian to the backbone. The King made the renunciation of Savoy with earnest exhortations to his dear ancestral people to be good subjects to their new ruler, but the pang was great.

When, for the first time, Victor Emmanuel spoke to the representatives of the new portions of his widened realm, it was the day after he had received news of his excommunication. He said to them : —

"True to the creed of my fathers, and, like them, constant in my homage to the Supreme Head of the Church, whenever it happens that the ecclesiastical authority employs spiritual arms in support of temporal interests, I shall find in my steadfast conscience and in the very traditions of my ancestors the power to maintain civil liberty in its integrity and my own authority; for which I hold myself accountable to God alone, and to my people. . . . Our country becomes henceforth the Italy of the Italians."

In April, 1860, Victor Emmanuel and Cavour set out on a journey through the King's new dominions. Such joy as was everywhere displayed was unprecedented. "What are you clapping so frantically for?" asked a foreigner of a young lad in Florence, who seemed out of his senses at the sight of the King. "We are eleven millions of Italians!" was the answer. All the men of letters in Italy contributed to Victor Emmanuel's triumph, — "and yet I am nothing but a soldier," he repeatedly said.

GIUSEPPE GARIBALDI.

CHAPTER XI.

GARIBALDI.

TO effect the union of eleven millions of Italians into one Kingdom of Northern Italy had cost terrible sacrifices. The Emperor Napoleon, who had begun his schemes for interference in the affairs of Italy with a project for establishing French influence in the peninsula, in place of that of Austria, had at first planned to place a Murat on the throne of the two Sicilies, and Prince Jerome Napoleon on that of Tuscany (the Napoleonic kingdom of Etruria), while he himself maintained an army of occupation in Rome. Events had not moved exactly as he wished, and he perceived that if he hoped to establish French influence in Southern Italy he would have to give up the duchies (Tuscany, Parma, Lucca, and Modena) and the northern legations. It would, he found, be impossible to stem the current of popular feeling in these provinces, which had been wisely governed *ad interim* by friends or agents of Victor Emmanuel. These States had all sent deputations to the King of Piedmont, imploring annexation to his kingdom. He had not granted their request, but had advised the formation of temporary provisional governments, while he sent agents or commissioners into each of these States. The Emperor Napoleon had seen one of these deputations, and had dismissed it with assurances of his support; but after the Peace of Villafranca, which provided that these duchies and legations should return to their former rulers, but made no provision for placing them there, the Emperor changed his attitude to Victor Emmanuel. He consented not to oppose the will of the people, which he could only have done by pouring French troops into the Roman States; but he demanded, as the price of acquiescence in the popular will, a renewal of the agreement that the King of Northern Italy would cede to France, Nice and Savoy. At Plombières Cavour had agreed to give up Savoy. He had not stipulated to surrender Nice; and when Louis Napoleon had to stop short in what seemed a career of victory after Solferino, he had said at parting, "We will talk no more of Savoy and Nice." But early in 1860 he proposed to make a new bargain. If he allowed Victor Emmanuel to add six splendid provinces to his kingdom on the south, he must have in exchange the rocks of Savoy and the harbor of Nice.

Words cannot express the indignation of Garibaldi when this arrangement was made known to him. He was born at Nice, though his boyhood was spent in Genoa. Never would he forgive those who by the cession of his birthplace "made him a foreigner!" He hurried to Turin, and had an interview with the King, who said to him sadly that his own sacrifice of Savoy, the cradle of his race, was greater than his sacrifice of his birthplace, — that they must both be willing to give up what was dear to them for the sake of Italy.

But Garibaldi was not to be restrained. He believed himself to be animated by righteous wrath, and to the day of his death exhausted his vocabulary of vituperation on what he called "the low intrigues of Cavour," and of "his cowardly tail," who had sold themselves into the hands of "that vulpine knave," Napoleon.

It had been stipulated that according to the Napoleonic policy, a *plébiscite* should be held in Savoy and Nice to certify the willingness of the population of those countries to be united to France. We know well enough now the hollow sham of a *plébiscite* as conducted under a French administration. Before, however, the *plébiscite* in Nice could be taken, Garibaldi was elected deputy from Nice to the Parliament at Turin, the first held in Victor Emmanuel's enlarged dominions.

In that Chamber, soon after its opening, April 6, 1860, Garibaldi rose to do battle for his birthplace. He had no knowledge of parliamentary rules, and was little of an orator, but he denounced the Treaty which ceded Savoy and Nice to France, as a violation of the Constitution, — at least that was what he intended to say, it was the strong point in his case, but he soon wandered from it into invective and abuse of diplomacy.

Cavour replied that the true ground for the treaty was that its provisions formed a portion of the integral policy of the government. It was the logical and inevitable consequence of a past policy, and an absolute necessity for the carrying out of this policy in the future.

When a vote was taken, Cavour had a majority of one hundred and ninety-six, and Garibaldi at once proceeded to act upon a plan which in Nice at least should prevent any count of a *plébiscite* from being taken, till he had sent political missionaries and agents all through the little State to stir up hostility to annexation.

There are few more charming books of stirring experiences by flood and field than Lawrence Oliphant's "Scenes in a Life of Adventure," first published in Blackwood's Magazine as "Moss from a Rolling Stone," and one of its chapters relates how he was in Turin in April, 1860, — how he was introduced to Garibaldi and a number of other Nizzards (*i. e.*, men of Nice), and how, with his love of adventure, he was more than ready to take a hand in the game. When Garibaldi's motion in the Parliament had failed, it occurred to him that if he and a party of his friends could seize and destroy the ballot-boxes before the count, another *plébiscite* would have to be held, thus gaining time to work upon the peasantry. So, with Oliphant for company, he went from Turin to Genoa. All the way he was very silent, reading and destroying an immense quantity of letters. At Genoa they were to be met by about two hundred men, old members of the Legion told off to take part in the plan. The first thing to be done was that Oliphant (while Garibaldi met his followers) should go to the diligence office, and secure a whole diligence for Nice. His account is very amusing, of how he failed to persuade the office clerk that he and his friend, a rich Englishman, travelling with no luggage but a portmanteau apiece, wanted to pay for sixteen places for the satisfaction of being able to change from one seat to another. However, failure to secure a whole diligence proved not of any consequence, for, on joining Garibaldi, he found all his plans had been changed. Nice was given up. The two hundred gentlemen assembled at Genoa were all from Sicily. "I find," said Garibaldi, " that if we are to relieve their country from the oppression of Bomba, we must go at once. I had hoped to be able to carry out this little Nice affair first, for it is only a matter of a few days; but, much as I regret it, the general opinion is that we shall lose all if we try for too much, *and, fond as I am of my native province, I cannot sacrifice the greater hopes of Italy to it.*"

It probably did not strike the General that the words I have put in italics would have come equally well from the lips of Victor Emmanuel or Cavour.

So Nice and its *plébiscite* were left to their fate, and thus was begun the first act of the Sicilian campaign.

Lawrence Oliphant, to the end of his life, regretted that he did not accept Garibaldi's invitation to take part in the affray. As it was, the eight hundred who embarked for Sicily were all Italians, though they were joined afterwards by volunteers from many nations.

The expedition to Sicily had, indeed, been planned during the summer of 1859, as early as the days of Villafranca. The most active and trusted agent of Mazzini in the island was Francesco Crispi, well known to all of us in 1896 as Italy's long distinguished Prime Minister. He travelled in all parts of Sicily, and sent in reports to Mazzini that the island was prepared to welcome a republic. But Mazzini curbed his zeal, and told him only to aim at Italian unity.

Meantime Rosalino Pilo, a Sicilian of a noble house, and on his mother's side descended from the royal house of Anjou, had organized the first steps toward revolution.

He and Mazzini had held communication with the angry lion at Caprera. They had stored arms in the convent of La Gancia, near Palermo; the conspiracy was discovered, the convent attacked, and all the monks would have been slaughtered had not one of them pointed out to his comrades a secret issue from the chapel.

Rosalino Pilo, arriving in Sicily just after this event, found only a few armed bands of conspirators roving in the mountains. These he concentrated, and he sent back letters to Garibaldi which convinced him that the right time had come for the enterprise which had been already prepared for. We have seen how embarkation was undertaken, on the spur of the moment, by the General, who found things in readiness when he arrived at Genoa.

An officer of the Red Shirts, high in the confidence of Garibaldi, and employed by him when any enterprise demanded especial daring, — and, it might be added, exceptional severity, — was Nino Bixio. He, like Garibaldi, had been a sailor, — indeed he had served as a seaman in the Sardinian navy, which he had been forced to enter by his family, who professed themselves unable to control him. When, in 1847, Charles Albert, on the eve of his declaration of war, was entering Genoa, it was Bixio who stopped the royal carriage, and thundered out: "Sire, cross the Ticino, and we will all be with you!" A year earlier, when deserting with three others from an American merchant ship on the coast of Sumatra, he fell into the hands of the savages of the island, and, but for the humanity of the Quaker captain, who reclaimed his runaways with risk to himself and his ship, it might have gone hard with the young rascals.

When Bixio, in March 1848, heard of the rising at Milan, he started to play a part in it. There the young poet Goffredo Mameli took him in hand, and he joined the volunteers, but when the war came to a close he refused to be disbanded. It was then that he was first brought into close personal relations with Garibaldi. He served with distinction against the French at Rome, where he was badly wounded and his poet friend was killed. Next we find him in command of a fine clipper, which he named the Goffredo Mameli, starting from Genoa on a voyage to Australia.

He served in the war of 1859, contemptuously approving the French alliance, and quoting Dante's saying: "We must create Italy,—even were it by help of the devil!" (*Facciam l'Italia, anche col diavolo!*)

When Garibaldi had resolved to start on his Sicilian expedition it was to Bixio that he intrusted the task of embarking his volunteers, the celebrated Thousand, who were waiting in small parties all along the coast, though the chief part had assembled at Genoa. The arms and ammunition for the enterprise had been got on board an old hulk which was lying in the harbor between two passenger-steamers. By the tacit consent of their owner, these steamers (subsequently paid for) were selected to transport the filibusters. At dusk on May 4, 1860, forty men, the flower of the Garibaldian expedition, stepped on board the hulk, where Bixio assumed command as naval captain and lieutenant-colonel. The arms and ammunition were transferred to the steamers, and by early dawn they were under way for a small port where Garibaldi was waiting for them with a large party of his Thousand.

After some hours of anxious suspense, which Garibaldi in his book, "I Mille," has graphically described, the "Piedmont" and the "Lombard" hove in sight, and the embarkation was accomplished in two hours. Bixio commanded the "Piedmont," Garibaldi the "Lombard." The latter was the faster sailer, and soon in the darkness the "Piedmont" lost sight of her. Suddenly through the gloom a black mass was seen right in her course. Bixio at once resolved to run down the strange vessel. His volunteers seized their arms with cries of "Board her! Board her!" The ships were on the point of a collision, when a voice hailed from the steamer which was lying to. "Captain Bixio!" It was the voice of Garibaldi. "What are you about there? Do you want to send us to the bottom?" "General, I saw no signals." "Eh! Signals? don't you see we are within the enemy's lines? Make for Marsala."

It is marvellous that they were not discovered by the Neapolitan fleet, but the proximity of an English squadron is thought to have paralyzed the Neapolitan commander. The ships reached Marsala, a small port on the west coast of Sicily, and landed their thousand Red Shirts in safety.

At once Garibaldi marched his men to Calatafimi, where the Neapolitan army was intrenched in a very strong position. The "Thousand" was really eight hundred, together with a few bands (*squadri*) of Sicilian insurgents, called *picciotti*, who had joined him. These men proved fierce fighters, but they were also fierce with all the cruelty of savages. The fighting at Calatafimi was desperate. Garibaldi's men carried position after position with the bayonet. But at last even Bixio despaired, and whispered to his chief: "I fear we must retreat." "Never say that, Bixio," was the answer, "Here we die." With this he cried to his men:

"Five minutes' rest! Five minutes' rest! — and then we charge!" With loud cries they dashed up the mountain, and in a quarter of an hour Calatafimi, Garibaldi's most important battle, was won.

It was a great assistance to Garibaldi that the Sicilian priests were nearly all upon his side. His own chaplain, Father Pantaleone, by what Mr. Bent calls a "spiritual *coup de main*," professed to relieve his general from the ill effects of the Pope's bull of excommunication. This had a most happy effect on the minds of the Sicilians.

Garibaldi's next move was to take Palermo. He got into the town without a battle by a piece of masterly generalship, but once there he found hard street-fighting, ending however by the Neapolitan garrison retreating to the palace and the citadel.

Palermo went mad with gaiety; every scrap of a red fabric, whatever its material, was brought forth on the occasion. But rejoicing was soon turned into terror. The Neapolitan ships and the soldiers in the citadel bombarded the town. The English admiral, who with his squadron was in the harbor, wrote to his government: —

"A whole district, one thousand English yards in length, by one hundred wide, is in ashes. Families have been burned alive, with the buildings, while the atrocities of the royal troops have been frightful. In other parts, churches, convents, and isolated buildings have been crushed by the shells, eleven hundred of which were thrown into the city from the citadel. . . . The conduct of General Garibaldi, both during the hostilities and since their suspension, has been noble and generous."

Ten days later, the Neapolitan soldiers, who had surrendered, embarked on transports for the mainland, apparently in high spirits, notwithstanding their defeat, for the greater part were foreign mercenaries, and they carried with them considerable booty.

Every inhabitant of Palermo that same day set to work with spade and pickaxe to destroy the citadel. In such a population liberty meant license, and Garibaldi and Bixio had to make sundry severe examples before they could establish any authority.

Just then arrived an agent of Cavour from Piedmont. He came to take measures for promoting the immediate annexation of Sicily to the kingdom of Sardinia. This, too, was urged by Admiral Persano. But on this point Cavour and Garibaldi disagreed. The general had set his heart on presenting his conquests to his King, Victor Emmanuel, when Italy should be complete. There remained Naples, Venetia, and, above all, Rome to make it so. He did not wish to offer his great gift piecemeal. He therefore got rid of Cavour's agent, and proceeded to carry out his own plans. Meantime money and recruits reached him at Palermo. He won the hearts of the inhabitants. Even his piety increased his popularity, as he knelt among the crowd on the bare pavement of the cathedral, when thanks in a solemn mass were returned to God for his success. The desire of the better class of inhabitants of Palermo was for speedy annexation to Piedmont, that law and order might be restored and commerce and prosperity be re-established. Garibaldi had to explain to them that "he had come to fight for Italy — not alone for Sicily, and that until Italy should be entirely united and free, nothing could be done for individual parts of it."

The moneyed classes, however, in Sicily are said to have been for the most part apathetic in this struggle. Mobs in the cities cheered themselves hoarse on every occasion; the peasantry, already semi-brigands, joined the *picciotti;* and the clergy, curiously enough, did all they could to assist the insurrection.

By June, 1860, Garibaldi reigned as Dictator over all Sicily, except the citadel of Messina. He appointed a ministry, at the head of which was Signor Crispi; he also appointed as his substitute, or pro-Dictator, Signor Dupretis; but after the departure of the Red Shirts for the mainland, the task of bringing order out of anarchy in Sicily proved too hard for these subordinates.

Garibaldi fought another important battle at Milazzo before obtaining possession of the city of Messina. Early in July, when at the height of his fame and prestige, he suddenly disappeared for two weeks, he had gone no one knew whither. It was, however, to Sardinia, where a large force had been assembled under directions from Mazzini, ready to co-operate with the Red Shirts in an attack on Rome. Garibaldi, however, succeeded in persuading these men to join his own forces in Sicily. He had received intelligence from Cavour that if any invasion of the Pontifical States was made by this body of soldiers, they would have to fight not only the Pope's army, now under command of the French general Lamoricière, but the French army of occupation and the Piedmontese.

Garibaldi returned with these recruits to Messina, and at once organized his forces for an invasion of the Neapolitan kingdom. He took with him about four thousand men. Three thousand were his own Red Shirts, while Bixio's brigade consisted of one thousand volunteers brought from Sardinia, and seven hundred others. One of Garibaldi's chief officers was General Cosenz, whom we have before heard of in the siege of Venice. He was a Sicilian.

The aspiration of Sicily was, not for *Italian* unity, but for autonomy and separation from the kingdom of Naples. For centuries there had been bitter hatred between Sicilians and Neapolitans; and the feeling even now, at the close of the century, has not died away.

Garibaldi had by this time purchased a little fleet; two of his steamers, the "Franklin" and the "Torino" were anchored off Taormina, and there he and his men embarked, — four thousand volunteers, to encounter eighty thousand disciplined troops, that being the estimated strength of the King of Naples's army. "But," says Mr. Bent, "the soldiers were desperately afraid of Garibaldi's guerilla style of warfare, so new to them, and a sort of mysterious horror pervaded those who were not over-enthusiastic for the cause in which they were to fight."

Garibaldi's troops, — no longer called the Thousand, but the Army of the South, were landed at Melito, almost the extreme southwest point of the Italian peninsula. Leaving them upon the mainland, we will pause to say a few words concerning the situation from Cavour's point of view, of policy and diplomacy.

The great statesman's design was to be successful. He secured Italian unity. He baffled all those who would have defeated his plans, but the story of his triumph is not a pleasant chapter in Italian history. Our judgment goes with Cavour, our sympathies with the men against whom he intrigued; and while we cannot approve of them, we feel that the very policy of Cavour owes to them success and gratitude. As the Countess Cesaresco has said truly, "the Italian kingdom is the fruit of the alliance between the strong monarchical principles of Piedmont, and the dissolvent forces of the revolution."

Cavour had just succeeded in establishing his sovereign as King of Northern Italy, and in having him acknowledged such by the Great Powers. He had frustrated the French Emperor's scheme for establishing a kingdom of Etruria, at the cost of two provinces dear to the hearts of himself and his sovereign, and when the prospect opened before him of a war on the southern frontier of the new kingdom, war between Giuseppe Garibaldi, Francis II. of Naples, the French, and the newly raised army of the Pope, composed chiefly of Irishmen and Austrians, how should he act? Undirected by himself, such a struggle would throw Italy into anarchy and confusion, and if he and his sovereign assumed its direction, every court in Europe which had just entered into friendly relations with Victor Emmanuel would unite against him. The enterprise of Garibaldi in Sicily and his designs on the Pontifical States and on the Roman capital were believed in all the courts of Europe to be connected with the spread of the ideas of Mazzini. "In short, Victor Emmanuel and his government were pledged to the national cause, and they did not mean to stultify themselves by taking part with the enemies of that cause, even if they were Red Shirts and Garibaldians."

It was true that Garibaldi's war-cry was "L'Italia e Vittorio Emmanuele," but Garibaldi was a man easily influenced and persuaded. His programme was to conquer Sicily; then Naples; and then to march on Rome. This would upset all Cavour's carefully laid schemes of diplomacy.

He dared not oppose Garibaldi, a subject who, in popular estimation, was a man even greater than his sovereign, — he dared not openly countenance him. Yet the cause for which Garibaldi was to risk his fame and life was the cause for which he was quite as willing to imperil his own. But, as his King had said, "a man may risk his own life, but not the cause of Italy." Cavour, therefore, adopted an underhand policy. He would not oppose Garibaldi's expedition, he would even covertly assist it, — as he did by his orders to Admiral Persano; he would suffer him to conquer Sicily, and to land upon the shores of Calabria; there he trusted he might fall into a trap and his revolutionary rising be defeated. His King should then take possession of Sicily, and gain Naples, Rome, and Venetia at some future time, probably through diplomacy.

This offers the only comprehensible explanation of the

position of Cavour. He certainly encouraged Garibaldi's expedition into Sicily. He certainly never intended that his invasion of Naples should succeed; nor that he should draw down on the newly made kingdom of Northern Italy the wrath of all Catholic Europe by revolutionizing Rome.

Cavour said openly in Parliament that the kingdom of Italy would never be complete until its capital was the Eternal City; but the question involved so much delicate European diplomacy, complicated as it was by the French occupation of Rome, that Cavour and Victor Emmanuel were anxious to postpone the Roman question till Italy could recover Venetia. But Garibaldi was impatient of diplomacy, and the Roman people (especially those in the papal provinces since Piedmont had annexed Romagna) were impatient of the yoke. The whole scheme of United Italy might be put, by Garibaldi's expedition, into peril. In vain Victor Emmanuel issued proclamations against Garibaldi, and wrote him private letters, commanding him to stop. Garibaldi believed in the sword, and not in diplomacy. Victor Emmanuel had only the choice left him of putting down Garibaldi by force of arms, or assuming the direction of affairs in Southern Italy.

Garibaldi's campaign in the kingdom of Naples was a mere military promenade. Except at Reggio, he met with no resistance till his forces had made their way to the Volturno.

Bodies of Neapolitan troops, composed of several thousand men, surrendered or dispersed at the first sight of the Garibaldians. On one occasion seven thousand infantry, cavalry, and artillery yielded on being summoned by one English officer, who told them that the Garibaldians were near at hand.

There is an amusing anecdote told of Colonel Peard, a Cornish gentleman among the Red Shirts. Garibaldi had volunteers of all nations under him, — among them an English legion. His army had increased to about fifteen thousand men. The only point at which Garibaldi feared resistance was Salerno, where thirty thousand Neapolitans were massed around the town in positions of great strength.

Before the advanced guard of Garibaldi's army approached Salerno, Colonel Peard, riding forward with a few followers, reached the town of Eboli. Peard's features were not like those of Garibaldi, nevertheless he was very often taken for him, and on this occasion the terrified townsfolk of Eboli believed that they beheld the "conquering hero." Peard readily assumed the part, and, with Commander Forbes as his aide-de-camp, accepted all kinds of honors.

"Like wildfire spread the news. The whole population besieged the house of the Syndic, who had received the spurious general, brass bands sounded, Chinese lanterns were hung out; the Church, led by the bishop, hurried to the spot; the Law, with a judge at its head, closely followed; while the wives of the officials, gaily dressed, craved audience. . . . But all were assured by Captain Forbes that General Garibaldi was much fatigued and fast asleep, — as in truth he was, ninety miles away, — but that he would receive them the next morning. Meantime, Peard was in an inner room, where he had sent for the telegraph operator, and was sending off messages to Naples. The chief of these was to General Ulloa, who had just been made the Minister of War of King Francis. It was signed as if it came from one of his known personal friends at Eboli, and ran thus: 'Eboli, 11.30 P. M. Garibaldi has arrived with five thousand of his own men; and five thousand Calabrese are momentarily expected. Disembarkations are expected in the Bay of Naples and the Gulf of Salerno to-night. I strongly advise your withdrawing the garrison from the latter place without delay, or they will be cut off.' The message was hardly sent, when a real despatch came from the War Minister, asking the telegraph clerk at Eboli if news had been received from a division of the King's army under Caldarelli? To this Peard made answer that General Caldarelli and his division had gone over to Garibaldi yesterday and now formed part of his army. Similar information was sent to General Scotti at Salerno. Finally the Syndic of Salerno was asked if he had seen anything of the Garibaldian expeditions by sea.

"Satisfied with this work, Colonel Peard, who knew that there were Neapolitan troops within four miles of Eboli, and who did not think that things looked entirely reassuring, decided to beat a somewhat precipitate retreat. He told the Syndic of Eboli that he was going to reconnoitre in the direction of Salerno, and that his departure must be kept a dead secret, but as soon as he was out of town, he turned the horses' heads backward toward the Garibaldian lines. He was still accompanied by Captain Forbes, to whom, during their midnight ride, he related his performance on the telegraph wires. 'What on earth was the good of all that?' said Forbes. 'You don't imagine they will be fools enough to believe it?' 'You will see,' answered the Colonel. 'It will frighten them to death. And to-morrow they will evacuate Salerno.' And in fact at four o'clock in the morning the evacuation was begun, in obedience to telegraphic orders from Naples."

Then the King, Queen, and the Austrian, Prussian, Bavarian, and Spanish ambassadors left Naples for the strong fortress of Gaeta, on board a Spanish man-of-war, the King leaving behind him a proclamation to his subjects which would have been touching from a sort of simple eloquence had it not been for the memories of a hundred and fifty years. It was not, however, written by himself, but by his prime minister, Liborio Romano, who had just sent a telegram to the supposed Garibaldi at Eboli, invoking in Naples "the most desired presence" of the Dictator. With this document in his hand, Peard met the General, who received him (having already got news of his exploit) with a cheer and *Evviva Garibaldi!*

The invading army had only to walk into Salerno, and next morning at half-past nine, Garibaldi, with thirteen officers of his staff, took the regular morning train for Naples. It took them some hours to get there, however, the crowds of enthusiastic peasantry were so great along the road.

In Naples the population went mad with excitement, but cheers in Southern Europe seem to count for little.

Meantime, in Turin great fears were entertained that the freeing of the Two Sicilies would drift into a republican movement. Garibaldi's Secretary of State was Dr. Bertani, a pronounced friend and agent of Mazzini. Garibaldi had refused to give up Sicily to the King's government, as he now refused to give up Naples; and he declared without the least concealment that he intended to proclaim Victor Emmanuel King of Italy in Rome itself.

When affairs had reached this stage, Cavour decided that

it would be best for Victor Emmanuel to carry his army across his own frontier into Umbria and the Marches of Ancona, which still belonged to the Pope. The Pope had a little army of his own — five thousand men — drawn from France, Ireland, and Belgium. Their commander, General Lamoricière, had been one of the African generals, arrested by de Morny during Louis Napoleon's *coup d'État*, and imprisoned at Ham, where he contracted rheumatism which lasted him his life.

Before commencing hostilities, Victor Emmanuel proposed to Pio Nono that he should assume the administration of the papal provinces, leaving to the Pope their nominal sovereignty, and the control of Rome. This proposition was received with scorn; then thirty-five thousand men, under General Fanti (a soldier of the old school, particularly disliked by Garibaldi) crossed over the frontier, as was said, to re-establish order. The present Pope, Leo XIII., then Bishop of Perugia, did all he could to quell anarchy and prevent bloodshed.

The Sardinians and the papal troops met at Castelfidardo. The latter sincerely believed that a miracle would be wrought to save what they held to be the cause of God and the Holy Father. "In the battle the French fought with the gallantry of the Vendeans, whose descendants for the most part they were, and the Irish behaved as Irishmen will always do under fire, but the Swiss and the Romans mostly fought ill, or not at all. . . . The former had for some years served the Pope, and the latter, being Italians, and above all being Romans, were not sustained by one scrap of the mystical enthusiasm that animated the men from Brittany." Many of the French officers were killed, and Lamoricière lamented truly that much of the best blood of France had been spilled on that lost field.

The campaign had lasted eighteen days. The Piedmontese fleet, under Admiral Persano, came round from Naples to Ancona, to co-operate with Victor Emmanuel's land forces, which, holding Umbria and the Marches, left the way open for a march on Naples.

Meantime, news reached the King that Mazzini was with Garibaldi, and it caused great uneasiness at Turin. Garibaldi, indeed, though refusing to deny Mazzini permission to remain in Naples, had suffered him to be informed privately that it was his wish that he would go. "How could I have insisted on sending Mazzini into exile, when he had done so much for Italian unity?" he said afterwards to Victor Emmanuel. And the King owned that he was right.

The English government at this time tried its influence with Garibaldi, through his friend Admiral Mundy, who commanded the British squadron off Naples. But Garibaldi stood firm to his opinion that Rome was an Italian city, and that no emperor or any one else, had a right to keep him out of it. "He was," said Mundy, "not to be swayed by any dictates of prudence."

Meantime, the troops of King Francis were drawn up on the right bank of the Volturno in a long line of many miles, and the soldiers of Garibaldi on the other bank were facing them. At first, victory seemed assured to the Neapolitans, but the Garibaldians fought splendidly, and at the end of ten hours their chief was able to telegraph to Naples, "Victory all along the line!"

There then remained only the fortresses of Capua and Gaeta to be taken. All the rest of the kingdom of the Two Sicilies had submitted to the Dictator. But Garibaldi now knew that he must give up his favorite dream of proclaiming Victor Emmanuel King of Italy within the walls of Rome.

In October, 1860, Victor Emmanuel set out for Naples, through the newly won provinces that connected his northern kingdom with Southern Italy. He visited the sick in the hospitals, who had been wounded at Castelfidardo, and spoke words of kindness to his own soldiers, and to those who had fought them as enemies; only one man refused him gratitude, a Belgian, who drew his coverings over his face, that he might not even see "the robber king."

Victor Emmanuel also visited the Holy House of Loretto, which is near the battlefield; and, like a pious Catholic, he there performed his devotions. He was determined on a *plébiscite* in his new provinces, saying to those around him, "Italy must be made by us, or it runs the risk of being unmade forever. Garibaldi is a hero, but he does not know how to combat the difficulties of the situation. We alone can meet them."

He made the whole journey on horseback, starting at daybreak every morning after a cup of coffee and a roll, and riding on till evening, when he dined at some country house.

"One bright morning, as he was starting on his day's march, he saw a body of horsemen drawing near. They proved to be the Red Shirts, with their leader in their midst, come to lay down his dictatorship at the feet of his constitutional sovereign. The two leaders rode rapidly forward, and when near enough to salute, Garibaldi reined up his horse, and in a voice of much emotion, said simply: 'King of Italy!' Victor Emmanuel answered as simply, 'Thank you,' and the two clasped hands. They remained silent a few moments, then the Sardinians and the Garibaldians rent the air with their cries, *Viva Vittorio, Rè d'Italia! Viva Garibaldi! Viva l'Italia!* "

This was the proudest moment of Garibaldi's life. He had laid aside all feelings of personal ambition. He had given a kingdom to his sovereign, or rather to one who was no longer his sovereign, for was he not a native of Nice? He had done his duty for love of Italy, — and "nothing for reward," and he asked for but one recompense, favor to be shown to his devoted followers, his Red Shirts and his Calabrese. This was denied him; even in this first interview a cruel note was struck, when he asked that, in the impending battle on the river Garigliano, his volunteers might have the honor of fighting in the first line, — and the King answered, "Your troops are tired; mine are fresh. It is my turn now." Garibaldi said sadly to an English friend that evening, "They have sent us to the rear." Did he remember what Mazzini had told him, — "If you are not on your way to Rome or Venice before three weeks are over, your initiative will be at an end"?

Garibaldi's last act was to issue a proclamation to the citizens of Naples : —

"Tomorrow Victor Emmanuel, the elect of the nation, will break down the frontier that has divided us for so many centuries from the rest of the country, and, listening to the unanimous voice of this brave people, will appear among us. Let us worthily receive him who is sent by Providence, and scatter in his path, as the pledge of our redemption and our affection, the flowers of concord, — to him so grateful, to us so necessary. Let there be no more political colors, no more parties, no more discords. Italy one (as the metropolis has wisely declared she should be), under the King Galantuomo, who is the symbol of our regeneration and the prosperity of our country.

"GARIBALDI."

The King, with Garibaldi at his side, made a triumphal entry into Naples, but as the sovereign had kept the population waiting several hours for his appearance, their patience and enthusiasm were a good deal worn out, and what they had was bestowed more on their own hero than on Victor Emmanuel, who to the multitude was far less an Italian than a foreigner.

It is said that Garibaldi, who may not unreasonably have imagined himself entitled to name any boon he wished in requital of his services, asked that Cavour should be dismissed, and that the King would march on to Rome. But Victor Emmanuel answered peremptorily: "I will not dismiss Cavour, and I will not march on Rome." Nor did he review the volunteers, the Army of the South, as he had promised, nor incorporate them into his regulars, though some of their officers received rank in his army. Garibaldi's troops were really an undisciplined horde, who, except on the Volturno, had hardly seen regular warfare, and there the brunt of the engagement had fallen upon Bixio's command, which included the remnant of the Thousand and many foreigners. No wonder that Fanti and La Marmora were not disposed to run the risk of disorganizing their Northern army by incorporating into it such an element of disorder. But surely, had Cavour been with his master at Naples at that moment, something diplomatic, if not gracious, might have been done.

As it was, Garibaldi, with admirable self-control in all his words and acts, but with bitterness in his heart, left the kingdom he had conquered, and over which at one word he could have reigned, to the guidance of men whom he distrusted; and on November 9, 1861, having had to borrow twenty pounds to pay his debts in Naples, and with little more than three scudi in his pocket, he embarked on board an American packet ship, — the " Washington," for Caprera.

As he passed out of the Bay of Naples he went on board Admiral Mundy's flag-ship, the " Hannibal," to take leave of his friend. "He was sadly out of spirits," says the Admiral, who replied to an invitation given him to pay a visit to Caprera: "I shall be on this station for the next eighteen months. By that time you will be away from Caprera." "Yes," rejoined the General, with a bright smile, "before five months I shall be again in the field." "Advice to him was fruitless," adds the Admiral. "He was bent on the mad project of his life. Rome, and nothing but Rome, would satisfy his aspirations."

The internal affairs of the Two Sicilies, when Garibaldi turned them over to their new administrators, were in frightful confusion. Garibaldi was no organizer. He could not even rule his family with ordinary prudence and discretion. He was a patriot soldier. He was fond of quoting a Spanish proverb to the effect that "A man is a true man only in war." He was a man of the sixteenth century interjected into the nineteenth. There was sixteenth century work still to be done in our own day; it was his task to do it, and he fulfilled it nobly; but when he came in contact with the nineteenth century it "broke his head." He could not understand its methods, — he could not act with its men.

It was just before Garibaldi's retirement, when he had openly announced his hostility to Cavour, that Cavour, in a private letter, thus wrote of the situation: —

"To construct Italy at the present moment it is needful not to set Victor Emmanuel and Garibaldi in opposition. Garibaldi has an immense moral power. He exercises an immense prestige, not only in Italy, but above all in Europe. If to-morrow I entered into a struggle with Garibaldi, it is probable I should have with me the majority of old diplomatists, but European public opinion would be against me. And public opinion would have the right on its side, for Garibaldi has rendered to Italy the greatest services that a man could render her. He has given Italians confidence in themselves. He has proved to Europe that Italians know how to fight and die on a field of battle to regain a fatherland."

In vain the King offered Garibaldi a dukedom, and the collar of the order of SS. Annunciata, which would have given him rank in Italy equal to that of princes of the blood. He might have known beforehand such honors would be rejected. A few months later he sent General Türr to Caprera to present to Theresita, Garibaldi's daughter, a magnificent diamond necklace as a wedding present. Theresita's husband, Captain Canzio, before long had disposed of the valuable stones.

Meantime, the war ended in Italy. The Neapolitans, under the eye of their young king, had at last fought bravely, but Capua was taken, and then Gaeta. Owing to British intervention, the French fleet withdrew its protection from Francis II., who took refuge in Rome. The first act of the conquerors of the half-ruined town of Gaeta, which they had bombarded, was to attend mass for the repose of the souls of the brave men, friends and foes, who had fallen during the siege.

The Countess Cesaresco tells an anecdote of Garibaldi in Caprera, after his first rejoicing that the war had ended, and that Italians would not kill each other any more. In the evening he seemed so depressed that one of his friends thought him ill. "I am thinking," said Garibaldi, "of Francis II., that poor boy. Born to a throne, and perhaps not by his own fault hurled from it. He, too, will have to feel the bitterness of exile." "Is that all?" asked Garibaldi's friend. "Do you think it nothing?" was the answer. "Why, then, did you go to Marsala?" "It was my duty to go," Garibaldi said quickly; "else how could there have been one Italy?"

So Garibaldi returned to his island of rocks — to dig and to eat, as he said himself, the potatoes he had planted in the spring.

But what marvellous work had been done by him whilst those potatoes had been growing! At Caprera he had to take charge of an ill-regulated family, and to marry his daughter Theresita to the man she had chosen, — a man brave, indeed, but in other respects more like the sordid, grasping villain of old romance than the fitting son-in-law of a great hero.

Naples, when the King assumed its administration, became a serious subject of anxiety for Cavour. Every element of anarchy that had for a century and a half been accumulating under a wretched government, was now let loose. A political cloak was given to brigandage, for the brigands proclaimed themselves soldiers of King Francis and his fallen *régime.*

"Then, too, there was the Army of the South, — Garibaldi's own army, — which General Fanti, the War Minister, refused to recognize in the interest of his own army; and in the interest of diplomacy, such an army could not be permitted to hover upon the Roman frontier with Garibaldi not so far off, eager to lead them."

At that moment Cavour was conducting delicate negotiations to obtain peaceable possession of the Eternal City. "Had Cavour lived," said Victor Emmanuel, "we should have been in Rome in six months." But Garibaldi was wholly unable to appreciate the slower methods of statesmanship. He wanted eagerly to rush at everything. He had been elected a member of the Turin Parliament, and he went to it determined to beard Cavour. For some days after he reached Turin he was too ill with rheumatic fever to take his seat, but at last, in his red shirt and his poncho, and attended by crowds of his old legionaries, who had assembled at Turin to support him if their presence should be necessary, he appeared in the chamber and rose to make his speech.

Here is an account of the scene, as related by M. d'Ideville, who was present:

"Alas! the great actor did not know his part. He had scarcely pronounced a few words, when his memory failed him, . . . but suddenly abandoning all attempts to conform himself to the rules of parliament, he angrily flung his notes away and spoke out bluntly. With threatening voice and gestures he addressed himself to the ministerial bench, declaring that never would he clasp the hand of the man who had sold his country to the foreigner, or ally himself with a government whose cold and mischievous hand was trying to foment a fratricidal war.

"Cavour restrained himself with an effort, and made no allusion in his reply to the accusations of Garibaldi. Baron Ricasoli administered the rebuke, affecting to defend Garibaldi from what he declared to be a calumnious report of an intemperate and unbecoming speech that the General had made a few days before to a deputation from Genoa. 'I know this man,' he said. 'I know how dear to him is his country. I know the sacrifices he has made. As for me, I dare assert that it is impossible that the odious words attributed to him should have fallen from his lips. For who, great as he may be, would dare in his pride to assign himself in our country a place apart? Who would dare to claim for himself a monopoly of devotedness and patriotism? Among us a single head should tower above all others, — that of our King.' Then Nino Bixio, Garibaldi's *Secondo nel Mille*, rose and apologized to the Assembly for the strong language used by his chief; appealing to Cavour's generosity to forget what had happened. Garibaldi, who by this time had cooled, ended the debate, saying: 'I am sure Count Cavour loves his country; let him therefore use his influence in support of my bill for arming Italy; let the volunteers of the Army of the South be called into service; thus we shall be reconciled.'"

A few days later, Cavour and Garibaldi, by desire of the King, had an interview, which Cavour, in a letter to a friend, has thus described: —

"My interview with Garibaldi was courteous though not warm. We both kept within the limits of reserve. I acquainted him, however, with the line of conduct which the government intends to follow as regards Austria, as well as France, assuring him that on these points no compromise was possible. He declared himself ready to accept the programme, and to be willing to pledge himself not to act contrary to the views of the government. He only asked me to do something for the Army of the South. I gave him no promise, but I told him I would seek means to provide as well as might be for the future of his officers. We parted, if not good friends, at least without any irritation."

But this semi-reconciliation was one of the last acts in the noble life of Cavour. The winter of 1860-61 was for him full of incessant labor and incessant anxiety. The difficulties of his position were enormous. He had written in January : —

"The King does not look upon his task as finished. He knows that he must labor to constitute Italian independence and unity on solid grounds, — an end which will not be attained until the questions of Rome and Venice have received a complete solution, conformable to the wishes of the Italian people."

Alas! the solution of the Roman question was one to tax to the uttermost the skill of any statesman, and it cannot be held to have received its "complete solution" even now. But Cavour was determined to have Rome in due time for the Italian capital, and he carried through the Chambers a declaration that Rome was the true capital of Italy. "When I once see the King enthroned in the Capitol," he would say, "I will retire to Leri, to plant cabbages, tend my vines, and repose myself for the rest of my life."

Alas! he was to find that repose, not at his country seat, but in his grave.

Early in June, 1861, it was rumored that he did not seem well, and on the 6th of that month he died.

"I have never worked so hard as I do now," he had said sadly to a friend during the week before he broke down. "His brain and frame," writes the Countess Cesaresco, "worked without rest, without recreation, broke down at last, and would work no more."

On May 29 he had returned from the Chamber after speaking. He seemed much agitated, and in the night was taken very ill. The evening before his death, the King, unannounced, entered his chamber, and stole up to his bed. Cavour opened his eyes, and had just strength to put out his feeble hand. Victor Emmanuel leaned over the bed and kissed him, then departed in tears, and with a heavy heart.

"The life of Cavour had been given wholly to the service of his country. As he said of Italy, she was *la sua sposa*. He wedded her in the hour of her extremest need; he left her equipped with freedom, dowered with hope, ready, after obliteration for centuries from the map of Europe, to take her place among the nations of the world."

He had long beforehand received a promise from a certain Fra Giovanni that, when dying, he would administer to him the last sacraments, and not let him die like Santa Rosa. This promise was fulfilled, and immediately thereafter Cavour was heard to murmur, almost his last words, "A free State, — a free Church" — and, "tell the people of Turin I died a Christian."

Garibaldi went back to Caprera, where presents poured in upon him from his admirers in all lands. On one occasion, when his heart had been moved by accounts of destitution among the peasants in some part of Austria, some valuable gifts being brought to him at that moment he asked leave to sell them, and devote the proceeds (two thousand francs) to these Austrian poor. But, from Garibaldi's autobiographical memoirs, published six years after his death, it does not appear that he ever forgave "that fox," as he continued to the last to call Cavour.

CHAPTER XII.

ITALY MADE — NOT COMPLETED.

THE death of Cavour, in June, 1861, threw heavier labors, heavier anxieties, and responsibilities without stint on Victor Emmanuel. When the great guiding hand was cold, the affairs of the new kingdom of Italy never worked so smoothly as when he held the helm. In a few years Italy gained all that had been the hearts' desire of her people, — Venetia, Rome, a welcome to a high place among European powers. Victor Emmanuel had the happiness of thinking that "he need not continue to hate any man," but national pride was mortified by the disasters to Italian arms at Custozza and at Lissa; the proud motto of Garibaldi and his followers, *Italia farà da se,* — which, though never accepted by Victor Emmanuel or his great minister, was at the heart of the nation, — had been singularly falsified. Venetia had not been *won*, it was a gift — a gift to be accepted from the hands of a man looked upon by Italy with detestation and distrust. To this hour Italy has never recovered from resentment for that gift. She may be free from the Alps to the Adriatic — the *straniero* may not own a foot of Italian soil, but Italian pride has been humbled. Oh! the pity of it that she could not have won the second battle of Custozza!

The year 1862 was a trying one to Victor Emmanuel. He had in that year constant changes of ministry. The successor of Cavour was the great Tuscan statesman, Count Ricasoli, whose health obliged him to resign in a few months. Honorable, upright, and acquainted with the management of affairs, he nevertheless found those of the new kingdom beyond his guidance. He was a thoroughly good man, — not only an earnest Christian, but an earnest Catholic, as was proved by his hesitation about taking his little daughter into Switzerland, lest she should form any associations that would taint her mind with Protestantism. But he most earnestly desired on religious grounds that the Pope should free himself from his temporal power. He believed, like Dante, that the obligations imposed on him as an Italian prince impaired his influence as a spiritual ruler. On Ricasoli's resignation, after holding office for a few months, he was succeeded by Rattazzi.

Rattazzi has been called the "man of splendid disasters;" he might also have been called the man of varied alliances. His political career began by his being a leader in the left wing of the Piedmontese parliament; he was next a strong opponent of the Anglo-French alliance, which led Piedmont to send troops to the Crimean War; he was in one or two ministries, but never remained long in office; he married into the Bonaparte family, and became thenceforth a strong adherent of the Emperor Napoleon. He liked to work underground, for his own ends, and showed considerable skill in doing so.

The restless Garibaldi at Caprera, the relations he kept up with the disaffected, and the designs he made no secret of harboring against the Papal States, continually disquieted Rattazzi. Then, too, there were two armies in the field, under different leaders and under different discipline. He was perplexed how to get rid of the volunteers. He appears to have conceived a plan for ridding himself of both embarrassments by appearing secretly to favor Garibaldi's designs for a new march on Rome, thereby leading him into a trap, in which he might be caught, together with the rasher portion of his adherents, and so put out of the way of creating further embarrassment.

This plan was promoted by Garibaldi's intense indignation and disgust at certain concessions made by the Rattazzi ministry to the French Emperor. It was reported that the Cabinet was in close alliance with Louis Napoleon for the

URBANO RATTAZZI.

division of Italy into three parts, — the northern one to belong to Victor Emmanuel: the Pope to rule in the centre; and the kingdom of the Two Sicilies (under what government it does not appear) to be restored.

Absurd as this rumor was, it had its effect on Garibaldi. As president of a rifle corps association he travelled through Lombardy and the newly annexed duchies, exciting the young men. The Rattazzi ministry did not oppose him. He was carrying out their policy; he was playing into their hands.

Mazzini, however, wholly disapproved the scheme of Garibaldi, and would take no part in it. He thought, — as, indeed, did Victor Emmanuel, — that the first step to gaining Rome should be to recover Venice.

So Garibaldi had his own way unopposed, and again landed in Sicily. At Palermo he found the two princes, Umberto and Amadeo, and passed some hours in their company. His reception in Palermo, and throughout Sicily, was triumphal. He was received as the Liberator, not as the leader of a revolt from the authority he had himself established. However, he never admitted that he was a rebel. He always said his only object was to make Rome a present to his King.

His claim to interfere in Roman affairs was founded on his having been made Dictator of the Roman Republic in 1849, when the triumvirate broke down. He said his appointment had never been reversed, and that legally he was still Dictator.

By what appears to have been connivance on the part of Rattazzi, an Italian ship of war in the harbor of Catania moved out of the way at the right moment, enabling Garibaldi to embark his Red Shirts on two merchant ships, which he seized by a *coup de main*. The Straits of Messina were safely crossed, and the expedition was landed as successfully as Garibaldi's first set of volunteers had been, three years before, at Melito, in Calabria. *Then* the enemy they came to fight was Bourbon tyranny. — *now* Garibaldi thus set forth his views in a proclamation: —

"I bow before the majesty of Victor Emmanuel, king of the nation, but I am hostile to a ministry which has nothing Italian but the name; . . . the livery of a foreign master will never be a title of esteem for any minister of ours."

General Cialdini was in command in Southern Italy. As a soldier of the regular army of Italy, he had the contempt of his class for volunteers and guerillas. He resolved to catch Garibaldi in a net, and took measures to prevent his re-embarkation.

For some days, Garibaldi, who had landed with three thousand men, wandered about in mountain passes, where half his force deserted him. No one joined him. He is bitter at all times in his posthumous biography against the Italian peasantry. His best men were always from the intelligent classes, and he deprecates the action of those who, with what he calls the "parrot cry of freedom for all," would put it out of the power of an intelligent minority to rule their country. Nevertheless, his last public speech in England, when he paid his visit to London in 1865, was to urge on all nations the adoption of universal suffrage.

Hungry, weary, and dispirited, the remainder of his forces encamped for the night of August 28, 1862, on the brow of the hill of Aspromonte (The Mount of Bitterness). "The night was wet and gloomy. The rain put out their fires, every rag on their backs was soaked, and they had no provisions."

Early in the morning the royal troops, under Colonel Pallavicini, ascended the hill. The forces were drawn up facing each other. Garibaldi and his son Menotti advanced before their men, ordering them to restrain themselves, and not to fire. Unhappily some men, young and inexperienced, were unable to control themselves; a few shots from their ranks were returned by a volley from the regulars. Garibaldi and his son were both wounded, — the General in his left thigh by a spent ball, and by a bullet which buried itself in his foot, and was not extracted for many months.

Wounded, and a prisoner, Garibaldi was carried to the

seaboard; his forces were disarmed and disbanded. At Silla, on the coast, he was separated from his staff, and put on board a man-of-war to be taken to the Fort of Varignano, on the Gulf of Spezia. Preparations had not been made for his arrival, and his quarters were far from comfortable for a sick man. The King sent him his own surgeons, but they failed to find the ball in his foot. It was removed by a French surgeon nearly a year later.

Every kind of attention was lavished on Garibaldi in his prison, especially by ladies and foreigners. His personal friends filled the hotels and lodging-houses at Spezia. He suffered terribly from his wound, in addition to which he was a martyr to rheumatism.

In October, however, came an amnesty, which released Garibaldi from Fort Varignano, and he moved to Spezia, where no king could have been surrounded with more enthusiastic courtiers; and the whole of the busy port, the modern naval arsenal of Italy, echoed from morning till night with the Garibaldi hymn.

The Rattazzi government seems to have done many little things to "spite" (if we may use the homely word) their illustrious prisoner. But Victor Emmanuel grieved bitterly over the affair of Aspromonte. "The Garibaldians were all in the wrong, still they were his subjects, and the thought that Italian blood should have been shed by his soldiers affected him deeply."

Bitter, indeed, must have been Garibaldi's memories of Aspromonte when he could speak thus in the memoirs he left behind him to be printed after his death: "The crime committed by me of having gained ten victories, and the insult of having aggrandized the King's dominions, have been things such as monarchs never forgive."

No less bitterly does he speak of the Calabrian peasantry, who, he says, refused his volunteers the most necessary food. "It was worse than if we had been robbers. It was not the first time that I saw an Italian population inert and indifferent to their would-be deliverers."

Of his treatment after his captivity, — while other accounts speak of it as full of generosity and sympathy, and although in after years he took pains to show regard and appreciation to the officer who had had him in charge, — he says: —

"I feel repugnance to speak of the miseries I endured. . . . Some rubbed their hands when they heard that I was sorely wounded. Others abjured their friendship for me, and there were others who said they had deceived themselves when formerly praising some merit of mine. . . . True, some commonplace civilities were shown me, such as are common in the case of great criminals when they are led to the scaffold. Yet, instead of leaving me in a hospital at Reggio or Messina, I was put on board a frigate, and carried to the Varignano, thus making me cross the whole Tyrrhene Sea, and inflicting the greatest torment on me through my wound."

The next event in Garibaldi's life was his triumphant visit to England, which took place in March, 1864. It was not the first time he had received a hearty welcome in "the land of the free," though on the former occasion he came only as master of a trading vessel and landed at Newcastle. He was then hailed as the man who had fought the French at Rome. Now he had won a kingdom for his sovereign, had presented it to him, and had then retired into private life. In return, the armed forces of that king had made him permanently lame, and had taken him prisoner. This was how the case presented itself to the minds of the great mass of Englishmen. He was to them a sort of demi-god. Had they not seen representations of his unrivalled feats of heroism at Astley's Circus, where the future triumphs of the Wild West Show were rehearsed night after night, in the winter of 1859-60, before crowded London audiences, with Garibaldi in his red shirt for their hero? Garibaldi flying across the Atlantic; Garibaldi's exploits in Uruguay; Garibaldi bringing bands of wild horsemen from the Pampas, and Charrua Indians, to fight the Austrians; all offered to crowded audiences, with daring feats of horsemanship, and the din of musketry? And did not mothers dress their little boys in "garibaldis"? What could popularity run rampant have done more?

There was considerable diplomatic discussion before Lord Palmerston could be persuaded to permit this visit, but at last Garibaldi came to Stafford House, as the guest of the Duke of Sutherland. He came by a P. and O. steamer, which picked him up at Malta; and, as a writer who relates his journey says, "happy were those who, returning from their Eastern travels, found themselves on board the 'Ripon' with a real lion for their fellow-passenger, and ten days in which to gaze on him."

The Duke of Sutherland and other friends, English and Italian, met him before he landed. Already there were dissensions in the ranks of his admirers. Some complained that he was being monopolized by the aristocracy.

The Mayor of Southampton officially received him, the town was dressed with flags, a public reception at the Town Hall took place, — well! we all know, when a hero is a nation's guest, what programme of receptions, dinners, deputations, speeches, etc., etc., lies before him. And when this hero reached the Nine Elms station on his entrance to London, where dense crowds had been waiting his arrival for hours, the English cheer that welcomed him was, as he said afterwards, like nothing he had ever heard.

Ladies dressed themselves in the Italian colors; men donned the *camicia rossa;* street singers bawled ditties in his honor; bands played the Garibaldi hymn and "See the Conquering Hero comes," till their brazen throats seemed hoarse. Every manner of society, — political, religious, literary, or philanthropic, — sent its deputation, with an appropriate speech and banner, to join in the reception. Poor Garibaldi, still lame, and weak from recent illness, must have had a trying day! One day of rest was granted him, and then the receptions and the speeches and the sight-seeing began again. The Italians in London presented to him a sword, and another was given to Menotti. Both father and son said in reply that they hoped to carry them to Rome and Venice.

In a great reception at the Crystal Palace, which was to have been a musical entertainment, the whole audience rose to their feet at the first strains of the Garibaldi hymn, and refused to hear anything else.

> "O Garibaldi, nostro salvator,
>   Ti seguiremo al campo d' onor!
>   Risorga Italia,
>   Il sol di libertà!
>   All' armi, all' armi, andiamo!"
>
> ("O Garibaldi, saviour of our land,
>   Lead us to honour's field, — a faithful band!
>   Revive our Italy,
>   Dear land of liberty!
>   To arms! To arms! To arms! Soldiers march on!")

"All, turning towards the hero of the occasion, men and women, artistes, orchestra, and conductor, joined in one overpowering demonstration of enthusiasm to that quiet demure-looking man, who sat there in a sort of glad but quiet wonder."

A month had passed with daily demonstrations on the part of Englishmen, and Garibaldi was preparing to set out on a tour through the North of England, when he suddenly renounced his design, and gave out that he should go back to Caprera. He said his health required rest, which one thinks might be true enough, but the real cause of his sudden return to Caprera, was a quiet intimation from Lord Palmerston that his visit had lasted long enough, and that it was desirable to calm the ferment it created, which was beginning to create disquietude in other countries.

So Garibaldi left England in the Duke of Sutherland's yacht, having made a little detour to Penzance to greet "his Englishman," — the Colonel Peard who had played his part at Eboli.

"Garibaldi would receive no purse from his English friends," says Mr. Bent. "They wished to subscribe a sum of money, which, if invested, would have kept him from want for the rest of his days, . . . but he gladly accepted the yacht 'Osprey,' which they offered him, for the old General loved to skim along the blue waters of the inland sea, and there it lay for a while at Caprera, until, as is the fate of most toys, the General got tired of it, and went out to sea in it less and less. Ricciotti Garibaldi looked on with covetous eyes at so much wealth lying idle in the harbor of Caprera, so he asked his father's permission to go a cruise one day in the 'Osprey,' which was readily granted, and since then the 'Osprey' has been no more seen in the waters of Caprera."

When Garibaldi died in 1882 the London "Spectator" spoke thus of him: —

"We ask ourselves the question, — Why did this man, with no claim of birth, no careful education, and no great power of thought, so enchant the European democracy that he was for a quarter of a century a perceptible force in Europe, that he was deeply reverenced by millions who had never seen him, and that, though he had no wealth, he was the single private man in Europe, in an age when private war is extinct, at whose bidding an army would spring up from the ground? The explanation is said to be his career; but not only was his best army raised before men knew that he was a great guerilla chief, but his career, though marked by *one* almost miraculous success, was by no means a successful one. In regular warfare he was always beaten. He failed entirely as a legislator; his dictatorship in Naples produced no civil fruit, and we can remember no great measure in Italy in which he took a prominent part. That Italians should love him for his action in Italy, for his defence of Rome, for his marvellous overthrow of the Bourbon dynasty, — a feat which stands alone in history, — for his still more marvellous surrender, for the sake of Italy alone, of the kingdom he had won, is intelligible enough; but why did other peoples love him? Patriotism does not necessarily endear the patriot to strangers, nor does all mankind always honor the deliverer of part of it.

"Wherein lay the charm of Garibaldi? We think it lay in two words, 'unselfishness' and 'heroism,' which, when found together under circumstances in which both can be fully perceived, exert over the masses of mankind a sort of supernatural charm, till they are content to believe without either seeing or knowing. To the multitude in all European countries Garibaldi was a figure nearly resembling that which Joan of Arc must have presented to the peasantry of Northern France, — a being so heroic as to be almost more than mortal, incapable of fear, incapable of mistake, incapable of final defeat, yet seeking nothing, asking nothing, desiring nothing, utterly devoted to them. . . . Nobody felt distrust of Garibaldi or rivalry towards him, or suspicion about him. Friend or enemy, detractor or worshipper, no European doubted that Garibaldi desired the good of mankind to the utter forgetfulness of self, and would, if once in motion, go forward to secure it, uninfluenced by any bribe, undeterred by any danger, unfettered by any fear. . . . That quality of disinterestedness excites in men reverence to all who possess it, and when seen in a great hero, a man who has done marvellous things in a marvellous way, who has, so to speak, walked up to the lion and rent him with his hands alone, who has personal dignity in its highest form, and a face that the ablest French caricaturist could make only heroic, it develops reverence to passion."

Sincerely grieved as Victor Emmanuel had been by the sufferings and humiliations of Garibaldi, he had about the same time to endure other great trials. The sympathy felt throughout Italy for the sufferer of Aspromonte, caused the ministry of Rattazzi to become intensely unpopular. Rattazzi was replaced by Farini, the Italian historian, who has written the story of this period in a book which has had the honor of being translated by Mr. Gladstone. Farini was soon succeeded by Minghetti, a patriotic and honest statesman, but one not qualified to fill the place of Cavour. Cavour had nearly succeeded in making an agreement by which the French troops were to evacuate Rome and the Papal States in a fortnight, Italy undertaking to guard the Papal frontier from invasion. The exploit of Garibaldi changed the situation. Minghetti could only obtain the Emperor's promise that his soldiers should in two years leave the Pope to himself to take care of his temporal power; and he exacted that in the meantime the Italian capital should be moved from Turin to either Florence or Naples.

When Signor Minghetti first broke this matter to the King, Victor Emmanuel was overwhelmed, and pleaded, even with tears, that his native city might be spared such a cruel sacrifice, at least until he could be proclaimed King of Italy at the Capitol. "You know I am a true Turinese," he said, "and no one can understand what a wrench it is to my heart to think that I must one day abandon this city, where I have so many affections, where there is such a feeling of attachment to my family, where the bones of my fathers and all my dear ones repose. However," he added, "if we cannot do otherwise, I will make even this sacrifice for Italy."

The sacrifice was made doubly hard by the indignation which the new convention with the Emperor Napoleon created in Italy. The ministry was forced to resign, and La Marmora was called to the helm of State, but when the decision of the King, his ministers, and parliament, was announced to the people of Turin, disgraceful riots took place. Guests going to a court ball were stoned as they left their carriages, and other popular demonstrations were made in various ways against the King. Deeply indignant, Victor Emmanuel set out immediately for Florence, accompanied by his prime minister.

It was some time before his anger cooled. He showed much reluctance to forgive his Turinese. The blow had struck home.

There came, too, in these days a domestic affliction, — Odone, the youngest son of Victor Emmanuel, a cripple and an invalid, died, to the great grief of his affectionate family, to whom his bright intelligence and gentle disposition had endeared him. The family circle was broken up. Princess Clotilde was away in Paris; Maria Pia had made a happier marriage, having wedded the young King of Portugal. The two robust and soldierly brothers, Umberto and Amadeo, remained as yet unmarried.

During the years 1862–64 a great many discussions unknown to the general public were going on in diplomatic circles. Poland in 1863 broke into revolt; Count Bismarck was laying hands on Denmark; Italy was eagerly assuring France and Prussia that she would assist both of them, or either of them, in a war with Austria, it being understood that the price of her help was to be the restitution of Venetia.

English statesmen were desirous of seeing Venetia given back to Italy, but not at the price of a Continental war.

Various ways of inducing Austria to part with Venetia were proposed by diplomatists. Austria might exchange it for Poland, or the Danubian principalities might be taken from Turkey, and offered her in its stead. But as time went on it seemed evident to Italian diplomatists that their cause was secondary in the eyes of European statesmen to others that they had more at heart. France wanted war for the liberation of Poland; England espoused the cause of Denmark; while the Emperor Napoleon continued to urge patience on the Italians, saying, "Have I not told you more than once already, — Austria and Prussia are now in accordance, but not for long. They soon will have to fight, and then will be Italy's opportunity."

As by degrees diplomatists became aware of the truth in these words, Italian statesmen endeavored through the mediation of Napoleon to obtain from Austria the cession of Venetia in return for Italy's promise of neutrality in the event of a Prusso-Austrian war.

Poor Maximilian, still contending with his own troubles in Mexico, had always urged upon his family the restoration of Venetia, which could never be otherwise than a dissatisfied, unrestful portion of the Austrian Empire. The government at Vienna did not, however, accept the Italian proposal.

Then the government of Victor Emmanuel sent a secret diplomatic agent to Berlin to negotiate an alliance with Prussia. Every day increased the probabilities of war, the great cause of dispute being the Schleswig-Holstein question. The Austrian government began to see that it would not be well to have war on the north, and war in the south of the empire at the same time, and at last intimated to Louis Napoleon that if he would remain neutral she would make him a present of Venetia. The Emperor at once communicated this offer to the Cabinet of Victor Emmanuel, but the treaty offensive and defensive had been signed with Prussia, and the Rè Galantuomo would not break his word. Possibly, too, the King and his ministers shared the popular Italian feeling, *Italia farà da se,* and were confident the valor of their troops would gloriously unite Venetia to Italy by force of arms.

La Marmora quitted his post as Prime Minister to take command of the King's army on the Mincio. Garibaldi received a message at Caprera from the King, urging him to take charge of the volunteers, who were to serve in the Trentino; and in June, 1866, while the Seven Weeks' War was in progress in Germany, the Italian and Austrian armies were in the field. The Austrians were commanded by the Archduke Albrecht, a general of military experience and high character. His troops had enormous advantages in organization and discipline, and were also in possession of the Quadrilateral fortresses, — but their numbers were very inferior to those brought into the field by the Italians. The Archduke's forces did not exceed seventy thousand men, including those in garrison; the Italian army was estimated at two hundred thousand, exclusive of Garibaldi's volunteers, who were estimated at thirty-five thousand, though probably the force available was not half that number.

General La Marmora crossed the Mincio (the boundary between Lombardy and Venetia) without opposition. Half the army under General Cialdini had been sent to the southward, their commander's headquarters being at Bologna. They were probably intended to draw off the Archduke, and to march direct to Venice. But the Austrian commander had no intention of being turned aside. His first object was to defeat La Marmora.

On June 21, war between Austria and Italy was declared; on the 23d La Marmora's army crossed the Mincio; on the 24th the battle began under a burning sun. Nothing could exceed the personal bravery of the Italians. No man bore higher testimony to this than the Archduke; but it must be added that the generalship on the Italian side seems on this occasion to have been deplorable. La Marmora, besides engaging with only half his forces, the other half being with Cialdini far away, did not call into action two large bodies of troops that were near at hand. For the second time Italians and Austrians encountered each other on the plain of Custozza, the scene of Charles Albert's defeat in 1848. Up to 3 P. M. the battle was undecided. Then the Austrian general paused to rest his troops, and La Marmora, seeing the importance of getting fresh men into the field, rode *himself* to find and bring up certain reserves posted at a great distance, instead of ordering up others that were near at hand. "This inexplicable proceeding left the army without a commander in chief for several hours. The battle was renewed; the generals of division followed their individual inspirations, but the Austrians steadily gained ground. Toward sunset, the Archduke, persuaded that the Italian reinforcements, whose arrival he had so much feared, were never coming, prepared for a final effort. At 7 o'clock in the evening his soldiers succeeded in storming the heights of Custozza, and Austria could write a second battle of that name among her victories."

It is wonderful that no attempt was made to retrieve the disaster. But some irresponsible person had telegraphed to Cialdini, as if from an authoritative source, "Irreparable disaster. Cover the capital"; and consternation seems everywhere to have reigned.

Ten days later came accounts of the battle of Sadowa or Königgrätz, in Bohemia, in which Prussia vanquished the Austrians. Sadowa was one of the decisive battles of the world. The Emperor Napoleon intervened to prevent the Prussian army from marching on Vienna. The price of his intervention was to be the gift of Venetia. Napoleon always exacted pay for his services, and it is said this was the reason why England refused to accept his aid in settling the Schleswig-Holstein question.

This cession of Venetia to Napoleon was part of a former treaty, but, as the secret of that treaty had been well kept, this cession, less than two weeks after the battle of Custozza, while two large Italian armies were still in the field, was a surprise to Europe, and not less so to Italy, where in the public mind it produced embarrassment and mortification, rather than joy. Italy had lost her military prestige —

the object of her heart's desire had been, at it were, tossed over to her. It had not been won, as she had hoped, by the valor of her sons.

Here is contemporary opinion as to this campaign. It is from the pen of Charles Lever, at that time British consul at Trieste, who had, from his official position, a certain inside view of the state of affairs.

"Napoleon's policy amounted to this: 'It is impossible to say what result of this war will most serve or disserve me. A victorious Austria might undo all I have done in Italy, and send me in a bill for the damage besides. Prussia successful means a strong and united Germany on my flank, more than a rival for the supremacy I have exercised in Europe. The great point, therefore, is that the war should end without any overwhelming results, — that all the powers engaged should be weakened by the struggle, and none be a great gainer.' ... A plan of campaign was drawn out, and given to La Marmora, a man who, though a brave soldier, was constitutionally fashioned to be a dupe. ... La Marmora had received his orders from the Tuileries, and Archduke Albrecht had also his instructions. He was to beat the Italians, but not to follow up his victory. ... General Fanti, La Marmora's countryman and colleague, always said: 'One of these days he is sure to run his stupid head against the Quadrilateral'; but even Fanti never suspected that that 'stupid head' would be dashed at it by Louis Napoleon."

Only two things might have consoled Italians for the unwelcome gift of Venetia and the loss of the battle of Custozza, — a great naval victory in the Adriatic, or the success of Garibaldi's volunteers in the Trentino.

Italy had hurried into the war with an inadequately organized commissariat, which would have told more had the war lasted even a few weeks; she had also paid little regard to her naval preparations; all was confusion in her dockyards, and in her fleet disorder. Admiral Persano had been pressed to take command in the Adriatic. He objected that he had for some time retired into private life, and was a stranger to the officers and men he was to command, but he yielded to his sovereign's wish, and accepted the position. The fleet placed under his orders comprised thirty-three vessels, of which twelve were ironclads. The Austrians had twenty-seven ships, including seven ironclads; they were commanded by Admiral Tegethoff, the same who eighteen months after brought from Mexico the body of the unhappy Emperor Maximilian. Tegethoff worked with might and main to get his ships in order; Persano does not seem to have appreciated the haste that was necessary. Depretis, the Minister of Marine, was a lawyer, unacquainted with the sea. After some weeks of inaction, Persano, under direct commands from Depretis, decided to attack Lissa, a fortified island on the coast of Dalmatia. He reached it July 16, and began a heavy bombardment, which was measurably successful. On the morning of the 19th the captain of the "Esploratore" signalled to the Admiral that suspicious vessels were in sight. The Admiral returned for answer, "Probably fishing boats" But soon the truth was revealed: they were ironclads. The Admiral had not anticipated the arrival of the hostile fleet. He was intent on landing troops to attack a fort on Lissa. His own vessels were scattered and in disorder.

The battle is described as the naval counterpart of a charge of cavalry.

"Tegethoff's aim was to come to the relief of Lissa, and, as the Italian ships lay between him and that place, he charged through them. Being totally inferior in number and weight of guns, he dashed prow on to force his way, and went head-foremost at the 'Rè d' Italia,' because he believed her to be the flagship. She was scarcely moving at the time, having stopped her engines to enable Admiral Persano to change his flag to the iron ram 'Il Affondatore.' Being, besides, an ill-built ship, she gave way at once, and, cut down from bulwark to water-line, with a yawning gap sixty feet wide in her flank, she heeled over and sank in thirty-four seconds with all on board of her."

After the "Rè d' Italia" was disabled, one of her seamen, thinking to assert a claim for pity, began to pull down her flag, but a young officer pushed him aside, and hoisted it again. She went down with the Italian colors flying, and cheers from all on board. There were five hundred and fifty men in her, and although Admiral Tegethoff sent all possible assistance, very few lives were saved. Soon after, the gunboat "Palestro" caught fire and blew up, with over two hundred men on board.

When the Austrians avowed that the suddenness and completeness of the calamity, when the "Rè d' Italia" sank, almost stunned them, we may imagine the horror and consternation that were felt by the Italians. Indecision and confusion reigned throughout their fleet. Their ships were scattered without being dispersed. It was scarcely a naval action, though Tegethoff did all a man could do, with a force so disorganized to oppose him. Finally Persano collected together his ships, and led them out of action. He sailed back to Ancona; as he entered the harbor, his flagship, the "Affondatore," sank, from injuries received during the battle.

"The rage and sorrow throughout Italy defies description. Persano attempted to explain what no man can explain — a scene of confusion, misunderstanding, and blunder. The nation was not in a forgiving mood, — in fact, the people had pardoned too much already, and in such cases the last offender pays the penalty for all."

In spite of his past services, Persano was heavily dealt with; he was dismissed the service and degraded.

Garibaldi's expedition into the Trentino, with the ultimate object of capturing Trieste, was not more successful. He had hoped to be sent into Dalmatia, to raise that old Venetian province; then to march on and attack Vienna; instead of which he was shut up in the mountain passes of the Alps. In Naples he had had an enthusiastic people with him. They gave him little military or material aid, but more than enough cheering. The mountaineers of the Alps were loyal to their Austrian rulers. They liked better light taxation and an orderly administration than the conscription, the taxes, the sacrifices demanded by the Italian government. *Italia Irredenta* it has been of late years the fashion to call this mountain province, and many unsuccessful attempts have been made to revolutionize it. Again, Garibaldi's volunteers had never been opposed to regular soldiers, except in the case of the half-hearted Neapolitans. The regular troops of Austria were quite another foe. Garibaldi in his previous military operations had the freedom of action of a guerilla commander, now he was under orders from a war department, — a department that seemed to care little for his wants and mismanaged his supplies, so that his soldiers were compelled either to pillage or to starve. Garibaldi cannot find words hard enough, in his posthumous biography, to describe his contempt for the rank and file of his Trentino army. Of the thirty-five thousand volunteers of whom it was supposed to consist, not half joined, and out of those in one day three thousand were dismissed as bad characters. They fought, however, bravely when occasion offered ; and Menotti and Ricciotti Garibaldi distinguished themselves on several occasions as commanders. Canzio's better qualities also came out when there was no opportunity for plundering his facile father-in-law.

The Garibaldians met with some successes, but these had no results. "If ever I lose my senses," wrote Garibaldi, "it will be in this campaign." He could no longer sit a horse, being crippled with rheumatism.

The battle of Lissa was fought five days before the Prussians signed the preliminaries of peace with Austria, in which no mention was made of Prussia's Italian ally, and thus the combined armies of the Empire of Austria, three hundred and fifty thousand men, were set free to make war upon Italy. Such was the wrath and disappointment of the Italians at their defeats by land and sea, that a large part of the population, and even some of the leading statesmen of Italy, were eager to continue the war at all risks and against all odds. But La Marmora played the same part that was played by Thiers at Bordeaux after the Franco-Prussian war ; he acted as a true patriot by forcing his country against her will to cease hostilities. "They will say that we are traitors," said the King. "Come what may," answered La Marmora, "I take the whole responsibility on myself." "This is too much," answered Victor Emmanuel, with tears brimming in his eyes, "I too must have my share."

Garibaldi's volunteers, who had accomplished nothing though they had fought bravely, were thrown into a ferment by orders to evacuate the enemy's territory. Their leader, who had hated the expedition from first to last, wrote one word in answer to the telegram commanding him to retreat. "*Obbedisco.*" "Do you obey," he said to the would-be mutineers around him; "I have obeyed — do likewise." One of them cried out: "To Rome!" "Yes," said their chief, "we will march to Rome together."

Peace was signed October 3. The animosity between France and Prussia was increased by the pretended good offices of the French Emperor. The Countess Cesaresco tells us that —

"The comedy of the cession of Venetia to Napoleon, was enacted between General Le Bœuf and the Austrian military commandant of Venice. Among other formalities, the French delegate went the round of the museums and galleries to see that everything was in its place. Suddenly he came upon a most suspicious blank space. 'A picture is missing here,' he said. 'It is,' blandly assented the Austrian officer. 'It must be sent back immediately; where is it?' And the reply was, 'In the Louvre.'"

At last Austrians and French departed, and Italy shook off her mourning. The object of her desire was accomplished. The stranger had gone!

Venetia held a *plébiscite*, and voted to implore Victor Emmanuel to be her king. One does not place much dependence upon *plébiscites*, but on this occasion there was no need to coerce votes, or to tamper with the ballot boxes. Out of six hundred and forty-two thousand votes cast, sixty-nine only were against offering Venetia to the King. The day when the result of this *plébiscite* was presented to

Victor Emmanuel, he exclaimed, "This is the greatest day of my life. Italy is made, though not yet completed."

On November 7, 1866, Victor Emmanuel made his public entrance into Venice, hailed by the Bride of the Sea with all such displays of rejoicing as she had the means to make. A month later he congratulated his Parliament in Florence on representing twenty-five millions of Italians.

The Iron Crown of Lombardy, the crown of the Kings of Italy, which the Austrians had carried off in 1859, was brought back and restored to its old place in the Cathedral of Monza. But Victor Emmanuel never gave himself the empty triumph of placing it upon his brows. It was, however, carried after his coffin at his funeral.

Garibaldi retired to Caprera, where he passed some months in writing two books, — both autobiographical novels. One was "I Mille" (The Thousand), — the other "The Rule of the Monk." "I Mille" relates the exploits of his thousand brave Red Shirts in Sicily. "The Rule of the Monk" is a bitter invective against Roman priests, from the popes to the meanest friars. Hatred of priests had become with him monomania. The days were changed since his dearest friend was Ugo Bassi.

CHAPTER XIII.

SADOWA. AUSTRIA-HUNGARY.

THE history of the expulsion of Austria from Italy, and the triumph of Victor Emmanuel as King over twenty-five millions of Italians in 1866, though that triumph was not completed by the acquisition of Rome, can hardly be understood without reference to the battle of Sadowa, on which hinged the fate of Europe, which transferred to Prussia the supremacy in Continental affairs that had for centuries been disputed between Austria and France. Yet, strange to say, general readers in this country know comparatively little about Sadowa, — less than they do about the fights of the great Frederick, far less than about the campaigns of Napoleon. The reasons for this are probably manifold. First, the extreme brevity of the Seven Weeks' War; and secondly, that it took place when the interest of the American public was absorbed in other things; our Civil War had just come to a close, our nation had to be reconstructed. I allow myself, therefore, to interrupt the tortuous course of modern Italian history, and to interpolate a few words concerning an event which served more to " make " Italy than the bravery of her own soldiers or the wisdom of diplomacy.

In a few words I will here try to make clear the downfall of Austria as the arbiter of European affairs and leader of the German people, which was the outcome of the Seven Weeks' War. That war ended with the battle of Sadowa, July 3, 1866, and prepared the way for the moment when the crown imperial of Germany was, five years later, set on the head of King William of Prussia in the Prefecture of Versailles.

Nor are there many picturesque figures or incidents that stand out conspicuously in the Seven Weeks' War to enliven the story. The history we really need to know is that of how the balance of power changed from Austria to Prussia in the latter half of the nineteenth century.

To the eight provinces of which Prussia consisted in the spring of 1866, the Seven Weeks' War added Hesse-Cassel, Nassau, Hanover, Schleswig-Holstein, and Lauenburg, thus raising her population to between twenty-three and twenty-four millions. In 1866 there had been for sixty years no Emperor of Germany, — the last one was Francis II., who, by the will of his future son-in-law, Napoleon, took the title of Emperor of Austria, and announced his resignation of that of Germany to the Diet at Frankfort, August 10, 1806. By this act the Empire of the Cæsars in Central Europe, — old as the days of Augustus, the oldest political institution in the civilized world, — was extinguished by the power of Napoleon. Its partial restoration in our own day may be said to be indirectly due to the second Napoleon.

Up to the early part of the present century, the German Empire consisted of no less than three hundred States, large and small, governed by secular or ecclesiastical princes, each independent of the other, but subject to the Emperor as their federal head; besides which there were free cities, and a class of nobles, chiefly in Swabia and the vicinity of the Rhine, who, without enjoying the title of princes, acknowledged no superior but the Emperor. These were called freiherren, whose strong castles, together with the free cities, made up the sovereign States of Germany to three hundred and sixty.

When Napoleon swept with his armies over Germany, he made short work of these tiny sovereign princes, dukes, landgraves, counts, pfalzgraves, freiherren, and barons. They became what are called "mediatized" princes, — received pensions in exchange for power, and descended, from being reigning sovereigns, into the rank of nobles.

EMPEROR WILLIAM I.

German geography must have been awful to learn in the days of those free cities and sovereign princes. Thanks to Napoleon, they were reduced to thirty-nine, and Prince Bismarck has since cut them down to twenty-six, for which he deserves the gratitude of all students of geography.

In far-back times the Emperor of Germany was elected by nine electors, — the electors of Cologne, Treves, Mayence, the Palatinate, Hanover, Prussia (*i. e.*, Brandenburg), Saxony, Bavaria, and Bohemia (*i. e.*, Austria, whose only connection with the German Empire was through her possession of that subject kingdom). But after 1438 the imperial crown of Germany became hereditary among princes of the house of Hapsburg, rulers of Austria.

As our federal representatives meet in Washington, so the German federal representatives met at Frankfort. The Diet was composed of three Chambers. The first was composed of the nine electors (or their representatives); the second of the various princes, and imperial prelates, counts, and barons; the third consisted only of the representatives of the free imperial cities, — fifty at one time, and subsequently only six.

Out of the thirty-nine countries composing Germany seventy years since, only five had as much population as the city of New York has to-day.

Close beside Prussia, and guarding all the passages from the Baltic to the North Sea, lay the little kingdom of Denmark, which contained the fine ports of Kiel and Altona, greatly desired by Prussia. Denmark is a kingdom largely made up of islands. Its foreign possessions are all islands; its home territory is now all islands, except the peninsula of Jutland, which a narrow strip of country connects with the mainland. Up to 1864, Jutland stood, as it were, upon a pedestal, formed of two provinces called the Elbe duchies, —*i. e.*, Holstein and Schleswig; Denmark also. in 1815, by bargain with Prussia, acquired the Grand Duchy of Lauenburg in exchange for a piece of Pomerania, which she ceded to Prussia at the Congress of Vienna. Lauenburg and Holstein were parts of the German Empire, having votes in the German Diet, — and thus Denmark had her share in the affairs of the German Empire.

A diplomatic agreement, drawn up in London in 1852, had secured the throne of Denmark, together with the duchies of Holstein and Schleswig, to Prince Christian of Glücksborg, on the death of the reigning king. It was stipulated that Schleswig should not be incorporated into the Danish kingdom, but should retain home rule, and live under its own Constitution. However, King Christian, as soon as he came to the throne, set this agreement aside. A certain Duke of Augustenburg conceived that, the diplomatic arrangement having been broken, he was at liberty to claim the right to rule Schleswig and Holstein in virtue of a stronger hereditary claim than King Christian. He laid the matter before the German Diet, and the Diet was ready to support him. The duchies, it may be added, were in favor of his claim to be their ruler.

The result of the dispute was that German federal troops were quartered in the duchies, and that a war took place there in 1864. Denmark had expected to receive help from England, but England did not support her, and, in despair, she gave over to the Diet Schleswig, Holstein, and Lauenburg, to be held in trust till the dispute should be adjusted. Austria was to quarter troops in Holstein, Prussia in Schleswig.

Then began quarrels between the two Great Powers. Prussia governed Schleswig with a very high hand. Austria's rule in Holstein was milder and more popular. Prussia accused Austria of advocating the claims of the Prince of Augustenburg, and stirring up popular opinion in Schleswig in his favor. This was in 1865.

Prussia, which had become so great under the Great Frederick, came out of the wars of Napoleon a very small Great Power, — not that Prussia had become less, but that the four other Great Powers had risen to be more. The ruling spirit of the German people at this time was the Austrian Prince Metternich, whose conscience demanded of him to put down everything that tended to progress, as being dangerous and devilish, and whose mandates the King of Prussia, Frederick William III., accepted without remonstrance or misgiving. Frederick William was a good man, and a pious one, but entirely without force of character.

In 1830 the French revolution which deposed Charles X. sent an electric shock through Europe. Brunswick opened the ball with a little local revolution, which unseated her duke and set up a new duke, who gave his people a Constitution. Hesse-Cassel, Hanover, and Saxony followed suit, though King Ernest, who mounted his throne in 1837, revoked the constitution of Hanover soon after assuming the crown.

Prussia remained quiet, but it chafed her people to be obliged always to follow the lead of Austria, and a strong feeling grew up in Germany that Prussia's aspirations were for progress, Austria's for old-time obstructiveness and conservatism. However, Prussia had the satisfaction of leading the new Zollverein, a league which did away with custom-house duties between the little states and left Germany with only one line of federal custom-houses on her frontier.

In 1840, Frederick William III. died, and more liberality, if less piety, was expected from Frederick William IV., his successor. This king was an accomplished gentleman, but no statesman, — timid, vacillating, never sure of his own mind, and unfitted for an emergency. So far from granting the desired Constitution, "No power on earth," he declared, "shall ever succeed in persuading me to change the natural relation between king and people into a conventional and constitutional one, — and never, never, will I yield to the demand that, between our Lord God in heaven and this country, a written paper shall interpose itself to take the place of the old sacred ties of loyalty by which the people of Prussia are bound together."

Frederick William IV., by his vagaries, nearly drove Prince Albert frantic, as we may see in his letters. It was he who was very unwilling to allow his heir to brave the dangers of London at the time of the Great Exhibition.

In 1848 another French revolution occurred. This time its shock sent Prince Metternich into exile, and with astonishment the upper classes of the Viennese beheld a mob of students, followed by troops of ragged artisans, marching through the streets, shouting for "Liberty!" In our brief notice of this insurrection in the chapter on Kossuth, we have seen how this revolution was ended by the army of Prince Windischgrätz and the gallows.

Next, a self-constituted Diet met at Frankfort, and debated the formation of a new German Empire, with a new Liberal Constitution, and a new Emperor. The Emperor decided on was the King of Prussia, who had quieted a revolution in Berlin by the words "henceforth Prussia is merged into Germany." Yet he steadily refused to accept the Imperial crown; and the whole project of a new German Empire fell to pieces. His subjects, however, managed to secure from him a modified form of Constitution. He died in 1861, after having been insane for some years, during which time the heir presumptive, his brother William, ruled as regent of his kingdom. King William was sixty-four years of age when he came to the throne. Above all things he was a soldier. He meant to build up Prussia, to make her the centre of German unity, and to that end he was resolved to organize a military system that should give her preponderance, not only in Germany, but among the other Great Powers. He was not a man of distinguished talent, but of wonderful sagacity and firmness. Some writer elaborately compared him to the Duke of Wellington, and, indeed, it was no desire for personal popularity or aggrandizement that actuated both of them to impress on other men their own opinions, but a genuine wish to do, in whatsoever circumstances they might be placed, what they deemed best for their country.

King William was soon involved in a fierce dispute with his Parliament, which was not at all inclined to give way to his views concerning the organization of the Prussian army.

"But at the very moment when the course of the political drama seemed most perplexed, a 'heaven-born minister' appeared upon the scene. This was Count von Bismarck, who, with a strong will and a firm hand, piloted his sovereign triumphantly through the troubled seas of parliamentary conflict, and carried on the government of the country on the basis of forced grants, without asking Parliament for its annual vote of supplies."

It was a high-handed measure, one that, two centuries and a half before, had cost a King of England his life; but Charles I. had no Bismarck; moreover, unlike King William, he was not the man to subordinate his ideas of prerogative, when the right moment came, to the good of his country.

Otto Edward Leopold von Bismarck was born a few weeks before the battle of Waterloo. He had the clever mother usually attributed to great men, and she set her heart on his becoming a diplomatist, which in European countries is a profession. But, first of all, he started in life as a very naughty, troublesome boy. He was a noted duellist in his university career; indeed he fought twenty-eight duels during the three years he spent at Göttingen. Till he was twenty-five, there was reason to think he might come to no good, but he then, like Count Cavour at the same age, retired to the country and devoted himself to the care of his father's estates and to husbandry. He had studied, however. He had learned several languages, and had fitted himself for his future career by the great interest he took in history and political economy.

In 1851 he wrote thus to his wife: —

"The day before yesterday I was at Wiesbaden, the scene of former follies in my early life. May it now please God to fill the vessel, — where the champagne at twenty-one uselessly frothed, leaving only empty dregs, — with His own clear and strengthening wine."

He first entered public life as a member of a provincial diet, and made his first speech on the over-consumption of tallow in a poor-house. He soon, however, attracted attention, was elected into a more prominent deliberative body as a strong Conservative, and became a favorite adviser of

Frederick William IV. On one occasion he made a speech to prove that there could be no German Confederation that excluded Austria.

He was next appointed Prussia's representative in the Federal Bund, or, as we more usually call it, the Diet, at Frankfort. There he remained eight years, during which time he changed his views with regard to Austria.

In every way Prussia was thwarted by Prince Schwarzenberg, the Austrian representative, who used the numerical strength of the little States to outvote Prussia, and tried by every means to weaken her influence with the rest of Germany.

It is said that one of the arrogant ways by which Austria tried to show her supremacy over other German States was that, in the sittings of the Military Commission, only the Austrian representative was accustomed to smoke. Bismarck coolly brought out his cigar, and asked the astonished Austrian for a light. After this, the representatives of other States timidly asserted their right also to smoke.

"Only Würtemberg and Bavaria were left out," said Bismarck, " because their representatives did not smoke. But the honor and dignity of their States required it, so the next time we met, Würtemberg produced a cigar, — I see it now; it was a long, thin, light yellow thing, — and he smoked at least half of it as a burnt-offering to the Fatherland."

In 1859, Bismarck was sent as ambassador to St. Petersburg, where he became a favorite; but he had contracted ill-health during his eight years of hard work at Frankfort, — and his tendency to neuralgia and erysipelas has never since left him.

In 1862 he went as ambassador to Paris. During his ambassadorship he joined the Emperor Napoleon III., at Biarritz, and, in quiet walks with him along the seashore, laid the foundation of that personal knowledge of his character which served him so well in the struggle between Russia and Austria in 1866, and subsequently in the Franco-Prussian war.

On his return from Biarritz, Bismarck was recalled to Prussia. There the new king, William, was in conflict with his parliament and needed a wise counsellor by his side. Bismarck was appointed at once Prime Minister and Minister for Foreign Affairs, and was launched upon an angry sea of Prussian politics.

The struggle on which he now entered ended only with Sadowa. What I have said thus far of Prussia, Denmark, Schleswig-Holstein, and Count von Bismarck is but introductory to the subject of Sadowa. It was that victory over Austria that silenced opposition in Berlin, and justified the monarch and his minister in their desire to raise to a high pitch of efficiency the Prussian army. But the fight was hard. Bismarck in after years did not hesitate to say, when asked the question, "You wanted Schleswig and Holstein, did you not, from the beginning?" — "Yes, certainly I did, immediately after the King of Denmark's death. But it was a difficult job. Everybody was against me, — several coteries at Court, Austria, the petty German States, and the English, who grudged us the harbor of Kiel. Crowds of the Liberals were opposed to it, who all of a sudden discovered that the rights of princes were matters of importance (in reality it was only envy and hatred of me), and even the Schleswig-Holsteiners themselves did not want it. I had to contend with all these difficulties and plenty besides."

A great deal of diplomacy was necessary to prepare the way for war. Bismarck paid another visit to the Emperor of the French, and gathered, from conversations with him, that he was not likely to interfere in any contest between Prussia and Austria. Indeed, such a quarrel was to the advantage of the French Emperor. If Austria won, and he believed she would, unless attacked fiercely on the south by Italy, which might stir up Hungary on the east, the rising power of Prussia would be broken, and France might gain the Prussian Rhine provinces which she so much desired. It was therefore very much to be wished that Italy could be induced to take no part in the strife, and very improbable that she would consent to remain neutral when such an opportunity to fight Austria with advantage was opened to her. Austria had become willing to relinquish Venetia. She agreed to give it up to the Emperor Napoleon to do what he liked with it, provided he would guarantee that no part of her German possessions should in any event be alienated from her. Thus Austria's remaining hold on Italy would be lost, and Venetia might complete the kingdom of Italy; the Emperor Napoleon would have redeemed his promises; Italy would be "free from the Alps to the Adriatic," and he would be relieved from his early obligations as an Italian Carbonaro.

But part of this scheme was defeated by a premature alliance, offensive and defensive, between Italy and Prussia. The King of Prussia had long shown himself friendly to Victor Emmanuel, and when Venetia was offered to Italy, on condition that she would keep out of the coming conflict, Victor Emmanuel and La Marmora, his prime minister, pleaded the necessity of keeping faith with Prussia, besides which they knew the feeling of the Italian people. *Italia farà da se*, was in every Italian heart. They did not wish to receive Venetia as a gift, — to complete the kingdom of Italy by diplomacy, — they wanted to triumph by arms over Austria; they wished that the last bit of Italian soil she owned should be wrenched from her by the hands of Italians. Their defeat a second time on the field of Custozza, close under the walls of one of the fortresses of the Quadrilateral, and the disastrous engagement which destroyed their navy at Lissa, were the outcome of this revolution.

It is impossible not to sympathize with the disappointment of Italian patriots on this occasion, or with the spirit that prompted the feeling *Italy herself will make herself;* but patriotism needs to be guided by statesmanship, especially in a young nation, — a lesson Italy was slow to learn, an axiom never in favor with Garibaldi or Mazzini. "Young Italy!" said d'Azeglio, "Lack of wisdom must be always pardoned in the young."

Early in 1865 it became evident that the Diet at Frankfort, under the leadership of Austria, was going to oppose the very singular claim which Prussia had set up to the Danish duchies. This claim was, that since the Prince of Augustenburg had surrendered his rights in Schleswig *temporarily* to Prussia, Prussia succeeded to his rights when the disposition of the duchies should be arranged.

Bismarck then proposed a reorganization of the German Confederacy. This was opposed by all the South German States, and by the North German States of Hanover, Saxony, and Electoral Hesse, which took part against Prussia. The brother of Prince Albert, Duke Ernest of Saxe-Coburg-Gotha, was in Prussia's favor. Both Austria and Prussia, all through the spring of 1866, were making preparations to take the field against each other, and the armies of Italy were put on a war footing at the same time. But Austria had taken the initiative, and began some weeks before Prussia the work of mobilization. Mobilization means getting an army all ready to enter on a campaign, with its transport, artillery, supplies, ammunition, hospital train, and reserves, prepared for action. Prussia has so complete a military organization that she can mobilize her army in less time than any other Power.

In fourteen days the Prussian army was all ready to march at fourteen hours' notice. They carried no tents. Each soldier had a tin pan for cooking. Each regiment had only one waggon for its officers' baggage, two waggons with hospital supplies, and a few pack-horses.

On June 14, 1866, Prussia sent word to Hanover, Hesse, and Saxony that she expected them to dismiss the armies they had been assembling in obedience to the Federal Diet, and in twelve hours give her an answer, whether or not they would submit to her demands.

The sovereign of Hanover was King George, grandson of George III. of England. He was blind, good, musical, and dearly loved by his subjects. Saxony was governed by King John, a man of taste and culture, who made the best translation of Dante's " Divina Commedia " ever made into the German language; and Hesse was governed by the family into which Princess Alice of England had married.

The three States so peremptorily summoned to take part with Prussia, or against her, in the coming war, replied that they would not reduce their armies, and did not propose to join the new North German Confederation. Twenty-four hours later Prussia declared war against them, and five days later Italy made her declaration of war against Austria.

The army of Saxony had been mobilized, but that of Hanover was wholly unprepared. Every exertion was made by King George to get it into order, but Prussia attacked Hanover both by land and sea, and in less than one week after the declaration of war (*i. e.*, on June 22, 1866) Prussia had taken possession of the whole of Hanover, except a small portion of territory round Göttingen, where the Hanoverian army was assembled. Prussia had also secured possession of all depôts of arms in Hanover, and all its other munitions of war.

The Hanoverian army lay almost paralyzed. Its object now was to break out of Hanover and to unite if possible with the Bavarian troops, and those of Hesse-Cassel. To do so, it would have to pass through a small portion of Prussian territory, and then through a part of Saxe-Coburg-Gotha.

In vain the King of Hanover sent to the prince who commanded the Bavarians, asking help to enable him to push his way through the enemy. No help was sent, and the King of Hanover, with his unprovided army, had to meet the emergency as best he might. On June 27, — twelve days after the declaration of war, a battle was fought at a place called Langensalza, where the Hanoverians distinguished themselves by their loyalty and bravery, and they won the battle. But their triumph was not of long duration. They were but nineteen thousand, wholly unprovided even with food, and in an enemy's country. A force of forty thousand Prussians was sent to hem them in, and two days afterwards, King George, seeing his situation was hopeless, and unwilling uselessly to sacrifice the lives of his brave soldiers, offered to accept terms of capitulation. Arms, carriages, and military stores were handed over to the Prussians; the Hanoverian soldiers were dismissed to their homes; the officers were allowed to retain their horses and their swords, on condition of not again serving against Prussia in the war. The King himself and the Crown Prince were permitted to depart whithersoever they pleased, except within the borders of Hanover.

Thus, less than three weeks finished the war with Hanover, and gave Prussia that little kingdom, which for one hundred and thirty years had belonged to the crown of England, and had involved Great Britain in several European wars. It had a Salic law, and on the accession of Queen Victoria, in 1837, fell to her eldest uncle, Ernest, Duke of Cumberland.

The deposed king lived as a private gentleman quietly in Paris. The conduct of Prussia was always harsh to him. He had been blind from early boyhood. He left one son, the present Duke of Cumberland (or King of Hanover), who made a love-match (opposed by Prussia) with Princess Thyrza of Denmark, sister to the Princess of Wales, and the dowager empress of Russia. The daughter of King George married, with the approbation of Queen Victoria, as head of the house, a private gentleman, her beloved father's secretary. They reside in England.

I have not been willing to interrupt the story of the war in Hanover by recounting that of the simultaneous and more important campaign in Saxony and Bohemia. The moment the declaration of war was made by Prussia on June 14, 1866, the Saxon army, already mobilized, began to evacuate Saxony, and fall back to join the Austrian army under Field-Marshal Benedek in Bohemia. They had first attempted to tear up the railroad which connected Prussia and Saxony, but the Prussians came upon them so rapidly that they could only do their work very imperfectly. In three days the Prussians had possession of Dresden, the capital of Saxony. It must be said, in justice to the discipline of the

Prussian army, that the order it maintained in Saxony was admirable, and that the proclamation of Prince Frederick Charles of Prussia to the Saxon people was carried out to the letter. It said: "Private property will be everywhere respected by my troops, who are also directed to protect every peaceful citizen from injury."

"In most of the villages and hamlets of Saxony, certainly on all those that lay on roads leading to the frontier, Prussian soldiers were billeted; cavalry and artillery horses filled the barns of the border farmers, and field guns and artillery carriages were parked on many a village green. But the Saxons had no complaints to make, and, as far as could be judged from appearances, seemed highly to approve the occupation of their country by the Prussian army. The Saxon peasantry and the soldiers were on the most friendly terms, and a stranger who did not know the Prussian uniform, in passing through the villages would have supposed that the troops were quartered among people of their own country. . . . In some places the men were helping the peasantry to get in the hay harvest, in others they might be seen working in the cottage gardens, and nearly always they were spending money in the village shops; the bare-legged country urchins got taken up for rides on the artillery horses, or were invited, half afraid, to peep into the muzzles of the rifled cannon. Passenger traffic was resumed upon the railroads, and telegraphic messages were regularly sent."

The theatre of this War of Seven Weeks was the valley of the Elbe. The Elbe flows out of Bohemia, a land walled in with mountain ranges, into Saxony, and continues its progress northward through West Prussia.

The Austrian army in Bohemia consisted of about three hundred and ten thousand men. The Prussian force was divided into three armies; one under the command of the King; one under the Crown Prince; one under Prince Frederick Charles, — known as the Red Prince in the army. These three armies consisted of about two hundred and eighty thousand men, but they had about two hundred more guns than the Austrians.

On June 22d, a week after the occupation of Dresden, the Prussians began to pour through the mountain passes

PRINCE FREDERICK CHARLES.

from Saxony into Bohemia. The day was very hot, and the dust of the roads was choking, but the men stepped out cheerily, proud of themselves, and with full confidence in their commanders. On the night of June 22 the division of Prince Frederick Charles was at the quiet little village of Zittau.

"Its resources," says the war correspondent from whom I have been quoting, "were sorely tried by the sudden inroad of hungry men. The common room of the inn was filled with a multitude of soldiers hungry with the day's march. Each man brought a large piece of bread and a junk of meat, and, retiring to a side table or bench, cut it up with his pocket-knife and made a hearty meal. The regimental officers fared no better than the men. The campaign had shaken off many outward distinctions, though discipline was unimpaired."

The next morning, June 23, Prince Frederick Charles stood on the border line between Saxony and the Austrian dominions, and saw all his soldiers pass by him on the march. A week from the day when the Prussians entered Saxony their helmets were over the border into Bohemia.

The small successes of the next week were all with the Prussians. The divisions commanded respectively by the King and the Crown Prince followed Prince Frederick Charles rapidly, and on July 3, 1866, was fought the great battle called the Battle of Königgrätz by the Germans, but which we call Sadowa. Königgrätz was a great fortress near the battlefield, Sadowa a picturesque village with pine-log farmhouses that lay near.

The attack was a surprise to the Austrians, who were lying around Königgrätz, on the bank of the Elbe. They had no idea that the Prussians were so close to them. Prince Frederick Charles was determined to attack on the morning of July 3, and sent an aide-de-camp to tell the Crown Prince his plan, and to beg him to bring up his army to his help in the course of the day. The fighting began at dawn and lasted till about 3 o'clock in the afternoon. The battle was very bravely contested. Field-Marshal Benedek was a skilful general, and his Austrians were tried troops, though they were less sturdy men than the Prussians. Backward and forward swayed the tug of war until midday. Prince Frederick Charles saw nothing of the Crown Prince, and for some hours believed that his advance had in some way been prevented. At last, to his astonishment, he perceived Prussians *before him* driving the Austrians towards the Elbe. The Crown Prince had taken the enemy on the flank, and after a hard contest the Austrians were almost surrounded. The Elbe was in the rear of the Austrian army, but Benedek had taken the precaution to throw several bridges over it, and across them the remains of his army made their retreat. Great numbers of Austrians were taken prisoners. Hundreds who had been wounded remained upon the field. It was remarked that the Austrian prisoners seemed dazed by their defeat, but Italians who were serving in Austrian regiments looked joyful.

There is a certain interest in knowing how Count Bismarck fared that day, for he was with the army. To him the importance of victory in that battle was immense. He had urged his King, almost against his own judgment into the war, and a lost battle would — to himself — have been ruin. He had said to a friend on starting for headquarters: "We shall conquer, or I shall fall with the last charge of cavalry."

All day, during the fight, he sat on his big chestnut horse, and that night he had prepared to bivouac, like the combatants, on the field, with his head on a carriage cushion, when the Duke of Mecklenburg sent him word that he had a bed to offer him. The bed proved to be a child's bed. The Count put a chair at the end to make it longer, but his position was so cramped that he suffered from it for days after.

The next day an Austrian proposal for peace was received, but could not be entertained as Prussia had pledged herself to enter into no negotiations for peace without consulting Italy.

In a few hours the victorious army (Prince Frederick

Charles's division still in advance) was proceeding through Bohemia, the Austrians retreating as it came on.

We are told that the royal family of Saxony, escaping from Dresden, reached Vienna by railway on the morning of the 4th of July. The station was brilliantly lighted, and decorated in their honor with flags and flowers. The Emperor of Austria met them with a face as white as his uniform, and told them of the terrible disaster of Sadowa the day before.

Field-Marshal Benedek was adored by his army, but public clamor demanded his dismissal, after the lost battle, and he was superseded by the Archduke Albrecht, who had commanded in the Italian campaign and won the battle of Custozza. The imperial family determined to abandon Vienna, and to leave it open to the enemy, should he advance, instead of subjecting it to bombardment. They took refuge at Pruth.

We have seen how the Prussians marched through Saxony; here is a little picture of their march through Bohemia: —

"The villages along the road had been mostly deserted, for the inhabitants had fled south with the retreating Austrian army. The houses looked desolate, with their doors and windows wide open, and shutters flapping in the wind. A stray dog or two, here and there, stood and barked at the soldiers as they marched past, but even these were rare. For twenty-five miles the army passed through a luxuriantly fertile country, but almost entirely deserted. Sometimes one or two peasants stood by the side of the road, staring vacantly at the passing troops, or a few women might be found in a village, who, half-frightened by the sight of the soldiers, supplied them with the drinking water they everywhere requested. The children did not seem so timid; they were present along the roads in large numbers, for the cherries were just ripening, and they took advantage of the panic among their elders to make a raid on the trees alongside the road. With them the soldiers soon became good friends. The boys ran alongside of their battalions with their caps full of fruit and got coppers for handfuls, exulting in the coins they collected in so unexpected a way. But, for the most part, the country in front of the army was still and silent.

No church clocks sounded; the guardians had fled. No horses neighed; they had been taken to carry away the inhabitants, or to drag the Austrian artillery. Broad belts of corn, trodden flat to the ground, showed the march of the retreating Austrians. The Prussian infantry tramped steadily, keeping to the road, while the cavalry spread in bending lines through the fields; and behind the combatants toiled long trains of waggons, carrying the stores of this long army. Every column was headed by Uhlans, the black and white flags of whose lances waved with an almost funereal aspect above their smart caps and gay red or yellow facings."

In eight days the army entered Brünn, the capital of Moravia, having marched, always in perfect order, thirty miles a day. When they came in sight of Brünn they stopped outside the city to brush their clothes, refold their blankets, and enter smartly and in good trim.

At Brünn they halted, and Benedetti, the French ambassador, had his first interview on the subject of peace with Bismarck in a chamber of the upper story of the town hall.

The Emperor Napoleon was now desirous of stopping further warfare. The war had not turned out as he expected. He was not likely to wrest the Rhine provinces from the victorious Prussians. Their successes had added immensely to their strength and their prestige. He now saw how dangerous to France would be the powerful North German Confederation, under the supremacy of Prussia. It was too late to stay the march of events in Northern Germany, but he was desirous above all things to prevent further reverses to Austria. He believed he had put Italy out of the war by the sudden gift of Venetia, two days after her armies, which had fought for it, had been defeated at Custozza. He had pledged himself that the hereditary dominions of the Emperor Francis Joseph should not be torn from him, meaning by that, that he would encourage no revolutionary rising in Hungary, and would oppose, by force of arms if necessary, Count Bismarck's scheme of annexing Bohemia to his Confederation. Victorious Prussia must be content with having annexed Hanover, Hesse,

Anhalt, Nassau, Oldenburg, and the Danish duchies to her own dominions, and with having forced reluctant Saxony to join the North German Confederation. The German Empire would be reconstructed, consisting only of those States that joined with this confederacy, and in due time an Emperor of Germany would be elected, who, of course, would be the King of Prussia. These were the terms of peace. Its arbiter, the Emperor Napoleon, got only the *prestige* of dominating the diplomacy of Europe. He had hoped for much: he received nothing. But doubtless he consoled himself with visions of "à Berlin!" in the near future, for all the world believed that France and North Germany were soon to be at war.

The peace between Austria and Prussia is called the Peace of Prague. It was signed August 23, 1866, two months and eight days after the Prussian troops attacked Hanover. On the 20th and 21st of September grand preparations were made in Berlin to receive the troops home-coming from the war. All that evergreens and banners and military bands could do to express popular delight was done, but the wildest cheering was for the King, the Crown Prince, and Prince Frederick Charles, who rode together. The King stopped a few moments to speak to the wounded, who, unable to march in the procession, were seated in a group in an open square, and then he rode out of the city to place himself at the head of his troops, with whom he entered the town. There, cheered all the way, they formed in one of the great squares, and King, generals, soldiers, and people, united their voices in the national hymn of praise to the God who giveth victory.

We cannot here follow out the making of Germany. We turn rather to the making of Austria-Hungary, concerning which I should like here to say a few words.

"It would be difficult to point to any country," says a writer in the "London Quarterly Review," "in the course of the world's history which, in the short space of four years after defeat and loss of territory, so completely cast away old traditions and assumed a new political and social character, as

Austria, the old home of despotism, the last depository of the traditions of the Holy Roman Empire. Finally excluded from Italy and Germany, by the campaign of 1866, Austria cast aside her dreams of foreign domination, and set herself manfully to the task of making a nation out of the various conflicting nationalities over which she presides."

In 1850 a deep gloom had settled over all the nations under Hapsburg sway. The policy of reaction had been carried to an extreme, and, for all who had set themselves against it, punishment was most severe.

There never was a nation composed of more conflicting nationalities than Austria. Roughly, it might be divided into the States that formed part of the Reich, — the old German confederacy, — of the States that did not, and of the provinces of Italy. The States that formed part of Germany were Austria, Bohemia, and some minor towns and dukedoms. The non-German States were Hungary, — a separate kingdom, with her various dependencies, Croatia, Transylvania, and so on, — Austrian Poland, the Tyrol, Styria, and the Lombardo-Venetian kingdom. The inhabitants of all these countries had different languages, were all of different races, and each race cordially detested the others.

The new Emperor, Francis Joseph of Austria, having, in 1849, put down rebellion in his Italian States, turned his attention, as we have seen, to stamping out rebellion in Hungary. The old Constitution of the kingdom, so dear to every Hungarian heart, he had never sworn to observe, as his predecessor had done. He declared that it had been forfeited by the adoption of the Declaration of Independence, in 1849; and the Austrian armies, as we have seen, under Haynau and Windischgrätz, proceeded to take vengeance on all who had promoted or favored the establishment of a republic. In Vienna, leading men concerned in the brief rising of 1848, lawyers, publishers, jurists, and wise men who had hoped to effect, not revolution, but reform, were shot by court-martial. In Italy the work of reconquest was completed leisurely by *fusillades*; and on

EMPEROR FRANCIS JOSEPH.

the gallows erected at Arad, in Hungary, were strung up Magyar magnates, statesmen, and generals by the dozen. By drum-head law, men were condemned to be hung. Occasionally an imperial "pardon," as it was called, permitted them to be shot. For women there was the whip of Haynau. In Lord Palmerston's private correspondence we find a letter, speaking of the atrocities of the Austrian government at this period in Hungary, styling its agents "the greatest brutes that ever called themselves by the undeserved name of civilized man." He adds: —

"Their latest exploit of flogging forty-odd people, including two women, at Milan, some of the victims being gentlemen, is really too blackguardly and disgusting a proceeding. As to acting on their feelings of generosity and gentlemanliness, that is out of the question, because such feelings exist not in a set of officials who have been trained up in the school of Metternich, and better men can only blush in private for the disgrace such things bring upon their country; but I do hope you will not fail to express openly and decidedly the disgust which such proceedings excite in the public mind of England."

For several years Prince Schwarzenberg was governor of Hungary, and pursued this policy to the utmost. His rule failed so utterly that another man was put in his place. His rule was based on the methods of the Dark Ages. Then a system parliamentary in form, but without power, was tried, and failed like the others.

The government, in despair, invoked advice and help from Francis Deák, a leading Hungarian. He repeatedly declined to give them aid, declaring that, so long as Hungary had no Constitution, he could do nothing.

Deák was a Magyar, a year younger than Kossuth, and his course in the Hungarian parliament had been very much the same as that of Kossuth had been. Like Kossuth, he took a prominent part in the Diet in 1848; like him, he was a member of the Committee of Defence, or provisional government; but he was a reformer, not a revolutionist. He respected old forms, and clung to old rights. Trial by jury, freedom of the press, and similar questions of justice and reform he firmly advocated; but in matters affecting the political situation at large he was a strong Conservative. "I love progress," he used to say, — "not revolution."

When race hatred and the power of Russia brought about the downfall of the Hungarian cause, Deák retired quietly into private life, and lived for ten years in obscurity. In 1860 the Austrian government began to be utterly discouraged by the failure of whatever policy it tried in Hungary, and then first wished to consult Deák, who refused to interfere. Nevertheless, some of his sayings became largely quoted in Vienna, and helped on the cause he had at heart, especially his remark that "the Austrian government had wrongly buttoned its political coat, and there was now no help for it but to unbutton and button over again."

Kossuth had in 1858 great hopes of a new rising in Hungary. He had been summoned to Paris by Mazzini to meet Prince Napoleon, and the result was a secret interview with the Emperor. Some steps were taken, agents were sent into Hungary to corrupt Hungarians serving in the Austrian army, and a rising was planned to take place, which was abruptly put an end to by the Peace of Villafranca. Kossuth was heart-broken, and retired to Turin.

When the Prussians defeated the Austrians at Sadowa; when the peace of Prague was signed; when Austria had renounced her supremacy in Germany, and had given to Louis Napoleon her province of Venetia as the price of his good offices, the Austrian empire might have been thought to be on the road to dissolution. Something, its rulers felt, had to be done. The statesmen of Austria at that period had the calm sense to see that the only way to restore Austria was to strengthen her by conciliating the various heterogeneous parts of her great empire. They resolved to restore the Constitution of Hungary, — that is, not the old Constitution, but one that secured to Hungary freedom and self-government, while it bound her more closely to Austria. In short, in the new Austro-Hungarian empire and kingdom the two countries were to be like Siamese twins. Austria was to include all the German part of the empire, Hungary its own various Slavonic dependencies. Over Austria Francis Joseph was emperor; over Hungary he was king. Each country has now its own parliament, and each has what is called its delegation. The delegations arrange all federal affairs, peace, war, military matters, and federal expenditure. But these questions are discussed by each delegation in its own house. They must then be accepted by both delegations, and then go back to their respective parliaments for final decision. If no decision on matters of common interest can be thus reached, the Emperor-King decides the matter.

The result of this arrangement is that, as Hungary contains exceptionally fine men, and the Magyar race has been long accustomed to self-government, Hungary, in all federal matters generally takes the lead from Austria, though the two nations seem to dwell together on the most friendly terms.

This arrangement has been in force more than twenty-five years. Under it the Emperor Francis Joseph was crowned with the crown of St. Stephen, which for a quarter of a century had disappeared. All efforts to induce Kossuth to reveal its whereabouts were unavailing, but some one else surrendered the secret, and it was dug up in a forest under a mighty tree. With the crown, Francis Joseph took the coronation oath to observe the Constitution.

Deák, whose advice and assistance brought about all this good for his country, died ten years after this Constitution was established. His body lay in state at Pesth with every demonstration, not only of a nation's sorrow, but with a laurel wreath sent by the hand of the Empress Elizabeth, that beautiful and eccentric imperial huntress, who dearly loved and honored him.

Deák lived during the last ten years of his life, while compatriots and strangers pined to do him honor, in the simplest manner possible, at Breda. He had given up his estates to his next heirs for a small annuity. He was a bachelor and had rooms in a hotel, — the " Queen of England." He was a small, thick-set man, looking far more like a German than a Magyar. He was called the Father of the restored Constitution of Hungary, in public speeches, but in private life people loved to speak of him by endearing names. *Der alte Mann* was their favorite epithet. The Queen-Empress Elizabeth, who had a country seat near Pesth, called him " Uncle Deák."

"His modesty, his retiring disposition," says Karl Blind, "never forsook him. Having nothing about his personality that could be called impressive, he might, in his *sombrero* hat and his Neapolitan cloak, have passed unobserved in a crowd; but a nation's admiring looks followed his steps in spite of his occasional strong protests against every ovation. Repeatedly the Court confidentially approached him to know what he would accept that it was in the power of the sovereign to bestow on him. His answer was uniformly: 'I am not in want of anything.' At last Francis Joseph, on the advice of one of his ministers, sent him a Royal Family portrait, in a frame of gold, set with costly gems. 'It would look like a present in money,' said Deák. 'I cannot accept that.' Taking the picture out of its setting, he sent back the frame, with his thanks and compliments. All decorations he also refused to accept, much to the annoyance and discomfiture of the King-Emperor. Deák's constant resolve was to remain independent. No calumny could touch so disinterested a man."

Alas! — the pity of it. While Deák was thus honored, Kossuth lived in exile, wounded to the quick by what he deemed the ingratitude of his countrymen. He had imbibed the ideas of Mazzini. He was no friend to constitutional reforms, or to constitutional government. He endeavored to defeat the plans of Deák in 1868, and the followers and admirers of Deák found it hard to pardon him. Nevertheless, he could have returned from exile (as his son, since his father's death, has done) by going through a simple acknowledgment of the *de facto* government of Austria-Hungary. He died in 1894, aged 92, with his faculties still unimpaired. His body was brought back to Hungary with every demonstration of affection and respect. He is buried in the land he loved.

"To-day," says Karl Blind, writing of Francis Deák, " Hungary has once more her old landmarks, and her time-honored ground law, modified by the reforms of 1848. Her ruler — placed under an especial coronation oath — is recognized only as her *king*. The name of Hungary figures in all State documents on equal terms with that of Austria. The Honveds, who had fought against the Kaiser, are acknowledged as having merited well of their fatherland. The rank of general was given back to Klapka and two other generals, once foremost amongst the military chiefs of the revolution. Men who once narrowly escaped the gallows have been placed in the highest positions. Andrassy, Austria-Hungary's leading statesman, belongs to that class, — in short the restoration of self-government was as complete as, under existing circumstances, was possible."

As I write, in 1896, the great fête is going on in Hungary which is to last a year and celebrate the thousandth anniversary of the formation of the kingdom of Hungary under its beloved, time-honored Constitution. The King-Emperor joins with his Hungarian subjects in their national rejoicings. He is present at the unveiling of statues to men who once refused him their allegiance, and takes a foremost part in the rejoicings of a people who have long learned to love and honor him.

Alas! that two men who would have made such worthy successors to the present Emperor have been cut off by violent and premature death, — the Crown Prince Rudolph, who, in spite of his lax morality, would have made a liberal and noble sovereign, and Maximilian, who would have been the next heir. Maximilian had the good word of all who knew him, save those who shot him in cold blood at Queretaro.

CHAPTER XIV.

MENTANA.

THE year 1867 opened with rejoicings. On the 7th of November, 1866, Victor Emmanuel had made his triumphant entry into Venice, and the day on which Venetia had been offered to him he had declared to be "the happiest day of his life." But that happiness was soon at an end; no year of his troubled reign proved so unhappy as the year 1867, as he said subsequently with a sigh. "You are at least more fortunate than I," he wrote to a minister who had resigned his office, "you can send in your resignation."

The French Army quitted Rome, in accordance with the convention of 1864, on the 4th of December, 1866. The Pope and his advisers did not seem much discomposed by its departure. Pio Nono had been raising a Roman legion. In addition to his Swiss Guard and Garda Nobile, he had his Papal Zouaves. Men of all nations and languages, Irish and French predominating, enlisted in his service, — foreigners who knew the Holy Father only as their spiritual head, not as their temporal ruler. The population of Rome, and of the restricted papal territory that surrounded it, was six hundred thousand. The Pope's army amounted to twenty thousand, and the priests who had hastened into the city as a refuge, were computed at twenty thousand, while a monsignor high in office confessed to a Spanish traveller that it was believed that seventy thousand men belonging to revolutionary societies were in the city. The Convention of 1864 bound Victor Emmanuel, when the French garrison should be removed, to protect the papal frontier from invasion. "This would take two hundred thousand men," La Marmora said at the time, disapproving the Convention.

Garibaldi, mortified and furious at the way in which Italian unity had been achieved, not by arms but by diplomacy, made up his mind that the moment was propitious for another attack on Rome. His life was now drawing, as he thought, to a close, and its object was unaccomplished. Even more than the expulsion of the Austrians, he desired the annihilation of the Pope's temporal power. Unlike Victor Emmanuel, who was a Catholic and a Christian, Garibaldi was a rabid opponent of all priests, and had no sympathy with religious feeling.

"However we may admire the expediency of trying to make Rome the capital of Italy," says Mr. Theodore Bent, " we cannot forget that Garibaldi, in pursuing his desire, set at defiance the authority of his country and his king; disregarded the will of a parliament elected by well-nigh universal suffrage; and urged Italy to break her pledge with France, by which she had agreed to leave the Pope in possession of Rome, if France withdrew her troops as the convention of September, 1864, required. Hence France was at liberty, in accordance with a clause in that convention, to return to Rome, and to protect the hierarchy if attacked by Garibaldi."

Many Italians of the moderate and constitutional party considered the departure of the French as the first stepping-stone to the acquisition of Rome. At the time the convention was under discussion in 1864, Monsieur Drouyn de Lhuys, the French prime minister, who was engaged in the negotiation, so spoke of it: —

"A revolution, however, so great, naturally required time before it could be brought about; and Italy had gone through so many revolutions during the last twenty years, that anything rapid might be detrimental to her welfare; she wanted rest, and common-sense; neither of which Garibaldi would allow her to have. He was determined to precipitate matters in the face of every far-seeing statesman, long before affairs were ripe, confusing thereby all their manœuvres by cutting across their most skilfully arranged preparations."

Mazzini wholly disapproved of Garibaldi's plans. His scheme was a republic; the overthrow of Victor Emmanuel's government; the retention of the Pope in Rome, with a sort of nominal supremacy over Italian affairs, though with no power. He was even, possibly, afraid of Garibaldi's extreme hatred to priests, proclaimed in an address he made from a balcony to an excited crowd: "We must go to Rome to clear out that den of vipers, to make soapsuds, and scour out and wipe off that black stain; for without all this cleansing our nation will never be itself, and if this Italy does not occupy the place it ought, it is on account of that black race of priests, a worse plague than the cholera."

There were fierce disputes in Rome itself between the two sections of the revolutionary party. Arms were stored for use when the time for action should arrive, nor were there wanting dynamite and Orsini bombs.

Meantime, during the first months of the year, there was anything but harmony in the Italian government. Prime ministers were several times changed, and Parliament twice passed a vote of "No confidence" in the Ministry. The financial condition of the country was in an alarming state. Taxes were six times as heavy as they had been in former years, yet in the treasury there was a deficit of forty million dollars, and no visible means of supplying it, unless, indeed, by the suppression of convents, and the confiscation of much of their property.

Garibaldi, during these early months of 1867, was making an electioneering tour through Central Italy, — an electioneering tour he called it, but it was in reality a tour to call up and enlist volunteers for his projected expedition. The Pope quietly regarded these preparations, believing firmly that a miracle would be worked to save his temporal throne. In France, though the French garrison was removed from Rome, the Emperor encouraged the enlistment of Frenchmen in the Papal Zouaves, and the fine body of troops in the Papal army called the Antibes Legion was composed almost entirely of French soldiers, allowed to volunteer from the regular army.

On the other hand, volunteers for the Garibaldian army began to collect from all sides as Garibaldi approached the Roman frontier. Never had Italy more needed the strong hand of her great statesman Cavour. Ricasoli, having no majority in Parliament, had been forced to resign. Rattazzi, who was more of a shifty politician, took his place. Apparently he was giving to the great agitator a free hand. Garibaldi had taken on himself the title of General of the Roman Republic, and assumed to have legal authority in virtue of the decree of the Roman Constituent Assembly, which in its dying moments had made him Dictator. While he believed himself in full career, however, he was suddenly arrested at Sinalunga, and carried off, half-dressed, and with no hat upon his head.

He was taken to Alessandria, but contrived on his way to scribble a few lines in pencil, by way of proclamation, to his followers: "The people of Rome have the right of slaves, — to rise against their tyrants. The Italians have the right to assist them, if even fifty Garibaldis were in prison; so, *avanti, Italiani, avanti!*"

The Minister of Marine hastened to Alessandria to make terms for Garibaldi's peaceful retirement to Caprera. He was told not to consider himself a prisoner; but the government stationed four steamers and a frigate off the island of Caprera, to make it impossible he should escape.

Meantime, volunteers continued to assemble. The ministry was forced to resign under the pressure of a storm of unpopularity consequent on Garibaldi's arrest; and one or two important events took place during his enforced retirement. One was a little rebellion in Sicily, engaged in by the bands of brigands who still infested the mountains and were stirred into action by the intrigues of Francis, their ex-king. They threatened Palermo, in which there was a very small garrison, but the courage, skill, and firmness of General Cadorna, and of the Marquis di Rudini, then in command there, put the rising down. Another event was the blowing up of the barracks of the Serristori in Rome, by which fifty of the Papal Zouaves perished. All my readers will remember the account of this in Mr. Crawford's "Sant' Ilario."

Victor Emmanuel issued a proclamation on October 27, 1867: —

"Italians! Bands of volunteers, excited and seduced by the work of a faction, without authority from me or my government, have violated the frontier of the State. The respect due equally by all citizens to the laws and international conditions sanctioned by the parliament and by me establishes on me in these grave circumstances an inexorable obligation of honor. Europe knows that the banner raised in the neighboring lands on which was written the destruction of the supreme spiritual authority of the head of the Catholic religion, is not mine. This attempt places the common country in great peril, and imposes on me the imperious duty of saving the honor of the nation, by not allowing to be confounded in one two causes absolutely distinct, two objects totally different. Italy must be secured against the dangers that may come. Europe must be convinced that Italy, faithful to her engagements, does not wish to be, and will not be, a disturber of the public order. . . . I am the depository of the right of declaring peace or war for the nation, and I cannot tolerate the usurpation of it. I trust, therefore, that the voice of reason will be listened to, and that the Italian citizens who are violating that right will quickly place themselves in the ranks of our troops. . . . When the excitement has calmed down, and public order is fully re-established, then my government, in agreement with that of France, and in accordance with the vote of parliament, will try sincerely, by every loyal effort, to find a solution which will put a termination to the grave and important question of the Romans. Italians! I have, and always will, put confidence in your good sense, as you have done in the affection of your King for this great country, which, thanks to our common sacrifices, we have at last placed upon the roll of nations, and which we ought to transmit to our sons honored and entire.

"VICTOR EMMANUEL.

"FLORENCE, October 27, 1867."

Victor Emmanuel found the Emperor Napoleon as hard to deal with as Garibaldi, and the clerical party in France as unmanageable as the revolutionary party in Rome. He was very desirous to prevent the return of the French garrison, and made the most earnest representations to the Emperor, assuring him that the ruin of Italy would be the ruin of France. But the Emperor showed even more than his usual vacillation on the occasion. He was tired of interference in Italy. He was ill. He was perplexed by changes which he was pondering in his own system of government. He was haunted by the ghost of Maximilian. And since the death of de Morny he had had no confidential adviser. There was indeed a power behind his throne, the Empress Eugénie, who was in her turn under the influence of the clerical party, and the clerical party had long before formulated the relations it desired to establish with the Emperor: "Do you keep the Pope on his throne, and we will keep you on yours."

From October 19 to October 26, Napoleon again and again ordered and countermanded the departure from Toulon of the transports that were to carry back a French army to Civita Vecchia.

There is a story, which is hardly probable, though told by General Menabrea in his posthumous memoirs, that the Emperor went so far as to threaten to pour a large army into Italy and break up Italian unity, since Victor Emmanuel did not seem able to restrain his rebellious subjects from violating faith with foreign lands.

This threat, it is said by Menabrea, had its effect on the prime minister, Ricasoli, and led to Garibaldi's arrest at Sinalunga; but the volunteers continued to gather, and on October 14, 1867, their chief made a daring escape on a dark night, alone in a fishing skiff, from Caprera. He reached the neighboring island of Maddalena, thence passed over to Sardinia, and thence sailed for the Tuscan coast in a boat managed only by himself and his son-in-law Canzio. The sea was rough, the wind unfavorable, it took them many hours to make land; then they ran the boat ashore among some reeds, and wandered some hours in the dark in a trackless swamp. "Of all the risky and dangerous enterprises that I have undertaken in my life," said Garibaldi afterwards, "the most arduous, the most beautiful, and that of which I am most proud, is my escape from Caprera."

He went openly to Florence; he harangued a crowd of people in a public square, and no man arrested him, for the Rattazzi ministry had resigned. Menabrea, who succeeded Rattazzi, had not yet been appointed, and there was no one to give the order. The general took the train for Turin, and entered the Papal States on the same day that the first instalment of the French troops reached Civita Vecchia.

The volunteers were numerous, but for the most part were mere boys. They were undisciplined, ununiformed, and ill-armed. Their officers could only be distinguished by each carrying a green bough in his hand.

The point that Garibaldi desired to reach was a town and fortress situated on a hill commanding a magnificent view over the valley of the Tiber. It was called Monte Rotondo.

Garibaldi with his men attacked the place, the volunteers fighting with great bravery. The besieged had cannon, the besiegers none. They fought till nearly midnight, when, the gate of the little city being destroyed by fire, the Garibaldians poured into the town, and the next day Garibaldi found himself comfortably lodged in Prince Piombino's beautiful palace, looking down on his beloved Rome. His men committed many sacrilegious acts in the cathedral, and drew down on themselves the indignation of the inhabitants of the little city. Garibaldi had seven of the worst marauders shot, but this did not allay public feeling.

There had been a gallant attempt made to supply the revolutionists in Rome with arms, by bringing them in boats up the Tiber. Enrico and Giovanni Cairoli undertook this enterprise. They had almost succeeded when their party was attacked and cut to pieces. A body of papal troops had come out to attack the Garibaldians, but, finding Monte Rotondo taken, they retreated, burning all the bridges (except one at Mentana) by which the invading force could approach Rome. To Mentana Garibaldi advanced, three days after he had taken Monte Rotondo. There he halted, only four miles and a half from Rome. This halt was incomprehensible to many persons. They did not know that the papal commandant at the Castle of St. Angelo, was ready to deliver up that fortress for twenty thousand dollars. That sum (four thousand pounds) had been raised by some English friends of Garibaldi, and the transaction was about to be completed, when the first detachment of French troops arrived in Rome. The French government had in its service, as a spy, a man trusted by Garibaldi, placed by him in charge of his camp post-office, and intrusted with his cipher. This man had occupied the same position with Garibaldi in the Tyrol; had fought by his side bravely, and the chief would listen to no suspicions concerning him. It was not until the secrets of the Paris Prefecture of Police fell into the hands of French republicans in 1871 that it was discovered that for four years this man had been in receipt of a thousand francs a month for secret services to the imperial government.

Due notice of the projected treachery of the governor of the Castle of St. Angelo having been thus furnished to the French, the governor was removed at once, and the garrison in the fortress was changed.

On the failure of his plan, Garibaldi resolved to retreat to Monte Rotondo, a retrograde movement which caused the desertion of a large number of his followers. His army was one that could be held together only by success. It is probable that with all troops belonging to the Latin races, success is essential to preserve steadiness and constancy.

At Monte Rotondo, Garibaldi issued an address to his army, informing them that the government of Victor Emmanuel had just sent troops over the frontier.

" If these troops come to join us in the design of taking Rome," he said, " they are to be looked upon as friends: but if they come to sustain tyranny, and to enforce the base convention of September, 1864, then I will let all the world know that I alone, a Roman general with full power, elected by the universal suffrage of the only legal government in Rome, — the Republic, —

have a right to maintain myself armed in this, the territory under my jurisdiction!"

But with an Italian army behind him, a Papal army confronting him, and a French army disembarking at Civita Vecchia, — with his own men disaffected and dispirited, with his prestige impaired, and with no unanimity among the revolutionary party within the walls of Rome, Garibaldi felt that he must not stay long at Monte Rotondo, but must hasten to act, if anything was to be done. With a force of four thousand seven hundred infantry, one squadron of cavalry, and only four guns of small calibre, to assault the walls of a great city, he moved forward a little before midday on the 3d of November. The troops were to have started before dawn, but they were delayed by the advice of Menotti Garibaldi, who suggested that, as many of them marched barefoot, and a consignment of shoes had just arrived at headquarters, the advance had better be delayed till all were shod.

This mistake was fatal. The battle began near the hamlet of Mentana, a little village with a single street, nestled in a valley.

"This village in the Roman Campagna," says the Countess Cesaresco, "sprang into history on a November day one thousand and sixty-seven years before, as the meeting-place of Charlemagne and Leo III. Here they shook hands over their bargain, — that the Pope should crown the great Charles Emperor and that the Emperor should secure to the Pope his temporal power. And now a ragged band of Italian youths was come to say that of bargains between popes and emperors there had been enough."

The fortunes of the battle at first varied. At the first onset the volunteers fell back in confusion. Then they rallied and with the bayonet retook the principal positions they had lost. About two o'clock, the enemy's fire slackened; something was evidently taking place in the papal ranks. An unfamiliar whirring sound soon told that the French with their new *chassepôts* had come up.

A hailstorm of bullets decimated the Garibaldians. The cannon they had captured at Monte Rotondo were useless. They had exhausted their ammunition. They fought on till four o'clock, and then retreated. The *chassepôts*, as the French general reported, "had done wonders."

Next day the Garibaldians were in retreat. The castle of Mentana, in which they had left some men, capitulated, and eight hundred ragged prisoners were taken in triumph into Rome.

"It would have been wiser to let them go. The Romans had been told that the Garibaldians were cut-throats, incendiaries, human bloodhounds, waiting to fly at them They saw a host of boys, with pale, wistful, very youthful faces. If anything was wanting to seal the fate of the temporal power it was the sight of that procession of famished and wounded Italians brought to Rome by the foreigner."

Garibaldi, haggard and aged by this reverse, led the remnant of his volunteers over the frontier. His hat was pulled down over his eyes. "It is the first time they make me turn my back like this," he murmured. ". . . It would have been better. . . ."

He was preparing to go back to Caprera when he was arrested. It was the Italian government's response to an angry and insolent letter from the French Emperor, reproaching Victor Emmanuel, and telling him he did not know how to govern.

To govern! Were ever tasks so hard thrown upon a sovereign at one time? To fuse into one nation twenty-five millions of people, separated for centuries by race hatreds from each other; to give them equal laws; to raise money for the expense of wars, revolutions, and good government; with ex-rulers, and a French Emperor of vacillating views to be dealt with; with Rome a thorn in the side of Italy, with the head of the Catholic Church and his most ardent adherents conscientiously opposed to him; with a new Constitution to make "march," and all the complications arising out of relations to France and the Roman question?

Garibaldi retired to Caprera after a brief imprisonment at Varignano. As far as Italy and Rome were concerned, the star of the old hero had set forever.

Victor Emmanuel was made furious by the battle of Mentana. He had pledged himself that if the Garibaldians were repulsed by the papal troops, his soldiers should disarm them. He had never expected that the French, in alliance with the clerical party, would mow down his subjects, — even his rebellious subjects, — with *chassepôts*. He said plainly to the Emperor, "The late events have suffocated every remembrance of gratitude due to you in the heart of Italy. It is no longer in the power of the government to maintain the alliance with France. The *chassepôt* gun at Mentana has given it a mortal blow."

Sorely tried as Victor Emmanuel had been during this year, some events in his own family had given him pleasure. His second son, Prince Amadeo, Duke d'Aosta, wounded at Custozza, had been married in May to Princess Maria Vittoria, daughter of a prince of ancient family, though not of royal descent. This marriage was very acceptable to the Italian people, and in due time a little son was born, named Filiberto Emmanuele.

The Crown Prince Humbert remained unmarried until April, 1868. The bride intended for him was an Austrian archduchess, who met with a shocking and accidental death.

But as time went on, it became necessary for the future of Italy that he should give to his country a direct heir to the crown. There was a charming princess living with her mother in Turin, a princess of the house of Savoy, daughter of the Duke of Genoa, Ferdinand Alberto Amadeo, King Victor Emmanuel's beloved brother, who, dying in 1855, had left two children, a daughter and a son. To Margherita might be applied Wordsworth's lines: —

"None saw her but to love her,
None knew her but to praise."

In 1868 some preliminary steps had been taken to secure the hand of this pearl of Italy for the Prince of Rou-

PRINCESS MARGHERITA.
(Afterwards Queen of Italy.)

mania, who subsequently married a hardly less charming princess, Elizabeth of Wied.

The marriage of the cousins was celebrated at Turin. Prince Napoleon and Princess Clotilde came from Paris, Queen Pia came from Portugal, and the Crown Prince Frederick of Prussia was present. He loved Italy, and had formed a strong personal attachment for Victor Emmanuel. At the beginning of the year 1869, the present heir to the throne of Italy was born, Victor Emmanuel, now Prince of Naples. But he came into the world while all Italy was agitated by dread of a great calamity. His grandfather, King Victor Emmanuel, lay sick of a malignant fever, in a country seat near Pisa. He had twice before suffered from a similar attack, and his physicians believed that he could not resist a third one. He thought himself dying, and sent for the parish priest to give him the last sacraments. It is said that the priest used every argument, and even threats, to induce the King to restore Church property. Be this as it may, he could extract no promise from his penitent on matters relating to politics, but when he spoke of his personal sins, and, above all, of his *liaison* with Rosina, Countess of Mirafiore, who had been his mistress many years, and by whom he had children, Victor offered no opposition to his demand that he should marry her. The lady was in the house; she was called to the side of the sickbed, and the religious ceremony was performed, though it was never, I think, followed by a civil marriage.

Absolution was given the King, — and, in the absence for a few moments of other attendants, his valet administered to him a glass of port wine. The stimulant, aiding a salutary revulsion of feeling, had an immediate effect; the King rallied at once, though for some time he remained too weak to take part in politics, and ministerial crises continued to go on.

Victor Emmanuel always took pleasure in travelling about his dominions. He did so without the pomp of a royal progress. He liked, too, to receive visitors. Several members of the imperial family of Russia came to see him; and also some distinguished Austrians. "Your sovereign is a true king," said one of them to General Menabrea, the prime minister.

The Empress Eugénie, when, at the close of 1869, she made her triumphal journey to Egypt, touched at Venice, where Victor Emmanuel and his ministers courteously greeted her; and Count Beust, the Austrian prime minister, on his way back from the festivities at the opening of the Suez Canal, called, by his master's wish, to pay his respects to the King of Italy. The heart of Victor Emmanuel rejoiced over the friendly advances made to him by the Austrian Emperor, and the renewal of family ties.

The Spaniards, who had found great difficulty in obtaining a king after the flight of Queen Isabella in 1868, offered the precarious honor to Prince Amadeo. Amadeo did his duty nobly by his Spanish subjects. No one has ever found a flaw in his career or in his character; but the crown proved a very uneasy one. His young wife's health failed under the burthen of royalty; he became convinced that no sovereign but a Spaniard could hope to rule Spain satisfactorily; and in February, 1873, he abdicated, taking back with him to Italy the love and admiration of even the most disaffected of his subjects.

When war became imminent between Prussia and France, there were proposals for a triple alliance between France, Austria, and Italy. But Italy could not forgive the *chassepôts* of Mentana, and Victor Emmanuel's ministers dreaded that the fortunes of war would impair Italian unity. Besides, Napoleon would not consent to withdraw his troops from Rome as the price of Italy's realliance with France. Nevertheless, when disaster after disaster fell on the French Emperor, the generosity of the Savoyard's heart would have induced him to hasten to the relief of the man who had once befriended him. But the Italian ministry would not consent, and events marched too rapidly to give time to overcome their opposition.

There was one man, however, in Italy, who, as soon as

France was declared a Republic, hastened to aid her. Garibaldi was now much broken in health, and much changed in disposition. What Scripture calls "the gall of bitterness" seems to have been infused into his soul. Much of what he wrote during the last years of his life is mere raving.

A few days after he had openly declared himself in favor of establishing a European Areopagus which should keep the world in peace, he set off to offer his sword to the new Republic. It was at the close of September, 1870; the Prussians had just completed the investment of Paris. Garibaldi had already written to the Committee of Defence, offering his services, but he had received no answer. His arrival might form a new embarrassment for the provisional government. It had enough upon its hands already, and the Italian government feared lest Garibaldi might involve them in new diplomatic complications, for it was believed that the ultimate object of his offers of service was the recovery of Nice, either by force, or as a gift of gratitude.

He reached Tours at nearly the same moment as Gambetta, who dropped out of the clouds. No party in the Republic was very much obliged to the foreigner who had taken upon himself the mission to save France. In his autobiography he complains bitterly of the indifference shown to him by members of the provisional government, by "Gambetta most of all, — he from whom I ought to have expected, if not personal sympathy, at least active and energetic support."

France, besides having plenty to attend to at home in the latter months of 1870, held, as a national axiom of diplomacy, the opinion of M. Thiers, — that a united Italy was a danger for France; that France ought to be surrounded only by nations with loose federative constitutions. Italian revolutionists might be enthusiastic over the triumph of the "good cause" in France, but French republicans were not sympathetic or enthusiastic over the "good cause" as desired by Italians.

Mazzini wrote to Garibaldi: "We want Rome and Nice. Aid us, and reckon upon us. But if help is to be useful to us, it must come with lightning rapidity."

In March, 1871, there had been a rising stirred up by Mazzini's agents among the garrison of Milan. The ringleaders were shot, among them a corporal named Barsanti, — a dull, ill-looking fellow with dark skin and hair, whom it pleased Italian sympathizers to make into a hero and a martyr, endowing him with golden curls, a fair blond face, and a despairing mother.

Garibaldi was first offered the command of two or three hundred volunteers assembled at Chambéry. He refused indignantly, and threatened to return home. Then Gambetta, fearing lest any slight to Garibaldi should be resented by the radicals, offered him the command of the irregulars in the Vosges district, and a brigade of the Garde Mobile. Garibaldi's friends had desired for him the command of the whole Eastern Army; but Gambetta feared, as he said, the remonstrances not only of the generals of his regular army, but of the clergy; whom it was the wish of the provisional government to conciliate.

Garibaldi's command consisted of four brigades, one commanded by Menotti, one by Ricciotti, one by a Polish patriot, and the fourth by another unimportant general.

Some one, describing the assemblage of these troops, says : —

"We seem here in the midst of a *bal masqué;* thousands of different costumes are to be seen. Boys, at most sixteen years of age, are camping in the mud of the fields, scarcely covered by a thin blue blouse, like those worn by carters. The Bretons and French Garibaldians wear low brimmed hats, like those in the opera 'Dinorah'; the *franc-tireurs* all dress unlike each other; the mobiles are mixed with last remnants of the line; there are a few hussars among the dragoons and chasseurs d'Afrique who have escaped from the Prussians at Sedan and Metz; hospital attendants with the red cross on the white field; and, amid this mass of soldiers (not soldiers in the true sense of the word), are women and children, who wander about the fields to escape from the enemy."

The troops of Garibaldi were a horde and not an army; and they everywhere brought down upon themselves the indignation of the country people. If they were ragged, like Falstaff's men, they had, like Bardolph, no scruple about stealing pixes, desecrating churches, and piercing altar-pieces with their bayonets. Besides which, Bordone, the chief's quartermaster, was a rogue, implicitly trusted, as Wolff, the French spy, had been at Mentana, by the too confiding general.

It is not surprising that, with such forces, Garibaldi may be said to have accomplished nothing in the campaign. When peace was made at last at Versailles, Bismarck tried hard to have Garibaldi and his horde excepted, saying he should like to take him to Berlin and exhibit him as a monster of ingratitude. It is rather hard to imagine on what grounds Bismarck based this character of Garibaldi; but the two men could never have loved or served each other.

The campaign closed with a gleam of success on the 20th of January, 1871, when a large force of Prussians was driven off from Dijon, and Ricciotti Garibaldi distinguished himself.

The French National Assembly, which met at Bordeaux in February, 1871, was very far from grateful to Garibaldi, and threw great blame on him, which was wholly undeserved. They expected from him apparently all that could have been done by a disciplined and well-appointed army. But Frenchmen at that moment were ready to throw blame on any one.

Garibaldi took leave of his army of the Vosges and retired to Caprera. A complimentary letter followed him, signed by all the members of the provisional government.

Shortly after that, he was elected to the French Assembly from Algeria, but when he presented himself to take his seat a violent scene took place in the Chamber. It was moved that General Garibaldi was ineligible, being a foreigner. Victor Hugo sprang to the tribune, and exclaimed: "Not a king, — not a state, — *no one* came forward to help France, which had done so much for Europe, — only one man!" Here ironical applause interrupted the orator. "Well!" he continued, " no Powers interposed, but a man came forward, — that man was a power. He came. He has fought. I speak but the plain truth. He was the only general who fought for France, and was not conquered!"

Those only who know Frenchmen, and have seen what the French Chamber is like in a moment of excitement, can imagine the tumult created by these words. The fury of the deputies became so great that Victor Hugo found it prudent to leave the hall.

A few weeks later the Commune of Paris offered Garibaldi the command of the National Guard, but Garibaldi declined at once. "What you need," he said, " is an honest dictator who can choose honest men to act under him. If you should have the good fortune to find a Washington, France will recover from shipwreck, and in a short time be grander than ever."

Garibaldi returned to his island home, and worked off some of his superfluous energy with his pen. Almost every week some writing of his, warning, appealing, or vituperating, found its way into print, and was read throughout the reading world.

For twenty years Garibaldi had been endeavoring in vain to get divorced from his bride of an hour, whom he had married at Como during his campaign in 1859. But on January 14, 1880, the good news reached him that the divorce had been obtained. Como, where the marriage ceremony had taken place, was, at the time of the marriage, Austrian soil, subject to the laws of Austria. The marriage laws of Austria differed from those of Piedmont, and Garibaldi had cause to thank his enemies that through that circumstance his relief had been obtained.

He had for many years considered himself the husband of Francesca, the nurse brought over to Caprera much against his will by his daughter Theresita; they had had several children, whom, despairing of obtaining his divorce, Garibaldi had implored the King to legitimize. The thing, however, was impossible. "I would have done it myself long ago — if it could have been done," was the answer of Victor Emmanuel.

Ten days after the receipt of the news of the divorce, Garibaldi and Francesca were legally married. The crippled general sat in his bath chair; Theresita and her husband Canzio, Menotti and his wife, and as many of Garibaldi's old friends as could be assembled, were present on the occasion. Telegrams of congratulation flowed in, among them one from Victor Emmanuel.

In 1875, after Rome had become the capital of Italy, Garibaldi revisited it as a deputy to the Italian Parliament. His journey to Rome from Civita Vecchia was a triumph, but the Romans found him physically greatly changed. He was a very old man, crippled with gout and rheumatism, and he could move only with crutches. Some one has said, "He was the idol of Italy from the throne to the cottage; Italians worshipped him, but they did not know what to do with him." He still wore the red shirt and the gray cloak, and his smile lit up his face as sunnily as ever.

When, on assuming his seat in the Senate House, he took the oath of allegiance, the whole house rose and cheered him frantically. His intercourse with his King was friendly and affectionate; for one whole month, — his "honeymoon" as he afterwards called it, — he was on good terms with his government.

He threw himself ardently into a plan for diverting the course of the Tiber, thereby making Rome more healthy, and improving the agricultural conditions of the Campagna. Victor Emmanuel, Prince Torlonia, and Garibaldi were at the head of this plan. "We must do it," cried the voice of Rome, "because Garibaldi wishes it." "I thought we were two powers in Rome," said Pio Nono kindly, "myself and the King; now I see that there are three of us." But the question of money rose, — the state of the finances of Italy did not justify the project. It was never carried out, and the whole world may regret the non-discovery as yet of the relics of old Roman art and greatness that still must lie deep in the bed of Father Tiber.

In 1880, a few months after his marriage, Garibaldi became enraged with the ministry of the day, then presided over by Benedetto Cairoli, brother of the three gallant Cairoli who had died for Italy. Benedetto Cairoli was a man who commanded universal respect and love. He had been a dear friend of Garibaldi, until suddenly this friendship was broken off by a scrape into which Canzio got himself in Genoa, which landed him in prison. Garibaldi denounced his old friend, who had sanctioned the arrest, as "a lackey who had thrown off his mask," and he then resigned his seat in the Senate Chamber.

Garibaldi died at Caprera, June 2, 1882, worn out by the hardships of his life, its excitements, its disappointments, and its honors. He was seventy-five years of age, not old as compared with some living statesmen. He had desired that his remains should be cremated, but they were buried at Caprera.

On March 19, 1895, the corner stone of a national monument to Garibaldi was laid at Rome by the King and Queen of Italy, in the presence of the Cabinet Ministers, and innumerable dignitaries. The day was selected as the twenty-fifth anniversary of the reunion of Rome to Italy, and the site of the monument was appropriately chosen on the Janiculum, because Garibaldi's defence of Rome against the French in 1849 was there most furious, and most successful. The monument itself is by a Florentine sculptor, Emilio Gallori, and is nearly completed. Inserted in the foundation stone is a splendidly wrought casket, with coins, medals, and inscriptions attesting the great deeds of Garibaldi, with the appropriate dates. The casket contained also the arms of Nice, Savoy, Rome, and Sicily, and a medallion portrait of Garibaldi in high relief. It was reverentially placed in the excavation made for it, by Crispi, then Prime Minister, and the Syndic of Rome. The hands of Umberto and Margherita did the rest.

CHAPTER XV.

THE LAST YEARS OF VICTOR EMMANUEL'S REIGN.

VICTOR EMMANUEL never wholly recovered from the effects of the malarial fever, which had so nearly ended his days at his hunting seat at San Rossore in the autumn of 1869. But the crowning triumph of his life was yet to come.

Garibaldi, again released from prison, was banished and sorrowful, though honors were showered on him the moment he set foot upon Italian soil as a free man. He had failed to crown his life-work, — that glory was reserved for the sovereign whom he had always loved, yet sometimes distrusted; to whom he always rendered homage, yet whom he often disobeyed; whose plans he crossed, yet to whom he gave a kingdom. As he quitted the prison-fortress of Varignano, he wrote these words: "Farewell, Rome ; farewell, Capitol ; who knows who will think of thee, — and when?"

This was at the close of 1867. Before three years were out, Rome was the capital of the kingdom of Italy. Pio Nono had yielded to an overwhelming force, and had retired to his prison, — as he ever afterwards designated the palace, gardens, and adjoining demesnes of the enormous Vatican.

When news of the repulse of Garibaldi's volunteers at Mentana reached Paris, it gave rise to an exciting debate in the French Chamber of Deputies. Jules Favre proposed a vote of censure on the ministry for their Roman policy. Thiers, though no friend to the government of the Emperor, gave the ministry his support on this occasion, while M. Rouher, the prime minister, asserted with emphasis, as the resolve of the French nation, that Italy should *never* get possession of Rome! "Is that clear?" he cried vehemently. And the Chamber acquiesced in his "*never*" by a vote of two hundred and thirty-seven ayes against seventeen noes.

But a storm-cloud was darkening over France.

"Prussia, or rather the great man who was the brain of Prussia, took, of all that was happening, attentive note," says the Countess Cesaresco. "He was convinced that the 'wonders' accomplished by the *chassepôts* at Mentana would soon lead France to try the effect of the new rifle upon larger game."

In view of an impending war with Prussia, the Emperor Napoleon sought alliances with both Italy and Austria. Informal negotiations on the subject passed between Victor Emmanuel and the Emperor, and lasted from 1868 to June, 1869. The King could never forget his personal friendship for Napoleon III., nor the gratitude he owed him for the help that had been given him in his time of need. It cost him much not to repay that service by hearkening to his fellow-sovereign's appeal. But he was bound by the Constitution to be guided by the opinion of his ministers; and the Cabinet, with General Menabrea at its head, steadily refused to engage in a war so unpopular that it would imperil the new kingdom of Italy, unless the Emperor would consent to propitiate the Italian people by withdrawing his troops from Rome, and ceasing to protect the Pope as a petty temporal Italian prince. This the Emperor and the French ministry refused to do; and, when overtures of the same nature were made by France to Austria, the same answer was returned. Prussia was then in alliance with Russia, and Austria was unwilling to provoke war upon her northern and eastern frontiers with the great Slav empire, besides which "from the moment that Austria resigned the Iron Crown, the symbol of her Italian power, she had acted towards Italy with a loyalty that has few parallels in history. And she, too, replied to Napoleon, 'Rome capital of Italy, or no alliance.'"

So, in the early summer of 1870, the Emperor Napoleon, without condescending to give notice of his declaration of war to the Powers who had refused him their alliance, undertook to march his armies to Berlin without assistance.

Meantime, the finances of Italy caused her rulers great embarrassment. From that day to this Italy might have echoed the old colored woman's cry, "Money don' make happiness; but not to have it, honey, is mos' times a mighty ill-convenient thing." Everything that promotes material prosperity had been lacking in Italy when she became a kingdom; roads, railroads, lines of steamers, schools; water, lighting, and sanitary regulations in the cities; while vast unprofitable sums had to be spent on the army and navy; and thus it was that Italy went on light-heartedly, accumulating debt without thought of the day of reckoning.

In 1869 came a financial crisis. The Cabinet of General Menabrea was overthrown on a question of the budget, and Giovanni Lanza was made prime minister, with Sella, another Piedmontese, as his minister of finance. So long as they were in power a course of retrenchment was entered on, which, had it been pursued by their successors, might have repaired the financial situation, which, at the present day, is the despair of Italian statesmen.

Almost simultaneously with the outbreak of war between France and Prussia, in the summer of 1870, Christendom was excited and astonished by the declaration of the Twentieth Œcumenical Council, then assembled in Rome, that the Pope was infallible. Early in August, the Emperor Napoleon began to perceive the worthlessness of his military preparations, and the strength of his opponents. After the defeat of the French army at Wörth, and their failure to gain any decided success at Gravelotte, he renewed his entreaties to Victor Emmanuel to come and help him. Prince Napoleon was sent to his father-in-law with a sheet of blank paper, signed by the Emperor, on which Victor Emmanuel was entreated to write down his own terms. It was too late!

Victor Emmanuel was eager to march his troops into

France to the aid of the Emperor. In vain his ministers told him that his army was not prepared for an immediate campaign. He urged the cause of Napoleon so earnestly, that they at last consented to act, if Austria would coöperate, and reconsider her decision. But Austria repeated "It is too late," and the only help that came to France from Italy was from the single arm of Garibaldi. We have seen already how little that help served the cause of France, and how the man who offered it was subsequently slighted.

Rome had been evacuated by the French before the final catastrophe at Sedan. The French garrison was needed to reinforce the armies at home. The little army raised by the Pope, amounting to thirteen thousand six hundred men, of whom five thousand three hundred were foreign volunteers in his service, was manifestly inadequate to oppose the Italian army, should it cross the frontier and lay siege to Rome. The King wrote a moving letter to the Holy Father, entreating him to consent to the new order of things, declaring at the same time that, as a Christian and a Catholic, he willingly bowed to the Pope's spiritual authority, and should ever continue to do so.

The only answer the Pope would give to the nobleman who brought this letter was: "Signor Conte, I am not a prophet, but I dare to foretell that the Italian troops shall not enter Rome."

He was, at least, a brave old man. In spite of events, he believed in his infallibility to the last moment. Strange that we all, — Pope, penitent, and unbeliever, — will persist in clinging to our own ideas of what God ought to do, and both Pope and penitent conceive that He will accommodate His will to their own wishes!

A few months earlier Lord Clarendon had arrived in Rome. He was an English statesman for whom Victor Emmanuel entertained profound respect.

"The King talked freely to him of his difficulties and perplexities, and asked him to be the bearer of a message to the Pontiff. He begged him to assure his Holiness of his affection, which no political dissensions had power to change; to lay before him the true state of affairs, and to say that the longer the policy of resistance lasted, the more painful would be the inevitable end. Lord Clarendon delivered the message. 'They are strange people, these Italians,' said the Pope, 'pretending to unite Italy without my aid.' Lord Clarendon suggested that his Holiness might aid in the process by sending his blessing to the King of Italy. But Pio Nono was obdurate. He said he was not trusting in foreign interventions, but in some miracle of Providence. 'Providence has worked miracles, your Holiness, during the last ten years, but all in favor of Italy,' was the prompt reply of the English statesman."

Meantime, the Italian army had been massed along the Pontifical frontier, and only waited for an order to march on Rome. It consisted of about sixty-five thousand men, and ten thousand more subsequently reinforced them. It was under the command of General Raffaele Cadorna, and was in five divisions, two of which were under the command of old officers of the Red Shirts, Bixio and Cosenz. On the 12th of September, the Italian troops crossed the Pontifical frontier. It was one week after the surrender at Sedan. There was no regular declaration of war, — the theory being that Rome was a part of Italy, and that the King of Italy had a right to reclaim it as such. The Italian army surrounded Rome, and closed in upon the city, the Papal army retiring before it, having orders to do so from its commander-in-chief, General Kanzler. Bixio's division was stationed between Rome and the sea. Into Civita Vecchia, one of the first objects of attack, Colonel Charette, a Breton, and a tried leader of the Papal Zouaves, threw himself by a wonderful forced march through by-ways and over mountain passes, but he was at once ordered by General Kanzler to bring his men to Rome. The commandant in Civita Vecchia promptly capitulated to Bixio, to avoid, he said, the bombardment of the city. Civita Vecchia was that part of the Roman dominions most favorable to the cause of the unity of Italy. It is emphatically asserted by writers who sustain the cause of the temporal power of the Pope, that the native population in his dominions was not enthusiastic in the cause of the invaders. This view seems supported both by passages in Garibaldi's "Rule of the Monk," and in his autobiography.

"In Rome," he says, "and in the Campagna, the population is composed of priests, of some honest middle class families, some boatmen, and the lazzaroni. In the country, where ignorance is fostered by the priesthood and has struck deeper root, the people side with the clergy, but especially in the Roman Campagna, where all the landowners are either priests or powerful friends of the priesthood."

Then, too, the country people were in great fear of the Italian troops. They remembered the raid of the Garibaldians three years before, and the reputation they had left behind them at Monte Rotondo, for sacrilege, plunder, and insults to women. These memories, of course, had not been allowed to die out, and were cherished in the hearts of the citizens and peasantry when the day came for the invasion of the Papal territory. Added to this, in Rome all the men of the upper classes who had liberal tendencies were either in exile or in the Italian army; and those who have had an opportunity to watch an urban population, in times of revolt or revolution, know well that the chief feeling among citizens is to hold aloof, and let the conflict be decided by men who have no domestic responsibilities.

The Pope's army, as I have said, appears to have consisted of between thirteen and fourteen thousand men. Of these, eight thousand five hundred were enrolled as "Romans," — that word covering all Italians, and not being exclusively applied to the inhabitants of Rome; while more than five thousand were foreign volunteers, of whom it must be said that they maintained good discipline, and fought with devotion and bravery.

On the same day that Civita Vecchia capitulated, *i. e.*, September 14, 1870, the main body of the Italian army, under General Cadorna, beheld from the Alban hills, as they advanced, the dome of St. Peter's glittering on the southern horizon. They did not, however, attack the city for several days, though brisk skirmishing went on in every direction. There were still attempts made to effect a compromise by the efforts of diplomacy. Count Arnim, the Prussian Ambassador at Rome, was especially active. A proposition was made by the Italian government to leave to the Pope the Leonine City,— that is, the part of Rome lying on the right bank of the Tiber, including St. Peter's and the Castle of St. Angelo; but Pio Nono would not accept what would seem to acknowledge any right on the part of the conquerors. His instructions to General Kanzler were as follows : —

"GENERAL : At this moment, when a great sacrifice and a most enormous injustice are about to be consummated, and the troops of a Catholic King, without provocation, nay, without even the least appearance of any motive, surround and besiege the capital of the Catholic world, I feel in the first place the necessity of thanking you, General, and our entire army, for your generous conduct up to the present time; for the affection you have shown to the Holy See; and for your willingness to consecrate yourselves entirely to the defence of the metropolis. May these words be a solemn document to certify to the discipline, the loyalty, and the valor of the army in the service of the Holy See.

"As regards the duration of the defence, I feel it my duty to command that this shall only consist in such a protest as shall testify to the violence done to us and nothing more, — in other words, that negotiations for surrender shall be opened as soon as a breach shall have been made. At a moment when the whole of Europe is mourning over the numerous victims of the war now in progress between two great nations, let it never be said that the Vicar of Christ, however unjustly assailed, had to give his consent to a great shedding of blood. Our cause is the cause of God, and we put our whole defence in His hands. From my heart, General, I bless you, and your whole army.

Pius P. P. IX.

"FROM THE VATICAN, Sept. 19, 1870."

The O'Clery, an Irish gentleman, then serving in the ranks of the Papal Zouaves, who has since written a book on the Pope's side of the controversy, called "The Making of Italy," thus writes : —

"The night between the 19th and the 20th was an anxious one. There were numerous alarms caused by the enemy's scouts (*i. e.*, the Italians) appearing near the walls. The sentries on the old ramparts of Rome could see lights flashing in the vineyards and gardens, and could hear the sound of pick and shovel preparing positions for the artillery which was to open for the invaders a way through the walls of Rome. In the city the chaplains were busy through the night hearing the confessions of men who were preparing for a death, which they believed to be inevitable, for all looked forward to a struggle *à l'outrance*, against sixfold odds, — a struggle, not on the walls alone, but from house to house. 'We will all die for the Holy Father,' said a brave Dutch Zouave, in broken French, to a chaplain, speaking the mind of the whole army. At the early masses said before daybreak, at various points near the walls, officers and soldiers received the Holy Communion. The Red Cross of St. Peter was affixed to every uniform. At half past four all were at their posts. Along the far extended lines of the Italians, drum and bugle notes, the galloping of estafettes, and the rumbling of cannon wheels told that all was fast preparing for the attack. The sun rose that morning in the full brilliance of the early Italian autumn; and through the still air, which was peculiarly clear that day, the officers and men of the Papal army stationed on dome and church tower to observe the enemy's movements, could see far over the Campagna, and up to the blue Apennines on the one hand, and out to the sea-coast on the other."

At nine o'clock on the morning of the 20th, the whole diplomatic body assembled in one of the halls of the Vatican. The Pope entered looking serene, though the thunder of the Italian cannon was in his ears. He said it was twenty-two years since a similar assemblage had waited on him under almost similar circumstances in the Quirinal. He alluded to a threat attributed to Bixio when he served under Garibaldi in days gone by, that he would throw the Pope and all the cardinals into the Tiber. He told how he had visited the American College the previous day, and that when the students asked for arms he had refused them, but had told them to help in taking care of the wounded. As he was thus conversing, he was called out to receive a messenger from General Kanzler, who brought news that a break had been made in the walls. "I have given the order to capitulate," said the Pope, returning to the ambassadors, with his eyes full of tears. "The defence could not be prolonged without bloodshed, and I wish to avoid that. I will not speak to you of myself. It is not for myself I weep, but for those poor children who have come to defend me as their father. You will each take care of those of your own country. There are men of all nations among them." Then he dismissed the ambassadors, and withdrew.

The *corps diplomatique* went at once in a body to Cadorna's headquarters, in order to beg him to give favorable terms to the Papal army. Cadorna was quite willing to grant their request. The capitulation stipulated that all Rome except the Leonine City was to be put into the hands of the Italians, that the Papal troops were to receive the honors of war, and the foreign volunteers were to be sent to their own homes.

The Zouaves and the Legion had made many friends in the Eternal City, and there was sorrow at their humiliation as they marched forth to Civita Vecchia, first having, with flashing swords waved in the air, received the Holy Father's blessing from a balcony of the Vatican. Their journey to Civita Vecchia was long and weary, but a few hours after they got there the French Zouaves and the Legion of Antibes were shipped to their own land, where they joined the army of the Loire, and fought bravely for France, many of them being killed by Prussian balls. The Irish, English, and Americans were shipped to England; the Belgians and Dutch were sent over the frontier into Switzerland, and there were left to beg their way home. The Italians were sent to the fortress of Allessandria, whence small parties of them were despatched to various parts of Italy, — all but the *squadligieri*, a corps of peasants largely consisting of bandits, who, on the principle of set a thief to catch a thief, had been enlisted by the Pope to put down brigands. These, till the country grew more quiet, were detained in prison.

As soon as possible a *plébiscite* was held in Rome. We know how to appreciate the value of a *plébiscite*. This one gave forty thousand seven hundred and eighty-five votes for annexation to Italy, forty-six votes against it. The Leonine City was not called upon to vote, but did so on its own responsibility, and sent up its ballots — all ayes — in a glass jar. Meantime crowds poured into Rome, calling themselves "exiles." A very large number of these so-called exiles were roughs, and came from other Italian cities. Disorder became so great that the military had to put it down, and General Cadorna was requested to extend his protection even over the Leonine City.

All the courts of Europe acquiesced in the changed state of affairs in Rome, and, on the 9th of October, King Victor Emmanuel received a Roman deputation headed by the Duke de Sermoneta, which came to present to him the result of the *plébiscite*. In reply, while rejoicing that the name of Rome was reunited to that of Italy, "the two names dearest to my heart," he said: "I, as a King and a Catholic, in proclaiming the unity of Italy, remain firm in the determination to secure the liberty of the Church and of the High Pontiff; and with this solemn declaration I accept at your hands the Roman *plébiscite*, and present it to the Italians, trusting that they will know how to show themselves equal to the glories of our past and present fortunes."

In conformity with these sentiments, the Italian Parliament, which met for the last time in Florence, December 5, 1870, drew up what was called the Law of the Papal Guarantees.

It was divided into two parts: —

I. The Prerogatives of the Sovereign Pontiff and of the Holy See.

The provisions in this were substantially as follows: —

I. The inviolability of the person of the Pontiff.

II. All acts either of violence or insult, by word or deed, offered to the Pontiff to be severely punished, the discussion of religious subjects being left free.

III. Royal honors in the Italian kingdom to be paid to His Holiness, his guards and his palaces being recognized as belonging to himself alone.

IV. An endowment of three millions and a quarter of francs to be paid to him per annum. This to be an unalienable revenue, never to be taxed, to meet all the needs of the Roman Church and other expenses.

V. The Vatican, the Lateran, and the Villa Castel Godolfo are assured to him, with all their belongings, gardens, museums, libraries, etc.

VI. During the time of the election of a new Pope, no judiciary or political authority shall interfere with the cardinals. The same in the event of an Œcumenical Council.

VII. No Italian official shall have any right to intrude into the Pope's palaces, unless authorized by the Sovereign Pontiff, by the Conclave, or by the Council.

VIII. Visits, perquisitions, or seizure of any papers, etc., are forbidden in any pontifical congregations invested with purely spiritual functions.

IX. The Pontiff to be free to fulfil all the functions of his spiritual authority; and to have affixed to the doors of all churches in Rome notice of such acts.

X. Ecclesiastics who are officially in Rome attendant on the acts of the Pontiff's spiritual ministry are not to be molested.

XI. Foreign envoys to the Pope shall be treated in all respects like foreign ambassadors.

XII. The correspondence of the Pontiff is not to be interfered with. He may have his own post-office, couriers, and telegraph service, without tax or charge.

XIII. In Rome and in its six suburban sees, ecclesiastical institutions for the education and culture of priests shall not in any way be interfered with by the scholastic authorities in the Italian kingdom.

II. THE RELATIONS OF THE STATE WITH THE CHURCH.

XIV. No restriction is placed on the right of meeting of members of the Catholic clergy.

XV. The Italian government renounces its right to be temporal head of the Church in Sicily. Bishops shall not be required to take the oath of allegiance. Italians only shall be appointed to sees, except in Rome. The King renounces the right of nominating or presenting to the higher sees.

XVI., XVII., XVIII., and XIX. are articles referring to ecclesiastical property, the State retaining some power over Church temporalities, while giving up all right to interfere in matters purely spiritual.

"Such full liberty," says Mr. Probyn, "is not accorded to the Roman Church either by France, Spain, Bavaria, or Austria, for the consent of the government is required to confirm appointments to the episcopate. So, too, in the latter countries the government has a right to prohibit the publication of papal bulls, briefs, etc., whereas in Italy all such rights have now been renounced by the civil power."

Pio Nono and his advisers protested earnestly against all that had taken place, including the guarantees, and Catholics were forbidden to take part in any election or *plébiscite*, — a prohibition in force until the present day; thereby depriving the government of a valuable element in parliament, often in need of what was once happily called "His Majesty's opposition." "Nè elettori, nè eletti," — neither electors nor elected, — has been the *mot d'ordre* from the Vatican, responded to by the cry of the advanced Republicans, "Neither guarantees, nor guaranteed."

There were three courses open to Pio Nono. He could submit to events; he could quit Rome; he could shut himself up in the Vatican, — containing, it is said, eleven hundred rooms, with its gardens and its villas, — and then consider himself a prisoner. He chose the latter course, and posed before the world accordingly.

Victor Emmanuel's first visit to Rome was made *incognito*. A terrible overflow of the Tiber had desolated the surrounding country, and caused great distress among the poor, both in the city and in the Campagna. The King went to the scene of desolation, and did all he could to mitigate the calamity. Early in July, 1871, he made his public entry into Rome, and took up his residence in the Quirinal. "We are here, and we intend to stay here," he said to his first Roman parliament, which he opened in November. The Florentines, to whom the loss of King and Court and parliament was a great blow, behaved very differently from the Turinese under similar circumstances. They made every demonstration of loyalty, rejoicing that Italy was now "complete."

Victor Emmanuel, before taking his seat upon his throne in Rome, assisted at the opening of the Mont Cenis tunnel, and was fêted in his own Turin with much enthusiasm. But this great triumph having crowned his life-work, the props of his throne began to fall away from it one by one. Cavour was dead, so was d'Azeglio. Manzoni died at a great age ; then Cavour's successor, Rattazzi, died also. Louis Napoleon's death in 1873 was a personal sorrow to the Rè Galantuomo, who loved him far better than the Italian people did. Mazzini died in 1872.

"He was," said the London "Spectator," speaking of his death, "that rare character, a political idealogue. . . . It was on an Italian Assembly, sitting in Rome, and reigning by the full consent of Italians over the whole peninsula, that he expected a divine influence to descend, which should make its proceedings as important to the world as the decrees of Councils once were to Christianity. That Assembly should make its laws the models for human legislation, and its resolves the basis for the grand code which should ultimately regulate our race.[1] . . . He had to fashion his tools, as well as to use them, and using, when compelled, materials like the Carbonari, the Secret Societies, and the Socialists, it is little marvel that he himself was believed for years to be the greatest of Revolutionists, Socialists, Terrorists, the chief and soul of all the parties which Continental statesmen hold in such abhorrence. . . . It was Mazzini who revived among Italians the idea of nationality, of the unity of their nation, . . . so that men, accustomed from their infancy to think of their next neighbors as foreigners, had come to long for the unity of their nation, to believe that Italy was above her

[1] As I was copying this passage, a Roman newspaper containing the last debate on the war in Abyssinia was put into my hands. Truly there is but one step from the sublime to the ridiculous! The world's regeneration will never come through parliamentary debates, unless indeed parliaments endure to the Millennium. — E. W. L.

provinces, to postpone hatreds and jealousies, and causes of division, some as old as civilization, to the one grand end, — the restoration of Italy to herself. . . . The political faults of Mazzini were all of the same type as his virtues. He was incapable of compromise. He could not accept those who differed from him except as instruments. He no more in his heart tolerated the house of Savoy than the house of Hapsburg, or thought Italy perfect as a monarchy than as a prey to petty despotisms. His ideal was always with him, and latterly, we suspect, events had only deepened the force of his convictions. As a young man he had seen three visions: — the unity of Italy; the enfranchisement of Rome; and the rise of his half-inspired Assembly. Two of the visions had come true, and till his death he labored for the realization of the third one, the ideal Republic."

In 1873, Victor Emmanuel accepted an invitation to visit his relations in Vienna, with whom he had been at war almost ever since he ascended his father's throne. He stayed four days with the Emperor of Austria, greatly enjoying his visit and the resumption of friendly relations with members of his own and his wife's family. He next went to Berlin, where he won all hearts by his simple *bonhomie*. He had wanted, as we have seen, to send aid to the French and their Emperor when in distress, but had not been allowed to do so by his ministers. At a Court dinner at Berlin, when sitting at the right hand of old Emperor William, he suddenly said to him, "Do you know I should have made war on you but for these gentlemen?" — pointing to his ministers; and then he went on to say that such had been his personal regard for Napoleon and his grateful remembrance of his services to Italy, that only a sense of his duty to his own country kept him from going to his aid in his hour of adversity. The old Emperor seemed charmed with his frankness.

In 1876, when Victor Emmanuel had been on his throne twenty-seven years, the Emperors of Austria and Germany came to return his visits. Neither came to Rome from motives of consideration to the Pope; and the Emperor of Austria chose Venice, his own city of old, as the place where to meet his old enemy, — now his host and friend.

"When the train was expected, Victor Emmanuel walked feverishly up and down the platform, and when the Emperor sprang out, the first face he saw was that of his host, his dear friend, ally, and brother. The sovereigns kissed each other and walked arm in arm out of the station."

The people of Venice left nothing undone to welcome and honor their former sovereign, whose rule had been so hated. The Italian tricolor on the great flagstaffs in the Piazza of St. Mark now floated peacefully with the black and gold banner of Austria. The visit of the Emperor of Germany, which took place at Milan was no less successful. Victor Emmanuel and the Crown Prince Frederick were personally attached to each other.

All the seven years that Victor Emmanuel reigned in Rome, Pio Nono remained within the limits of the Vatican. In his allocutions he called himself a martyr and a prisoner, but in reality he was a benign old gentleman, with kindly courteous manners. In politics he was wholly governed by Cardinal Antonelli. In private he always spoke with kindness of Victor Emmanuel, calling him sometimes a "good fellow." And once when Cardinal Antonelli was not upon the watch to prevent him, he wrote the King a letter with his own hand, ending, "Full of paternal affection, I pray God for your Majesty, I pray Him for Italy, and I pray Him for the Church."

This letter gave great comfort to Victor Emmanuel, the sorrow of whose life was to be disowned by the heads of the Church, while he said often of himself, "I am not a bad Christian."

On New Year's Day, 1878, the King held his reception, but was not feeling well. A day or two after, he was greatly affected by news of the death of La Marmora. There had been always a lack of cordiality between the two men. Each esteemed the other, but they were not *simpatico*. La Marmora had been deeply wounded by not having been asked in time to take part in the King's triumphal entry into Venice. The King had resented the publication by him of two pamphlets which La Marmora considered necessary for the defence of his own conduct in the campaign of 1866, — " Un po' più di Luce," and " Segreti di Stato " (" A little more Light," and " State Secrets "). As La Marmora said himself in the Chamber, speaking on this subject, " I do not want to pass down to posterity as a great captain or a great diplomatist, but I hold to living and dying as a good citizen, and as a soldier without stain." As soon as Victor Emmanuel had been made aware of his old friend's illness, he wrote to him in his old familiar, kindly tone, and affectionate messages were sent by Prince Humbert and Margherita. The poor general was consoled also by the many marks of sympathy and esteem that were showered on him from all parts of Europe, as well as from his own people, in the last months of his life.

The news of La Marmora's death completely prostrated the King, already attacked by inflammation of the lungs, and in a few hours he was no more. Prince Humbert and Margherita were beside his bed, but Amadeo, Princess Clotilde, and Queen Maria Pia were too far off to be summoned.

The Court chaplain applied to the parish priest for permission to administer the last sacraments to the dying King. The parish priest applied to Pio Nono, who granted the permission at once, and later in the day came a cardinal with the Pope's especial benediction. Thus Victor Emmanuel's most earnest earthly wish was granted. He died as a good Catholic as well as a good Christian. His last words were, " My children ! My children ! "

The new King, Humbert or Umberto, issued the next day a very affecting proclamation : —

" Italians ! An immense calamity has befallen us. Victor Emmanuel, the founder and uniter of the kingdom of Italy, has been taken from us. I received his last sigh, which was for the nation, and his last wishes, which were for the happiness of his people. His voice, which will always resound in my heart, imposes on me the task of vanquishing my sorrow, and points out to me my duty. At this moment there is but one consolation possible for us, that is to show ourselves worthy of him. . . . Italians ! your first king is dead. His successor will prove to you that constitutions do not die. Let us unite in this hour of

CARDINAL ANTONELLI.

great sorrow and strengthen that concord which has been the salvation of Italy."

Victor Emmanuel's funeral in Rome was magnificent. Among the garlands laid upon his coffin was a wreath sent by Queen Victoria. On his tomb is inscribed: —

"VITTORIO EMMANUELE II., THE FATHER OF HIS COUNTRY.
ITALY, WITH THE PRIDE OF A MOTHER
AND THE GRIEF OF A DAUGHTER, BESEECHES FOR HER GREAT KING,
WHO WAS A FAITHFUL CITIZEN AND A VICTORIOUS SOLDIER,
THE IMMORTALITY THAT IS DUE TO THE GOOD MAN
AND TO THE HERO."

The anecdotes of Victor Emmanuel in private life are very numerous. We have space only for a few, but many are told in his "Life" by G. S. Godkin.

He rose early, and spent the first two hours of the day in exercise. By the time most men begin to awake he was ready for a hard day's work at his "profession," as he always called his kingship. He was very hardy, and never wore flannel, which may have been the cause of the chill which resulted in his death. He never had more than two suits of clothes at a time beside his uniforms, and one day at Naples a *gamin* called out: "See how our ministers treat our good King! With all the money we pay in taxes they don't give him money enough to buy a new pair of pantaloons!"

His "heart was kind and soft," and his hand only too freely open in charity. He had a quick temper, and quarrelled not infrequently with his best friends, but he was always ready and eager to "make up." He detested unpunctuality. Once a young engineer kept him waiting ten minutes, and was received with considerable fierceness. The young man was overwhelmed, which the King perceiving turned from him and went into his chamber, whence he returned with a beautiful gold watch saying, "Keep this, and remember it always keeps time with my own."

One evening, as his carriage was driving up to the door

of the theatre, he was struck in the face by a hard cushion flung by a woman in the crowd. He was very angry, and his attendants were much alarmed. The cushion was suspected to contain bombs or dynamite. He entered the theatre, however, holding it in his hand; and sent at once a gentleman in attendance to see who and what the woman was who had so outraged him. The messenger returned, saying that the woman was overwhelmed with a sense of the impropriety she had committed, but the sofa cushion had been intended as a gift to the King. "Well, take it back, then," said the King, "and tell her I have no need of any such articles." But as he was handing it to a servant he saw a note pinned to the tassels. It was a begging letter. "Ah! — as usual," said the King, and recovered his good humor.

The next day he inquired after the woman, who was a seamstress at the theatre, and heard she had been dismissed by the manager. "Ah! — I am sorry for that," said the King. "Go to the manager and ask him to pardon her, and take her two hundred and fifty francs, and tell her never to throw anything in my face again, — at least without warning me!"

He was devoted to horses, and kept splendid ones of every kind in his stables. A little English terrier, called Milord, was his constant companion. When the King died, his attendants had hard work to save poor Milord's life, so bent was he on dying of grief and hunger.

CHAPTER XVI.

THE PAPACY.

ON the 20th of September, 1870, when all eyes were fixed on the last acts of the great drama of the Franco-Prussian war, Pio Nono proclaimed himself a prisoner in the Vatican, and General Cadorna, in the name of Victor Emmanuel, took possession of the Eternal City.

The fall of the Pope's temporal power took place nine months after his spiritual power had received supreme exaltation and recognition in the Catholic world. In 1864 he had published his celebrated Syllabus, and on June 29, 1868, he issued a summons to cardinals, bishops, and prelates throughout the world, to send representatives to Rome to an Œcumenical Council, which was to meet on December 8, 1869, — for the purpose of confirming it.

In the church of Santa Maria Maggiore, at Trent, is an elaborate inscription, saying that "within those sacred walls the Divine Spirit spoke for the last time." For three centuries that boast had been maintained, and, at length, when Rome was threatened within and without by enemies, when the Pope was sustained upon his throne by foreign soldiers, and when his temporal power was impaired, the moment was chosen for a new Œcumenical Council, — and the dignitaries of the Catholic Church were called to assemble in the Eternal City.

The original idea of an Œcumenical Council was that it should be a parliament of the civilized world, held in the interests of religion, and to this end the first seven general councils were convoked by Roman emperors. But this idea of a parliament of religion was not that of Pius IX.

and his advisers. The General Council of 1869 was to be of the nature of the parliament of Paris before the Revolution, which was called together only to register, or not to register, the ordinances of the King.

Down to the days of the Council of Trent, the rulers of Christian States, or their representatives, were admitted to the council. In a still existing picture of the Council of Trent in session, the representatives of all the European sovereigns are shown, with their suites in attendance; the Spanish envoy, however, sits apart, surrounded by his people, because the question of his precedence over France and Germany could not be settled to his satisfaction.

The Council held in Rome, December 5, 1869, could not, therefore, in a proper sense be called a general council. It was not a council of the old Roman empire, that institution being a thing of the past. It was not a council in which the laity were represented with the clergy. It was not a council at which all parts of Christendom were to assist. It was a council of the clergy of the Latin Church, and nothing more.

During the months that elapsed between the summoning of the Council and its assembling it came to be generally understood that it was called together simply to ratify the eighty-four propositions in the Syllabus, of which Archbishop Manning foretold: "'The Syllabus will become the rule of thought with respect to the eighty-four errors which it condemns; and the eighty-four truths which are condemned by those errors will become the rule and law of the intellectual belief of man."

But there was strong opposition to the principles laid down in the Syllabus, throughout the Roman Catholic world. Earnest remonstrances were published, intended to prepare the minds of the prelates expected to assemble at the Council for what was before them. Among the most earnest writers were Monsignor Dupanloup, Bishop of Orleans, and M. de Montalembert, writers well known and honored, not only in their own but other countries, and whose opinions carried weight beyond the walls which excluded from the public the deliberations of the Council.

The Syllabus combated eighty-four errors, — errors, that is to say, in the opinion of the Pope and his advisers; and it consisted of five principal propositions.

I. It asserted the power of the Church to inflict temporal punishment, including death.

II. It asserted the political supremacy of the Pope, as King of kings, including the power of deposing refractory rulers.

III. It called for the "correction of history," with a view to proving that the clergy could not lawfully be made amenable to the civil law.

IV. It pronounced all freedom of conscience and of worship to be unlawful.

V. It condemned modern civilization, and constitutional government.

Besides giving assent to these propositions in the Syllabus, two other matters were to be acted upon by the Council.

It was to put forth as an article of Catholic belief an assertion of the bodily assumption into heaven of the Mother of Our Lord, — a belief not heard of till the fourth century, when it is to be found in two apocryphal writings, one attributed to St. John, the other to Bishop Melito of Sardis. It had, however, been generally received by Catholics after the seventh century.

The third and most important subject which required the assent and endorsement of this Œcumenical Council, held nearly two thousand years after the Apostles first preached Christianity, was the doctrine of the Pope's personal infallibility. The Roman Catholic Church has always claimed to be infallible; in its dogmas it cannot err, but the question had never been settled where and with whom did this infallibility reside, — with the Popes, or with the Councils? The last three Councils had emphatically pronounced against the Pope. His decision *ex cathedra* was only that of the most learned and exalted doctor. As such, apparently, Pius IX. put forth his Syllabus, and desired to have the propositions it contained confirmed by the Council. But he wanted it to go further and to pronounce his future opinions and decisions infallible. He desired that his power of issuing infallible decrees under the inspiration of the Holy Spirit should be an article of faith throughout Catholic Christendom.

Now, as there was a wide-spread feeling amongst men of enlightenment in his own communion that the Syllabus was a mixed collection of general truths, empty truisms, incorrect statements, and unmeaning phrases, it was hard for such men not only to accept it as a rider to their faith, but to declare themselves and others bound to accept any more such utterances put forth by the same authority.

The party that supported the views of Pio Nono, who, it must be said, sincerely and earnestly believed in his own pretensions to infallibility, was the party of the Jesuits, with a contingent of prelates who held ultramontane views.

The dissentients were the majority of foreign cardinals and nearly all the foreign bishops. Archbishop Manning, not then invested with the purple, was active and emphatic in support of the Pope's views.

It is, of course, impossible for me to go into any argument concerning the dogmas brought forward for the consideration of the Council. I can only tell facts.

On some points the Council seems to have been called upon to place itself in the position of King Canute when he sat upon the sands and commanded the advancing tide to fall back from him; while the Pope, as his views were interpreted by Archbishop Manning, seems to say "I acknowledge no civil superior; I am the subject of no prince, and I claim more than that, — I claim to be the supreme judge and director of the consciences of men; of the peasant that tills the field, and the prince that sits on the throne; of the household that sits in the shade of privacy, and the legislature that makes laws for the kingdoms; I am the last, sole, supreme judge of what is right and wrong. What you call 'progress' is a departure from

Christian civilization. In that path you will have many companions, but me you will not find."

The great struggle in the Council was over the Pope's views respecting the world's progress and the doctrine of his infallibility, — an assuredly most comfortable doctrine, could it have been established, — "a soft cushion for the head troubled by doubts to rest upon."

As the objects of the Council were known generally among the clergy some months before it met, the opposition found voice in books and pamphlets before the day appointed. The Pope and his advisers, warned of what they might expect if they permitted free discussion, decided to smother it. Not only was it made unlawful to report the words uttered by the speakers (a precaution many may consider hardly blameworthy), but the names of those who spoke were to be withheld. The opposition party in the Council was reckoned at something like two hundred bishops, including several cardinals. Persistent efforts were made to induce the seven hundred and fifty bishops present to sign a petition in favour of the Infallibility dogma, but only one hundred signatures could be secured. Archbishop Darboy of Paris (the martyr of the Commune), Bishop Dupanloup, and Archbishop Strossmeyer, of Bosnia, led the opposition.

The Council was coerced, not by force but by pressure, into adopting the views it had been called together to endorse. By arbitrary authority unofficial meetings of bishops were forbidden, even in private houses, and a board of nine bishops that had been organized, — three French, three German, and three English — were warned not to assemble. Books that opposed the dogmas the Council had met together to enforce were seized by the Roman government.

As I have no right to print anything in this connection on my own authority, I will add a letter written by Archbishop Strossmeyer, already mentioned as one of the leaders of the opposition party. It was published in a German paper, Nov. 27, 1870, and republished 1881.

"My Honored Friend, — Some time ago I received a communication from Bonn, in which some distinguished Catholics put the question to me, whether I, as a member of the minority in the Vatican Council, persisted in the conviction which I there expressed and defended. Permit me, my dear friend, to make you the medium of the following reply, — to the effect that my conviction, which I shall uphold before the judgment seat of God as I upheld it in Rome, is firm and unshakable. And this conviction is, that the Vatican Council was wanting in that freedom which was necessary to make it a real Council, and to justify it in making decrees calculated to bind the consciences of the whole Catholic world. . . . Everything which could resemble a guarantee for the liberty of discussion was carefully excluded. Everything calculated to convert discussion into the mere expression of preconceived opinion was brought into play in the most lavish, and I might say, most shameless manner. And, as though all this did not suffice, there was added a public violation of the ancient Catholic principle, *Quod semper, quod ubique, quod ab omnibus*. In a word, the most naked and hideous exercise of papal infallibility was necessary before the Infallibility could be elevated into a dogma. If, to all this, be added that the Council was not regularly constituted; that the Italian bishops, prelates, and officials were in a monstrously predominating majority; that the apostolic vicars were dominated by the propaganda in the most scandalous manner; that the whole apparatus of that political power which the Pope then exercised in Rome contributed to intimidate, and repress all free utterance, you can easily perceive what sort of *liberty* — that essential attribute of all councils — was displayed at Rome."

It should be said, in justice to Pio Nono, that he was a very weak man, and a man of whom it has been said that, like Louis Napoleon, he was so anxious to satisfy and please others, that those nearest to him were always those who could influence him to do what they wanted. He also sincerely believed himself, by virtue of his office, to be under especial divine guidance. He referred all things to God, and then did what those about him persuaded him to do. The Jesuit party, which controlled him, received a crushing defeat by the election of the next pontiff.

We have no means of knowing what part Cardinal Pecci

took in the proceedings of the Council, but we cannot suppose he endorsed all the propositions in the Syllabus, or accepted the decree that subsequently conferred upon himself infallibility. Nevertheless, he has boldly insisted on submission to papal authority, and to himself as its representative. In 1885, when he could no longer put up with the opposition shown to him by the ultramontane party, he addressed a letter to the Archbishop of Paris, defining his views as to the duty of submission on the part of the clergy to their ecclesiastical superiors, and defining his own views of the doctrine of infallibility.

He enforces obedience and subordination to the chief pastor of the Church, saying that "upon these two virtues depend the order and life of the Church. They are the indispensable conditions for doing right, and arriving happily in port." He goes on to say that it is a proof of insincere submission to the pastor in charge " to establish an opposition between sovereign pontiff and sovereign pontiff. Those who, in the case of two differing directions, reject the present one and hold to the past one, give no proof of obedience to the authority which has the right and duty of directing them." In fact they are no better than those " who after condemnation would appeal to the next council, or to a better informed pope." The person to be obeyed is the pope for the time being, not a pope who has passed away, or a pope who is yet to come. Each pope is " free to follow the rule of conduct which he judges best for the times and the other circumstances of the case."

Both Pius IX. and Leo XIII. revived the ancient custom of jubilee. The first jubilee began in the year 1299, when Dante was present and described the crowding of the pilgrims on the bridge of San Angelo. So many pilgrims flocked to Rome on that occasion that the jubilee was prolonged into the following year.

"At Christmas of 1299," says an authority, "thousands of strangers thronged the churches, and the question arose whether it would not be advisable to take advantage of this outburst of devotional fervor. After due examination of precedents and consultation with cardinals, the Pope, on the feast of St. Peter's Chair, Jan. 18, 1300, solemnly proclaimed the first jubilee, — with plenary indulgence for all who during that holy year should visit the basilicas of St. Peter and St. Paul on thirty days, if residents of Rome, on fifteen days if strangers. The experiment proved a great success. No less than two millions of pilgrims, of all ages and both sexes, and from all parts of Europe, are said to have visited Rome during the year, and as many as two hundred thousand were constantly to be found gathered in the holy city."

It had been originally intended to restrict the Sacred Year to the first year of every century, but subsequently it was changed to every fifty years, and then to every thirty-three years; that being the received term of the life of our Saviour. The pilgrims brought large offerings to the Holy Father, and the papal coffers in these years overflowed. Sometimes monarchs were admitted to share the benefit of the indulgence without leaving their States. This was the case with King John of France, and Richard II. of England. After a while, such indulgences were sold; as, for instance, by the "gentil pardoner, that streyt wes comen from the court of Rome," of whom Chaucer writes in the " Canterbury Tales." This practice created great scandal, but was reformed by Nicholas V., who held his jubilee in 1450.

The last jubilee solemnized under the old *régime* in Rome was in 1825, in the reign of Leo XII., when the number of pilgrims amounted to four hundred thousand. Pio Nono had a jubilee, and Leo XIII. has already had two; one to celebrate his fiftieth year of admission to the priesthood; the other his first communion, seventy-five years ago. On the first occasion personal gifts from nearly all the rulers on the earth flowed into the Vatican. President Cleveland sent a superbly bound copy of the Constitution of the United States. Queen Victoria sent a royal gift; associations, companies, and private persons brought presents to the Pope, as well as offerings in money to his treasury. The halls of the Vatican where these presents were displayed, are said to have resembled a museum.

But to return to Pio Nono. His daily life, after he constituted himself a prisoner in the Vatican, was of the simplest kind. He was an early riser; at an hour when all Rome was asleep, lights were to be seen in the windows of the Vatican. Filippiani either died or quitted his master's service; a new attendant named Zangolini succeeded him. When dressed and shaved, the Pope remained always alone till seven (probably engaged in private devotion), when he went to his chapel to hear mass and to celebrate the communion; it was then that he administered the sacrament to foreigners of distinction visiting Rome. Leaving the chapel, the Pope went to his breakfast; a Pope always takes his meals alone. Soup, wine, and biscuits were served to him. Then he went to his cabinet, where official business was daily transacted with Cardinal Antonelli. This over, he would read his letters, and look over the papers, till it became the hour when he had to give audience. Ladies visiting the Vatican must always wear black silk, the head covered with a black veil, and no jewelry. Gentlemen must be in strict evening costume, with a white cravat. The audience over, the Pope would walk with several cardinals, or familiar friends, in the garden of the Vatican, when they would tell him, for he dearly loved a dish of gossip, all the news of the day. A very simple dinner was always served to him; generally he ate none of it but soup and fruit. After dinner came the siesta, after that, personal friends visited him in his library, on his way to which Pio Nono would bless the mountains of rosaries, chaplets, crosses, and scapularies which every day are sent from Rome to all parts of the globe. Kindly, genial, and witty, as he was, it was not hard to keep him amused. He closed the day with religious affairs, with the business of the secretaries of various congregations, and if he had a discourse to prepare, this was the time he generally took to do it. When at last he went to bed, a prelate would read to him, and when he perceived the Pope falling asleep he would drop on his knees and say "Holy Father — your benediction!" Pio Nono would then lift his hand, comply with the request, and the day was over.

He was a very handsome man in his youth, and retained his comeliness even to old age. To his Protestant visitors he was always very courteous and invariably produced on them a most favorable impression. Englishmen who during the furor about Garibaldi had wished him all sorts of evil, in his latter days looked on him as a man who had lost a fine property and might be excused and pitied if he bemoaned his misfortunes sometimes too loudly.

His will showed that he left little money behind him. He directed that his monument should not cost more than five hundred dollars. He left a few legacies, none of them exceeding fifteen hundred dollars, to friends, and three thousand dollars to be divided among his servants. The residue of his estate, barely ten thousand dollars, went to his family. But he was rich in relics, which he left to various churches, not forgetting a cathedral in Chili where he had preached in his missionary days. He had two pieces of the true Cross, and one of the Crown of Thorns, besides numerous relics of St. Peter, St. Paul, and St. Damaso.

Barely a month after the death of the first King of Italy, he who was (probably) the last pope-king of Rome also died. After the death of Cardinal Antonelli, who, in homely language, may be said to have had Pio Nono in charge for almost thirty years, all things in the Vatican fell into confusion.

"The mind of the aged pontiff was tossed to and fro by a perfect tempest of accusations, recriminations, calumnies, and innuendoes, raised up around him by the fury of rival factions, so that it is scarcely too much to say that, whatever may be the degree of papal command over the purgatory in another world, it did not, during the last fifteen months of Pio Nono's sojourn in this life, exempt him from the experience of something very like purgatory here."

During his early manhood his health was thought too delicate to warrant his admission into the Garda Nobile, but he lived to a ripe age, being in his eighty-sixth year at the time of his death. In his latter years, however, he had been so completely prostrated several times by attacks of illness that his physicians and attendants had despaired of saving him; but when death came it was at a moment when he had been professionally declared to be remarkably well. During the months that preceded this event, the question that agitated, not only Catholic Christendom, but European courts was, Who would be his successor? Some cardinals (Cardinal Manning, it is said, among them) urged that the Conclave should be held out of Rome, but this was contrary to all precedent, and the cardinals met, not in the Quirinal, but in the Vatican, on February 20, 1878. There were sixty-two cardinals present, of whom about one-third were foreigners. The determination of the body was known beforehand to be that the new pontiff must be an Italian.

In thirty-six hours the Conclave had made choice of Cardinal Gioacchino Pecci, who had been made cardinal *camerlingo* a few months before. It is not usual for the choice of the Conclave to fall on a cardinal *camerlingo*, so that it is possible that this consideration may have guided Pio Nono in the appointment. The new Pope was born March 10, 1810, the son of Count Ludovico Pecci, a nobleman in the papal province of Umbria. He entered the Church at eighteen, became a priest at twenty-seven, a prelate at twenty-eight, and was at once appointed Delegate successively of Benevento, Spoleto, and Perugia. He was next raised to the rank of Archbishop of Damietta, and went to Belgium as nuncio for Gregory XVI. In 1846 he was made Archbishop of Perugia, and in 1853 was promoted to be a cardinal.

"He presented in his own person," says the Italian statesman Borghi, writing in the "Contemporary Review," "a complete and splendid example of what an Italian priest may become under favorable circumstances. A member by birth of the lesser provincial nobility, a man of good natural capacity, and of high culture, an admirable Latin and a good Italian writer, devout in spirit and rigidly orthodox in opinion, a sincere and entire believer in the past and future of the Church and in the importance of its influence on society even in the present day, accustomed to command, familiar with the habits and methods, as well as with the international relations, of the court of Rome, advancing year by year in experience, in dignity, and in authority, — such was Cardinal Pecci."

He was born at Carpineto, a smoke-blackened little town among the Volscian hills, to whose rugged rocks and olive gardens his heart returned all his life. The first letter he wrote after he had been proclaimed pope was to his brothers at Carpineto.

"DEAR BROTHERS, — I give you news that the Holy College of Cardinals has this morning raised my unworthiness to St. Peter's See. This is the first letter I write. It is addressed to my relatives, for whom I beg all happiness from Heaven, and to whom I lovingly send my episcopal blessing. Pray much for me to the Lord.
"LEO XIII."

The house, or castle, as it is called by courtesy, of the Pecci family towers above the hamlet of Carpineto. The Pecci have been hereditary lords of the district for centuries. They are considered rich people by their neighbors, and were noted for their piety. Gioacchino was the second son of his parents, who had seven children. Giuseppe, another son, entered the Church as well as Gioacchino.

As a boy, the future pope gave signs of thoughtful piety. He would wander out under the beech and chestnut trees, Bible in hand, to study the Scriptures. He early learned three valuable rules in life, — orderliness, steadfastness, and self-control. When he was eight years of age, he and his brother Giuseppe were sent to a school of the Jesuits at Viterbo. There he acquired such admirable proficiency in the use of the Latin tongue that both his prose writings and his poetry in that language are models of elegance. Viterbo, where he remained six years, is full of memories of past pontiffs, some of whom are buried there. When he was fourteen, he was sent to Rome to the College of the Jesuits. The first pope he saw was Leo XII., who had but a brief pontificate, ascending the papal throne in 1823.

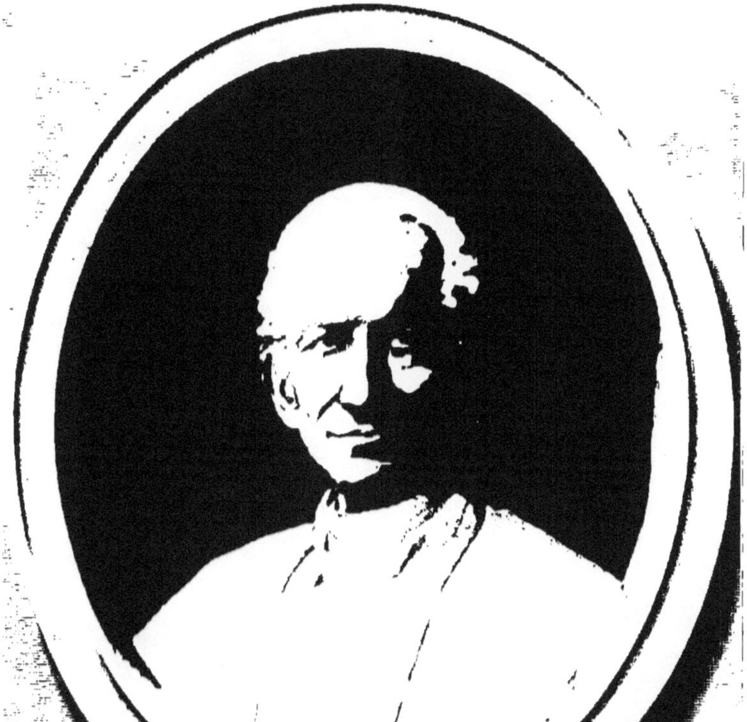
LEO XIII
PONTIFEX MAXIMVS

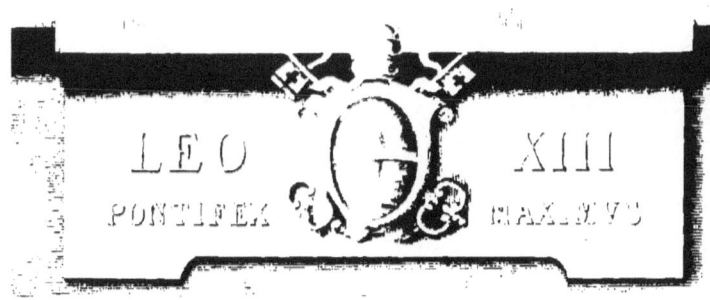

The personality of this pope made so deep an impression on the young student that he took him as a model for his own life, and, in his remembrance of his youthful enthusiasm for this pontiff, he took his name when he himself was called to wear the papal crown. At the age of twenty he fell ill, having injured his health by overstudy, and turned his attention to poetry, writing an autobiographical account of his feelings and experiences in Latin verse. He did not anticipate recovery, and in his poem expresses his longing, after his brief voyage of life, to steer his bark into an everlasting haven. But fulness of years, — years of industry and honor, — were in store for him.

"The success which had attended his career as a legate and diplomatist, had, in accordance with the almost invariable practice of the Apostolic Court, ensured his promotion to the purple. But it was notorious that Gioacchino Pecci was not a man after the heart of Pius IX.; that Cardinal Antonelli distrusted him, and that his archbishopric of Perugia was, in fact, an honorable exile from the court of Rome. After having represented Gregory XVI. for three years at the court of Brussels, to the entire satisfaction of King Leopold I., who always entertained a high respect for and kindly remembrance of him, he was appointed to the see of Perugia, and continued for thirty-two years to administer that important diocese in a manner which secured the esteem and affection of a population not much prone to respect ecclesiastical rulers."

As Archbishop of Perugia the future pope sat on a seat that had been occupied in the past by men whom history and legend have proclaimed heroes and martyrs.

"If he left his episcopal palace for the neighboring Cathedral of San Lorenzo, he could pray beside the ashes of three popes, one of whom had surpassed all his contemporaries in power and energy, — namely Innocent III., who deemed the world too small to hold the Church, and who now sleeps his last sleep in one single little coffin, in company with two pontiffs of minor fame. . . . The nature that surrounded the mountain see of Perugia, — how splendid it was! When the Archbishop gazed down into the valley at his feet, clad with vineyards and olive groves, his eye could range far away over one of those rich landscapes that fill the soul with yearning. Lost in dreamy solitude, Assisi, the city of St. Francis, sits throned on her proud height, and many a place is there of which Dante's muse has sung. . . . The very air of Umbria seems permeated with religious thought; for has it not been the great domain of the Romish Church, — the province aptly termed the 'Italian Galilee'?"

The history of Perugia from 1846 to 1878, — the years of Cardinal Pecci's episcopate, — is the history of Italy in miniature. When he entered on his life there, it formed a portion of the States of the Church; when he left it, it was an Italian city, one of the hundred cities of which the kingdom of Italy is proud. Naturally, the future pope could not go all lengths with the national spirit then awakening in Italy, but he recognized it as legitimate, so long as it was hostile to the "stranger," who was holding the peninsula in subjection.

When, after the defeat of Lamoricière and his papal army at Castelfidardo, Umbria was united to the kingdom of Victor Emmanuel, its cardinal-archbishop reaped the fruits of the personal good feeling which he had exhibited towards the oppressed members of the Liberal party during the period from 1849 to 1860.

"Men felt grateful for the good he had done, without too closely calculating its amount, for they could not refrain from bearing in mind all the evil which it had been in his power to have performed."

In 1847, both Pio Nono and Archbishop Pecci had been greatly attracted by the book of Vincenzo Gioberti (subsequently a member of the Piedmontese cabinet) on the reforms needed in Church government. The book was called "Il Primato," and was taken to Rome by Cardinal Mastai-Ferretti in 1846, to be presented by him to whoever should be chosen Pope. Gioberti, whose theory at that time was of a federation of the Italian States, was the personal friend of Monsignor Pecci, who received him at Perugia as his guest.

A remarkable book published by Father Curci, a Jesuit,

made a great stir in 1874 in Rome. Curci had formed the acquaintance of the Cardinal-Archbishop of Perugia, during one of his brief visits to Rome, and had been on terms of considerable intimacy with him.

Father Curci's pamphlet, which was republished as a preface to a translation made by him of the Gospels into Italian, not only led to his expulsion from the Society of the Jesuits, but brought down on him the indignation of Pope Pius, who required him, by way of retractation, to sign his assent to three propositions, as fundamental doctrines of the Roman Catholic Church: 1. The speedy re-establishment of the temporal power of the popes. 2. The duty of all sincere Catholics to abstain from political elections. 3. The impossibility of co-existence for the Papacy and the kingdom of Italy.

"These propositions," said Father Curci, "I am resolved not to subscribe; and rather than do so I would be cut to pieces. It is high time to recognize the fact that Italian unity cannot be broken up; for, whatever may be the form of government destined to rule the country, the nation will not consent to be again divided into different fractions. Such being the undoubted state of matters, the duty of all Catholics is to come forward and play their part in political life, unless they are content to see morality and religion go to the dogs."

In consequence of these sentiments, Father Curci was subjected to much persecution during the later years of the pontificate of Pius IX. Nor did the relations supposed to exist between him and the Cardinal Archbishop of Perugia tend to make that prelate a favorite at the papal court.

"In Rome, while Archbishop of Perugia, Cardinal Pecci was rarely seen, and very little known or heard of. A few months, however, before the death of Pius IX., when he was appointed to the high office of *camerlingo*, he came to Rome, where his tall spare figure and homely though kindly features were seen in Roman drawing-rooms with a frequency unusual with his brethren of the Sacred College in these latter days." This was thought indeed, by many, to indicate his dissent from the policy of seclusion adopted by Pope Pius and his cardinals. When elected by the Conclave (February 20, 1878) and it became his duty to go forth and give his first pontifical benediction to the people, he was about to proceed, in accordance with immemorial custom, to the balcony on the outside of the west front of St. Peter's, when those about him hurriedly interfered, assuring him that this could not be done; that all those forms were now in abeyance, and that the blessing must be given from the interior balcony, looking into the church. Leo XIII. yielded, and from that day to this the theory of the pope's imprisonment in the Vatican has been maintained. Many think, however, that this would not have been the case had it not been for the disgraceful scenes that took place when the body of Pio Nono, three and a half years after his death, was transferred by night through the streets of Rome to its last resting-place in the Church of San Lorenzo. Instead of the splendid ceremonies that had attended the removal of the bodies of other popes to the tombs prepared for them, the funeral services within St. Peter's were performed in strict privacy, and the procession outside the church was simplicity itself. There was no saluting, no tolling of bells, even at St. Peter's, as the bier moved away. There were crowds, however, on hand to witness what was taking place (it is said one hundred thousand people were abroad that night), and the weather was warm and fine. The Italian government had offered Italian soldiers to keep order in the streets, but this offer was refused. The funeral car was drawn by four black horses, — the first pair ridden by a postilion wearing a cocked hat, — and it had a lamp at each of its corners. Over it was thrown as a pall a red velvet cloth, which dated from about the year 1200, in the days of Innocent III. Beside the car walked priests carrying lighted candles. Then followed the carriages of cardinals and prelates and members of Catholic associations on foot bearing torches.

From the first there was confusion, there being neither soldiers nor police to maintain order; but at the angle of the Castle of St. Angelo a disgraceful scene began, which was continued up to the very door of San Lorenzo. A group of youths, who at first did not number more than fifty or sixty, forced their way among the torch-bearers, shouting "*Viva l'Italia!* Down with the priests!" Some even cried, "Throw him into the river!" but receiving no encouragement from the rest of the crowd, who only cried, "*Canaglia!*" they ceased operations till the procession entered some narrow streets, when a regular scuffle occurred. All up the Via Nazionale the same scenes were repeated by the same turbulent set. They sang Garibaldi's hymn to drown the prayers, and not infrequently gave, or accepted fights with the bystanders. At last the military had to be called out, for the mob was pelting the carriages. With difficulty the coffin was got into the church of San Lorenzo, and the mob was finally dispersed.[1] But it is little wonder that since that day Leo XIII. has renounced all inclination or intention of exhibiting to the Romans a live pope in their streets, surrounded by the pomp and majesty befitting his position. The government has guaranteed protection to his person, but to invoke that protection would be to acknowledge the authority of the Italian government; besides which, as earnest Catholics would drop on their knees as he passed, the roughs and scum of the city (unrestrained by the civil authority, which, as I have said, the Pope would not willingly call to his help), would doubtless ill-treat and molest them. So Leo XIII. has ever since remained firm in his determination to continue a prisoner in the Vatican, not even going (I believe) in the unhealthy season to the Villa Gondolfi, which was guaranteed to him as a retreat from Roman malaria. The bitterness with which he spoke of the cruel insults offered to the remains of his predecessor, in an allocution he put forth a week after the funeral, and certain words addressed a few months earlier to Cardinal Lavaletta, vicar-general of Rome, on the subject of the unbridled insults showered on

---

[1] This account is that of an eye-witness, who sent it at the time to the "St. James's Gazette."

the Catholic religion by the press, and what he considered the indecent erection of Protestant chapels within the walls of Rome " raised by the gold of Bible societies," — are almost the only indignant utterances of Leo XIII. His mission has been one of peace and conciliation.

One of his first acts was to revive the authority of the Sacred College, — that is, the body of cardinals, which in theory, was the privy council of the Pope. Many persons seemed to think that this act of invoking advice and assistance from his brethren of the Sacred College would limit his authority, and obstruct him in carrying out his own views. Apparently this has not been the case. The cardinals, with few exceptions, have rarely opposed him.

It is impossible not to acknowledge the marvellous spread of this pope's personal influence. Relieved from the embarrassments of his position as a petty Italian ruler, he has found compensation in becoming virtually the foremost standard-bearer of Christianity throughout the world. When he speaks, — and he speaks frequently, — he speaks as one having authority. Whether, as Protestants, we accept what he says or not, we ponder his words. They have weight with us, not only from his official position, but from his earnestness, his wisdom, his large-mindedness, and his piety. No longer a pope-king, he holds, as spiritual head of his ancient Church, a position with reference to the world at large such as none of his predecessors have held for centuries. He has effected reconciliation between foreign States and the Catholic Church, in Belgium, Germany, Austria, Hungary, and Russia. He has extended his influence in South America and into Eastern lands. Towards the two great Republics, France and the United States, his tone is always that of " high consideration." We all know with what interest his views are read, when he gives them to the world, on socialism, family life, marriage, and the relations of employers and employed. He is effecting a great change in the sentiments of devout Protestants towards the religion of which he is the head. The Church unity of which he has been said to dream in England can surely never be accomplished, since Papal authority has never been submissively accepted by Englishmen ever since England became a nation. But unity in Church government and the unity of feeling that binds together devout Christians — all who fulfil the definition of Church unity laid down by Saint Paul, " those who love the Lord Jesus Christ with sincerity " — have been largely promoted by what the world knows of Leo XIII. No doubt, as Dr. Watts tells us, —

> " One army of the living God,
> At His command we bow,"

but that army is divided into brigades and regiments. Unity may consist in the whole army fighting one enemy, in all struggling to attain one end; yet the officers and men of each regiment may at the same time be zealous for its discipline and its honor; nay, may even have firm faith in the superiority of its efficiency.

One great difficulty in Pope Leo's way has been the narrowness of his income. The three million and a half of francs guaranteed to the Pope by the Italian kingdom, neither Pope Pius nor Pope Leo has been willing to receive. The financial deficiency in the days of the former was made up by the revival of the old custom of Peter's Pence, and for a time much money flowed into Pio Nono's coffers. By degrees, however, the amount fell off, and, a few years since, not only gross mismanagement of the fund, but peculation and embezzlement were discovered at the Vatican. Leo XIII. himself is a very poor man. A few years after his elevation one of his nephews was about to be married, and craved his assistance. The Pope had nothing to give him; but he borrowed a thousand crowns, and then made over to his relatives his small patrimony, telling them that it was all he had, and that even after his death they could expect no more from him.

In June, 1881, Father Curci published another book, — *La Nuova Italia ed i Vecchi Zelanti*, — in which the opinions expressed in his former work were set forth at greater length, and with greater urgency. The history of this book and of its author is somewhat curious, and may deserve a little space in this brief sketch, into which so many and great things have to be crowded.

Father Curci, as we have seen, was expelled from the order of the Jesuits after the publication of his first pamphlet; but he trusted that under the new pontiff his views, which he knew in a great measure coincided with those of Leo XIII., would be better received. He was also personally acquainted with Cardinal Giuseppe Pecci, the elder brother of the Pope, who had been made librarian of the Vatican. Giuseppe Pecci had himself been a member of the Society of Jesus, but had quitted it on account of some diversity of views. A storm having arisen on the publication of the *Nuova Italia ed i Vecchi Zelanti*, Father Curci was advised to go into retirement for a time, and preparations were made for his retreat in the Basilian monastery of Grotta Ferrata. But, under pressure, the Superior at the last moment refused to receive him. The Pope, on learning this, allowed Cardinal Pecci to offer him hospitality in his own apartments at the Vatican. During his stay there Father Curci had several interviews with the pontiff, who, while Archbishop of Perugia, had purchased a number of copies of his former work for distribution. Father Curci earnestly upheld the necessity for the reconciliation of Rome with constitutional Italy, believing that the Pope's duty as a Christian and a priest was to submit himself to the "powers that be, as ordained of God."

The Pope was vehemently urged to condemn the views of Father Curci, and that immediately. His only answer was, "There is a Congregation whose business it is to see into and judge this. It is for them to do their duty." The body referred to was the Congregation of the Index, whose office it is to pronounce whether a book is heretical, not whether it is good or bad. The passage selected for attack was one that spoke of the doctrine of Infallibility as a stumbling-block placed in the way of the spread of the gospel, and affirmed that the Council which decreed it had been deprived of liberty of discussion and decision. The Congregation did not find anything heretical in the book, but declared that they were incompetent to pronounce judgment on it. The matter was then referred to the Inquisition, which gives no reasons for what it says or does; and with little delay the book was condemned as a libel on the Church and Holy See. The sentence was forthwith submitted to the Pope, who, to avoid a serious schism in the Church, was forced to sign it.

It must have been terribly painful to Leo XIII. when he found himself compelled to acquiesce in the condemnation of a book with which he in the main agreed; but he was angered at the moment by the insults offered in Rome to the corpse of Pio Nono, and had come to the decision that the relations between the Papacy and the kingdom of Italy, as established by Pio Nono, must be maintained. A year later, however, he put forth a remarkable encyclical. After severely criticising those " wicked ones who declare war against Christ, and endeavor to rob the people of their Christian privileges," he goes on to reprove the clergy for not having done their duty as teachers; and then, without openly combating Pio Nono's dictum of *nè eletti nè elettori*, he allows it to be plainly perceived that he thinks it the duty of true Catholics to take part at least in the municipal elections. He urges Catholics to make use of the press, and, far from re-echoing Pio Nono's condemnation of all progress, all advancement in science and civilization, he calls upon priests to cultivate sound learning, " embracing not only sacred, but philosophical, physical, and historical studies." " Besides graver studies," he says, " young clerics should be instructed in other branches of knowledge, which cannot be fitly ignored at the present day, — such as natural science, and whatever serves to illustrate the authority and interpretation of Holy Scripture." In short, the encyclical seemed to prepare the way for the withdrawal of the self-denying ordinance by which Pius IX. deliberately placed the voting urns at the permanent and exclusive disposal of his assailants.

Leo XIII. is an earnest disciple of the Angelical Doctor, Saint Thomas Aquinas, the schoolman loved and praised by Dante; and he not only has urged the study of his writings and those of his followers, but he has founded an institution of learning especially for that purpose, and devoted some money that came into his hands by way of gift to the publication of a superb edition of his writings. Leo XIII. is said to know all Dante by heart. His knowledge, too, of history and general literature is varied and profound, as may be seen in the quotations he makes in his encyclicals. His use of Latin is said to be most elegant, and a rather large volume of his verses has been published. These are written chiefly in Latin. He is not the only pontiff who has been a poet. Leo the Great in the fifth century, Gregory I. (though he despised pedantic learning), and Gregory VII., the great Hildebrand, all wrote verses. Pius II. received the Laureate's crown from one of the German Emperors, while Urban II. used, it is said, to put off business to be transacted with his cardinals till they had given him their opinion of his latest sonnet. About two years ago Pope Leo sent to a friend, who was about to attain his ninetieth birthday, some verses which he had written on his own advancing age. They were this time in Italian, soft and sweet, to which justice can hardly be done in a translation.

"The sinking sun, descending into night,
Sheds on thee, Leo, its last rays of light.

"In thy dulled veins the blood creeps day by day
Slowly, — more slowly, — as life ebbs away.

"Death casts his dart; thy mortal form, when cold,
Earth shall receive, the funeral shroud enfold.

"But from its prison thy glad soul shall rise,
Stretch wide its wings, and, soaring, seek the skies.

"Then, when life's long, hard road has all been trod,
Ah, if it be Thy blessèd will, O God,

"Grant me — if counted worthy of Thy grace —
In Thy most blessèd heaven to see Thy face!"

CHAPTER XVII.

BRIGANDAGE AND SECRET SOCIETIES.

THE tendency to organize into secret societies was always strong in Italy. Before the Christian era, in the days when the Senate at Rome ruled the world, its power was insufficient to induce members of such societies to reveal secrets they had made oath to keep; while in after years the emperors were "fain to wink at what they would not sanction and could not extirpate." Subsequently, wherever the Romans founded colonies, they established clubs and associations *de sodaliciis et collegiis*, having their own by-laws, officers, and organizations, which, if they did not break the laws of the State, frequently took occasion to circumvent them. In the Middle Ages men in cities formed themselves into guilds, honored and accepted institutions; but the idea was taken up by what we call the "dangerous classes," and turned to their own purposes. Italians have always had a talent for conspiracy, and the stronghold of a conspiracy is the secret society to which it belongs. "There is," said Massimo d'Azeglio, "some instinct of civil war in the heart of every Italian." When an Italian's political aspirations have no outlet in that direction, he is quite ready to embark on a little illegal warfare to forward his own social, commercial, or criminal purposes. Even to the present day these secret societies protect their members against the operation of the laws of the State; for in the courts the odds are that juries and judges will be always in their favor. "If," says a leading newspaper in Rome (October 26, 1879), "a member of such a society commits a crime, his associates defend him by manufactured evidence, intrigues, or intimidation."

Italy is a difficult country to make laws for. The laws of justice which do well for the orderly Lombards or Piedmontese, by no means suit the semi-barbarians of Apulia and Sicily. Philanthropy abolished the death-penalty for murder, and substituted for it imprisonment for fifteen years. The number of victims at once increased, nor did the law result in length of days to the murderers, the police shooting down suspected criminals on any excuse. And we are told that "whenever a crime has been committed, even before the circumstances are known, the sympathies of the community are invariably enlisted on the side of the accused."

But it is in the old kingdom of the Two Sicilies that the operations of secret societies may be best observed; and there, too, brigandage long existed in force, notwithstanding the persistent endeavors of the government to put it down. The two principal societies in the province of Naples are the Camorra and the Mafia; the latter, however, is the most powerful in Sicily. The Camorra is said at one time to have been divided (some say it is still) into the *Camorra alta*, or, as it was sometimes called, "the Camorra in kid gloves," and the *Camorra bassa*. The Camorra alta busied itself chiefly with elections and jobbery, using, when violence was needed, members of the Camorra bassa as its tools. It was in full force as late as 1877, and boasted of the control it could exert over elections.

The Camorra bassa is well supplied with funds levied upon the peasants, who bring their produce into the cities (in addition to the unpopular legal gate tax on eggs, vegetables, etc.). Large sums are also paid to the society by all sorts of men and women, who find protection for illegal modes of life by numbering themselves among its *clientèle*; especially does it claim a portion of the winnings of any of its members at the gaming table, — leading us to the conclusion that the Camorra originated in Spain, since Sancho Panza banished from his island a band of rascals who claimed a similar right to take toll of his subjects' winnings.

The Mafia is a less organized society than the Camorra. It has no entrance initiation, and no visible head. It has, however, many secret maxims, which are to be learned by heart by each new member. Here are some of them: "The poor resort to force; fools have recourse to law. — Take the life of whoever makes you lose the means of living. — Be respectful to officers of the law, but stand afar off. — If I die, I shall be buried; if I live, you will be. — Of what does not concern you, say neither good nor ill. — If needful, bear witness; but take heed that what you testify does no harm to your neighbor. — He that dies is buried; he that lives gets married. — An influential friend is worth more than a thousand lire in your pockets. — Imprisonment, sickness, and misfortune test the hearts of friends."

The idea of such associations as the Camorra and the Mafia (frequently classed together under the general name of *Mala Vita*, — that is, " Evil Life ") was to form a State within the State, — a State having its own rulers, its own code, its own power of punishment, its own finances; a State framed in the interest of evil-doers, and which forbade its members under any circumstances to have recourse to the laws of the land. "The true Mafiosi are polished villains. They assume towards their enemy the language and bearing of fraternal good-humor, and write the most threatening letters in terms of bland politeness." The keynote of of the whole alliance is *omerta*, — a word derived, some say, from *uomo*, or *omo*, — that is, "man," — the leading principle of the order being that a man must depend on himself for all he needs (support, justice, etc.), without regard to the laws of society. Some, however, think that the word *omerta* is derived from " humility," — an explanation that finds support both in the assumed humility of the Mafiosi, and also in the terms of the oath by which they bind themselves " to make war upon the infamous [that is, those who have property], and to protect the humble." License to rob is given to all members; but they are expected to divide the spoils with their associates.

Brigandage ("old as the hills" in Southern Italy) allies itself more or less with the societies of the Mala Vita; but it was of itself, up to twenty years ago, a recognized institution. Early in the century it existed in the peninsula, principally in the mountains of Calabria and Apulia. It flourished under Italian princes, — the Pope and the kings of Naples; but the parts of Italy that were more directly under Austrian rule were comparatively free from it. In 1817 there were said to be seventy thousand brigands, or their secret accomplices, in one province of the kingdom of Naples alone; and their chief had a plan of uniting all brigands into an army, marching against the king's troops, and making terms with the Bourbon government.

Under these circumstances, King Ferdinand employed an English gentleman — General Church — to do his best, with a strong force of carbineers, to put the brigands down. General Church's narrative of his extraordinary adventures while endeavoring to carry out this mission was published in "Blackwood's Magazine," in 1892,[1] by a surviving relative. Unfortunately, General Church's interesting reminiscences cannot, for want of space, be given here.

The brigand chief against whom he was especially employed was Ciro Annichiarico. This man was a priest, and sometimes exercised the functions of his priesthood in the midst of his bloody exploits. We hear of his celebrating mass before starting on his wild expeditions, and he complained of the mission priests that they did not preach the pure gospel, but disseminated *illiberal* opinions among the peasantry. At the same time he was cruel, sparing neither

[1] Also in Miss Yonge's "Monthly Packet." When I was a child — say in 1830 — the number of children's books published was small. One of my chief favorites was "The Stories of Old Daniel." Old Daniel was supposed to have been the body servant of an English officer, who travelled, in search of health, into all parts of southern Europe. His narratives were manifestly genuine reminiscences. A great many related to Italian brigands; and in nearly all of these a priest and a landlord bore chief parts, either as accomplices or leaders.— E. W. L.

age nor sex; his life was openly immoral, and he boasted of his infidel opinions. "He was," says General Church, "a good horseman and a capital shot; strong and vigorous as a tiger, and equally ferocious. His countenance was bad; he had large features, a very ordinary face, never without a sinister expression, quite unlike the manly countenance of Don Gaetano Vardarelli (another brigand chief, also a priest). Ciro had friends and protectors in all the towns and villages of the province of Lecce, and had the effrontery at times to show himself in broad daylight, apparently unaccompanied. He was a perfect Proteus in disguises, — as a woman, as a beggar, as a priest, as a friar, as an officer, as a gendarme. His usual dress was of velveteen, highly faced with many rows of buttons, and belts in every direction; and he was always armed with pistols and stiletto, carbine, or rifle. He always carried poison with him in a small case, within a red pocket-book. He also always wore several silver chains, to one of which was attached a silver death's-head, the badge of the secret society (the Decisi) which he had founded, and of which he was the recognized head, — that terrible society whose first condition for admission into its ranks was that the candidate must have committed two murders with his own hand, and whose decrees and patents were written in blood. On his breast he wore rows of relics, crosses, images of saints, and amulets against the evil eye. His headdress was a high-peaked drab-colored hat, adorned with gold band, buckle, and tall black feather, and his fingers were covered with rings of great value."

Ciro was born of well-to-do parents, respectable people of the farming class, who early destined him for the priesthood. His first murder was that of a young girl who had repelled his advances, being betrothed to a fellow-townsman. This man he also murdered, together with his sister and his three brothers. The only member of the family he left alive was a little boy, who was hidden away by a faithful servant in his own desolate house, and who grew up there, barred and bolted in, for fifteen years, never stirring beyond the door. One day a party came in broad daylight to the house, knocking, and clamorously calling on him to admit them. He shrank back, fearing a snare. At last, however, he was persuaded to come forth into the light, which dazzled and bewildered him, and was taken by his friends to the city gate, where the head of his enemy was shown to him, hung up in an iron cage. He stood dazed at first, then falling on his knees, with tears and wild laughter, he thanked the Madonna and the saints; then rushed off to General Church's quarters, to thank him too.

Ciro's most notorious crime was committed on a night in December, 1814, and led to the employment of General Church with orders to extirpate him.

A young and amiable princess lived in the strong castle of Martano, apparently without a male protector, though she had faithful servants. Late one night a traveller presented himself at the gates, asking hospitality for his excellency the commandant of the province, who had been belated on his way to Otranto. The moment the gates were opened, a large body of horsemen poured into the courtyard, and some, dismounting, followed their leader into the hall. The old steward was stabbed as he came forward hospitably to receive the unexpected guests. Every other man-servant was swiftly murdered. None were spared, not even the white-haired chaplain, nor an old lady the princess's duenna, nor her waiting-women. Then Ciro made his way to the chamber of the princess, cut down a maid who stood before her door, and entered. He demanded a sum of money that she was known to have in the house. She pointed to an iron chest that stood near. He asked, "Where are the keys?"

"On the table by the chimney-piece."

"Where are your jewels?"

"In a small box on that table."

"Have you any others?"

"Not in this house."

"Very well. Then allow me to examine them."

He opened the chest, which contained thirty-six thousand gold louis; then he opened the jewel-case. It was full of sparkling gems. He closed the box, and, crying fiercely, "Philosophers tell us that dead dogs cannot bite," he stabbed the princess and a second maid with his poniard. Then the brigands feasted in the hall, and, after some quarrelling about the division of the spoils, departed, setting fire to the furniture in the great hall, and carefully closing the gates, so that no passer-by might suspect that there was anything wrong within. They thought that every soul in the castle had been murdered. They were mistaken. A small boy, cousin of the princess, had run into her room, and had hidden himself under a table covered with thick drapery. After seeing his cousin fall, he fainted, but came to life again, and found the castle full of smoke. Active as a cat, he got out of a window, and made his way into the town that was clustered under the castle wall. Here he roused the syndic and the townsmen. The only creature found alive in the castle was one of the maidservants, who lived just long enough to depose to what had happened.

Ciro's activity was as astonishing as his artifice and his intrepidity; and as he was always well mounted, and found concealment and support everywhere, through fear or inclination, he succeeded in escaping from the soldiers repeatedly, even when confidential spies had discovered his place of concealment only a few hours before. This singular good fortune acquired for him the character of a magician, and he neglected nothing that would confirm this idea.

After General Church commenced his campaign, Ciro complained bitterly that he could no longer corrupt the soldiers sent against him. "I have tried," he said, "but to no purpose. Even the gendarmes, half of whom are Carbonari, are my bitter foes now that this Englishman has come into Apulia." He was taken at last and shot, February 8, 1818, after the formality of a trial, which General Church insisted on. The soldiers maintained that he could be killed only with a silver bullet; and as he stirred on the ground after he fell, one who had prepared a silver bullet, rammed it into the criminal's own carbine, and sent it through his body. "How many murders have you committed with your own hand?" was asked him after his trial. He answered carelessly, "Sixty or seventy."

Such was brigandage in the kingdom of Naples up to the year 1818. We may now see what it was in the States of the Church at a somewhat later period, when the present Pope, Leo XIII., was sent as papal delegate into the province of Benevento, which, "although it formed part of the States of the Church, was wholly inclosed within the territory of Naples. There, cut off from the central authority, situated among the Apennines, and remote from any of the great lines of communication, the little province formed the headquarters of the brigands who infested the neighboring Roman and Neapolitan territory. The ease with which malefactors could slip across the frontier, together with the lawless propensities of the feudal nobles of the country, rendered the task of governing it an extremely difficult one. The owners of the castles among the hills found it easier and more profitable to live on good terms with the brigands than to side with the pontifical authority against them. They audaciously claimed for their mountain fortresses immunity from the authority of the magistrates, and afforded to the brigands an inviolable asylum; and these lawless feudal nobles were supported by very powerful friends at Rome.

"The new delegate began by obtaining from Gregory XVI. a very capable man as head of the civil force in the province. He then procured from Naples orders to the Neapolitan police authorities on the frontier to support him to the utmost of their power. Thus prepared, he sent a force of gendarmes to one of the hill castles, in which several brigands were known to have taken refuge, seized them, and safely lodged them in prison. The owner of the residence thus violated was one of the most powerful men of the province. On the morrow he visited the delegate in the city of Benevento, and with extreme anger intimated that he was on his way to Rome, whence he should soon return with an order for Monsignor Pecci's recall. 'That you can do, Signor Marchese,' said Pecci quietly, 'but you must put off your journey for three months, since I am going to put you in prison for that period, during which I shall give you only bread and water.' And he was to the letter as good as his word. He was thanked by Gregory XVI.; he was invited to Naples to receive the expression of King Ferdinand's approbation, and Benevento was, for the time, cleared of brigands."

Not long since there was published in Florence (1892) a small pamphlet, being the autobiography of Colonel Michele Zambelli,[1] who, during thirty-two years of active service in the *gendarmeria* of the Papal States, was the scourge of banditti, and the most active uprooter of the secret societies with which they associated themselves. His work lay in Romagna, where the peasantry are a bold and handsome race, with considerable natural intelligence and great activity. Impetuous, quick-tempered, and excitable, they are more governed by their emotions than their reason. They are kindly and considerate to the old and to women, and remarkably affectionate to their children. The autobiography of this Italian Inspector Byrnes is very brief, but it contains material out of which a literary workman of the "blood and thunder" school might construct a dozen dime novels. Yet Romagna has no world-wide reputation as the especial *habitat* of the Italian brigand.

Stories of Italian brigandage and secret associations were so long stock properties belonging to a certain class of writers that we are apt always to class them with sensational fiction. There is no sensational writing, however, in the little narrative of Colonel Zambelli. It is a simple chronicle of facts connected with his experience. The *gendarmeria* to which he belonged is a body of police, uniformed and under military discipline. In France the police service is divided into two branches, — agents of

[1] I made a translation of a portion of this narrative, which appeared in the New York "Sun." — E. W. L.

police, who are organizers and detectives, having *mouchards* (or spies) under them; and gendarmes, who do active police work, make arrests, and maintain order. In Italy, at least during the days of which Colonel Zambelli writes, the gendarmes, or carbineers, seem to have united both these functions. If an organized band of brigands infested any district, a trusted officer of gendarmes, like Zambelli, was sent to take up his quarters in its chief town, with orders to extirpate the band or the secret society, and bring to justice all aiders and abettors of the same. Apparently no warrants were necessary. Shooting at sight seems to have superseded the ordinary course of law; indeed, on one or two occasions, Zambelli excuses himself for prompt measures by saying that criminals, if taken to prison, might have escaped through the meshes of the law, or by the law's delays.

The father of Michele Zambelli had been a soldier under Napoleon, and his tales of adventure so stimulated a martial spirit in his family that all his sons became soldiers. Michele, the youngest, tells us that he dreamed of battles from his infancy; and finding that his father meant to retain his services at home, he ran away to enlist when fifteen years old. Crossing a mountain range, he came near losing his life in a snowstorm; but at last, by following some mule-tracks he reached a hospice, where the brothers treated him with every kindness, — " gratefully remembering which," he tells us, " I have never omitted, when fortune smiled on me, to give to the Capuchins abundant alms." His enlistment took place in 1831, when all Italy was in the throes of that abortive revolution in which Napoleon Louis and Louis Napoleon took part.

The first raid against any noted malefactor in which Zambelli was engaged was in 1832, when a brigand named Cavalli was secreted with a small band of followers in the Apennines, and harried the neighboring villages. A movable column of soldiers had been hunting these outlaws for some months; but one day, when Private Zambelli was going, unaccompanied by any of his comrades, to a town in the district to draw the pay of his company, he received information that Cavalli was hidden in a neighboring mill. The young soldier endeavored to persuade the villagers to assist in arresting him, but their dread of retribution was too great. "I knew," says Zambelli, "that Cavalli had a gun with which he had been shooting little birds, then roasting in the miller's kitchen. He was also in possession of a sabre and a pistol. I hastened to the place, and from a loop-hole I could see the bandit in the stable. I made a sudden spring, and was so quickly upon him that he had no chance to use his weapons. For this arrest the government awarded me a silver medal, which I received with great satisfaction."

Two years later, hearing that a district called Saluduchio, in the province of Forli, was infested by two bands of banditti, Zambelli asked to be transferred to that new field of activity. In three months he had arrested three murderers, who made a dogged resistance. This broke up one band; but not long afterwards he was secretly informed that the other, which consisted of seven robbers, besides many who aided and abetted them, had formed a scheme to plunder the residence of a rich proprietor. Their leader was a man named Buratone, an escaped convict under sentence of close confinement for ten years. At midnight, Zambelli and two carbineers under his orders repaired to the house that was to be attacked, and waited some time before the ruffians arrived. These at once broke down the door. The carbineers sprang into their midst, and a rough-and-tumble fight ensued, at the end of which the carbineers, though victorious, had only made two prisoners, — one of whom was the chief, who was mortally wounded. His capture, however, was of great importance, for, out of revenge for the desertion of his band, he gave them all up to justice. By dawn they were arrested and marched to the nearest prison, amid the wildest exclamations of satisfaction on the part of the peasantry, half of whom, in spite of these demonstrations, were probably more or less accomplices. Among those arrested was a miller in good circumstances and highly respected by his neighbors. Zambelli's reward for this service was a very large silver medal.

In 1840 Zambelli was in command of a considerable number of men. He was secretly informed that a band of armed outlaws, the boldest rascals in Romagna, was in the vicinity of the town of Civitella, engaged in transporting contraband merchandise of great value. "I had only three men with me at the moment," he says in his narrative," all the rest having been detached from my command by a certain tobacco inspector, ostensibly to assist him in a search for illicit salt-works in the hills. Later I found that this inspector had an understanding with the banditti, whose chief had paid him to get my carbineers out of the way. I also discovered that other soldiers in the district had been tampered with, as well as the revenue officers."

With his three men, Zambelli planned and executed a successful ambuscade; a sharp fight followed. The night was very dark. Only the flashes of light from their firearms revealed the combatants to one another. The muleteers in alarm cut the girths that bound the burdens on their mules, and, mounting them, made off, consulting only their own safety. Four outlaws, two mules, and goods to the value of eight thousand dollars were captured. Then six other bandits, believing themselves to be surrounded by soldiers, surrendered; but the greater part of the band made their escape. For this service Zambelli received a gold medal.

He seems also to have been employed in putting down revolutionary movements in Romagna when Italy became agitated in 1845. Early in the following year he was sent to Imola, where the Cardinal-Archbishop Mastai received him with great kindness. Cardinal Mastai won praise, even from his enemies. Felice Orsini, the man who threw bombs at the Emperor Napoleon III., speaks of him thus: "He was charitable; his character was unspotted; no one could say a word against his morality. He was handsome, studious, and retiring, but he had also all the prejudices of his caste." When, after the death of Gregory XVI., Cardinal Mastai journeyed to Rome to attend the

Conclave, Zambelli with his carbineers wanted to escort him; but the cardinal declined his services, and went accompanied only by his own people, and by the famous white pigeon which persistently followed him to the end of his journey.

When Cardinal Mastai became Pio Nono, one of his first acts was to make Zambelli a lieutenant, and to order that his son Paulo, then three years of age, should be admitted into his own bodyguard with pay and privileges till he became twenty-one, when he would receive a commission as an officer.

Zambelli tells several stories illustrating the abject fear which men in authority felt of the vengeance likely to fall on them if they interfered with the operations of the banditti. He put them to shame, however, and was rewarded for his successful exertions by official congratulations and public dinners. At Sinigaglia he put down a band called *La Macchia*, or the Bewitched, who had just murdered both the Marquis Consolini and a poor old man recently released from prison in virtue of the Pope's amnesty. The Macchia vowed to take Zambelli's life, but only succeeded in wounding him.

The troubles that convulsed Italy in 1846–47 produced such general social anarchy that little could be done to put down murderers and robbers. Zambelli and his carbineers were therefore transferred to Rome. He was there when Count Rossi was murdered, but not on duty in that part of the city. When the Republic was proclaimed he retired from active service, but resumed his old position when the authority of Pio Nono was restored. With the assistance of a band of Austrian soldiers, he scaled the walls of Monturano, a small fortified city which had been taken possession of by robbers; and having taken the precaution to bring a judge along with him on this expedition, thirty robbers whom he captured were condemned before nightfall and marched to prison.

But the most celebrated bandit with whom he measured his strength was Stefano Pelloni, better known as the Ferryman (*Il Passatore*). The most celebrated exploit of this man was the capture of the town of Forlimpopoli. He had accomplices within its walls who kept him informed of the movements, habits, and circumstances of the principal inhabitants. There were only six carbineers at that time in Forlimpopoli. Two patrolled the streets; two stayed in the guardroom; and two were stationed at the theatre. At dusk the band of outlaws entered the little walled town, once defended by a now ruined castle built by Cæsar Borgia. They came in quietly by different gates, but uniting at a preconcerted spot, surprised and captured the patrol so quietly that no alarm was given. They then marched to the barracks, and obliged their prisoners to call out their two comrades, who the moment they appeared were also captured. The four were then fast bound, and left under guard in their own quarters. The rest of the band of outlaws then went to the theatre, where a large part of the population of Forlimpopoli seems to have been assembled. Several of them contrived to reach the side scenes; others quietly captured the two gendarmes on duty. When the curtain rose, it disclosed, with fine dramatic effect, the Passatore and ten of his men upon the stage with guns in their hands. The audience fancied at first sight that it was part of the play, and vehemently applauded; but when a voice exclaimed, "I am the Passatore! I am master of your city. Here are its keys. I have locked the gates. Let no one move. This theatre is surrounded by my men," — an indescribable panic seized the spectators. The captain then producing a list of the wealthiest inhabitants proceeded to read it, ordering each person, as his name was called, to come up on the stage. Each man was then escorted to his home, where he was forced to find the ransom for which the Passatore had assessed him. These sums amounted in all to about ten thousand dollars in money and jewels. The robbers likewise attempted to force open the safe of the Mont de Piété, but could not succeed in doing so. They held possession of the town for about three hours, during which time no man was suffered to leave the theatre, except those sent forth under guard. They had thus all the well-to-do population in their power, while the lower class did nothing to oppose them. The mail-carrier from Rome arrived at the gate during their occupation, and was informed that the key of the gate had been mislaid, and that to avoid delay he had better throw his mail-bag over the wall. He did so without suspicion, and went on his journey. No sooner was he well out of the way than the brigands beat a retreat, carrying with them the six gendarmes as prisoners. About two miles from the town they turned the gendarmes loose, and the band made their escape in safety. Two of their accomplices in the town were discovered, tried by court-martial, and shot. The scene of this exploit was a town containing about six thousand inhabitants.

The Passatore, like Robin Hood, robbed only the rich, and did not molest the poor; this gave his men the sympathy of a large part of the population; and, the police being as much employed against revolutionary associations as against robbers, the robbers and revolutionists often made common cause.

The Passatore was chief over three bands, — his own, and those of two lieutenants, one of whom was famous for the numerous murders he had committed. These bands had innumerable sympathizers in the towns and villages. They had fictitious names for everything and everybody; so that when two of the initiated met in public, they could talk freely without fear of being understood by a third party. They were well armed, and each man carried on his back an enormous sack, in which he could hide himself if necessary. The band frequently passed from Romagna into Tuscany, and from Tuscany into Romagna. They often set out upon their raids in carriages, that they might the more quickly be transported back over the frontier. When the zeal of Zambelli had succeeded in breaking up the main band of outlaws, those who were left took refuge in Tuscany out of his reach.

It was Zambelli's policy to secure the services of *manutengoli* — that is, hand-claspers, or honorary members of some robber-band — by promises of pardon and reward. "Some," he says, "served well; but some deceived me, and betrayed my purposes." So great, however, was the terror of all good citizens lest the brigands should suspect them of sympathy with the cause of justice, that it was harder to get information from them than from the *manutengoli*, who were confederates of the robbers.

In 1860, Zambelli joined the papal army under Lamoricière, and was in the battle of Castelfidardo with his carbineers. He speaks of Lamoricière's force as an undisciplined and heterogeneous horde of warriors; his own regiment, which was in excellent order, received high praise from the general. After Castelfidardo they took possession of Ancona; but the town was forced to capitulate, and the carbineers with the other papal troops were disbanded and dispersed. Zambelli retired into private life, having received many wounds from attacks made on him in the dark, as well as many medals. He was eighty-six years old in 1892, when his autobiography was published. It was a brief record of his adventurous life, written for his family; but, having been seen by a literary man in Florence engaged in catering for the public taste, its author, with some difficulty, was persuaded to consent to its publication.

It may be gathered from Zambelli's narrative that during the years of anarchy and civil war that preceded the unification of Italy, brigands and revolutionists often lent assistance to each other. When, in 1860, two armies were disbanded in the kingdom of Naples, — the volunteers of Garibaldi, and the forces of King Francis,— about fifty thousand men, more or less desperate, and all used to bear arms, were let loose upon society. Some enlisted in the papal forces, but a large part took to the mountains and became banditti. This state of things, both in Naples and Sicily, made the establishment of good government in the Two Sicilies the despair of the ministers of Victor Emmanuel. Piedmontese troops were sent into the south to put down the brigands, while Neapolitan regiments were quartered in the north, lest the soldiers should show sympathy with relations and old comrades engaged in brigandage.

The ex-king Francis took advantage of this state of affairs to annoy and embarrass the King of Italy. He sent agents into the mountains of Calabria and Apulia; he attached robber-chiefs to his service, and, exasperated as they were against the Piedmontese government, which was using every effort to restore law and order, they were glad of a political cloak under which to shelter their crimes. The peasantry too, who, as we have seen, were always, from fear or sympathy, more or less in alliance with the outlaws, were anything but satisfied with the results of the revolution. The misgovernment of the Bourbons had not borne hard on *them*. They cared nothing for what the educated classes called "liberty." The liberty they wanted was to be left in peace, independent of the law, and to be, above all things, unburdened by taxation.

The Sicilian and Neapolitan peasantry have been a disaffected population ever since the formation of the kingdom of Italy; and the power of the brigands soon became so great that there was talk of a brigand-rising in favor of the former government. It became absolutely necessary for the Italian authorities to put down the outlaws. It must be owned that the task was hard enough to fill them with despair; but it must also be added that their methods were quite as barbarous as anything we read of under the rule of the Bourbons.

There is no question, that, whatever may be the testimony of *plébiscites*, the rural population of the late kingdom of Naples soon became hostile to the new regime, — to its enforcement of law, its taxation, and its conscription. It was impossible to carry out the principle that governments that have not the consent of an unintelligent majority are illegitimate, and yet preserve the unity of Italy. "In Naples," said d'Azeglio, "we have made a change, and have sought to establish our government on a basis of universal suffrage; but sixty battalions are required to hold the kingdom, and it seems that even these are not enough."

To take advantage of this state of things, Spanish officers were sent over to Calabria under the secret sanction of the exiled dynasty. About twenty of them landed in the extreme south of the peninsula, under General Borjes, a Catalan who had distinguished himself by deeds of daring in the first Carlist war. They hoped soon to collect an army; but the brigand chiefs, on whom they had relied, declined to submit to their authority and, as winter was approaching, their best plan seemed to be to make their way over the frontier into the Pope's dominions. They were arrested, however, when only a few miles from safety, and summarily shot.

The generals sent into the Abruzzi and Calabria to put down brigands issued proclamations whose brutality called forth remonstrances in the English Parliament, where, in 1863, Mr. Baillie Cochrane quoted one put forth by a Major Fumel, remarking that " a more infamous proclamation had never disgraced the Reign of Terror." It ran as follows : —

" The undersigned, having been commissioned to destroy brigandage, promises a reward of one hundred lire for every brigand, alive or dead, who may be brought to him. This reward will be given to any brigand who shall kill his comrade; moreover, his own life shall be spared. Those who, in defiance of this, give shelter, or any means of subsistence or support, to brigands, or, seeing them, or knowing the place where they may have taken refuge, do not give information to the forces, and to the civil or military authorities, will be immediately shot. For the custody of animals, it would be well that they should be brought into several central spots, with a sufficient armed force, because it would not be of use unless the force were sufficient. All straw huts must be burned. The towers and country houses which are not inhabited must be, within the space of three days, unroofed and their entrances bricked up. Otherwise, after the expiration of that time they will, without fail, be burned, and all animals which are not under proper guard will be killed. It is prohibited to carry bread, or any kind of provisions, beyond the habitations of the communes; and whoever disobeys this order will be considered an accomplice of the brigands. Provisionally, and under these circumstances, the syndics are authorized to grant permission to carry arms under the strict responsibility of the land-owners who shall make the request. Shooting as a sport is also provisionally forbidden; and therefore no one may fire off a gun, unless to give notice to the armed posts of the presence of the brigands, or of their flight. The National Guard of each commune is responsible for its own district. The undersigned does not mean to recognize under present circumstances more than two parties, — brigands and anti-brigands. Therefore he will class among the former those who are indifferent; and against these he will take energetic measures, for in times of general necessity it is a crime to stand apart. The disbanded soldiers who do not present themselves within the space of four days will be considered brigands.

When these and similar documents were brought to the notice of the Emperor Napoleon III., he addressed the following letter to his confidential friend and agent, General Fleury: —

"I have written to Turin to remonstrate. The details we receive are of such a kind as to be calculated to alienate every honest mind from the Italian cause. Not only are misery and anarchy at their height, but the most culpable and unworthy acts seem matters of course. A general, whose name I have forgotten, having forbidden the peasants to take provisions with them when they go to work in the fields, has decreed that all on whom a piece of bread may be found shall be shot. The Bourbons never did anything like that."

It may have been hard to persuade the Neapolitan peasantry, who had been assured of peace and plenty under Italian unity, that the best means of promoting liberty and prosperity was laying waste their farms, villages, and even their market towns by fire and sword. But the only answer to remonstrances both from abroad and in the parliament at Turin was, that brigandage *had* to be put down, and *that* by the armed hand. It was almost impossible in Naples, quite impossible in Sicily, to procure either a judge or jury who would convict a brigand. The only way of getting rid of him was to imprison him for months without trial, or to have him summarily shot.

The prison system in Naples had not been reformed during the early years of the new government. It was as bad as in the days when Mr. Gladstone wrote of it. The prisons contained, indeed, few gentlemen of education and refinement, but those therein were loaded, as Poerio and Settembrini had been, with chains, and forced to associate with criminals. Lord Henry Lennox, who, as an ardent sympathizer with the Italian revolution and an admirer of Garibaldi, visited the southern provinces in 1863, was permitted to visit the prisons, and in very temperate language gave an account of what he had seen in them to the House of Commons. His speech was a repetition of the statements of Mr. Gladstone twelve years before.

It was not long, however, before brigandage, as associated with insurrection, met with its fall. Only a few scattered bands, brigands in the true sense of the word, kept the hills. These carried on predatory brigandage for years after. Some of them do so still.

The ancient brigandage, which the Italian government likes to claim that it has now suppressed, has lost its picturesque character, and is mere highway robbery. "What has become of all the brigands?" asked a traveller of an Irishman who had long lived in Italy. "Shure, and hav' n't they all intered into the service of the railway companies?" was the reply. A correspondent of the Baltimore "Sun," recently writing from Italy says: —

"A few years ago I fell in with one of the old-time brigands, at Melfi, — a man who in his day had done great deeds, when highway robbery seems to have risen to the dignity of a fine art. His name was Francesco Fonzella, but he was known by the name of Fina. He had long given up business as a brigand, and was engaged in the harmless and necessary occupation of a water-carrier. He had begun his career as a soldier in the army of Francis II., King of Naples. He was one of the last to leave the fortress of Gaeta when the defence was led by that heroic woman the young Queen of Naples, sister to the present Empress of Austria. The Italian army was successful, and the fortress capitulated. Fonzella returned to his native place a disbanded soldier, and was maltreated by every new official, who sought to retain his post by being harsh to the soldiers of the defeated king. A lieutenant of the new National Guard was particularly severe to Fonzella, and one day struck him. Fonzella returned the blow with interest. Conscious that it would go hard with him if the case came before the courts, Fonzella fled, and joined the forces of the noted brigand Crocco, who, from having once been a peaceful shepherd, had become the terror of southern Italy. The wife of Fonzella found means to communicate with her husband. This fact was discovered, and she was with especial harshness and cruelty condemned to be shot in the public square, — a sentence solemnly carried out to the end.

"The newly-made brigand thirsted for revenge. He attributed the death of his wife to the lieutenant. When it was night in the village of San Fele, near Melfi, Fonzella, disguised as a woman, entered the little café of the place, and there discharged two shots from a revolver at the lieutenant. The disguised brigand, in the confusion that followed, made his escape. The lieutenant's wounds were not mortal, and he recovered. The proximity of the brigands to this village created alarm, and guards were posted to protect the place. The brigands approached. Fonzella was on the watch for his victim. This time his shot was deadly. His career was fixed. He was an outlaw and an assassin.

"The usual occupation of Crocco's band was robbery of the wealthy Italians of the vicinity, battles with the Italian troops, and the seizure and robbery of rich foreigners, for whose deliverance heavy ransoms were demanded. When a detachment of troops was sent against them, they showed considerable courage. As they knew the country well, with its hiding-places and points of vantage, it was not easy to capture them.

"On the feast of the Carmine, July 16, a detachment of cavalry, commanded by a young lieutenant of the Italian army surprised these brigands. Crocco did not like to fight because it was a feast day, and proposed that the battle should be postponed. The young lieutenant answered, 'No truce with brigands!' The scruples of Crocco were cast to the winds, and the fight began. Not a man of the Italian cavalry was left alive.

"The old water-carrier of Melfi, with his thick bushy eyebrows overhanging his small bright eyes, his tufted hair and beard, now so silent and absorbed, admitted he had killed twenty-two persons, — two through his especial vengeance, twenty in the way of business.

"The band at last capitulated. Their lives were spared, but they were condemned to imprisonment. Fonzella spent twenty years in prison, and then returned to his native place."

Doubtless, hundreds of the brigands who infested southern Italy could have told very much the same tale as this Fonzella.

Some one in the year 1881 took the pains to ascertain how many British subjects had been captured by brigands and held for ransom during the preceding twenty years, — that is, from 1861 to 1881. In all there were thirteen captures, and twenty-nine captives, — three captures in Mexico, two in Italy, one in Sicily, four in Spain, two in Greece, and one in Turkey.

Mr. Beale was captured near Florence, in July, 1864. Twelve thousand scudi were demanded for his ransom; but, happily for him, he was released the next day, his guards being under a mistaken impression that the sum had been paid.

Mr. and Mrs. William Moens, and the Rev. Mr. Aynsley and his wife were taken near Battipaglia, in May, 1865. The ladies were released the same day, and Mr. Aynsley the day following, to make arrangements for the ransom; £8,500 was demanded, but the British consul at Naples succeeded in effecting a compromise for £5,000, and Mr. Moens, who had been left in pawn during three months, was released. He subsequently gave an interesting account of his experiences.

The Sicilian victim, Mr. Rose, was taken in November, 1876, close to a railroad station near Palermo; £5,000, then £2,000, was demanded for his release, but about £1,600 was finally accepted.

Such exploits as the recent one, when the Duke of Saxe-Weimar was "held up" on the road between Rome and Albano by a ruffian with a handkerchief tied over his face, can hardly be called brigandage; they are vulgar highway robberies.

Brigandage of the old sort still exists, however, in Sicily;

and there the Mafia has its roots in the very soil. Every ship-load of Sicilian or Calabrian immigrants landed on our shores is doubtless a satisfaction to the Italian government. The southern Italians are attracted to New Orleans by the climate. The greater part of the Piedmontese and Lombards, an industrious and thrifty class, land in New York. Many from Sicily and Naples go to Buenos Ayres.

The Mafia, as it now exists, is hardly a *secret* society. "It is," says an Italian, writing of it in 1887, "rather the development (the blossom) of arbitrary violence, directed to criminal ends of every kind. It is the instinctive, brutal, sordid solidarity that unites itself against the State, the laws, and the constituted authorities." But the most discouraging circumstance in connection with this society is that its working is, even by honest men, accepted as the inevitable. "It would take a volume," says a writer in the "Fortnightly Review," "to specify all the modes in which, without violating the letter of the law, the Mafia can make things comfortable for its subordinates."

The Mafia is organized upon the feudal system. Members of the High Mafia — the "Mafia in kid gloves" — have each their subordinates; these have their clients, and so on. "Even by the various governments of Sicily, up to 1877, the High Mafia has been shielded, it never having suited any ministry or ministerial functionary to bring home to its members crimes for which it was well known they were responsible. So great has been its political influence, that it has frequently controlled the elections, parliamentary and municipal, not only in the small towns and villages, but also in Messina and Palermo."

Mafia in Sicily, Camorra in Naples, are two names for the same thing. But the word "Camorra" has now come into use as a term in Italian politics. It means what we call "The Ring." The Camorra, indeed, as a last resort, has recourse to the stiletto; in other respects the Camorra and the Ring are the same thing. In 1877 the Italian government roused itself to action, and endeavored to put down red-handed Mafiaism in Sicily. It flattered itself that it had driven every suspected member of the Mafia out of the island, — many of them to our own shores. But the spirit of the thing remains, though its methods are somewhat changed. The Mafia and the Camorra have adapted themselves to the ideas of the nineteenth century.

Sicily and Naples are to the kingdom of Italy what Ireland has been to the English government. Their deputies in the Italian parliament make noise and trouble, like those of the sister isle at Westminster. Absenteeism, as in Ireland, is a principal cause of Sicilian destitution, and the land question is at the root of the peasants' discontent. Sixty-five per cent. of the acreage of Sicily consists of immense estates, varying in size from three thousand to fifteen thousand acres. The landlord rarely lives on these estates; he employs an agent, called a "gabellotto," who lets the land to those who sublet it at a rack-rent to others, who again sublet it in small lots to men who pay rent for it by two-thirds or three-quarters of the crop they raise. "Tenant farmers, with capital or farm buildings on the holdings, are equally unknown. The tenant is almost always in debt to the gabellotto, who advances him food and seed-corn at an extravagant interest, and to whom he is virtually a serf. If the season is good, he barely pays his way; if it is bad, he sinks hopelessly into debt. Baron Mendola, a Sicilian landlord and a shrewd observer, has given it as his deliberate opinion that the average Sicilian peasant cannot make both ends meet. "Honest labor," he says, "seldom suffices for the maintenance of his family. He *must* steal." What wonder that brigandage has attractions for young men! With respect to local politics in Sicily, the situation was thus described by an English writer nine years ago. I quote the passage, rather than employ any words of my own : —

"In each commune there are two parties. One must crush the other, so as to monopolize all the spoils of local office, and, by the influence of the deputy which it elects, to deter the *prefetto* from looking too curiously into any little irregularities that may be committed under his jurisdiction. The struggle for the municipal purse is more ignoble and more injurious to public morality than even the disputes of rival families in former days; and in these struggles the Mafia, with its terrible power, is practically the arbiter. Willingly or unwillingly, the wealthy gabellotto must support it by his influence, providing its members with employment and wages, or pushing them into municipal offices, according to their wishes and social positions."

CHAPTER XVIII.

KING HUMBERT AND HIS REIGN.

VICTOR EMMANUEL, first king of Italy, died January 8, 1878, and his son Humbert, or Umberto, succeeded him, "as quietly as if the Italian kingdom had existed for generations under the princes of the house of Savoy." All foreign nations seem to have felt sympathy for the loss sustained by Italy in the death of Victor Emmanuel, and hastened to send tributes of respect and of good-will to his son. The first utterances of the new King did credit both to his heart and understanding; and during the eighteen years that have since elapsed he has endeavored to do his duty faithfully as a constitutional monarch, and, so far as opportunity has offered, to display a kind-hearted interest in his people. "My sole ambition," he said, on the day of his accession, "will be to deserve my people's love."

Humbert is not, apparently, a man of striking abilities, and he has placed himself always in the hands of his ministers. One after another they have governed Italy. He has nothing of the personal magnetism of his father, who attracted to himself almost the adoration of all who were brought into contact with him; besides which, the lax morality which was condoned in the father has told against the son, whose subjects are almost ready to worship his beautiful wife, born, like himself, a member of the house of Savoy. Humbert is not handsome; he wears the same aggressive-looking moustachios as his father, and his hair is now snow-white, though he is only fifty-two years old. His mother died in 1855, when he was only eleven; and his father, then in the very crisis of Italian affairs, could give

KING HUMBERT.

little time to the five children whom she had left him, — Umberto, Amadeo, Odone, Clotilde, and Maria Pia. But they were all early imbued with the traditions of their house, and with an eager desire for the expulsion of the stranger from Italy, while they were fast bound together by ties of family affection.

In 1859, at the age of fifteen, Humbert fought by his father's side in the campaign that ended at Villafranca, and very early he was employed on important political missions. He was at Palermo when Garibaldi landed there on the eve of his second invasion of the kingdom of Naples. The prince and the general dined together, and together went to the theatre, — the prince not suspecting, probably, what his father's restless subject had in his mind. Umberto was subsequently sent to Paris, shortly before the Seven Weeks' War, to sound the French government as to its sentiments concerning the alliance between Italy and Prussia. In the campaign of 1866 both he and his brother Amadeo fought as became the princes of their house. Amadeo was wounded in the shoulder; and at Custozza, Nino Bixio (Garibaldi's old lieutenant) was just in time to save Umberto from great peril, so fearlessly had he exposed himself to the enemy.

In 1868, General Menabrea, then prime minister, put it into Victor Emmanuel's head, if I may use a homely phrase, that the best bride for Umberto would be his first cousin Margherita, — a princess about whom the King, strange to say, seems to have known little, though she was the daughter of his beloved brother, the Duke of Genoa, who died in 1855, shortly before the Sardinian troops departed for the Crimean war. The idea at once commended itself to Victor Emmanuel, and Umberto became the husband of one of the most beautiful and well-educated women in Europe. They have but one child, Victor Emmanuel, now heir apparent to the kingdom of Italy, and Prince of Naples.

While Florence was the capital of Italy, Humbert and Margherita lived chiefly at Turin; but when Rome was united to the kingdom, they took up their quarters with Victor Emmanuel at the Quirinal. It had been hoped that the presence of the Princess might make more of an Italian court than had been possible while the King of Italy remained a widower; but on Victor Emmanuel's morganatic marriage with the Countess di Mirafiore, that lady desired recognition as a legal wife, and showed great jealousy of the Princess. As ladies of the Italian nobility could not be expected to recognize the Countess as first lady of the land, the attempt to hold a court was in a great measure frustrated; but the Princess Margherita became a favorite with Victor Emmanuel, and persuaded him to conform rather more than his inclination would have led him to do to the usages of society.

Queen Margherita has but one fault, the fault of all fascinating queens,— she is extravagant. Her husband, on the contrary, has always practised rigid personal economy. The civil list of Italy is large, and life at the Quirinal conforms to the tastes of the lady who presides over social functions. At Monza, the retreat to which the royal family retires every summer, etiquette is laid aside, and life is simple and domestic. The Queen is always attended by an elderly white-haired lady, her motherly duenna and friend, the Marchesa di Villamarina. Innumerable are the anecdotes of Margherita's kindly consideration for the wishes, the wants, and even the whims of others. She plays on all kinds of musical instruments; she knows Latin, Greek, and Spanish; she speaks French, English, and German. Her favorite jewels are pearls (Margherita means "pearl" in Italian); and she has a magnificent collection of them, for the king always gives her a string of pearls upon the anniversary of their wedding day. She has been ever the most loving mother to her son, whose health is delicate. She superintended his education, but was so long in providing him with a wife, that it was thought he intended to remain a bachelor. Should he die without children, the succession will pass to his cousin the son of Amadeo, who has just married Princess Hélène of Orleans.

On November 17, 1878, eleven months after King Humbert's accession to the throne, as he was making his entry into Naples, accompanied by the Queen, by his little son the Crown Prince, and by his prime minister Benedetto Cairoli, a petitioner approached the carriage offering a paper. The King stretched out his hand to receive it, when the man pulled out a dagger and dealt a blow at him. The King caught it on his arm, for the Queen had flung her bouquet in the assassin's face which made his aim uncertain. Then Humbert sprang to his feet, and struck his assailant with his sword. The man, Passamente by name, aimed then another blow, this time more surely, at the King's heart; but Benedetto Cairoli threw himself on the assassin, received the wound intended for his sovereign, and held the murderer by his hair until an officer rode up and secured him. In two minutes the royal carriage and the procession moved on, the occupants keeping their places. Cairoli was observed to be smiling radiantly, though he was bleeding profusely from the wound he had received, — almost on the same spot in which he had been severely wounded while serving under Garibaldi in Sicily. But though the Queen bore up bravely for the remainder of the day, the alarm and excitement brought on nervous prostration, from which she suffered for many months, and which seriously alarmed the court and those around her.

The death of the Count di Cavour in the prime of his life, and when the triumph of Italian unity was almost at hand, was a misfortune for his country when it took place, and has proved a still greater misfortune as years have rolled on. He was born in 1810, was a year younger than Mr. Gladstone, and in the course of nature might have been alive and at the helm of state to the present day.

The three things on which Cavour's great heart was set, the objective points to which he directed all his policy were — first, the making of Italy, including the making of an Italian people; second, a free Church in a free State; third, peace with surrounding nations, since peace would give Italy the best chance to consolidate herself, and to recover from the strain of her great struggle.

The policy of Italy has not run along these lines since the

death of Cavour. For fifteen years afterwards the reins of government remained in the hands of his disciple and colleague, King Victor Emmanuel, who, though strictly a constitutional sovereign, could not but impose his own convictions and the line of his life-long policy on the various ministers who too rapidly succeeded one another during the remainder of his reign. In those days there was very little distinction between Right and Left in the Italian parliament. All the deputies had worked together in the same cause. When one ministry went out and another ministry took office, little change of policy took place. All Cavour's successors were worthy of him on the side of patriotism and of sincerity, — Minghetti, La Marmora, Ricasoli, Lanza, Stella, and others. But although they were his honest disciples, men of his school, they did not add to their great honesty and often great capacity the firmness of character which had given Cavour such weight.

When Victor Emmanuel died and his son succeeded him, a new order of ministers had entered upon office, — men as talented, as patriotic, and as full of sincerity as their predecessors, but who had received their training in another school. From 1878 to 1896, all the statesmen prominent in Italian cabinets have been old Garibaldians, — Depretis, Cairoli, Nicotera, and, above all, Francesco Crispi. A man's policy may change with the times and with experience, but his political sentiments have been generally instilled into him by his early training. These men, who had followed Garibaldi to Sicily, and thought by force of arms to annex Rome to Italy, cherished projects of territorial enlargement for their country rather than plans for her consolidation. They were eager to make Italy one of the Great Powers, — not as a means to an end, as Cavour had planned when he sent Sardinian troops to join the French and English in the Crimean war, but for what is called in modern slang "jingoism," and in old times was called "vainglory." The Italians as a people are nourished and brought up on classical traditions, and cannot forget that Italy once ruled the world. They do not realize that she is now but a small country, with no dominant city to give laws to the whole earth; that, though Italy is "made," Italians at present are only in the making, and have not been trained to self-government; that Italy is territorially, not nationally (as yet), consolidated; and that sectional jealousies and dislikes largely prevail. "Italy," said a gentleman long resident in one of its chief cities, "is like a family living in an alley, who insist upon keeping a carriage and four."

Depretis, the minister who came into power in 1873, after the fall of Rattazzi, and who, his contemporaries said, held office too long (he held power for ten years, with short intervals), had been appointed by Garibaldi his vice-dictator in Sicily, when in 1862 he went from that island with his Red Shirts to conquer the kingdom of Naples. But as soon as Victor Emmanuel became sovereign of Italy, Depretis ranged himself on the side of king and country. His ministerial life was fraught with great difficulties, but he himself was always honored and esteemed. The difficulties were the usual ones in Italy, — that is to say, the weight of the debts which the country had accumulated in her great effort to secure her freedom, and of the new ones which it became necessary to contract. During the great and glorious struggle for Italian nationality a veil was cast by patriotism over the eyes of every Italian citizen; so that, proud of their own success, and secure of the sympathy of other peoples, they never admitted the thought that they might weep upon the morrow. Depretis found before him a task harder than that of those who preceded him. They had governed a people less under illusions than he found them. Being a man of sagacity and experience, he thoroughly comprehended that the Italian people had reached the measure of the weight their backs could bear; but he was pushed by his classical reminiscences, by his colleagues, and by his party beyond the point that he thought prudent. All urged him to do something great and imposing, which would add glory and renown to Italy, and make her name shine brightly in the eyes of the world.

Depretis had a real affection for the reigning family, — above all for King Humbert, whom at the outset of his regal career he deemed it his duty to assist and protect, as a tutor protects his pupil. He was more of a parliamentary leader than a statesman, and the deputies in the Italian parliament occupy themselves less with national affairs than with local interests, — such interests as with us are relegated to State legislatures. All accounts say that the deputies (those especially from the old kingdoms of Naples and Sicily) are servants of a Ring — the Camorra — which elects them; and they in return are pledged to promote the interests of these supporters, particularly in the matter of appropriations. Thence come the great sums voted for local improvements, especially for nearly useless lines of railway. No party in power hesitates to make an extravagant use of the national funds. Each party when out of power inveighs against extravagance and taxation. It was Depretis who brought his old Garibaldian comrades into prominence; but in time they turned against him. They were Crispi, Cairoli, Nicotera, Zanardelli, and some others.

Twice in brief periods, when Depretis was out of office, Benedetto Cairoli formed a ministry. Cairoli had never been presented to Prince Humbert till they met at Victor Emmanuel's last reception, on New Year's Day, 1878. He was prime minister under the new king in the March following; and in November, as we have seen, he saved his sovereign's life. He said of himself that he was more honest than skilful (*piu onesto ch' abile*); others said of him that "he soared in such heights of blue ether that he was unconscious of the needs felt in a lower atmosphere." On taking office he said to the Chamber: "Parties dissolve, one Assembly succeeds another, ministers pass away; but a nation born in tears, nurtured in martyrdom, built up by the valor of her sons, — this is an edifice which does not crumble or decay; this is a Pharos whose light cannot grow dim."

Cairoli remained in office only till December, 1878, but returned to it in the summer of the following year, and held it till 1881, when the French surprised all Europe by entering Tunis as it were by a back gate, and taking possession of what was the bit of Africa coveted by Italy, — an acquisition that would have been really of use to her, a country in which she already possessed a railroad, and which was divided by only ninety miles of water from Sicily. Italy had been waiting for an opportunity to acquire Tunis. France, it was believed, had been debarred from doing so by treaty — when, lo! France caught her rival asleep, and in 1881 carried off the prize. Italians turned their indignation against Cairoli. He quitted office rather than make explanations in public which would have further embittered the feeling between the two countries; but he said to the French ambassador the day before he resigned, "I am the last Italian minister who will be friendly to France."

Benedetto Cairoli was the survivor of four brothers, all of whom had been devoted by their heroic mother to the liberation of Italy. All served under Garibaldi in each one of his expeditions. One died in battle; two were treacherously stabbed by Papal Zouaves as they lay wounded a few days before Mentana; and Benedetto, crippled for life by his wounds, lived to save the life of his sovereign. " He belonged to the party which, had it been theirs to choose, would have established Italian unity on a republican basis, but which maintained that ' no one has a right to substitute his own will, or that of his section, for the national will.' " When his Garibaldian hopes had passed away, his heart cried to Victor Emmanuel as Mazzini had once done to Carlo Alberto, " We must have one United Italy! Will you unite her? If so, we will stand by you."

Cairoli's gospel was one of concord. Since Italy was united, why, he thought, should not Italians be? He was never tired of urging that, without moral unity, political unity could avail nothing. Alas! his wounds too early sapped his strength, and not long after his retirement from office he died, beloved by all who had ever been brought into personal contact with him, and attended by the wife he loved. No grandchild was ever granted to the widow

Cairoli. When Benedetto died, it was found that during the time he was prime minister he had drawn on his own capital for more than fifteen thousand dollars, having devoted his official salary to pay expenses commonly borne by the State, — such as the payment of secretaries, the cost of carriages, etc.

To Cairoli and Depretis succeeded Mancini, to whom, and to the Marquis Robilant, Italy owes the millstone of the Triple Alliance, and her unhappy possession of Massowah.

In 1887, Francesco Crispi came into power, and has held it almost continuously till a few months ago. He has, indeed, been displaced by occasional political crises, when the cards would be shuffled, and possibly a new premier would take office; but Crispi would resume his place at an early day. He is a Sicilian both by birth and character. In early life he was a conspirator, a follower of Mazzini. Subsequently he threw himself heart and soul into the enterprises of Garibaldi. He was with him in 1862, and at Aspromonte and Mentana; but twenty years later he found himself a cabinet minister under a constitutional king of Italy. He has since taken Prince Bismarck for his model, — and in this has not departed far from the traditions of Garibaldi, who maintained that a republic needed a dictator. As a follower of Garibaldi in his latter days, Crispi held the pope and all the priests in holy horror, — nay, even religion itself, whether Papal or Protestant. Nor has he been a man who has escaped domestic scandals; he had at one time one legal and one illegal spouse, and lived openly with the latter.[1] He is a man who loves show and tinsel. Italy has had a great deal of glitter to be proud of under Crispi, — but, alas! we in the United States know how enormous is her emigration, not because of any overplus in her popula-

[1] Signor Crispi has been three times married. His first wife died young. While in exile at Malta he was married to Rosalia Montfasson. The union not having proved a happy one, the parties sought a divorce, when they learned that no divorce was needed, certain acts necessary to make the marriage legal not having been complied with. Signor Crispi afterwards married another lady, who, I believe, is still living.

tion, but because her peasants have no money to pay their taxes; and this wholesale emigration leaves entire fertile regions desolate, which ought to laugh and sing with ripening grain.

Crispi is represented as being gifted with a strong will, much audacity, and (what is sometimes a strength in politics) unlimited confidence in himself. His temper is fiery, and he often loses it in parliamentary debates. With his Garibaldian detestation of the Papacy, he by no means gives a cordial support to the Papal guarantees. "A free State, and down with all ecclesiasticism!" would probably be his motto. His policy, foreign and domestic, has been planned with a view to effect; he has sought to tickle the vanity of the Italians. But his enemies cannot deny that he has fearlessness, energy, and rapidity of action, — qualities especially valuable when dealing with a parliamentary assembly, apt (unless individual members are aroused on questions of local appropriations) "to fall into that condition of uninterested lassitude which is the dominant note in the Italian political world." Italians have not been educated to parliamentary life, and unless they can get something out of parliament they do not "like the bother" it entails on them. This was not Cavour's idea of how Italy was to be governed by a parliamentary system. Young Italy is not the Italy of Cavour.

An English writer who in 1891 put forth a book on "The Sovereigns and Courts of Europe," under the *nom de plume* of "Politikos," praises highly King Humbert's good heart and courage. "But Italy," he says, "is a poor country, impoverished also by the struggle it has had to pass through in order to effect its unity. It has, besides, many provinces which civilization has hardly reached, and where education is but commencing its labors. Such a land has need of rest, of quiet work, of wise and practical administration. It has need of statesmen of superior intelligence and acumen. Louis Philippe used to say, 'All tell me to do my duty; but the difficulty does not consist in doing my duty, but in knowing what that duty is.' These words might be echoed by the King of Italy. He is most sincerely anxious to do his duty, but he is tormented by uncertainty. He solves the situation by following closely the sentiment that is given by the passing vote of the Chamber, and in accordance with the solicitations of his ministers, who are naturally more inclined to favor the temporary interests of their own party than the permanent interests of the State. It is said that King Humbert is always enthusiastic about the prime minister in office. He was so for Cairoli, for Depretis, and for Crispi. . . . To his thirst for heroic deeds Italy is perhaps indebted for her hapless African policy, where she has been carried into adventures beyond her strength to conduct or carry through. One of the King's indubitable merits is to know how to deal with the masses. He always speaks to them the right word."

"The house of Savoy," says another English writer, "is the cement of Italy. Were it to disappear, then indeed would come disintegration with a vengeance; and the second state of Italy would be worse than the first."

It is not to be denied that Italy of late has fallen upon evil days; and that she pains and surprises us, when we remember how, half a century ago, her struggle produced a band of men, each in his way of extraordinary powers, — Mazzini, the dreamer of an ideal republic; Cavour, the master statesman; Manin, the dictator of Venice; d'Azeglio, the thinker, the statesman, and the artist; Ricasoli, the "Iron Baron"; Gioberti, the priest who roused in his church the first cry for reform; Garibaldi, the prince of guerilla captains; Ugo Bassi, the monk and martyr; Minghetti, the Cairoli, and many others. Of all these the story has been told too briefly in these pages.

The perilous financial condition of Italy, with its continually returning deficits, the burdensome taxation, the riotous protestations of the suffering poor, and the extraordinary emigration of its rural population were things all too likely to check the prosperity of the country, especially when we remember the sore always kept open by the relations of the Quirinal with the Vatican. But, in addition to these things, during the past two years there has been added a series of bank scandals, accompanied by serious failures, in consequence of which, ruin, suffering, and distrust have been spread widely everywhere, and have culminated in insinuations reflecting on the honesty of conspicuous and trusted men in power. There has lately come also a shock to Italy's colonial ambition, — a result that might have been expected when she endeavored to force herself upon a people nominally Christian ; a people who possessed a government, which, however imperfect, had lasted from before the days of Solomon ; a people intrenched in strongholds which thirty years ago were pronounced inaccessible unless the advance of an invading army could be made through the territories of a friendly chief in rebellion against his emperor. *Que diable allait-elle faire dans cette galère ?* is the motto that ought to preface every book that undertakes to tell the story of the Italians in Abyssinia.

"The explanation of Italy's many mistakes," says a writer in "Macmillan's Magazine," "is that the past is the seed-bed of the present." Under the excitement of the revolutionary struggle, Italians roused themselves to great deeds that their aspirations might be realized ; but when the making of Italy was accomplished, Italian politicians sank into lassitude, into the *dolce far niente* which characterizes their nation. Add to this that one-third of the population of Italy is composed of southern Italians. Garibaldi's conquests of Naples and of Sicily may possibly have been premature. Italy, though incomplete, might perchance have been stronger without them, at least until fulness of time enabled her to annex them to an established, well-ordered kingdom. The unprepared-for acquisition of these provinces does not seem to have been altogether satisfactory to Cavour.

We who deal only with domestic affairs soon learn to know that our foremost need as heads of a household, or as members of a community, is to maintain what is called "a good standing" among our neighbors in money matters. We must be prompt in our payments, ready to meet all legitimate obligations, and must not suffer ourselves to be involved in crushing debts; or, if we have them through misfortune, our whole strength must be exerted to pay them speedily. Society will not excuse us for heaping on ourselves new obligations. We have to care for those of our own house before we endeavor to increase our importance in the eyes of others.

Even so it is with nations. What money they can command should be appropriated first of all to making a contented prosperous people. No people can be either prosperous or progressive borne down by tyranny or taxes. This has not been the policy of Italy; and while her parliaments have been factious and indifferent, local administrative bodies have abused their powers, till corruption in many places has reached an aggravated form.

There is no reason to despair. Happily, Italians are becoming more and more aware of these evils. The disasters in Abyssinia have shaken the nation out of its slothful and selfish indifference. "The Italians are a people who require the strain of circumstances to bring out the heroic qualities which they undoubtedly possess." This was the opinion of Sir James Hudson, who was for many years English minister at Turin, and whom Cavour used to call *Italianissimo*. Sir James used also to say that he never knew a people who so easily collapsed as the Italians. This seems to be so far true, that, after a period of heroic effort, they have sunk into a state in which mean and petty objects have thrust out of sight the higher interests of life.

Mr. Gladstone, who revisited Naples in the winter of 1888-89 after an interval of thirty-eight years, has recorded his impressions. He was astonished and delighted to perceive the great change for the better that had taken place in the material condition of the population of Naples. "The basking, loitering, lolling, loafing population so completely Neapolitan seemed," he said, "to have become extinct. The filth in a great measure had disappeared. In all the frequented parts of the city the population was well clad.

... There was a free press, free speech, free worship, and freedom of person." He adds: "Never were sovereigns more honest than Victor Emmanuel and King Humbert. ... But in southern Italy an ingrained corruption, which, under the old system had become the ruling motive-power of public transactions, could not but exhibit itself even after the revolution. ... There were many old agents of administration whom it must have been necessary to retain, and there were doubtless crowds of new ones who had been bred in an atmosphere of prevailing laxity, and amidst a general absence of public spirit and civil manhood."

After speaking of this crying evil of political corruption,— which, since 1889, when Mr. Gladstone wrote, has received the name of the "Rule of the Ring," or "Camorra," — he goes on to speak of what he terms a matter which calls for the most grave and urgent anxiety, that of the Italian finances. He takes his facts from a report made to the English parliament in March, six years ago. The national debt of Italy, which in December, 1861, stood at £120,000,000, had in 1889 reached the portentous figure of £520,000,000. Its interest annually was £23,000,000, nearly two-fifths of the annual expenditure of the country. To this debt must be added forty-one millions more of provincial and commercial obligations. Some years earlier the minister of finance in Italy had been able to announce, with pride and pleasure, an equilibrium on his balance-sheet between receipts and expenditure. Reckless expenditure since then on the army and navy (requirements of the Triple Alliance), colonial schemes on the east coast of Africa, great outlays on railways, and other public improvements, — very many of them set on foot in the interest of private speculators, — account for the extraordinary increase in national outlay, while the revenue from taxation has steadily fallen off at the rate of several millions of pounds sterling a year. It is true that the grist-tax, which was terribly onerous to the rural population (a tax on all the corn ground into flour), has been taken off.

Italian commerce has been greatly curtailed by the quarrel between France and Italy, which, aggravated by the riot and massacre of Italian working-men at Aigues Mortes, led to the breaking up of a commercial alliance advantageous to both countries.

An English writer in the "Quarterly Review," a few years ago, speaking of taxation (and, except in the matter of the grist-tax, matters have not since improved), says: "Let us suppose an Italian is entitled to £100, and only £100 per annum from the public funds,—£13 4s. is deducted for the income tax. If he has £100 from the profits of trade, he has to pay £9 15s. If it comes in the form of salary, he is mulcted of £8 5s. A professional man in London making £300 a year, pays only £1 16s. A professional man in Rome earning the same income has to hand over £24 15s." This seems a great sum to pay yearly towards national expenses, a large part of which is incurred for the honor of being considered a Great Power, and as such liable to invasion from France by land and Russia by sea in the event of another European war.

Italy is essentially an agricultural country. Out of her thirty millions of inhabitants, barely four hundred thousand are employed in factories; and of these not a third are male adults.

"Any one who has seen King Humbert of Italy ride up the Via Nazionale in Rome, upon his birthday, surrounded by a splendid staff, and followed by some fifteen thousand troops of all branches of the service, or has been present at one of the reviews held periodically in the meadows between the Tiber and Monte Mario, can hardly fail to have been struck by the excellent physique and soldierly bearing of the rank and file. But these constitute the garrison of Rome, and are not a fair sample of the Italian army, any more than the garrison of Paris in the days of the Second Empire accurately exemplified the forces with which Napoleon III. rushed to his destruction at Sedan. Though the minimum standard for recruits is only five feet one inch, the average height of the Italian army is five feet five inches. But, while native thews are not wanting, the necessity of economizing in every branch of the service causes parsimony in the feeding of the army. Many of the soldiers have a rickety and half-starved appearance; and persons who ought to know assure us that, though drill is far more severe than it used to be, diet is precisely the same as it was before harder work was imposed on the raw recruit. The Italian soldier has allotted to him only half as much meat as is served out to the English soldier. His rations are smaller even than the French, and he has to find his own wine." The Duke of Wellington's doctrine of the three B's (Beef, Bread, and Beer), on which he based the efficiency of the English army, has not spread into Italy. In Germany the diet of the private soldier, his beer, and his tobacco are very carefully attended to.

It remains to say a few words on the Triple Alliance, that so-called Peace League, which has succeeded in obtaining the adhesion of Italy. Such an alliance had long been the cherished policy of Prince Bismarck. He used his utmost endeavors to persuade England to join it; but England held aloof from entangling alliances, preferring the position of friend and arbiter between all parties, in the event of a European war. An alliance between Germany, Austro-Hungary, Italy, and England would, Bismarck represented, be so formidable that no combination would dare to defy it, and he urged that there was not one chance in a hundred that these allied Powers would be called upon to go to war. But England preferred to remain free, even from the one risk in a hundred that might be involved in a strict alliance with this or that great Power, — though it is thought that in the event of a Continental war she has made some conditional promises to Italy; for Italy listened to Prince Bismarck's voice when he told her that alliances should be made between nations not already connected by close neighborhood or ties of blood, for such things in nations, as in households, too frequently afford cause for family jars. In the alliance he proposed, Germany, he said, should be mistress of the Baltic and Italy of the Mediterranean, in the event of war.

In the Italian parliament, though there are many minor political divisions, parties may be roughly divided into the Left, the Left Centre, and the Right, — the Right and the Left having each an extreme wing of irreconcilables. The chief matter that divides the Left from the Left Centre is foreign policy. The sympathies of the Left are anti-French, they are for alliance with Germany; the Left Centre is accused of a predilection for France, and of no cordial acceptance of the Triple Alliance. The ministries of Italy, since King Humbert's reign began, have been chiefly taken from the Left. Crispi, from 1887 to almost the present day, has been Italy's leading statesman. He has always been considered a disciple of Prince Bismarck. One of his first acts, when he came into office, was to accept an invitation (refused by Depretis) to go to Berlin, and exchange views with the great chancellor.

In 1886 Count Robilant was the ambassador of Italy in Vienna. He was thoroughly acquainted with Austrian politics, and in sympathy with Austrian views. Mancini, who had become prime minister on the fall of the Depretis ministry, recalled him to Rome to take charge of the portfolio for foreign affairs. The negotiations that were to make Italy a member of the Triple Alliance had almost been completed when Signor Crispi came into office, and under him the treaty of alliance, offensive and defensive, was signed. It has to be renewed from time to time, and has been so during the present year (1896). It places all central Europe as a barrier between Russia and France, — powers which, although they are said to have no counter alliance on paper, are understood to be in accord. The Emperor William says that the Triple Alliance preserves peace. If it does so, it is at a cost equal to that of war, — a cost prolonged from year to year, whereas war is soon over; and in Europe, though a heavy burden is laid on future years, countries are not so overwhelmingly borne down by an extravagant pension list as our own.

To make such a league as the Triple Alliance, presumes an enemy, or enemies, against whom it has been formed;

and that enemy naturally views with hostility the parties who make the league. In this case the feeling of hostility existing naturally between France and Germany could hardly be increased; Austria entered the league as a silent partner; besides which, her foe, in case of war, would be, not France but Russia. The wrath of France has therefore fallen upon Italy. In 1889 she broke off commercial relations with her, greatly to the disadvantage of both countries; she hurries on her fortifications and improvements at Biserta, which will make that naval station, within ninety miles of Sicily, the finest in the Mediterranean; and, above all, there is growing up between the two nations a bitter national dislike, which loses no opportunity of displaying itself in petty ways.

The extreme Left in the Italian Parliament has, on the other hand, political sympathies with the French Republic; it cherishes a traditional hatred of Austria, and aspires to the annexation of the Trentino and Trieste, which are entirely loyal to the Austrian Emperor, but which would give Italy the frontier of the Alps complete. With that frontier and Nice, Italy would, as she expresses herself, hold the keys of her own house, and be almost as safe as if she were an island, though she has a very extended sea-board. If, in case of war, the fleets of France and Russia should attack her coasts, she may heartily wish she had remained a neutral power, and had not provoked hostility by allying herself to their foes.

The Triple Alliance binds the three powers, — Germany, Italy, and Austro-Hungary, — to keep their armies and nations on a war-footing, and to hold in readiness vast reserves.

The available forces of the Triple Alliance, in the event of being at once called into action were, according to Mr. Probyn (or rather Signor Bodio, from whom his statistics are taken), as follows: Germany, one million men; Austro-Hungary, nine hundred and forty thousand; Italy, six hundred and ten thousand, — with reserves of about seven million men for Germany, nearly two millions for Austro-

Hungary, and more than two and a half millions for Italy. Whittaker's almanac, however, speaks of the Italian forces in 1895 as considerably more. The army, now on a war-footing, he places at 839,354.

The navy, assuredly the most important branch of the war service for Italy, consisted in 1891 of two hundred and sixty-nine ships, — eighteen of them enormous iron-clads, with torpedo boats, etc., in proportion. These are manned by about twenty thousand men. Naples is fast becoming the chief naval and military port of the kingdom.

These expensive armaments have at least the merit of introducing ideas of discipline and nationality among the peasantry of remote districts. "But the sight of Europe, thus armed to the teeth," says Mr. Probyn, "with its people ever more and more heavily burdened in consequence, gives a handle to the propagators of anarchy, and is only a sorrow and a hindrance to the advocates of a wise and reasonable progress, by which anarchy and violence are best resisted and defeated."

It must be acknowledged that in 1861, when Victor Emmanuel was first saluted King of Italy, ports, roads, and railways were all wanting to the young nation, and all had to be provided. Sanitary measures and modern improvements of all kinds had to be introduced into the cities, and an immense amount of work has been done, as well as money expended, in these ways. It is, indeed, acknowledged that much of the money spent, especially on railroads, has been wasted upon small branch-lines, not likely to pay, and of little service, but whose promoters have obtained appropriations from the State to advance their own interest or that of some petty locality.

The kingdom of Italy began its career with a forced paper currency. This was abandoned in 1886; and deficits made by the change, and by the abolition of the grist-tax so hateful to the peasantry, were made up by a loan, raised in London, by Finance Minister Magliani, who succeeded in impressing his optimistic views of Italy's prosperity and future progress on those who had money to advance in that

THE PRINCE OF NAPLES.

way. Italy has recently returned to her paper currency. The circulating medium is now paper lire, and the paper on which the notes are printed is so flimsy that they crease and fall to pieces in the purse.

Meantime, primary education is doing its work among the masses, and Italian writers and scientists are more and more numerous. Intellectual life in Italy has certainly not stood still within the last twenty years, though no world-famous books during that time have been published.

The Crispi ministry was shaken out of office in 1892 by the scandals that followed an examination of the affairs of the Banco Romano. It soon came back to power, however, Crispi being what some one has called him, an "indispensable man." The terrible disasters in Abyssinia, to which will be devoted our next chapter, broke up his cabinet again in March of this year (1896). He has been succeeded by the Marquis di Rudini, who is also a Sicilian.

We ask ourselves, How can Italy escape the consequences of her engagement to the Triple Alliance, — the Dreibund? To renounce it would be to make for herself two very powerful enemies; to continue it, is still more to impoverish her people, and a State staggering under taxation never can make progress. Is the Triple Alliance really a league to promote peace? It certainly does not do so among the populations who murmur under the sacrifices and privations it entails. Italy is not the only country which carries on her shoulders an Old Man of the Sea whom she cannot get rid of. But there is a burden from which Italy *may* release herself, and she seems to be preparing to do so at the present moment. Mr. Grant Duff, writing about her twenty years ago, said: "Italy, if she does not go forth in search of new adventures, which I trust she is very unlikely to do, has every chance of a future which will compensate her for all the miseries of the past." May we not say the same thing of her now? She has had experience of "new adventures," and has paid dearly for them; is it too much to hope that she will now learn a lesson from the bees, whom Archbishop Leighton tells us to take for our example, since, "when it is foul weather abroad, they are most busy in their hive." It is not foreign policy that will make Italy prosperous and great, but close attention to all that will diffuse health, wealth, and contentment among her people.

CHAPTER XIX.

THE ITALIANS IN ABYSSINIA.

ITALY claims that her explorers in the seventeenth century were the first to penetrate into central Africa, and to bring the world news of the great city of Timbuctoo; and when the European Powers in 1884 endeavored to mark out what were called " spheres of influence " on the map of Africa, so as to come to an understanding concerning the future division of Africa among themselves (Africa not being at this time a " sick man," but a child who had not arrived at years of discretion), Italy desired to have her share. She would probably have renounced colonial ambition had the treaty of Berlin given her the Alps for a frontier, restored her Nice, or made over to her the old Venetian province of Dalmatia; but disappointed in these plans, she fixed her hopes on Africa. Tunis was what she wished for. France had by treaty bound herself not to enlarge the limits of Algeria — either on the east, to the prejudice of Tunis, or on the west, to the prejudice of Morocco. Not a thousand Frenchmen were in Tunis, while Italians there numbered fifteen thousand, and possessed a railroad between Tunis and Goletta. With these things in their favor, they bided their time.

A miserable Arab tribe living in Tunis, finding scant pasture for their flocks during the dry season strayed over into Algeria. This was at once made a pretext for a French advance into their country. French forces marched at once to Tunis, and imposed a French protectorate upon the Bey. Italy made bitter complaints to the European Powers.

She turned Benedetto Cairoli out of office for a want of diplomatic forethought, and she set herself to seek compensation to balance the new acquisition of her rival. This is the modern spirit of international policy, — the very spirit of our nursery and childish days. "You gave him a bit of cake; now you've got to give me one, to make us even."

Italy has never ceased to remember that her language is the language of commerce in the Levant, having been that of those princely traffickers, the Venetians, whose sails for three centuries whitened the eastern waters of the Mediterranean; while, as far back as the thirteenth century, Venice had extended her commerce to the shores of the Red Sea, having commercial agents at Suakin, Massowah, and Mocha, who forwarded Indian products to Cairo, and thence to Europe via Alexandria.

In 1870 the Italian government sent a traveller named Sapeto to Africa, who obtained from a local petty prince, the Sultan Berehan, permission to make a settlement on an island in the Bay of Assab, not far from the Strait of Bab-el-Mandeb; while at the same time a portion of the coast was leased by the Italians from another local sultan, which included Ras Buia, which they made the capital of their little acquisition. In 1879 an Italian fleet was sent into those waters ostensibly to promote commerce and science. The commander easily induced Sultan Berehan to sell some more territory to the Italians, renouncing all rights over it for himself and his successors. In this way Italy obtained all the islands in the Bay of Assab, and a considerable strip of coast-line, lying south of Abyssinia, in 1880, some years previous to her acquisition of that province, north of Abyssinia, now called Eritrea.

For many years the barren strip of coast-line lying between Egypt and Abyssinia had been claimed by both. In 1876 a large army was sent against the Abyssinians by Ismail Pasha, who thought the time propitious for asserting his claims. This army, though it contained several European and American officers, was defeated and driven back;

and troubles multiplied so speedily around Ismail that no second expedition was planned.

In 1885, after the death of Gordon and the failure of the English expedition to bring away the garrisons at Khartoum, Kassala, and Sennar, the English, in virtue of the position they held as arbiters of the policy of Egypt, resolved to abandon the Soudanese provinces. King John was then King of Abyssinia and indebted to the English for his elevation to the throne. There was no hope for the Egyptian garrisons in Kassala and Sennar unless he would suffer them to retreat unmolested through Abyssinia to Massowah. An embassy was sent into Abyssinia by the English government, entreating this permission, and promising that the Egyptian troops should in return deliver up to the king all their ammunition and guns.

After the abandonment of the Soudan, Egypt no longer cared to hold Massowah. The European Powers did not wish to have it fall into the hands of the King of Abyssinia, and it was offered to Italy.

The intention of the Italian government when it made its first acquisition of territory on the shores of the Red Sea, was simply to found one or more commercial stations; but events hurried the colony into new responsibilities. The Abyssinians, who had been newly armed by the weapons surrendered to them by the Egyptian garrisons of Sennar and Kassala, were regarding the Italians in Massowah with a jealous eye. The French, who already had their settlement of Obok to the south of the Italian colony on the Bay of Assab, were anxious for territorial expansion; and Italy very soon perceived that, to hold Massowah, it would be necessary to come into conflict with the rulers of Abyssinia.

In 1883 a massacre of an Italian caravan took place at Beillut. In 1884 three Italian travellers, Bianchi, and two others, who had gone to the scene of the massacre hoping to recover the remains of the victims, met the same fate. Another Italian party under Captain Giullietti was similarly cut off when on an exploring expedition in southern Abyssinia. Meantime, there were complaints on the part of

Abyssinia that the Italians had not carried out the provisions of the treaty made through Admiral Sir William Hewett, which gave them possession of Massowah, but were levying custom dues on goods brought from the interior which it had been stipulated should be duty free. King John, however, never really admitted the right of the Italians to be in Massowah at all. He stoutly maintained, on the contrary, that Massowah, and all the southwestern coasts of the Red Sea, had for centuries belonged to Abyssinia. In the sixteenth century the Turks had, indeed, driven the Abyssinians from Zeila and Massowah, and had added these seaports to the possessions of the House of Othman. In 1866 Massowah was transferred by the Porte to the Khedive of Egypt for a tribute of sixteen thousand pounds a year; but the King of Abyssinia urged that, during the three hundred years of Turkish occupation, his ancestors had never given up their claim to the ports on the Red Sea, and that the Turks held them only by the power of the sword.

The irritation created by these causes rapidly increased, and reached a dangerous point when the Italians, in order to protect the caravan road between Massowah and the interior, on which murder and brigandage had become so common as almost to put a stop to trade, sent a couple of battalions to take possession of Sahati, a place about ten miles from Monkullu, the coast suburb of Massowah, which is built upon a coral island a short distance from the shore.

Abyssinia is a sort of federal empire. The country is divided into provinces or kingdoms, each nominally governed by its own prince, who is usually governed by his prime minister. The federated kingdoms are three in number, — Tigré, Amkara, and Shoa. These, again, are subdivided into districts, each with its own governor; while in the districts rule many lesser chiefs, each with his own following. Over all is the Emperor or Negus, to whom the sub-kings pay tribute. They are bound to follow him to war, and are in turn followed by their subordinates, — as kings and barons were in Europe in feudal times.

In 1890 the Great Powers of Europe made over to Italy the protectorate of Abyssinia and to France the protectorate of Madagascar; that is, so far as concerned the foreign relations of Madagascar and Abyssinia, — much the same arrangement as gave England authority to conduct the foreign relations of the South African republic of the Transvaal. The Queen of Madagascar never consented to this arrangement, and the Negus of Abyssinia vehemently declaimed against it.

The original idea of the Italian government was to make friends, and not enemies, of the native tribes. Instead, however, of forming treaties of friendship with them, as had been originally proposed, and peaceably exchanging European commodities for their products, or for coins of gold and silver, Italy was led step by step into taking military possession of what is now called Eritrea, which has as yet yielded her little or no profit, and has cost her millions of money and thousands of brave men's lives.

I have elsewhere[1] told of the English expedition into Abyssinia in 1868 under Sir Robert Napier, who destroyed King Theodore's hill fortress of Magdala. I then quoted Mr. Henry M. Stanley's account of the march. I venture to repeat it here: —

"Imagine three regiments, — two white, one dusky, — with miles of artillery, baggage-waggons, mules, and followers crawling after them, passing over mountains high as Mont Cenis, to halt at a point seventy-five hundred feet above the sea, — mountains behind, before, and around; mountains all conical. looking as if they belonged to another world: and, at the halt, only one wretched spring to be found, its water loaded, as such water always is, with the seeds of dysentery. It is hard to paint the frantic scene, — the rush to the spring, the confusion that followed, the trampling through the water, the angry craving of parched soldiers, and followers, and worn-out beasts."

And the men of the English army had met upon this toilsome march no foe to fire down on them from behind rocks and bushes. King Theodore had intrenched himself

[1] Europe in Africa in the Nineteenth Century, pp. 227-249.

at Magdala, and Ras Kassa (subsequently King John), through whose country they were passing, was their friend.

Ras Alala, ruler of the province of Tigré, and a successful warrior, had led an expedition against the Dervishes, who on the evacuation of Kassala took possession of it, but he failed to recover the city. Returning home, he found the Italians in possession of Sahati, ten miles, as I have said, from Massowah. He determined to assume the offensive, and in January, 1887, made an attack on the Italian works. His assault was unsuccessful; but the following day he intercepted a small body of four hundred and eighty men on their way to reinforce the garrison of Sahati, which was still threatened by the Ras with ten thousand men. I will take an account of this massacre from Sir Gerald Portal's very interesting book, "My Mission to Abyssinia," published in 1892.[1] In 1887, a few months after the affair of Dogali, he passed over the spot, and thus he describes what he saw and heard there: —

"After a couple of hours' good travelling from Monkullu we found ourselves passing through the now famous plain of Dogali, where the unfortunate Italian half-battalion of four hundred and eighty men had been annihilated by Ras Alala while on their way from Monkullu to relieve the garrison of Sahati. The place itself consists of a small plain, with a circular knoll in its centre about one hundred and fifty feet high, but commanded on every side, as was the whole plain, by a complete circle of volcanic hills. The path to Sahati enters this plain by a narrow gorge, passes the knoll, and leaves the plain by another narrow gorge. On the day of the massacre the Abyssinians were lying hidden on all these hills, but made no sign of their existence till the Italians were well within the circle of hills, and on the plain. The Italians, with the confidence of inexperience, and with misplaced contempt for the intelligence of their enemy, had no scouts or skirmishers, nor had they taken any steps

---

[1] I am greatly indebted to the pen of Sir Gerald Portal for much that is contained in this chapter; and also for his reports published in English Blue Books when I was writing, in "Europe in Africa," the story of Uganda. I was very sorry when news of his early death reached me. He died of African fever. I am also indebted in this chapter to some interesting articles in the "Nation." — E. W. L.

to ascertain that the hills were unoccupied. Hardly had the head of the Italian column reached the centre of the plain when the rattle of musketry was heard, and a shower of bullets was thrown among them from the rear. The Italians faced round, and answered their unseen enemy with volleys from their Wetterli rifles; but so well were the Abyssinians concealed that there was nothing to fire at except occasional little clouds of smoke, whereas the European soldiers on the bare and open plain offered a mark which could with difficulty be missed. Then was heard another volley, and another shower of bullets from the hills on the right, — and yet another from the left, from the front, from the rear. Verily the devoted band of Italians were caught in a cruel trap! Their men fell fast; in vain they tried to take shelter behind the knoll in the midst of the plain. Even there, if screened from one side, they were exposed to the fire from all the other hills. They continued their advance; but the hail of bullets became thicker. Few — very few — were now unhurt, and still nothing to fire at except those puffs of smoke. Ah! how those doomed and desperate men must have longed to see the face of an enemy; to have something tangible before them, instead of those incessant puffs of smoke from behind a distant bush or rock, too often followed by a thud, a groan, and the fall of a comrade! What a relief it must have been to the few still surviving, even though they knew it was their death-signal, when at last from every hill, from behind every rock, and from every side, there burst forth a cloud of fierce and dusky warriors, in red and white robes, casting away their guns and rifles, and whirling down to complete their work with sharp spear and glittering sword! It must have been soon over. At the moment of the final attack there were scarce thirty Italians able to wield a rifle. Their fate was never in doubt from the beginning; but they died fighting like men, and left their mark on many a soldier of Ras Alala's army. Subsequently I met and conversed with many of Ras Alala's soldiers who had taken part in this action, or massacre; they all had but one answer as to the conduct of the Italian troops upon that fateful day, that 'they fought like real devils till the last man fell.'"

Two days later the garrison of Sahati was withdrawn to Massowah, without meeting with opposition. Sir Gerald adds : —

"This battle, or rather massacre, of Dogali may be looked upon as the beginning of all the Italian troubles on the Red Sea coast, and in what is called in Italy the colony of Eritrea. Few people could then foresee how far-reaching would be its consequences, or how much it would eventually cost to the overburdened tax-payers of Italy; but even at the moment it was impossible, while admiring the courage and devotion shown by the Italian soldiers, to avoid criticising the rashness and over-confidence which allowed this half-battalion to be caught in a veritable rat-trap. It is the old, old story, — contempt of a gallant enemy because his skin happens to be chocolate, or brown, or black, and because his men have not gone through orthodox courses of field-firing, battalion-drill, or 'autumn manœuvres.'"

It is impossible to describe the cry for vengeance that went up when news of this massacre reached Italy. Preparations were at once made for an expedition on a large scale to inflict signal punishment on the Abyssinians. Massowah and its suburb Monkullu were both strongly fortified, and measures were taken to send at once by sea twenty or thirty thousand men to the scene of action. But the season for active operations was diminishing day by day, and more prudent counsels began to be listened to. "Men began to inquire more closely into the matter, and to count the cost; and as they did so the serious nature of the undertaking that lay before Italy became more and more apparent. A war of revenge could bring but little practical benefit, and would cost many millions of dollars, and probably thousands of valuable lives. In the meantime, Italy's action in Europe would be cramped proportionately to the magnitude of her task in Africa; and in the actual situation of European politics in 1887 it was most desirable, and might even at any moment become imperative, that the hands of Italy should be free."

Italy therefore consented to a proposal that an English embassy should be sent to King John to propose to him terms of peace, — it being supposed that English influence would be stronger with him than that of any other nation, since it was indirectly due to English influence and to gifts of military stores from Lord Napier in 1868 that he had risen from the position of Prince Kassa, Ras of Tigré, to sit as emperor on the Abyssinian throne. Unhappily the influence of England was not invoked till nine months after the massacre of Dogali, when both parties had made preparations for war, and King John would have incurred a great loss of popularity among his warriors had he balked them of their chance of attacking white men, rich in all that is most valuable to a semi-civilized soldier.

An Italian senator, who has written a book on "Gli Intenti Politici dei Diversi Stati d' Europa," quotes Marshal von Moltke, who advises Italy to strengthen her alliance with England on all questions relating to the Mediterranean, and with Germany on all those relating to Continental affairs. He insists that if Italy expects help in time of need from England, she must embrace any opportunity that offers of lending what aid she can to England in her African affairs. But when he spoke, Von Moltke did not foresee that Italy, impoverished, might prove unable to give such aid as she would gladly offer. Meantime, in Africa England has always to the present day been Italy's good friend.

A mission was therefore sent to King John and to Ras Alala bearing presents and letters from the Queen and Lord Salisbury; and the gentleman charged with this difficult and very dangerous mission was Sir Gerald Portal (then Mr. Portal), of her Majesty's legation at Cairo, subsequently agent and consul-general at Zanzibar. It was the close of October, 1887, when Mr. Portal set out on his embassy. He took with him only two Europeans,—his friend Major Beech, and his excellent servant, Hutchinson. Mules and mule-drivers, a guide and interpreters, were procured at Monkullu. The Italian government promised to abstain from acts of overt hostility for five weeks; but in that time it was very clear to Mr. Portal that he could not reach the interior of Abyssinia and return.

I may here say, *en passant*, that, during the absence of the embassy, Captain Lugard, since so well known in Africa, arrived in the Italian camp, hoping to be received as a volunteer. The Italians, however, refused his services, and he went forward to commence his splendid African career as an elephant hunter in Nyassaland. He speaks with admiration of the zeal, skill, and patience shown by Italian soldiers in digging earthworks and making fortifications, for which in the Italian service the regular soldiers, not sappers and miners, are employed.

Between the Italian outpost at Sahati and the forces of Ras Alala, encamped on the high plateau of Asmara, lay a sort of No Man's Land, given up to marauding parties and professional Arab robbers. Here is a description of the journey as they scrambled up to the camping-ground of the Ras Alala: "All through the night our unfortunate mules were clambering over impossible rocks, slipping and sliding down precipitous ravines, forcing their way through dense masses of unyielding mimosa thorns, and climbing range after range of black rocky mountains, on which no beast of burden but an Abyssinian mule could even obtain a foothold, while the mountains seemed to grow steeper and the country more parched as we went on."

The expedition, after incredible sufferings from thirst, heat, and fatigue, when their mouths and tongues grew black, at last reached Asmara, where on a plateau on the top of a mountain had been erected an immense earthen or mud pyramid, on which Ras Alala's own two large round huts were placed, and from which he could look down on the plain dotted with his troops, like an eagle from its eyrie. The Ras was bitterly opposed to their mission, and affected to believe that they were spies in the interest of the Italians. He held them prisoners for ten days, and then only suffered them to proceed on receiving the direct commands of his emperor. He put all kinds of obstacles in the way of their further progress, dreading apparently that the letters of the Queen and Lord Salisbury which Mr. Portal was charged to deliver might contain something about the massacre of Dogali which would irritate the king against him.

The king was on the march with from seventy thousand to eighty thousand followers, soldiers, or attendants, when the mission met him; and Mr. Portal, putting on his diplo-

matic finery, prepared himself to present his queen's letters to his majesty King Johannes, whose official title was the King of Kings of Ethiopia and King of Sion. The king received the embassy with civility; but they soon found that the greater part of his chiefs were of the opinion of Ras Alala, — that is, that they should be treated as enemies, loaded with chains, and decapitated secretly at a convenient season. They were detained as prisoners while their fate was under discussion, nearly all the chief men being against them; but King John stood their friend.

At Mr. Portal's first diplomatic interview, the king told him frankly that he could not grant peace on the Italians' terms. "By the treaty made by Admiral Hewett," he said, " all the country evacuated by the Egyptians on my frontier was ceded to me at the instigation of England, and now you come to ask me to give it up again." Mr. Portal remarked that no mention was made of Sahati or Wia in the treaty, that these places were necessary to the protection of Monkullu and Massowah, and that the king had already accepted the Italian occupation of those places. The king replied: "I did not give the Italians Massowah; the English gave it to them. I will not give them one inch of land. If they cannot live in Massowah and its suburb without Sahati, let them go." The interview ended by the king's repeating that he would give up nothing, but would stand by the treaty made with Admiral Hewett three years before.

The embassy marched as prisoners with the army. At last, on Dec. 16, 1887, the king sent for Mr. Portal for a final interview, and gave him permission to carry back his answers to the English Queen and Premier. The interview over, Mr. Portal was beckoned into a smaller tent, and he amusingly describes what took place there : —

" I found a complete *toilette* set out for me. I was first asked to take off my uniform coat, and to put on a pink-silk embroidered shirt reaching to my knees; over this was draped a 'shamma' of fine gauzy cotton, with a broad band of embroidery round the edges; and then over my shoulders was placed a fine lion' mane as a sort of tippet, the front part being decorated with gold filigree work, to which the forelegs were fastened and hung down in front, while the hindlegs dangled down my back. A long sword in a velvet and gold scabbard was then tightly buckled to my *right* hip; a shield covered with silver and gold *plaques* was hung on my left arm, and a long spear was placed in that hand. Finally a gold ornament in the shape of a double triangle was hung about my neck; and thus attired I entered the presence of the king for the last time."

This apparel cost him great embarrassment when he had to mount a beautiful Abyssinian horse with splendid housings, mounting in the Abyssinian fashion on the right side, like the illustrious Mr. Winkle; but it served him in good stead when he presented himself thus apparelled to Ras Alala, who could not resist this ocular demonstration of the favor of the king. After adventures, some of them more dangerous and exciting than those in the first part of their journey, they reached the Italian outpost Sahati on Christmas morning, and were received with great rejoicings by their Italian friends.

Nothing, one way or the other, came of the embassy. King John, at the head of his immense horde, found, when he reached the neighborhood of the Italian outposts, that the land was too poor to support his army. He also received news of the death of his only son in southern Abyssinia. Further news soon reached him that the Dervishes had attacked an Abyssinian army on the southwest, and had overpowered his followers. He marched at once against them with a large part of the force intended to operate against the Italians. A fierce battle was fought. The Abyssinians won the victory, and the contest seemed to be over, when King John was struck by a Dervish bullet, and the next morning died. Losing all heart, the Abyssinians flung away their victory and dispersed; even the coffin and dead body of their king fell into the hands of followers of the Mahdi, and were carried to Omdurman. The Abyssinians rallied after this, and drove the Mahdists over their frontier.

"The death of King John was the signal for the outbreak of a general civil war. The Italians at Massowah were forgotten. The succession to the throne was at once claimed by three or four powerful rivals. The most important of these was Menelik, king of Shoa, an extensive province joining the southern border of Abyssinia proper. Although a vassal of King John, to whom he paid a heavy tribute, Menelik had for a long time been in the pay of the Italian government. Italy, therefore, officially supported his candidature, and supplied him liberally with rifles, ammunition, money, and European advisers." Thus strengthened, Menelik advanced northward into Abyssinia, and after two years of desultory fighting, skirmishing, promising, and bribing, he succeeded in getting his authority at least partially acknowledged by rather more than half his countrymen.

Meantime, the Italians, encouraged by the situation, advanced their outposts and took possession of the plateau of Asmara, the camping-ground of Ras Alala. There they formed a military post, and proceeded to make preparations for advancing farther into the country.

Meantime, in 1890, by a new shuffle of the cards in the hands of European diplomatists, Italy was accorded all Abyssinia as her "sphere of influence," — the object of England, Germany, and Austria being to keep that country out of the hands of the French, who showed signs of extending their territorial possessions beyond Obok, and of Russia, which had all along held certain relations with Abyssinia as a Christian country whose church had in past ages accepted laws from the Byzantine fathers. A large tract of country running straight inland from Massowah was in those years of comparative peace declared an Italian crown colony, and received the name of Eritrea (Erythrea). In those years also a railroad was constructed from Massowah and Monkullu to Sahati, and had been projected to Keren, — so that the No Man's Land, between hostile outposts, travelled by night, swiftly and in silence, by Mr. Portal and his party for fear of brigands and scouting parties, is safe for the most unprotected traveller. The present Negus, Menelik, claims descent, like his predecessors, from Solomon and the Queen of Sheba; "and," says Mr. Portal, concluding his narrative, " though the question of the wisdom or unwisdom of the whole of the colonial policy of Italy on the eastern shores of the Red Sea is not one which it behooves me to discuss, I may say that, in assuming the protectorate of the whole of Abyssinia, Italy has undertaken a task of great difficulty and responsibility, in the performance of which she may find obstacles placed in her way by nations of Africa, and by nations of Europe as well."

As soon as Menelik found himself upon his throne he sent word to Ras Alala that he wished him to resign the kingly position of Ras of Tigré. Ras Alala was a man of low birth, who by his brave and successful campaigns against the enemies of King John had obtained great influence, and was made *ras*, though he was never crowned *king*. When Menelik summoned him to resign his province in favor of Ras Mangashah, a son of King John by a concubine, he was naturally indignant, and took to the mountains with the chiefs who adhered to him.

Such was the state of affairs in Eritrea and Abyssinia at the opening of the year 1893. But things changed greatly during that year. General Oreste Baratieri was made governor of the colony. A large army of natives (called Ankars by the Italians) had been organized, and under Italian officers was becoming a very efficient arm of the service. A brave and formidable Arab tribe, the Hadindon, who under Osman Digna had fought the Anglo-Egyptians, had given in their adherence to the Italians. General Baratieri had undertaken strongly to fortify Agordat, a place unheard-of in Europe till 1890, when two companies of native regulars surprised a column of Dervishes, and fought them with a steadiness and bravery that made a great impression on the Italians and other Europeans. General Baratieri, now that the western frontier of Eritrea extended into the Soudan, undertook to take possession of Kassala. The object of this was to prevent its falling into the hands of the Dervishes, who would have found such a stronghold a valuable possession, whence they could have raided and threatened the surrounding country. Many protests were made in Italy against this extension of Eritrea's western frontier; but Baratieri defended it on the ground of its being needful for security, though on military grounds the occupation was unintelligible.

Ras Mangashah, too, who in the early months of 1890 lost no opportunity of expressing friendliness to the Italians, was understood at the beginning of 1895 to be preparing to invade their colony. There was in General Baratieri's mind little doubt that Mangashah was acting on an understanding with King Menelik, and he thought it to be his duty to repel and chastise any chief who invaded what he held to be Italian territory. By some wonderful strategical movemente he won victories over the Dervishes at Coatit and Senafè. He was well aware, however, that the party in the Italian parliament which opposed colonial extension would not fail to blame his action. " I have done my duty; but if I succumb, no one will compassionate my death, or defend me if I survive." These words are pathetic, looked at in the light of late events, but in 1894 Baratieri was a popular hero. "The government summoned him to Italy in July, 1895, and he remained there till September, when he was recalled by despatches from Colonel Arimondi, which warned him of the hostile attitude of the Abyssinians. One of two courses was then open to the Italians, — either to insist on the total abandonment of the two great provinces of Tigré and Agame, or to forward to Abyssinia immense reinforcements of money, arms, and men." But Signor Crispi and his government hesitated to take either of these courses. They could not bring themselves to give up provinces already announced in the Almanach de Gotha to be portions of Italian territory,—provinces whose acquisition had been made dear to Italians by highly creditable feats of arms; but neither did it seem probable that the country, groaning under its financial difficulties, would patiently submit to increased burdens for colonial extension in Africa. At that very moment the minister of finance had been congratulating himself and the country that he had succeeded in laying the foundation for an equilibrium in the finances at some not very distant day.

But there was one man who could not bring himself to believe that the sentiment of the country was decidedly against the prosecution of the war, — a war that had brought glory to the Italian arms and revived the military spirit of the Italian people. King Humbert, who had for years chafed against the inaction forced on him by his scrupulous adherence to the duties imposed on him as a constitutional king, felt the spirit of a soldier of Savoy stir in his blood. In his eyes, the prestige of his house and of his kingdom was closely associated with deeds of arms and military glory. He wished to show the world that Italy could win victories, as much by the sword as by diplomacy; and now as she was beginning to realize these hopes, it seemed hard to turn her back in her career. The result was that no definite decision was arrived at. General Baratieri went back to Massowah, where he was hailed with enthusiasm, and where news of the most important battle yet fought by Italians in Africa awaited him.

It was the battle of Agordat, fought on the 21st of December. The fort was held by a garrison of two thousand men composed of eight companies of native troops, two squadrons of native cavalry, two batteries, and some Italians. A horde of Dervishes came down upon Agordat in a close column protected on the right wing by a large body of cavalry. Colonel Arimondi, who was in command, decided to meet them in the open plain. Leaving half of his force to hold the fort, he advanced with four companies and a battery. The fight began at eleven o'clock in the day, and at first the immense numbers of the Dervishes gave them the advantage. Seeing this, the reserves issued from the fort and fell on the right wing of the enemy. Their resistance was obstinate, and the battle lasted till three o'clock, the flying Dervishes being pursued for a considerable distance, and leaving the field of battle covered with their dead. The fight was a very brilliant one on the part of the Italians, but the people of Massowah in their delight magnified it in the most extraordinary degree.

General Baratieri had brought back from his government in Italy vague promises of support. They wanted to give him men, money, and supplies; but if they did, would not the public grumble at new taxes, and what would the minister of finance say? The telegraphic despatches exchanged between Crispi and the general after his return to Massowah, and published in the Green Books (the Libri Verdi), are very sad reading. Crispi's are full of exhortations to go on and conquer, but to spend as little money as possible; Baratieri's are urgent appeals for supplies. He knew that Menelik was joining all the forces of his kingdom to those of Mangashah. In one despatch Crispi suggests to the general to make war like Napoleon, and let the country support his soldiers. Baratieri replies that the country is too poor to support its own inhabitants. In one of his despatches Crispi makes so sure of victory that he wants to discuss with the general who had best be the successor of King Menelik. No orders seem to have been precise; no promises seem to have been fulfilled. "Go ahead, but don't spend money," seems to be the sum of what was said.

Goaded by these telegrams, and by his own sense of the perils and responsibilities of his position, General Baratieri seems in a measure to have lost his head. He had encountered and beaten the rear of Ras Mangashah's column at a place called Debra-Ailat, and seems to have considered that this victory gave him a firm hold on the great provinces of Tigré and Agame. The Italian Chamber of Deputies questioned the wisdom of this military occupation. The prime minister's answers " were curt and scornful. 'We are on the defensive,' he said; 'and if in defending ourselves we conquer, is this a crime? Are we to leave the field open to our enemy to come in and defeat us?'" One member accused the government of having totally changed the tenor of its instructions to General Baratieri; and, indeed, when we read those instructions in the Green Books, the suggestions and orders given him seem to have changed day by day.

A week later came news of the fight at Amba-Alagi, where a detached battalion of Italians was cut to pieces; and Major Toselli, who commanded it, after sending away a remnant of his men under an aide-de-camp to seek safety, faced twenty thousand foes till he fell dead at his post. Twenty million lire was reluctantly voted for the war by the Chamber, even the supporters of the ministry putting a veto on any further policy of "expansion."

The little force at Amba-Alagi was an outpost of General Baratieri's army, which he had not taken the precaution to call in, in the presence of an enemy with forty thousand well-armed men. The Abyssinian losses were greater than the entire force of the Italians, seven hundred of whom, under command of Major Toselli's aide-de-camp, escaped from the field, while a thousand lay dead among the corpses of their enemies. The remainder of the story, the terrible disaster in the battle of Adowa, or Abba Garima, I will tell in the words of a correspondent of the "Nation":—

"It was now evident that Baratieri had become so physically, morally, and militarily demoralized that he was unfit for command, and, but for considerations of his political influence, the ministry would have recalled him. He himself desired to resign; but the ministry contented itself with telling him to stand on the defensive. Meantime the Abyssinians took up a very strong position at Adowa. The Italian position was equally formidable, and there was a deep valley between them. The Italian troops reached their position after a long night march, weary and fasting, for three days before orders had been given to fall back, and all the provisions had been sent away to precede the retreat of the army. The officers did not know what to make of the indecision of the general. He seems to have been attacked by some illness,—something apparently like softening of the brain. He attacked the enemy in his strong position, and the result was the almost total destruction of the Italian army, the most disastrous defeat yet known in African wars. A report was published by the Italian government, drawn up on the evidence of some of the survivors, in which we find the following episode.

"Cut off (the enemy having broken through the centre), the Da Bormida brigade remained alone on the battlefield, fighting till night, bravely, heroically. Towards seven o'olock Da Bormida had sent up on a height to the left, perhaps to sustain General Albertone, the battalion of irregulars (that is, of native troops, fighting under their own chiefs and after their own mode of warfare). The battalion fought for half an hour against overwhelming forces, and then was obliged to retire with heavy loss. Two battalions sent to its support could not fire effectively without hitting our own men. Then Da Bormida, seeing that great masses of the enemy were moving on him from the right, attacked them, deployed, repulsed them, and advanced nearly to the camps of the commanders of the Abyssinians. For the moment our men believed that they had won the victory; but the enemy always increasing, General Da Bormida ordered a retreat in a direction diverging from the centre, and effected it in *échelon* with counter attacks at the point of the bayonet. The artillery had fired all its ammunition, and the infantry exhausted nearly all its cartridges. Da Bormida fell riddled with balls."

It was said by the officers who last saw their general, that when he gave the order to retreat, he said calmly, " Go on, my lads. I shall stay here,"— and, lighting a cigar, he faced the enemy, and was shot down.

"The force of the Abyssinian army in this battle, called by some Abba Garima, was six times that of the Italian, which had marched all night by moonlight, twenty miles, over a country cut up by ravines, mostly unreconnoitred, and so difficult that in places it was necessary to take the guns from the mules' backs and carry them by hand; while the whole army had been three days on short rations, owing to the provision reserves having been sent away. . . . The enormous superiority in numbers of the Abyssinians enabled them to outflank the Italians and to attack the reserve before it had formed or extricated itself from the ravines, and threw it into confusion, — all the greater because they were led to suppose that the main body in front, which was for a time victorious, had been annihilated. In confusion this portion of the army retreated, being the only division that moved from its position without orders to retreat, in spite of losses in the others in actual fighting quite unprecedented in modern warfare, except at Amba-Alagi. Several battalions were practically annihilated without moving from their positions, three-fourths of the officers falling, out of the total number in the battle."

Two thousand six hundred prisoners remained in King Menelik's hands. Intense was the indignation in Italy. The country was distracted with rival recriminations. Peasants in some places tore up the rails to prevent the departure of soldiers, their friends and neighbors, who were ordered to Africa. General Baratieri was tried by court-martial, but acquitted as being the victim of circumstances. The court-martial took place at Massowah. Had the unfortunate general been brought to Italy during the first days of excitement he might have been torn to pieces.

The Crispi ministry at once fell, and was succeeded by one formed by the Marquis di Rudini. He, like Signor Crispi is a Sicilian, but a man of a different type.

"While the one represented in an unusual degree the Sicilian type of character, — vigorous, aggressive, domineering, and at times violent, — his successor, who comes of another social class, is reserved, self-controlled, dignified, and has already had experience in the position which he now holds. Ten years ago he made public a programme which included the abandonment of enterprises in Africa, and economy and vigilance in finance. He is known also to favor the policy of allying Italy as closely as possible to England, a country which he is said to admire greatly. His enemies call him irresolute; his friends say he has the hand of steel in the glove of velvet. If he carry out his declared intentions he will minimize activity in Africa, enforce economies, give especial attention to the condition of affairs in Sicily and Sardinia, and follow more closely the lines of constitutional rule. But how far he will succeed in carrying out his own programme, in view of the various influences which will be brought to bear on him, remains to be seen."

"The Massowah expedition," says the "Nation's" correspondent, "was a blunder from the beginning; and so Crispi declared it when the first disaster in it called him to power; but after the affair at Dogali, military honor seemed to forbid retreat, . . . and the same motive will make it hard for the Italians to withdraw now."

This sentence was written early in April. Prudent counsels have since prevailed, and it has been decided to restrict Italian military enterprise strictly to the defence of the Italian colony. Aggressive operations in the "sphere of influence" have been renounced, and friendly powers are endeavoring to effect with Menelik a "peace with honor." Thus far the Christian barbarian has not proved tractable. The Italians still hold Kassala, which is nearly in a direct line west from Massowah, but very far in the interior. They have been encouraged to do this by the English, who conceived it might assist them in their present struggle with Africa. Before the Anglo-Egyptian march up the Nile began, the Italians were on the point of evacuating this outlying position, which was threatened by an immense horde of Dervishes; but suddenly these were called off to reinforce Kalifa Abdulla, the present Mahdi, and to oppose the English advancing on Dongola.

A few weeks ago, when negotiations with Menelik for the return of the two thousand six hundred Italian captives had produced no result, the "Osservatore Romano," the official organ of the Vatican, unexpectedly announced that "The Holy Father, Leo XIII., being affected by natural consideration for our prisoners in Africa, has adressed a letter to the Negus Menelik, asking for their restitution in pressing terms." This letter has been intrusted to Monsignor Cyrille Macaire, Patriarchal Vicar of the Copts of the Alexandrian mission, who set out at once upon his perilous embassy.

In December, 1878, before Menelik became Negus, and when he was only King of Shoa, he sent to Leo XIII., then recently made Pope, a letter of congratulation by the hands of Monsignor Massala (since cardinal), who was at that time Vicar Apostolic of the country of the Gallas, a province in southern Abyssinia peopled by Mahomedans, in which a very promising mission had been established by Jesuit fathers some years ago. Besides this, on the occasion of the Pope's jubilee, Menelik, in common with other potentates, sent him a gift, consisting of several valuable Abyssinian manuscripts, which are now preserved in the Vatican library. On both occasions the Pope expressed in his letters to the African prince his great pleasure and gratitude. The fact of these former relations between Pope Leo and the Negus might facilitate, it was hoped, the success of this new embassy.

The general sentiment throughout Italy on receiving the news that the Pope would interpose in favor of Italian prisoners, was one of surprise, admiration, and gratitude. Of course, in the Chamber, where everything is turned by one party to the disadvantage of the other, there were not wanting deputies to say that the interference of the Pontiff in Italian affairs was a menace to the stability of the Italian kingdom, and to take it as an insult that the announcement of the Pontiff's intervention should have been made on a day sacred to the memory of Garibaldi, being the fourteenth anniversary of his death. The Marquis di Rudini, having been questioned in parliament as to whether he had received any notice of the Pope's intended action, replied that he had only learned of it from the "Osservatore Romano." He said that "his own feelings in the matter were simply that the act was one to inspire at once a sentiment of gratitude. I believe," he added, " that the sovereign pontiff by doing this has obeyed a Christian sentiment and a feeling of humanity, both belonging to his sublime mission, and that he has also displayed his feeling of affection for the Italian fatherland. If this has been the sentiment of the sovereign pontiff, the sentiment of the Italian government can only be that of profound gratitude."

Thus, relieved from the complications and embarrassments of his position as a petty Italian prince, Leo XIII. assumes his place as the head of the largest division of the Christian Church throughout the world, and asserts his claim to lift up his voice to the nations in behalf of pity and humanity. Greater is he in this than any pope has been for centuries, — an example to the civilized world of Christian forgiveness of injuries.

Monsignor Macaire reached Adis Ababa, the present capital of King Menelik, on August 11, 1896. His journey

was arduous and dangerous, and, as another caravan, led by two priests, who were endeavoring to carry supplies to the prisoners, had met with misfortunes, it was greatly feared that Monsignor Macaire's embassy might have met a similar fate. A letter received by Cardinal Rampolla, secretary of state for the Holy See, on Monday, September 28, 1896, and published by order of Pope Leo in the " Osservatore Romano " the next morning, will give all that is thus far known of the expedition.

"ADIS ABABA, August 14, 1896.

" YOUR EMINENCE, — I write from Adis Ababa, the capital of the empire of Abyssinia, and have the honor to inform you that we have been here since last Tuesday, August 11. Our journey has been most fortunate, thanks to the protection of the Most High and to the benediction of the Holy See.

" His Majesty the Emperor Menelik has here received us with all the honors due to the dignity of the Apostolic Church. He sent to meet us, on the day of our arrival, a numerous escort of about one hundred and fifty soldiers, having at their head several native chiefs, and Monsieur Ilg, engineer in chief especially charged by his Majesty to bid us welcome in his name. The next day, Wednesday, August 12, at about eleven o'clock in the day, the Emperor gave us a solemn audience. I went to the imperial palace escorted by all the Abyssinian clergy of Adis Ababa, to the number of not less than fifty. I was received by the Emperor in the presence of his court. When I presented the pontifical letters to his Majesty, I stated to him the object of my mission; that is, that the Holy See placed confidence in the generosity of the descendant of King David, who is praised in Scripture for his lovingkindness and mercy. That the Sovereign Pontiff had chosen as his ambassador to his Majesty the head of the Coptic Church, both hoping thereby to avoid any suspicion of a political purpose in the mission, and because he thereby hoped to awaken, in the memory of the Emperor of Ethiopia, kindly thoughts connected with religion. Rome and Alexandria come before him, I said, on this mission. We present the united request of Saint Peter, foremost of the Apostles, and of Saint Mark, who was both his spiritual son and the spiritual father of both Copts and Abyssinians; in their name we solicit from his Majesty the release of all the prisoners. All Christian nations venture to hope that he who spontaneously gave to the Sovereign Pontiff marks of his royal courtesy on the occasion of his accession to Saint Peter's throne, will not refuse him the boon which his Holiness this day solicits by the mouth of an ambassador extraordinary. Then I ended by a prayer to God, in whose hands are the hearts of kings, to inspire in his Majesty all that might do honor to the greatness of a Christian Emperor, and to the dignity of the Holy See. The Emperor answered me in these terms: 'The Pope is the Father of us all. He has the right to write to us, and to express to us all he may desire. We will see each other again, and we will then talk further on this subject.' With that, I took leave of his Majesty, hoping that God would preserve his life for the glory and happiness of Ethiopia. These details may give your Eminence an idea of the delicacy of the great Emperor. That same day, the day of the audience, he sent us in the evening, to be attached to our service, a man who had been cook to General Baratieri. All the prisoners that we have seen are in good health, and speak in the most touching terms of the kindness with which they are treated by the Emperor, — indeed on every feast day a repast is prepared for them in the imperial palace. As for their liberation, we who have witnessed the greatness of the Negus, and the nobleness of his character, venture to hope that we may soon announce to the Holy See the happy news which will comfort so many poor mothers and will add to the glory of his Majesty.

"In conclusion, I beg your Eminence to lay this letter at the feet of his Holiness, and to solicit for us his apostolic benediction, that Jesus Christ our Lord may finish the work that He has thus begun.

"The very humble and devoted servant of your Eminence,

"✠ CYRILLE MACAIRE, Bishop and Patriarchal Vicar of the Copts."

The selection of this semi-oriental envoy, so skilled in compliments likely to be acceptable to such a monarch as the Negus, certainly shows the great care with which Pope Leo can choose his instruments, besides which, the hierarchical position of Monsignor Macaire, as the so-called successor of St. Mark, and the man who on the death of the present Patriarch of Alexandria will be his successor, must have lent an especial importance and interest to the mission in the eyes of the ruler of Abyssinia. The reply of the Negus was certainly somewhat sibylline, but, as the "Tablet" says, "is of a nature to afford grounds for hope."

What the Vicar Patriarchal of Alexandria says of the condition and treatment of the prisoners must be a great consolation to their families, being in direct contradiction to the reports, circulated for some months past in the Italian papers, that they were daily dying from hunger, hardships, fever, and suicide. Let us trust that before these pages reach the hands of my readers we may receive news of the release of all these unfortunates.

Unhappily, Italy pays no pensions to her maimed or disabled soldiers. Those who return thus afflicted from Abyssinia will have to be supported at the expense of their relatives, for the most part poor peasants hardly able to pay taxes and to support themselves.

Before the arrival of Monsignor Macaire at Adis Ababa, a society of Roman ladies had obtained from King Menelik the release of about fifty prisoners, who are described as having reached Italy in good health and good condition. It had been confidently asserted that the influence of Russia at the court of the Negus would be exerted to put obstacles in the way of the prisoners' release, and frustrate peace negotiations. But the interest taken by the Czar in the marriage of Princess Hélène of Montenegro with the heir to the throne of Italy, seems to indicate a desire to help Italy out of her difficulties rather than to aggravate them.

Meantime, however, the great question of peace or war, with its contingent considerations of taxation and conscription, appears to offer little promise of solution.

King Menelik's terms of peace were not considered such as could be entertained by the court and people of Italy, and General Baldissera, now governor of Eritrea, was in consultation during the summer with ministers at home. It seems decided that Eritrea shall be restricted within the frontier it possessed in 1892 before the military exploits, brilliant or disastrous, of General Baratieri. But Baldissera, who is a man of experience and moderation, stated openly his conviction that no less than 70,000 men, well supplied with all military stores, would be necessary to defend the colony, even within its restricted limits, if attacked by a large and determined force of Abyssinians. Of course, so large a body of men as General Baldissera considers indispensable to make the frontiers of Eritrea safe, could not be all Italians, but it would be necessary, in order to keep up the army reserve in Italy imposed by the terms of the Triple Alliance, to draw largely on the resources of the country for fighting men.

The statement of Baldissera's opinion on this subject reopened the difficult question of how to get rid of Eritrea without loss of honor, and how to retain Massowah as a commercial station, though its value in that respect has been considerably lessened by the opening of new ports on the Indian Ocean, more accessible to caravans from the interior.

Two articles recently published in the "Fortnightly Review" have attracted great attention to Italy. One is by Ouida, and is a passionate arraignment of Italy for her shortcomings. It cannot be denied that United Italy has greatly disappointed the hopes formed for her when Cavour held the helm of state and great men sprang up around Victor Emmanuel. The other article is by Mr. J. Theodore Bent, whose books on "The Ruined Cities in Mashonaland" and on "A Journey through parts of Abyssinia in 1893" have been of great use to me. He speaks of Eritrea as a colony perfectly worthless. It has neither mines nor agricultural facilities. The Italian government has spent large sums in agricultural experiments, without any prospect of making the colony anything but an enormous expense to the taxpayers in Italy. We call it a *colony*, but it contains no more than a handful of colonists, and there is nothing to attract them to its soil. Mr. Bent says that Northern and Southern Italy are sharply divided in opinion on the African question.

"Broadly speaking," he says, "the advocates of the Abyssinian colony, and the war-to-extremity party, are to be found in the southern provinces of Italy; the principal organs for the continuation of the war and the retrieval of the honor of Italy are the Neapolitan journals, whereas the advocates of peace at any price, and the abandonment of colonial honors, are to be found in the north of Italy, in the plains of Lombardy and Venice, where the newspapers are taking up a unanimous line on this point. The question is a burning one at present there, and it is distinctly assuming the aspect of a struggle between the north and south of the peninsula."

Italy has, as I have said, another African colony more fertile and promising south of Abyssinia, to which she has just despatched large military and naval reinforcements. She purchased a considerable tract of it from the Sultan of Zanzibar, and it is separated from British East Africa by the Jub, or Juba, river. It is in a dangerous position, however, being almost without defence if King Menelik, descending from mountains in the Galla country, should think good to attack it. It is also a near neighbor to Obok, that large district which the French hope to make some day not only an eastern outlet to a vast Saharian empire, but possibly a stepping-stone to great possessions in Western Asia. It had been hoped that Italy's African possessions might attract the emigration now overflowing into the United States and Argentina, but Eritrea offers too few attractions either to capitalists, artisans, small traders, or agricultural laborers. It is simply an unprofitable tract of country that absorbs soldiers who might be more profitably employed.

Ouida enlarges on the destitution and discontent of the laboring classes; on their inability to understand why revolt, to whose heroes statues are being erected and fêtes proclaimed, should have been right under the Austrians and Bourbons, and their imitation under the Savoy dynasty worthy only of fines and chains. She has a great deal to say, too, of the brutality and exasperating interference of the police, whose business it seems to be to treat all men as if they belonged to the criminal class in the absence of evidence to the contrary. This attitude of the police in Europe towards the general public, always impresses itself on an American or an Englishman. " I first felt I was in a land of freedom," wrote an Italian exile, " when, on landing at Dover, a policeman held out his hand and helped me up some slippery stairs."

Ouida gives, as an instance of police brutality, the story of a man killed this summer in Parma, whose murder excited a riot in that city. His name was Cassinelli.

"He had been in prison under frivolous charges and was subject to police surveillance, had lost work through this, and when a barber engaged him on the miserable wage of one meal a day, the police intimidated his employer, who discharged him. Then they arrested the unhappy man as a vagrant without employment. He resisted, was shot in the abdomen, and dragged over the stones towards the police barracks, dying on his way thither. The populace in the streets endeavored to rescue him, and when they found he was dead they attacked the police. . . . Harmless citizens are irritated, insulted and provoked about any trifle that presents itself. Any man who says an angry word to the police on such occasions is marched off to the police court, and from that moment is a marked man."

But, as I write, all causes of discontent are laid aside; the great African question is forgotten; all Italy is engaged in a *festa*, — for is not the heir of the house of Savoy celebrating his nuptials after great difficulty in finding a bride, for the Catholic Princesses of Europe were afraid to ally themselves with a royal house under the displeasure of the Holy See.

At the ceremony of the coronation of the Czar and Czarina, the young Prince of Naples, who was present, met the Princess Hélène of Montenegro. She was almost brought up at the Russian court, for the court of Cettinje offered few facilities for education. She was a great favorite with the Dowager Empress of Russia, widow of Alexander III., and formerly Princess Dagmar of Denmark, sister of the Princess of Wales. The Czar, observing that the Prince was attracted by the brunette beauty of the tall and stately Montenegrin lady, suggested that his marriage with one so nearly connected with the Russian court would be very agreeable to him. This seemed politically an offer of amity on the part of Russia to a member of the Triple

Alliance. The Prince spoke upon this hint, and was accepted. The Czar, as head of the Orthodox Greek Church, sanctioned the necessary change in the form of the Princess's religion. This pleased Pope Leo, who was anxious to draw closer the bonds of amity between Russia and the Holy See, — the Eastern and Western churches. The Princess is very accomplished, speaking fluently the four principal European languages. She has also written verses of more than average merit, published in the newspapers of St. Petersburg.

In a previous volume of this series,[1] I gave a brief sketch of the little principality in the Black Mountains, its reigning family, its people's brave resistance to the Turks, and its government, "carried on," said Mr. Gladstone, "like that of Greece in the Homeric age. The sovereign was priest, judge, and general, and was likewise head of the General Assembly of the people, in which were taken the decisions which were to bind the nation as laws." Mr. Gladstone said also of Montenegro in a sketch he published of it in the "Nineteenth Century": "It is a land which might have risen to world-wide and immortal fame had there been a Scott to learn to tell the marvels of its history, or a Byron to spend and be spent on its behalf."

The Princess is above the usual stature of women, — quite as tall as her bridegroom, who is under medium height. She has coal-black hair and flashing eyes like those of her people, and a superb figure. She landed at Bari on October 19, after a stormy passage across the Adriatic. She went straight to the Basilica of St. Nicholas, where the Saint himself is buried, and there before a silver altar, renovated for the occasion by silversmiths from the Quirinal, she made her abjuration, and heard mass according to the rites of the Roman Catholic and Apostolic Church.

Bari is a city which has more Greek associations than any other in the peninsula. To judge by a proclamation put forth by the municipality, it must have many other associations with the Middle Ages.

[1] Russia and Turkey in the Nineteenth Century.

Here is the edict, which was posted on the walls of the principal thoroughfares:

"CITIZENS OF BARI:

"It is your duty to clean the streets of all unseemly mud.

"Used and tattered washing linen must be taken away from the windows.

"Little children must no longer run naked in the streets.

"Goats, cows, hens, and drunken men must be kept at a proper distance.

"No dust bins may for three weeks be emptied in the streets.

"Licensed coachmen are forbidden to wear ragged liveries, and are advised to borrow police uniforms.

"Let these things be done, and our citizens will prove themselves worthy of their ancestors, and our city will be duly garnished for greeting our royal bride."[1]

The Princess went on the next day to Rome, attended by a large body of ecclesiastics, as well as her own friends and the nobles and ladies appointed to receive her. The Prince, who had crossed with her to Bari from Cattaro, was not present at her abjuration. He hurried on to Rome, where with his father, mother, relatives, and the Court he was ready to receive her on her arrival.

On Saturday, October 24, amid great rejoicings, the Prince and Princess were married at the ancient church of Santa Maria dei Angeli, which in some way is connected with the House of Savoy.

The altar was placed in the centre of the church, and under the transparent *baldacchino* hangings it was at first proposed to place Titian's great picture of the Assumption of the Virgin. "Modern ruins" were cleared away from the piazza before the church, an arch was erected at the entrance, and all the streets through which the bridal party passed were richly decorated.

Thus all in Italy for the present is merry with marriage

---

[1] "Quite as applicable to Brindisi," said a traveller, recently returned from the East, as I read out this proclamation with much amusement and some surprise. — E. W. L.

bells, and no doubt the *popolani*, who love festivities, and take little thought for the morrow, have enjoyed them greatly. But the expenses of the marriage must have been enormous, though King Humbert requested that no money might be spent on fêtes by the municipality of Rome. Still, one is sorry to see that Parliament is about to vote a million *lire* to the bridegroom, and a similar sum as dowry to the bride. There are so many suffering Italians that one would have been glad to know some were made happy by the expenditure of such millions in other ways.[1]

Let us hope, however, that a new and brighter day may be about to dawn on Italy, — that some friendly Power may intervene to help her out of her colonial difficulties in Africa. Already during the last weeks a little piece of better fortune has befallen her, — a treaty with France concerning Tunis, which restores to the traders of Italy important commercial advantages; and Menelik, on the birthday of Queen Margherita, released his prisoners.

[1] News has since reached me that King Humbert declined to sanction the dotation proposed for the Prince of Naples and his bride. It was, however, represented to him that this would establish a precedent which might prevent a proper provision for some future heir apparent. He has, therefore, consented to receive the two million *lire*, but proposes that they shall be spent on national objects by his son. — E. W. L.

POSTSCRIPT.

WHILE these pages have been going through the press, events have occurred which require some mention to bring this "History of Italy in the Nineteenth Century" up to date.

Monsignor Macaire reported to the Vatican that King Menelik, after protesting his devotion to the Pope, maintained that, while the Italian Government continued in its attitude of hostility toward Abyssinia, he was unable to sacrifice the sole guarantee of peace that he held by restoring to liberty the Italian prisoners. A few days, however, after the publication of this refusal in the American papers came news that peace had been signed with King Menelik, by which Italy renounced her nominal protectorate over Abyssinia.

The world has also been astounded by the revelation of a diplomatic secret by Prince Bismarck which has roused the indignation of the weaker partners in the Triple Alliance. The terms of that alliance were agreed on as early as 1882, and in the following year the treaty was practically made, though it was not till 1887 that it was formally signed. Italy had, however, since 1883, been straining her resources to meet the obligations of her engagement, while it now appears that Russia and Germany from 1884 to 1890 had a secret alliance, by the terms of which it was agreed that, in case France should attack Germany, Russia would detach herself from France and aid Germany; and, in case Austria should attack Russia, the Emperor of Germany would abandon the Triple Alliance and come to the assistance of the Czar, thus leaving the weaker Powers, Austria and Italy, to derive no advantage from the Triple Alliance, to maintain which they had made such sacrifices, and exposing them unaided to bear all the fatal consequences of a general European war.

I take this opportunity of offering an apology to my own sex, and to Miss Georgina Sarah Godkin, for having in early copies of this book, attributed her excellent "Life of Victor Emmanuel," which I have for some years known and valued, to an imaginary G. S. Godkin, Esquire.

INDEX.

INDEX.

A.

Abba Garima (or Carima), battle of, 412–414.
Abyssinia, 395–421; after King John's death, 407; Italian protectorate over, 399, 407; Italians invade, 398; Italian advance into, 407; proposals to restrict advances into, 411; Italian prisoners in, 414–419.
Adis Ababa, 417, 418.
Agordat, battle of, 410.
Alala, Ras, 400–405, 408.
Albert, Prince Consort, 213, 269.
Albrecht, Archduke, 257–259, 281.
Alessandria, 95, 204, 317.
Alexander, Emperor, 27, 60, 61.
Alison, Sir Archibald, *quoted*, 106, 108, 109.
Alliance, (1865) between Italy and Prussia, 274; declined with France by Italy and Austria, 310; Triple, between Italy, Germany, and Austria, 382, 387, 389–394, 426.
Amadeo, King of Spain, Duke d'Aosta, 175, 300, 302.
Amalfi, 11.
Amba Alagi, 412, 413.
Amnesty after the election of Pius IX., 43–46.
Angevin kings of Naples, 12, 13.
Anita, wife of Garibaldi, 139, 142, 144, 146, 149, 215.
Annichiarico, Ciro, 352–356.
Antonelli, Cardinal, 50, 58, 323, 335, 336, 339.
Arad, 169, 285.

Arnim, Count v., 315.
Arpad, 154.
Aspromonte, battle of, 248.
Assab, Bay of, 396.
Attila, 152.
Augustenborg, Prince of, 268.
Austria, 13, 15, 18, 20, 21, 26, 27, 56, 63, 64, 79, 80, 160, 173, 256, 265, 310, 312; after 1866, 283–286; Imperial family determine to abandon Vienna, 281.
Austria-Hungary, 283–289.
Azani F., 141, 142.

B.

Baldissera, General, 419, 420.
Bandiera, Enrico and Attilio, 37–39, 80.
Baratieri, General Oreste, 408–414.
Bari, 9, 10, 423, 424.
Barsanti, 304.
Bassi, Ugo, 123, 128, 129, 145–149, 384.
Batthyani, Prince, 162, 169.
Beauharnais, Eugène, 16–20.
Belgiojoso, Princess, 129.
Bem, General, 165, 169.
Benedek, Marshal, 209, 279, 281.
Benedetti, 282.
Bent, J. Theodore, *quoted*, 143, 145, 146, 227, 230, 252, 291, 420, 421.
Beust, Count, 302.
Biserta, 391.
Bismarck, von, 270–273, 280, 282, 310, 389.
Bixio, Nino, 225, 226, 242, 313, 316, 375.

INDEX.

"Blackwood's Magazine," *referred to*, 352.
Blind, Karl, *quoted*, 289.
Bomba. *See* Ferdinand II.
Bordone, 305.
Borghi, *quoted*, 337, 338.
Borjes, General, 366.
Brescia, 115, 116, 210.
Brigandage, 241, 352-370; political, 305, 366.
Brindisi, 424.
Broughton, Lord, *quoted*, 17, 20, 27; *referred to*, 180.
Browning, Robert, 84; Mrs. E. B. Browning, *quoted*, 112, 113, 118-121; "The forced Recruit," 210.
Byron, Lord, 20, 21; *quoted*, 79.

C.

Cadorna, General, 293, 313, 314, 317, 318.
Cairoli, brothers, 296, 308, 381; Benedetto, 308, 377, 380-382, 396.
Calatafimi, battle of, 227.
Camorra, 350, 351, 371-373, 387.
Campo Formio (1797), 21, 79.
Canzio, Captain, 240, 241, 262, 295, 307, 308.
Caprera, 147, 215, 241, 305-308.
Captures of British subjects by brigands, 370.
Carbonari, 21, 22, 32, 33, 36, 94, 98.
Carlyle, *quoted*, 29.
Caroline. Queen of Naples, 59-61.
Casa Guidi Windows, 118-121.
Cassinelli, 422.
Castelfidardo, battle of, 235, 364.
Castlereagh, Lord, 20, 25, 61.
Cavaignac, General, 126.
Cavour, Count Camillo, 29, 81, 100, 101, 178, 183-188, 196, 198-200, 203, 212-214, 229, 230, 238-245, 321, 377, 378, 384.
Central Italy, 15, 108, 212-221.
Cesaresco, Countess Martinengo, *quoted*, 22, 37, 51, 72, 73, 76, 83, 84, 104, 115, 116, 124, 125, 182, 210, 216, 240, 241, 243, 263, 298, 310.
Charette, Colonel, 313.

Charlemagne, 9, 14, 298.
Charles Albert, 25, 26, 28-30, 69, 83, 92-113, 120, 143, 173, 182, 183.
Charles Emmanuel IV., 24.
Charles Felix, 24-28, 92, 93, 94, 96, 97, 100.
Charles V., 159.
Chateaubriand, *quoted*, 94.
Charvaz, Archbishop, 174, 181.
Christian, Prince of Glücksborg, 268.
Christina of Courland, 92.
Christina of Savoy, 64.
Church, General, 352-355.
Cialdini, General, 248, 257, 258.
Ciceruacchio, 49, 56, 57, 123, 124, 125, 145, 149; his sons, 145, 149.
Clarendon, Lord, 312, 313.
Cleveland, President, 334.
Clotilde, Princess, 175, 201-203, 255, 301.
Cobden, Richard, 81, 184.
Confalonieri, 99.
Confederation of Italy proposed, 32, 33, 213.
Congress of Verona (1822), 26, 27; of Vienna (1815), 79.
Cosenz, General Enrico, 86, 88, 229, 313.
Crawford, F. Marion, 43, 294; Mrs. Crawford, letter from, 43-45.
Crimean War, Italian troops in, 90, 184, 185.
Crispi, Francesco, 224, 308, 378, 380, 382, 383, 390, 393, 409-411, 414.
Crown, Iron, of Lombardy, 17, 264; of St. Stephen, 154-158, 287.
Curci, Father, 340, 341, 345-347.
Custozza, first battle, 69, 106; second battle, 245, 257, 258.

D.

Dabormida, General, 174; in Abyssinia, 413.
Dante, 14, 15, 79, 275, 276.
Darboy, Archbishop of Paris, 331.
D'Azeglio, 81, 100, 101, 180, 183, 321, 384; *quoted*, 143, 178, 181, 349, 365.
Deák, Francis, 162, 285-289.
Dembinski, General, 165, 169.

INDEX. 431

Denmark, 267, 268, 273.
Depretis, 378, 379, 380.
D'Ideville, *quoted* 242.
Dogali, 400-404.
Drouyn de Lhuys, *quoted*, 291.
Dupanloup, Bishop of Orleans, 328, 331.
Durando, General, 84, 106, 111.
Durazzo, battle of, 12.

E.

Elizabeth, Empress of Austria, 287, 288.
Elizabeth, Queen of Hungary, 155-158.
Emilia. *See* Central Italy.
English expedition to Abyssinia, 399; advance on Dongola, 415.
Eritrea, 396, 399, 407, 409, 419, 420, 421.
Erythrea. *See* Eritrea.
Eugénie, Empress, 302.
Eugène. *See* Beauharnais.

F.

Fanti, General, 235, 238, 241.
Farini, 254; *quoted*, 63, 73.
Ferdinand Albert Amadeo, Duke of Genoa, 69, 70, 102, 110, 181.
Ferdinand I., King of Naples, 13, 27, 59-63.
Ferdinand II. (Bomba), 28, 64, 65, 66, 69-77, 83, 131, 132.
Ferdinand VII., King of Spain, 61.
Finns, 153.
Fleury, General, 210, 211, 367.
Florence, 97, 114, 117-121, 255, 321.
Fonzella, ex-brigand, 368-370.
Forlimpopoli, 362, 363.
"Fortnightly Review," *quoted*, 371, 420.
France and the Roman Republic, 57, 58, 126-130, 132-137.
Francis I., Emperor of Austria, 26, 27, 164, 165.
Francis Joseph, Emperor of Austria, 165, 210, 284, 287, 288, 322, 323.
Francis I., King of Naples, 28, 60, 61, 63, 64.

Francis II., King of Naples, 219, 231, 234, 240, 241, 364, 365.
Francis, Duke of Modena, 31-36.
Frederick William III., King of Prussia, 269.
Frederick William IV., King of Prussia, 269, 270.
Frederick, Crown Prince of Prussia and Emperor of Germany, 278-280.
Frederick Charles (Red Prince), 278-281.
Free Cities, 14, 15, 267.
French occupation of Italy (1797-1815), 15-21; in Rome (1848), 57, 58; land in Piedmont (1859), 205; quit Rome (Dec. 4, 1866), 290; troops again despatched to Rome (1867), 295; evacuate Rome (1870), 312.
Fuller, Margaret, Marchesa d'Ossoli, 30, 57, 119, 129, 130, 135.
Fumel, Major, 366, 367.

G.

Gaeta, 123, 131, 173, 179, 234, 236, 368.
Gambetta, Léon, 303, 304.
Garibaldi, Giuseppe, 29, 108, 122, 125, 127-131, 137-147, 149, 214, 215, 222-244, 246-254, 257, 259, 261-264, 291-300, 303-309; *quoted*, 314.
Garibaldi's hymn, 252.
Genoa, 14, 16, 25-29, 95, 178.
George, King of Hanover, 275-277.
Germany, before 1800, 266, 267; emperors of, 265.
Gibson, Mr., *quoted*, 130.
Gioberti, 178, 340.
Gladstone, W. E., 65, 66, 74, 75, 254, 386, 387, 423.
Godkin, G. S., 174, 426; *quoted*, 93, 178, 208, 209, 219, 237, 325.
Görgey, General Arthur, 165, 167-169.
Gregory XVI., 28, 40, 339, 357.
Guarantees, Papal, 318-320.
Guiscard, Robert, 11, 12; Roger of Sicily, 11, 12; Roger of Naples, 12, 50.
Guyon, General, 165, 169.
Gyulai, General, 205, 209.

H.

Hanover, 275; invaded, 276, 277.
Harcourt, Duc de, 52, 53.
Haynau, Marshal, 88, 115, 116, 166, 167, 170, 284, 285.
Hélène, Princess of Orleans, marries the Duke of Aosta, 376.
Hélène, Princess of Montenegro, marries Prince of Naples, 422-425.
Herwegh, Mrs. Emma, 192, 194.
Hewett, Admiral Sir William, 398, 405.
Hobhouse, John Cam. *See* Broughton.
Holstein, 267, 268.
Hudson, Sir James, *quoted*, 386.
Hugo, Victor, 305, 306.
Humbert of the White Hands, 24, 174.
Humbert, King of Italy, 175, 300, 301, 308, 324, 325, 374-378, 380, 383, 384, 387, 388, 410, 425.
Hungary, 150, 151; early history of, 152-159; parties in (1848), 162, 164; reforms in, 163; subject provinces, 163; declaration of independence, 165; raises an army, 163; Russia's intervention in, 164-166; after 1848, 285; Millennial Jubilee (1896), 172, 289. *See* Austria-Hungary.
Hungarian exiles in Turkey, 169; generals, 165; ladies, 166.
Hunniades, 158.
Huns, 152, 153.

I.

"I Mille" 264.
International Review, *quoted*, 97-99.
Ismail Pasha, 396, 397.
Italia Irredenta, 261, 262.
Italian troops in the Crimean War, 90, 184, 185; alliance with Prussia, 256; Ironclads, 260, 261; emigration to United States and Argentina, 371; army and navy, 388, 389, 391, 392; Parliament, parties in, 391.
Italians in Africa, Bay of Assab, 396; in Abyssinia, 395-421; in Somaliland, 421.
Italy, Central, 15, 108, 212-221; Northern and Southern contrasted, 371; estranged from France, 391; troubles in (1896), 384-388, 392, 414, 415, 420-422; opposed, 420, 421.

J.

Jellachich, Ban of Croatia, 163, 165.
Jerome Napoleon, Prince, 201, 202, 203.
John, King of Saxony, 275, 276.
John (Johannes), Emperor of Abyssinia, 397, 398, 400, 402-407.
Jub river, 421.
Jubilee, Papal, 333, 334; millennial, in Hungary, 172, 289.

K.

Kanzler, General, 313, 315, 316.
Kassala, 400, 408, 415.
Klapka, General, 169.
Komorn, 156, 157, 169.
Königgrätz. *See* Sadowa.
Kossuth, Louis, 150-152, 161, 162, 166-172, 288.
Kottenner, Helen, 155-158.
Krazinska, Françoise, Countess, 92.

L.

Ladislas, King of Hungary, 156-158.
La Gancia, monks of, 225.
La Marmora, General, 100, 103, 107, 146, 205, 255, 257, 258, 262, 263, 274, 291, 323, 324.
Lamoricière, General, 235; his army, 235, 290, 364.
Langensalza, battle of, 276.
Lauenburg, 267, 268.
Laybach, 62, 63, 95.
Ledru-Rollin, 126, 127.
Leighton, Archbishop, *quoted*, 384.
Leo IX., 10, 11.
Leo XII., 334, 338.
Leo XIII., 235, 333, 334, 337-340, 356, 357, 415-418, 423; as a poet, 348; on infallibility, 333.

INDEX. 433

Leonine City, 315, 317, 318.
Leopold, Grand Duke of Tuscany, 26, 69, 102, 116-121, 213.
Leopold of Belgium, 339.
Lesseps, Count Ferdinand de, 132-134.
Lissa, battle of, 260, 261, 262.
Louis Napoleon, Prince, 33-36, 57, 58, 69, 127, 134. *See* Napoleon III.
Louis Philippe, and non-intervention, 30, 31.
Lugard, Captain, 403, 404.

M.

Macaire, Monsignor Cyrille, 416-418; letter from, 417, 418.
Madagascar, 399.
Mafia, 351, 371-373.
Magenta, battle of, 207.
Magyars, 153-155, 159-161.
Mala Vita, 351.
Malghera, 85, 88.
Mangashah, Ras, 408, 409, 411.
Manin, Doge of Venice, 80.
Manin, Daniele, 80-84, 88-91, 186, 384.
Manning, Cardinal, *quoted*, 328, 330, 331, 337.
Mantua, 18, 20, 35, 80.
Manzoni, Alessandro, 15, 215, 321.
Margherita, Queen of Italy, 300, 301, 308, 324, 375-377.
Maroncelli, Pietro, 23.
Maria Adelaide, wife of Victor Emmanuel, 175, 181, 182.
Maria Louisa, ex-Empress, 27.
Maria Pia, Queen of Portugal, 255, 301.
Marsala, 227.
Massowah, 382, 396-398, 401, 402, 407, 414, 420.
Matthias Corvinus, 158, 159.
Maximilian, Emperor of Mexico, 80, 256, 260, 289.
Mazzini, Giuseppe, 28, 29, 30, 37, 46, 56, 108, 125-128, 130-136, 139, 142, 143, 190-193, 195, 196, 224, 225, 229, 231, 236, 237, 247, 292, 304, 321, 322, 384.

Menabrea, General, 295, 296, 310, 311, 375.
Menelik, Emperor (Negus) of Abyssinia, 407-409, 411, 414-419.
Menotti, Ciro, 33, 34, 35.
Menotti Garibaldi, 140, 262, 298, 304, 307.
Mentana, 296-299, 309, 310.
Messina, 70, 71, 229.
Metternich, Prince, 30, 46, 48, 93, 94, 99, 268, 270.
Milan (1815), 18, 19 (1848), 83, 103-109, 177, 323; rising in, 1871, 304.
Milazzo, battle of, 229.
Minghetti, 81, 254.
Minto, Lord, 68.
Mirafiore, Rosina, Countess of, 301, 376.
Mississippi, U. S. man of war, 170.
Moltke, Marshal v., *quoted*, 403.
Montfresson, Rosalia, 382.
Monkullu, 398, 402, 405, 407.
Mont Cenis, tunnel, 321.
Montebello, battle of, 206.
Montenegro, 423.
Monte Rotondo, 296-299.
Monthly Packet, 352.
Moro, Domenico, 38.
Mundy, Admiral, 236, 239.
Murat, 16, 17, 18, 60.

N.

Naples, Angevin kings in, 12, 13; given to Austria, 13; in 1848, 64, 65; reaction, 69; prisons in, 65, 66, 74-77, 368; constitution sworn to by Francis I. and Ferdinand I., 60-62; constitution sworn to by Ferdinand II., 64, 65; invasion by Garibaldi (1860), 229, 230, 232-234; second invasion, 248, 249.
Napoleon I., 15, 16, 17, 20, 21, 79, 268.
Napoleon III., 185, 186, 196-203, 205-208, 210-213, 218, 221, 246, 247, 256, 258, 272-274, 282, 283, 292, 294, 295, 299, 300, 302, 310, 311, 312, 367.
Napoleon Louis, Prince, 31-36.
Nardi, Anacarsi, 38.

28

434 INDEX.

"Nation," *quoted*, 412-414.
Nice, 111, 222, 223.
Nicholas I., Emperor of Russia, 185.
Nicholas II., Emperor of Russia, 422, 423.
Nigra, Count, 203, 204.
Normans in Naples, 9-12.
Novara, 25, 26, 57; battle of, 110, 111.
Nugent, General, 115.

O.

Obok, 397, 421.
O'Clery, The, *quoted*, 207, 208, 315, 316.
Odone, Duke of Monferrat, 255.
Œcumenical Council, 311, 327-332.
Oliphant, Lawrence, *quoted*, 48, 49, 64, 65, 223, 224.
Omar Pasha, 169.
Orsi, Count Joseph, *quoted*, 31, 32, 33.
Orsini, Felice, 188-199, 360.
Oudinot, General, 57, 128-130, 132-136.
Ouida, 420, 421, 422.

P.

Palermo, 66, 67, 68, 71, 72, 227, 228.
Palestrina, fight at, 131.
Palestro, battle of, 206, 207.
Palmerston, Lord, 46; *quoted*, 285.
Palffy, Count, 81, 82.
Panslavism, 164.
Pantaleone, Father, 227.
Papal Army under Lamoricière, 235, 250, 364; under Kanzler, 313-317.
Paris Commune, 306.
Passatore, Il. *See* Forlimpopoli.
Peace of Utrecht (1713), 13; of Paris (1814), 27.
Peace of Villafranca (1859), 213.
Peace of Prague (1866), 262, 283.
Peard, Colonel, 232-234, 252.
Pecci, Cardinal Giuseppe, 346.
Pellico, Silvio, 21, 22, 23.
Pepe, General, 61, 64, 69, 71, 84, 89; *quoted*, 112.
Persano, Admiral, 228, 235, 259-261.
Piedmont, 14, 16, 24, 25, 27; revolution in, 95.

Philibert Emmanuel, Duke d'Aosta, marries Princess Hélène of Orleans, 376.
Pilo, Rosalino, 224, 225.
Pio Nono, 41-56, 58, 69, 123-126, 141, 142, 179, 180, 189, 307, 312, 315, 316, 320, 323, 324, 329-336, 360, 361; his funeral, 342, 343.
Pius IX. *See* Pio Nono.
Plebiscite, in Nice, 202, 222, 223, 224; in Naples, 237; in Venice, 263; in Rome, 317, 318.
Plombières, 199, 222.
Poerio, Carlo, 72, 73, 75, 76.
"Politikos" *quoted*, 383, 384.
Pope's temporal power, 13, 14, 15.
Portal, Sir Gerald, 400-408.
Prina, 17, 19, 20.
Prisons, in Naples, 65, 66, 74-77, 368; in Sicily, 65, 66, 67.
Probyn, J. W., *quoted*, 16, 39, 61, 62, 137, 320, 391, 392.
Prussia, 265-283.
Prussians, on the march, 277-279; return to Berlin, 283.

Q.

Quadrilateral, 80, 105, 211.
Quarterly Review, *quoted*, 388.
Queen Victoria, 334.

R.

Radetzky, Marshal, 70, 82, 83, 90, 103, 104, 106, 109, 110, 143, 175, 176.
Railroads, in Venetia, 81; in Italy, 311.
Ramorino, General, 37, 38, 110.
Rattazzi, 184, 246, 247, 293, 296, 321.
Red Shirts, 130, 229, 237.
Restoration of Italian princes (1849), 173, 213, 214.
Revolutionary parties in Italy (1848), 83.
Ricasoli, Baron, 242, 245, 246, 293, 295, 384.
Ricciotti, 38.
Ricciotti Garibaldi, 140, 262, 304, 305.
Robert Guiscard, 11, 12.
Robilant, 382, 390.

Roger Guiscard, 11, 12.
Roger Guiscard II., 12, 59.
Romagna, 16, 33, 34.
Roman Republic, 56, 57, 58, 125; Constituent Assembly, 56, 124, 125, 128, 135, 136; deposes the Pope, 125; volunteers, 84, 106; relations of France to, 126.
Romans, 314.
Rome, (1846) 43, 44, 45, (1848) 48-52, (1849) 56-58, (1867) 290; besieged by the French, 126-129, 134-137; evacuated by the French, 312; entered by the Italian army, 314-318.
Rosas, 140, 141.
Rossi, Count Pellegrino, 46, 47, 48, 50, 51.
Roselli, General, 131.
Rouher, 309.
Rudini, Marquis di, 293, 414, 416.
Rudolph, Crown Prince of Austria, 289.
Ruffini, 37, 66.
"Rule of the Monk," 264, 314.
Russell, Lord John, 218.
Russia in Hungary, 164, 165, 166, 286; influence in Abyssinia, 407.

S.

Sadowa, battle of, 258, 265, 279, 280, 281.
Sahati, 400, 401.
Salerno, 11.
Sanfedesti, 46.
San Martino, 209.
Santa Rosa, 180.
Sardinia, 13, 24.
Savoy, house of, 24, 25, 174, 384; invaded, 37; and Nice, cession of, 201, 202, 218, 219, 222, 223.
Saxony, 275-278.
Schwartzenberg, Prince, 285.
Secret Societies, 349-351.
Senior, Nassau, *quoted*, 14, 60, 73, 74, 75, 180.
Settembrini, 75-78.
Seven Weeks' War, 265, 266, 278-281.
Sicardi Laws, 179, 180.
Sicilian Parliament, 62, 68.
Sicilian Vespers, 12.

Sicily, 10-13, 59, 66-72, 224-230, 247.
Sigismund, Emperor, 24, 155.
Slavs, 155.
Solferino, battle of, 209.
Somaliland, Italian possessions in, 421.
South American republics, war in, 139-141.
Spain, 13, 31, 58, 61.
Spanish Constitution (of 1820), 61, 95, 96.
Spaur, Count and Countess, 52-55.
"Spectator," *quoted*, 253, 254, 321.
Stanley, H. M., *quoted*, 399.
Stefani, Agostino, 85-88.
Stephen, Archduke and Palatine, 162.
Stephen, St., 154. *See* Crown of St. Stephen.
Story, Mrs. William, *quoted*, 129.
Strossmeyer, Bishop, 331, *quoted*, 332.
Sutherland, Duke of, 251.

T.

"Tablet," *quoted*, 418.
Tancred the Crusader, 12.
Tancred de Hauteville and his sons, 10-12.
Taxation in Italy, 292, 388.
Tegethoff, Admiral, 260, 261.
Theresita, Garibaldi's daughter, 140, 240, 241, 307.
Thiers, 309; *quoted*, 178, 303.
Thurn, General, 88.
Tommaseo, 81.
Toselli, Major, 412.
Treaty of Paris (1814), 27; of Campo Formio (1797), 79; of Villafranca (1859), 211, 213, 218, 221; of Prague (1866), 283.
Triple Alliance, 382, 387, 389-394, 426.
Tuckerman, Henry, *quoted*, 23.
Tunis, 395, 425.
Tunnel under Mont Cenis, 321.
Turin, 254, 255.

U.

Umberto. *See* Humbert.

V.

Vardarelli, a brigand, 353.
Velletri, fight at, 131, 132.
Venetia, 20, 21, 108, 212, 255, 256, 258, 259.
Venice, 14, 16, 20, 21, 68, 79–91, 212, 290, 322, 396.
Verona, Congress of, 26, 27.
Victor Emmanuel I., 24, 25, 27, 94–96.
Victor Emmanuel II., King of Italy, 78, 94, 98, 110, 111, 113, 114, 173–179, 181–187, 200–209, 211–215, 218–222, 235, 245, 249, 254–257, 264, 265, 274, 290, 291, 299, 300, 301, 318, 322–326, 374.
Victor Emmanuel, Prince of Naples, 301, 422, 424, 425.
Vienna, Revolution in, 164, 165, 270; Congress of, 79.
Villafranca, armistice, 210–213; peace of, 218, 221.
Villagos, 167, 168.
Volturno, battle of the, 236.

W.

William, King of Prussia, 273, 278, 283; Emperor of Germany, 322, 323.
Windischgrätz, Prince, 164, 270, 284.
Wolff, a spy, 297.

Y.

Year 1814, 19; 1821, 21, 22, 23; 1831, 28, 30, 31; 1846, 102; 1848, 102–108; 1849, 109, 114, 173; 1862–1864, 245, 255, 256; 1867, 292, 293.
Yonge, Miss C. M., "Book of Golden Deeds," *quoted*, 155; "Monthly Packet," 352.

Z.

Zambelli, Colonel Michele, 357–364.
Zollverein, 269.
Zouaves, French, 206, 207; Papal, 290, 293, 317.

By Mrs. Elizabeth W. Latimer.

Spain in the Nineteenth Century. Handsomely illustrated. 8vo. $2.50.

> With regret one notes that Elizabeth Wormeley Latimer's "Spain in the Nineteenth Century" is to be the last of her excellent series of Nineteenth Century Histories. We have come to look upon Mrs. Latimer as quite the most delightful purveyor of historical gossip to be found anywhere. In successive volumes she has sketched the external events of the century in France, Russia, England, Africa, Italy, and Spain; and this final volume is perhaps the most timely and the most needed of all. — *The Chicago Tribune.*

Italy in the Nineteenth Century. Handsomely illustrated with twenty-four full-page half-tone portraits. 8vo. 436 pages. $2.50.

> "Italy in the Nineteenth Century," is as fascinating as a romantic novel. Indeed every chapter is a romance from history made almost in our own day. It is hard to imagine a more difficult task than to compress into a single volume the richly varied stories of States and men and women that went to the making of the United Italy of to-day. — *The Press*, Philadelphia.

Europe in Africa in the Nineteenth Century. Handsomely illustrated with twenty-three full-page half-tone portraits. 8vo. 456 pages. $2.50.

> Elizabeth Wormeley Latimer has made a valuable condensation of the history of European exploration and conquest. She calls her book a volume of "short yarns," but this modest characterization does not do justice to the skilful summing up of achievement in the Dark Continent. — *The Advance.*

England in the Nineteenth Century. Handsomely illustrated with twenty-five full-page half-tone portraits. 8vo. 452 pages. $2.50.

> What a lot she knows! And how brightly she tells it all! We seem to be reading contemporaneous confidential letters to an intimate friend, written "not for publication" by any means, — the style is too good for that, — but simply because the writer is interested, and never imagines the reader to be otherwise. — *The Mail and Express*, New York.

Russia and Turkey in the Nineteenth Century. Handsomely illustrated with twenty-three full-page half-tone portraits. 8vo. 413 pages. $2.50.

> There is not a yawn in its four hundred pages. The author deals with the endless strife between the Ottoman and the Russian in the mood of a painter; and her word-painting is always bright and often brilliant and powerful. — *Chicago Evening Post.*

France in the Nineteenth Century, 1830-1890. Beautifully illustrated with twenty-two full-page half-tone portraits. 8vo. 450 pages. $2.50.

> For telling situations and for startling effects she certainly does not lack. . . . She is always picturesque. In her analysis of character she displays a thorough mastery of her subject. . . . Mrs. Latimer has written an extremely interesting book, which will be read with eagerness. — *The Daily Advertiser*, Boston.

Sold by booksellers generally, or will be sent, postpaid, on receipt of the price, by the publishers,

A. C. McCLURG & CO., CHICAGO.

By Miss MARGUERITE BOUVET.

Pierrette. Illustrated by Will Phillip Hooper. Small 4to. $1.25.

It is a charming little French story of the temptation, the victory, and the beneficent result thereof of a French sewing woman and her little daughter, and these simple materials are handled so delicately and attractively that the book possesses an unusual charm. It is pleasantly illustrated. — *Congregationalist*, Boston.

A Child of Tuscany. Illustrated by Will Phillip Hooper. Small 4to. $1.50.

It is a winsome tale of a Florentine peasant boy, a cheerful, unselfish little fellow, who was lost when very young but was restored to his family eventually. The author, who is unusually skilful in portraying child life, may fairly be said to rank with Mrs. Burnett as a writer of wholesome, charming juvenile stories. — *Public Opinion*, New York.

My Lady: A Story of Long Ago. Illustrated by Helen Maitland Armstrong. 16mo. $1.25.

The author of "Sweet William" has but to write, and she is read. There is no more universally beloved volume in the children's library, and none with more reason. "My Lady," a tender love story, is as charming as anything she has ever written.... It is exquisite. — *The Chicago Herald*.

Sweet William. Illustrated by Helen and Margaret Armstrong. Eleventh thousand. Small 4to. $1.50.

It is told with a grace of style that has not been surpassed in any of the juvenile fiction of the year. "Sweet William" is a charming little figure. The author has given her story a marked individuality that must ensure it wide popularity. — *The Boston Advertiser*.

Little Marjorie's Love Story. Illustrated by Helen Maitland Armstrong. Fifth thousand. Small 4to. $1.00.

It is one of the most fascinating tales for children of the season.... The beauty and pathos of the story are touching, and the delicate way in which the characteristics of the one child are contrasted with those of the other is as skilful as the management of the lights and shadows in an artistic picture. The illustrations by Miss Armstrong, it is needless to say, are exquisite, and the typography is a delight to the eye. — *The Philadelphia Press*.

Prince Tip Top: A Fairy Tale. With numerous illustrations by Helen M. Armstrong. Fourth thousand. Small 4to. $1.00.

It is a charming little fairy story.... Little folk will enjoy the tale hugely, and it will do them no harm. The style is simple and engaging, and the illustrations are all conceived in the spirit of the text, and daintily executed. — *The Commercial Advertiser*, New York.

For sale by booksellers generally, or will be sent, postpaid, on receipt of price, by the publishers,

A. C. McCLURG & CO., CHICAGO.

By Miss Elizabeth S. Kirkland.

A Short History of Italy. 12mo. 475 pages. $1.25.

The general reader will find in this book perhaps the best complete account of the events that have occurred in that peninsula whose priceless contributions to the world's civilization make its history of perennial interest. — *The Dial*, Chicago.

It is not a successive series of battles and descriptions of rulers, or dates of events, but an epitome of the spirit of the nation, with leaders in the front, the people as a background, and the whole a beautiful picture. — *Inter-Ocean*, Chicago.

A Short History of English Literature for Young People. With eleven portraits. 12mo. 398 pages. $1.50.

No better book could be placed in the hands of an intelligent boy or girl, as an introduction to a primary knowledge of the subject to which it is devoted. Miss Kirkland is to be complimented and congratulated on the skill and judgment with which she has performed her difficult task. — *Boston Gazette*.

The story of English literature has rarely been more delightfully told than in these pages. — *Journal of Education*.

A Short History of England for Young People. 12mo. 415 pages. $1.25.

"A Short History of England" is never trite, never dull; while its brief explanations of intricate systems — as, for example, the feudal system — and of great movements — such as the developments which led to the Restoration — are almost flawlessly clear — *The Evangelist*, New York.

It strikes the line between history and chronicle very happily. It is critical enough, without being so critical as to destroy the romantic glow of history which is so dear (and really so valuable) to a young reader. — *The Independent*, New York.

A Short History of France for Young People. 12mo. 398 pages. $1.25.

Miss Kirkland has admirably succeeded in her "Short History of France," in making a book both instructive and entertaining. It is not a dry compendium of dates and facts, but a charmingly written history. — *The Christian Union*, New York.

The little history may be commended as the best of its kind that has yet appeared. — *Philadelphia Bulletin*.

Six Little Cooks; or, Aunt Jane's Cooking Class. 12mo. 236 pages. 75 cents.

A lucky stroke of genius, because it is a good thing well done. It has the charm of a bright story of real life, and is a useful essay on cooking. — *The Times*, N. Y.

Dora's Housekeeping. 12mo. 275 pages. 75 cents.

We cordially recommend these two books ("Dora's Housekeeping" and "Six Little Cooks") as containing almost the whole gospel of domestic economy. — *The Nation*, New York.

Speech and Manners for Home and School. 12mo. 263 pages. 75 cents.

The author's theory of manners and of speech is good. Her modest manual might be read, re-read, and read again with great advantage in most American families. — *The Independent*, New York.

For sale by booksellers generally, or will be sent, postpaid, on receipt of price, by the publishers,

A. C. McCLURG & CO., CHICAGO.

By Mr. GEORGE P. UPTON.

The Standard Operas: Their Plots, their Music, and their Composers. A Handbook. 12mo. Flexible cloth, yellow edges. $1.50.

> Among the multitude of handbooks which are published every year, and described by easy-going writers of book-notices as supplying a long-felt want, we know of none which so completely carries out the intention of the writer as "The Standard Operas," whose object is to present to its readers a comprehensive sketch of each of the operas contained in the modern repertory. — *R. H. Stoddard*, in *The Mail and Express*, New York.
>
> The summaries of the plots are so clear, logical, and well written that one can read them with real pleasure, which cannot be said of the ordinary operatic synopses. But the most important circumstance is that Mr. Upton's book is fully abreast of the times. — *The Nation*, New York.

The Standard Oratorios: Their Stories, their Music, and their Composers. A Handbook. 12mo. Flexible cloth, yellow edges. $1.50.

> Nothing in musical history is so interesting to the general reader as the story of the great oratorios, — the scenes and incidents which gave them rise, how they were composed, and how first performed. These things are told in Mr. Upton's volume with a grace and charm comporting with the character of the subject. — *Observer*, New York.
>
> The book is a masterpiece of skilful handling, charming the reader with its pure English style, and keeping his attention always awake in an arrangement of matter which makes each succeeding page and chapter fresh in interest and always full of instruction, while always entertaining. — *The Standard*, Chicago.

The Standard Cantatas: Their Stories, their Music, and their Composers. A Handbook. 12mo. Flexible cloth, yellow edges. $1.50.

> This is a study of the cantata in its various forms, from its early simple recitative or aria style down to its present elaborate construction. The selections include quite all of the cantatas that rank high in merit. It is the only handbook and guide for musicians and their friends, and is as valuable as either of the two admirable works preceding it. — *The Boston Globe*.

The Standard Symphonies: Their History, their Music, and their Composers. A Handbook. 12mo. Flexible cloth, yellow edges. $1.50.

> The usefulness of this handbook cannot be doubted. Its pages are packed full of these fascinating renderings. The accounts of each composer are succinct, and yet sufficient. The author has done a genuine service to the world of music-lovers. The comprehension of orchestral work of the highest character is aided efficiently by this volume. The mechanical execution of the volume is in harmony with its subject. No worthier volume can be found to put into the hands of an amateur or a friend of music. — *Public Opinion*, Washington.

Woman in Music. 16mo. Gilt top. $1.00.

> Mr. Upton, in a series of comparatively brief chapters, has given us a kind of interior history of the domestic and heart relations of such composers as Bach, Handel, Beethoven, Mozart, Schumann, Chopin, and Wagner, filling in the larger sketches of these masters by lightly drawn but very interesting pictures of their relations with various gifted and unselfish women. — *The Book Buyer*, New York.

For sale by booksellers generally, or will be sent, postpaid, on receipt of price, by the publishers,

A. C. McCLURG & CO., CHICAGO.

www.ingramcontent.com/pod-product-compliance
Lightning Source LLC
Chambersburg PA
CBHW051234300426
44114CB00011B/735